THE
HEALING
٠ FOODS ٠
COOKBOOK
in Large Print

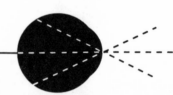

THE
HEALING
♦ FOODS ♦
COOKBOOK
in Large Print

400 delicious recipes with curative power

**By the Editors of PREVENTION Magazine
Compiled and edited by Jean Rogers**

*The Healing Foods Cookbook is in no way associated
with or related to the book The Healing Foods by
Patricia Hausman and Judith Benn Hurley*

G.K.HALL & CO.
Boston, Massachusetts
1992

Printed in Large Print by arrangement with
Rodale Press, Inc.

Prevention magazine is a registered trademark of
Rodale Press, Inc.

Recipe photograph on front cover: Grilled Chicken and
Artichokes with Mixed Greens (page 505).

G. K. Hall Large Print Book Series.

Printed on acid free paper in the United States of America.

Set in 16 pt. Plantin.

Library of Congress Cataloging-in-Publication Data

The Healing Foods cookbook : 400 delicious recipes with
  curative power / by the editors of Prevention magazine ;
  compiled and edited by Jean Rogers.—In large print.
    p. cm.—(G. K. Hall large print book series)
  Includes index.
    ISBN 0-8161-5520-8 (hc : lg. print).
    ISBN 0-8161-5521-6 (pb : lg. print).
    1. Cookery for the sick. 2. Diet therapy. 3. Nutrition.
  4. Large type books. I. Rogers, Jean, 1948–   . II. Prevention.
  (Emmaus, Pa.)
  [RM219.H39 1992]
  615.8'54—dc20   92-7949

The Healing Foods Cookbook Staff:
Editor: Jean Rogers
Senior Managing Editor: Debora Tkac
Writers: Jean Rogers, Sharon Faelten
Art Director: Jane Knutila
Designer: Lisa Gatti
Photographer: Angelo Caggiano
Photo Editor: Barbara Fritz
Food Stylist: Anne Disrude
Recipe Development: Rodale Food Center,
  Tom Ney, Director
Nutritionist, Rodale Food Center: Anita
  Hirsch, M.S., R.D.
Senior Home Economist, Rodale Food Cen-
  ter: JoAnn Brader
Research Chief: Ann Gossy
Senior Research Associate: Karen Lombardi
Production Editor: Jane Sherman
Copy Editor: Laura Stevens
Indexer: Andrea Chesman
Editor in Chief: William Gottlieb
Editor, *Prevention* Magazine: Mark Bricklin

Contents

Introduction   ix

PART ONE
    CHAPTER 1 *The Healing Power
                     of Food*   3
    CHAPTER 2 *100 Foods for Health
                     and Healing*   53

PART TWO
    CHAPTER 3 *Great Beginnings*   123
    CHAPTER 4 *Soups and Chowders*   159
    CHAPTER 5 *The Super Salad Bowl*   196
    CHAPTER 6 *Breads and Breakfasts*   244
    CHAPTER 7 *The Great Grains*   296
    CHAPTER 8 *Beans and Legumes*   344
    CHAPTER 9 *Vegetarian Main Meals*   388
    CHAPTER 10 *Fish and Seafood*   432
    CHAPTER 11 *Perfect Poultry
                    and Game*   475
    CHAPTER 12 *Lean Meats*   523
    CHAPTER 13 *Vegetable Side Dishes*   555

CHAPTER 14 *Grand Finales*   600

PART THREE
   CHAPTER 15 *Meals That Heal*   643

Index   785

Introduction

Eat food and prevent disease? Or better yet, eat food and *stop* disease! It's certainly a welcome concept in these times when we hear so much talk about what we *shouldn't* eat.

Too much fat, too much cholesterol, too many calories, too little fiber, not enough nutrients. The caveats about what we shouldn't eat for our health's sake go on and on . . . until now.

Here's the book that puts the emphasis on food right where it belongs—on the vast array of wonderfully delicious and highly nutritious foods that we *should* eat to promote super health.

As you'll discover right on page 3, thousands of studies now show that what you eat can have a significant impact on your health and even your longevity. And we're not talking about a few scrawny vegetables that'll just make you turn up your nose! We're talking 100 foods. Delicious foods. Varied foods. And that's just the cream, er, top of the crop!

As you read through chapters 1 and 2, you'll discover all the wonderful health benefits that can be derived by eating the right foods every day. And the 400 recipes that follow will give you delicious ways to enjoy them. *The Healing Foods Cookbook* isn't a diet cookbook. It's a growth cookbook—a growth in your knowledge about healthful food, a growth in your repertoire of fabulous recipes. The result will be a naturally new way of eating healthy foods prepared in ways you will savor and enjoy.

What you won't find in this book are calorie counts and cholesterol counts and saturated fat figures. They just aren't needed. That's because all the recipes were developed with low calories, low fat, and high nutrition as the top priorities. If your diet focuses on these foods, if you follow the fat-cutting tips spread throughout each chapter, and if you eat *all* foods in moderation, what you *shouldn't* be eating just won't be an issue.

Here's to your health!

Debora Tkac

Debora Tkac
Senior Managing Editor
Prevention Magazine Health Books

THE
HEALING
⬥ FOODS ⬥
COOKBOOK
in Large Print

PART ONE

PART ONE

CHAPTER ONE

The Healing Power of Food

Post this thought on your refrigerator: This is my "Food Pharmacy."

The idea that certain foods can prevent and treat disease is nothing new. As youngsters, we were told that chicken soup would help get rid of the flu, that roughage relieved constipation, that spinach made you strong. Compared with what we're told now, that's, well, kid stuff. During the past several years, the scientific evidence supporting the healing power of foods has turned from a trickle into a torrent—a convincing current even the nutrition naysayers can't dam.

"Hundreds—no, *thousands*—of studies have indicated that eating the right foods can prevent a host of ills," says William E. Connor, M.D., a nutritional scientist and professor of medicine at Oregon Health Sciences University. Most notable among them are high cholesterol, high blood pressure, gallstones, adult-onset (type II) diabetes, and cancers of the breast, ovaries, colon, and prostate. "This is significant, because these are the very conditions that send most people to their doctor," says Dr. Connor, who is also coauthor of *The New American Diet.*

But food doesn't only have the potential to stave off disease; it can help cure it as well. Studies have shown that eating certain foods can bring dangerously high cholesterol and blood pressure down to safe levels. The right foods can control diabetes, prevent osteoporosis, boost your immunity, and soothe a host of digestive woes. They can even ease painful conditions such as rheumatoid arthritis and gout. And that's just to name a few.

What exactly is a healing food? One that is short on elements we know are bad for us, like saturated fat, cholesterol, salt, and too many calories. And one that is chock-full of things we have learned are so good for us, like select vitamins and minerals, fiber, and fish oils. And the good news is that these healing qualities can be found in a bounty of foods readily available to us. (You'll learn all about the best of the bunch and what they can do for you in chapter 2.)

In terms of healing potential, Dr. Connor says, a representative meal might be 3 or 4 ounces of salmon or tuna, a helping each of broccoli and green beans, a sweet potato or white potato topped with yogurt and chives, a slice of whole wheat bread, and a fresh-fruit dessert.

What's so special about those foods? The fish is high in certain components of oil called omega-3 fatty acids that can help lower cholesterol and reduce the tendency for blood to clot. A growing body of evidence strongly suggests that the vitamins, fiber, and other substances found in dark green and yellow vegetables, potatoes, and certain fruits can help boost immunity, fight off cancer, or keep your arteries clear. As for yogurt, it's a rich source of calcium, which may help protect against high blood pressure and osteoporosis. Chives and other members of the onion family contain substances that help protect against cancer and heart disease.

Sound promising? Good, because there's more. Doctors and researchers have discovered a similar bounty of evidence about the healing potential of many other foods. Here, from A to Z, is what's happening on the disease front.

Anemia

Healthy blood depends on iron. It is the key component of hemoglobin, the substance in red blood cells that does the work of carrying oxygen through the bloodstream. If you have iron-deficiency anemia, it means your red blood cells are too scarce and too small—your body is starving for oxygen, and you feel tired and listless. Even a slight depletion of iron can hobble your energy. Women are the most common victims of iron deficiency, largely because of monthly blood losses through menstruation and their penchant for dieting.

Years ago, doctors tried to solve the problem of low iron by ordering their patients to eat liver. It's one of the most concentrated sources of heme (the most absorbable) iron, which is found only in flesh food. But they don't make that recommendation anymore. Doctors have since found that liver is loaded with so much cholesterol it can no longer be considered a healing food.

But you can get ample amounts of heme iron from other meats. Certain vegetables and grains also contain iron, but it is only in the nonheme form, which is not as easily absorbed as heme iron. Scientists have discovered, however, that non-heme iron is easier to absorb in the presence of certain substances, such as vitamin C. So if you're going to depend on grains and vegetables as your main source of iron, you might want to drink a glass of orange juice when you eat them.

To boost your iron intake or help fight anemia, reach for the following healing foods (to find out more about them, turn to chapter 2). And consult the diet plan for anemia on page 649 to see how to incorporate recipes from this book into your menus.

All low-fat meats, particularly beef
All poultry, particularly the dark meat of turkey
Beans (dried)
Cauliflower
Melons (cantaloupe)
Mollusks (clams only)
Seeds (sesame)
Tofu
Waterfowl (duck, goose)

Cancer

After decades of research, scientists and doctors have come to this conclusion: up to 50 percent of all cancers may be linked to diet. So what you eat and don't eat can tilt the odds of escaping certain types of cancer in your favor.

In fact, the evidence is so overwhelming that the National Cancer Institute (NCI) recommends a list of dietary guidelines for cancer prevention. And at the top of the list is reducing the amount of fat in your diet. There has probably been more research on the role of dietary fat in cancer development than on any other substance in the diet, says the NCI's Elaine Lanza, Ph.D.

How much fat is too much? You should get no more than 30 percent of your daily calories from fat, according to the NCI. Others suggest you should get even less than that. And you should get 10 percent or less of your calories from saturated fat. Using this rule as a guideline, nearly every recipe in this book is an anticancer weapon. All were developed to keep the amount of *saturated* fat at a minimum!

But excess fat is only part of the strong association between food and cancer. There are stacks of studies suggesting that you can cut your chances of developing certain forms of cancer by eating plenty of fiber, fruits and vegetables rich in beta-carotene, foods containing vitamins C and E, fish high in omega-3 fatty acids, and members of the allium (onion) and cruciferous (cabbage variety) families of vegetables. Even calcium-rich foods are intriguing scientists as potential protectors against some types of cancer.

Here are some examples of the cancer-fighting power of foods.

Several studies have linked diets rich in cruciferous vegetables with a lower incidence of cancers attacking the digestive system, such as bowel and colon cancers. Cruciferous vegetables are loaded with natural compounds called indole glucosinolates, which some researchers believe have protective action against cancer. (There is speculation, however, that cooking may break down glucosinolates, canceling out some but not all of their protective effects.)

A number of studies have found that people who eat a lot of fiber-rich foods have a lower incidence of colon cancer than those who don't get much fiber in their diet. Insoluble fiber, which is found in many fruits and vegetables and whole grains, seems to be the most protective type of fiber. Insoluble fiber encourages faster bowel activity, minimizing contact between the colon and cancer-causing substances.

Dozens of studies have found a protective link between beta-carotene—a precursor of vitamin A—and certain forms of cancers. These studies strongly suggest that the more foods you eat containing beta-carotene—chiefly green and yellow fruits and vegetables—the less likely you are to develop cancer of the lungs, stomach, or mouth. This is of particular significance to smokers, who are at high risk for lung and mouth cancers.

Beta-carotene, along with vitamins C and E, is an antioxidant, and scientists believe that antioxidants help protect the cells from cancer.

A study on lab animals found that fish oil can slow the growth of cancerous tumors. And another found that the cancer in the animals that were fed fish oils spread less quickly.

Members of the allium family, including onions, garlic, scallions, and chives, contain compounds that may reduce the risk of stomach cancer, according to a study sponsored by the NCI.

All in all, over a hundred food compounds have been credited with the ability to fight cancer, and the list you'll find in chapter 2 is teeming with foods that contain them. Also, you'll find a menu plan containing cancer-fighting foods on page 658. Here are some of the best cancer-fighting foods from chapter 2.

All cruciferous vegetables, including broccoli, brussels sprouts, cabbage, cauliflower, ruta-bagas, turnips

All dark green and yellow fruits and vegetables, especially apricots, carrots, pumpkin, spinach, sweet potatoes

All whole grains

Beans (dried)

Bran (wheat)

Citrus fruits (grapefruit, oranges, tangerines)

Fish, especially mackerel salmon, tuna

Melons (cantaloupe)

Milk (low-fat)

Nuts

Onions

Papayas

Peppers (chili, sweet)

Potatoes

Rice (brown)

Salad greens

Tropical fruits (guavas)

Celiac Disease

Also known as sprue, celiac is a malabsorption disease in which the body has an adverse reaction to gluten, the protein found in wheat, rye, barley, and, to a lesser degree, oats. Eating anything that contains gluten causes stomach distress, such as cramps, bloating, and diarrhea or constipation. Left untreated, this condition can lead to weight loss and malnutrition because changes in the intestinal tract can prevent proper absorption of key nutrients.

The obvious and most commonly prescribed treatment for celiac disease is following a gluten-free diet. But this is more easily said than done, especially when it comes to finding gluten-free products in the supermarket. Gluten is a common ingredient in commercially prepared foods and is found in such things as bread, cakes, cookies, crackers, pasta, cereals, and ice cream.

Avoiding gluten is difficult but not impossible. There are plenty of less-common grains that are gluten-free and can be used by those with celiac disease. Check the list in chapter 2 for these healing foods, all of which are easily digestible by those with celiac disease.

Buckwheat
Corn
Millet
Quinoa
Rice

Colds

When it comes to fighting disease with nutrition, there is probably no better-known couple than colds and vitamin C. But this marriage has been as controversial as it's been popular—at least until a few years ago, when researchers at the University of Wisconsin set out to get the cold facts once and for all.

They plied one group of students with large amounts of vitamin C and another with placebos (fake, look-alike pills), then they put them in an environment infested with cold virus. Most of them ended up with a cold. But those who had taken the vitamin C had less-severe cold symptoms than those who were not protected by the vitamin.

Other, though more speculative, research suggests vitamin C and vitamin A, which are both antioxidants, may even help squash cold germs before they bite by boosting the body's immune system.

And here's another food tip: A researcher affiliated with the UCLA School of Medicine has discovered that spicy foods can relieve nasal and sinus congestion.

How should you feed your cold when you feel the sniffles coming on? When your doctor tells you to consume plenty of liquids, take advantage of juices from fruits high in vitamin C. It's the easiest way to boost your vitamin-C count naturally. You'll find plenty of suggestions among the healing foods in chapter 2. And take advantage of the many Mexican dishes and other spicy recipes you'll find in this book. In fact, you'll find a complete meal plan high in cold-fighting nutrients on page 667.

These healing foods and juices are among the best of the bunch with cold-fighting punch.

Citrus juices (grapefruit, lemon, lime, orange)
Garlic

Herbs and spices (hot)
Kiwifruit
Mangoes
Papayas
Peppers (chili, sweet)
Pineapple
Salad greens
Strawberries
Tomatoes
Tropical fruits (guavas)

Constipation

You've known since the first time your mother put a bowl of stewed prunes in front of you that roughage, now better known as fiber, is the fastest cure for constipation.

Fiber is a substance found in many foods such as grains, fruits, and vegetables. It is difficult to digest. Fiber comes in more than one variety, and it is the insoluble form that works best for constipation. (The soluble form is helpful but to a much lesser degree.)

Insoluble fiber passes through your system virtually intact, taking other matter along with it for the ride. Because it's insoluble, this type of fiber has the ability to bulk up by absorbing water. This bulking action helps create movement in the intestines.

Good old-fashioned bran, particularly wheat bran, is one of the most concentrated sources of insoluble fiber. But it won't work alone. Doctors say high-fiber foods need to be paired with plenty of water for the best solution to common constipation.

The healing foods listed in chapter 2 are teeming with fiber. And a meal plan to improve digestive health using the recipes in this book can be found on page 683. Among the best foods to fight constipation are:

All whole grains
Apples
Artichokes
Beans (dried)
Blackberries
Bran, especially wheat
Figs
Nuts
Pomegranates
Prunes
Raspberries
Rice (brown)
Whole wheat flour

Dental Problems

If the Tooth Fairy gave a dinner party, what would she serve? Cheese. That's because cheese has been found to help fight tooth decay.

"Research suggests that certain cheeses—mostly the hard and aged Cheddar varieties—are beneficial to your teeth at the end of a meal," explains Irwin D. Mandel, D.D.S., of the Columbia University School of Dental and Oral Surgery. Apparently, when you eat cheese, the calcium and phosphorus it contains remineralize teeth eroded by acids emitted by plaque-forming bacteria. And it doesn't take a whole lot of cheese (which can be high in fat) to do it.

Cavities aren't much of a problem come adulthood. It's gum disease (like periodontitis, which can lead to tooth loss) that is. In addition to good dental hygiene, diet is believed to play at least a minor role in preventing this disease.

Periodontal disease is a bacterial infection that attacks the gums and eventually the underlying bone, explains James H. Shaw, Ph.D., professor of nutrition at Harvard School of Dental Medicine. He recommends eating a well-balanced diet high in the nutrients that fight infection by boosting the immune system. Vitamins A and C top the list. Other experts also recommend vitamin C because it helps in the production of collagen, which strengthens gum tissue. Some of the foods listed in chapter 2 that are high in both of these nutrients include:

Broccoli
Melons
Nectarines
Papayas
Peppers (chili, sweet)

Diabetes

At one time, doctors recommended a high-protein diet for those with diabetes and put bread, potatoes, fruits, and vegetables on the not-wanted list. Research over the last decade, however, has changed all that.

The American Diabetes Association now says diabetes is best controlled through a high-fiber, high-complex-carbohydrate, low-sodium, low-fat diet. In other words, bread, potatoes, fruits, and vegetables.

This reversal in thinking came about when researchers discovered that fibers in whole grains, beans, and many fruits and vegetables help stabilize glucose (blood sugar) levels. And that's important, because avoiding surges in glucose is crucial to controlling diabetes. A study by Canadian researchers, for example, found that the more whole, unmilled grain kernels in bread, the more slowly the bread is digested and the less it elevates glucose.

Similar studies have found that a diet high in fiber and complex carbohydrates also helps control weight. And overweight is one of the risk factors for adult-onset (type II) diabetes.

Another finding: Diabetics with retinopathy (inflammation of the eye's retina, which can lead to blindness) have diets significantly lower in fiber and carbohydrates than those with healthy eyes. So the same kind of foods that control diabetes in general may save a diabetic's vision.

But protein foods shouldn't be banned from the menu. Fish high in omega-3 fatty acids is encouraged eating for those with diabetes because of its heart-protecting ability. Research reported in the British journal *Lancet* concluded that eating fish as little as once or twice a week may help improve arterial health. And heart-healthy monounsaturated fats, found in oils such as olive and canola, are now believed to help control diabetes.

If you have diabetes, check out the following items on the healing foods list in chapter 2. And consult the menu plan on page 675 that uses the recipes in this book.

All fruits, especially oranges
All grains, particularly buckwheat
All vegetables
Beans (dried)
Bran (soy)
Fish, especially mackerel, salmon, tuna
Oil (canola, olive)
Pasta
Potatoes
Rice
Seeds
Whole wheat flour

Diverticular Disease

One out of every three Americans beyond age 60 is believed to have diverticular disease, a chronic condition characterized by the development of troublesome little pouches along the inner walls of the colon.

The collective wisdom of a past generation reasoned that the worst thing for a person in such a digestive state was fiber, an indigestible substance that would only get caught in the pouches and become abrasive, causing inflammation and pain. Then entered the age of serious fiber research. The result: Fiber is the food of choice, for both prevention and treatment.

Researchers found that many of those plagued with the problem had one thing in common: a low-fiber diet. They also found that sufferers improved when they added fiber to their diets. Doctors believe that the bulking action of insoluble fiber helps relieve strain on the colon's muscle walls.

One doctor's prescription for preventing diverticular disease: "Eat more all-bran cereal, whole wheat bread, and brown rice," says Marvin Schuster, M.D., chief of the Division of Digestive Diseases at the Francis Scott Key Medical Center and professor of medicine at Johns Hopkins University School of Medicine, both in Baltimore.

These are among the foods high in insoluble fiber listed in chapter 2. You'll also find a high-fiber menu plan for better digestive health on page 683.

All grains
Apples
Artichokes
Beans (dried)
Bran, especially wheat
Prunes
Rice (brown)
Whole wheat flour

Fatigue

Do you feel pooped out instead of pepped up? Did your get-up-and-go get up and go? If you're feeling tired all the time and it is not a symptom of an underlying disease (a determination that should be made only by your doctor), your diet could be to blame.

After all, food is energy, and if you're not eating properly, you're not going to feel energized.

For example, if you feel totally wiped out after

exercising, you may have what one medical expert calls "the mineral blues"—a deficiency of potassium and magnesium in muscle cells. Both minerals can be lost through sweat. When body stores of either potassium or magnesium drop below normal, even a mild deficiency can bring on fatigue.

But iron is the mineral most associated with fatigue. That's because iron is essential to the health of red blood cells. Without iron, blood cells get weak—and so do you.

Certain vitamins also help you maintain your zip and vitality. B vitamins, for example, help convert proteins, carbohydrates, and fats to fuel. Without the B's, you're sunk. Also, several studies suggest that people whose diets lack vitamin C grow fatigued more quickly than those whose C intake is high. And C helps boost your absorption of dietary iron.

Knowing all this, it's no wonder that your doctor is always lecturing you to eat a well-balanced diet! If you're looking for staying power, make sure that your "well-balanced diet" contains foods that are iron rich and high in B vitamins and vitamin C.

Better yet, go for the foods that contain a combination of all these nutrients. You'll find plenty in the healing foods list in chapter 2. And a menu designed to fight fatigue using the recipes in this book can be found on page 692. These are among the best fatigue-fighting foods.

All low-fat meats, expecially beef and pork
Beans (dried)

18

Bulgur
Corn
Milk (low-fat)
Millet
Oats
Potatoes
Poultry (chicken, turkey)
Quinoa
Sprouts
Tangerines
Wheat germ
Whole wheat flour

Fibrocystic Breast Disease

Fibrocystic breast disease is a catchall term for lumpy breasts, a condition that half of all women experience. And for a majority of these women, the lumps are painful, particularly right before their periods.

Doctors have found that many women with this condition also are big consumers of caffeine through coffee, tea, colas, or chocolate. Caffeine and other similar chemicals (called methyl-xanthines) activate breast hormones and promote buildup of cyst fluid, explains John Minton, M.D., Ph.D., professor of surgery at Ohio State University College of Medicine. Some women find that when they give up caffeine, the pain goes away. (It can take two to four months, however, to notice the difference.)

Other research has found that tyramines can also abnormally stimulate breast hormones. Tyramines are found in cheese, wine, spices, nuts, mushrooms, and bananas. Since salt promotes fluid retention, reducing sodium intake can help, too. And studies found that when women with fibrocystic breast disease reduced their fat consumption by 20 percent, their levels of prolactin, a hormone that contributes to cysts, also went down.

All that tells you what you *shouldn't* eat. But what *should* you eat? Fiber. Doctors say a fiber-rich diet can help escort excess estrogen out of the body so breasts don't become overstimulated.

Overall, a low-fat, low-salt, high-fiber diet is the prescription for women with fibrocystic breast disease. Most of the recipes in this book (none contain added salt) and a majority of the foods listed in chapter 2 fit that description. Among the foods to look for are:

All fruits, except bananas
All vegetables, except mushrooms
All whole grains
Bran
Herbs, but not spices

Flatulence

If you start eating healing foods, you'll automatically be increasing your intake of fiber-rich foods. But eating a lot of fiber has one drawback, at least initially. You may experience higher-than-usual levels of intestinal gas.

Among the healing foods, beans, onions, celery, carrots, raisins, bananas, apricots, prunes, wheat germ, whole wheat flour, cabbage, and brussels sprouts have been indicted as the biggest offenders.

Most flatulence is actually caused by colonic bacteria, which ferment undigested food and create gas as a by-product. To alleviate the problem, it is best to start adding fiber to your diet slowly.

"Start with a small dose of fiber, so the bowel gets used to it," says Michael Mogadam, M.D., of Georgetown University. Flatus production should drop to less-noticeable levels within a few weeks.

Flatulence, however, can be a symptom of an underlying condition, such as lactose intolerance (a sensitivity to a carbohydrate in dairy products). If you have flatulence that does not subside after moderating your diet, you should consult your doctor.

Food Allergies

If you break out in hives every time you eat tomatoes, chances are you should avoid tomatoes. If you start to wheeze when you eat puffed wheat cereal, you might switch to puffed rice instead. And if your throat swells when you eat shrimp or crab, you probably should steer clear of any kind of shellfish, no matter how tantalizing.

Experience has shown that, for some people, even nutritious foods can cause problems. While almost any food can trigger an allergic reaction, some foods cause more problems than others. Milk, eggs, wheat, and corn tend to cause chronic complaints. Legumes, like peanuts and soybeans, also cause a fair number of adverse reactions. And many people have problems with chocolate, citrus, or seafood. Some foods, like

21

raw apples or other fruits or vegetables, are less allergenic when they're cooked.

Allergies can trigger symptoms other than sneezing, itching, or wheezing, making diagnosis tricky. Other signs of possible food allergy include stuffy nose, diarrhea, nausea, bloating, headaches, mood swings, fatigue, and joint pains, among others.

If you suspect that a food allergy (or allergies) is responsible for any discomfort you may be experiencing, avoid recipes containing the most common allergy triggers—milk, eggs, wheat, legumes, and so forth—for two to three weeks. Then reintroduce each food, one at a time, every four or five days. Sometimes it takes a few days for a food to produce a reaction. Make sure you do this under the supervision of your allergist or doctor. If a "food challenge" provokes symptoms, you have reason to suspect food allergy.

Gallbladder Problems

Doctors have known for a long time that obesity is a major risk factor for gallstones. But a Harvard Medical School study of 89,000 women showed an exact match between overweight and gallstones—as weight increased, so did the risk of developing the nasty pebbles.

Most gallstones are made out of cholesterol, the same artery-clogging stuff that seems to be responsible for many cases of heart disease. When bile, the digestive juice in the gallbladder, contains too much cholesterol, it forms stones. And heavier people tend to have higher cholesterol levels. They also tend to eat fatty foods.

If you're having gallbladder trouble or are prone to gallstones, try making low-fat foods the cornerstone of your diet. Also, increase your intake of fiber. Doctors have found that fiber seems to help prevent the formation of gallstones. And if you're overweight, gradual weight loss, based on a low-fat diet, may help reduce your risk of gallstones.

You can achieve this by decreasing your intake of fatty meats, butter, and high-fat cheeses and increasing your intake of fiber-rich vegetables, fruits, and grains. Look in the healing foods list in chapter 2 for these foods:

All fruits, except avocados
All grains
All vegetables
Beans (dried)
Cottage cheese (low-fat)
Crustaceans
Fish (low-fat varieties such as cod, flounder, haddock)
Mollusks
Pasta
Popcorn
Potatoes
Turkey
Yogurt (low-fat)

Gout

Gout is a royal pain—in the toe. This form of arthritis was once known as the royal disease because of the belief that it was brought on by rich food and drink.

Doctors now know that the source of this very painful disorder is the prickly movement of needlelike crystals lodged in a joint, usually the big toe. These microscopic meddlers are solidified uric acid, a normal body substance that some gout sufferers amass at abnormally high levels.

A healing foods diet for someone with gout is mostly one of avoidance—avoid foods that raise uric acid levels. A sample of such a diet using the recipes in this book can be found on page 701. (Some people claim they have found great relief by eating cherries every day. This is only a folk remedy; there is no scientific proof that it works. But it is certainly worth a try.)

"Foods high in purines contribute to a higher uric acid level," explains Robert Wortmann, M.D., associate professor of medicine and co-chief of the Rheumatology Division at the Medical College of Wisconsin. Foods such as anchovies, consommé, mincemeat, and organ meats (liver, brains, and kidneys) have the highest purine count and are most likely to induce an attack. (So, too, can alcohol.) But you'll find none of these foods listed in chapter 2.

Other purine foods, found in certain vegetables, grains, and meats, should be eaten only in limited amounts. These do include some of the healing foods listed in chapter 2. If you have gout, *limit* your intake of these healing foods:

All low-fat meats
All whole grains
Asparagus
Beans (dried)

Cauliflower
Crustaceans
Fish
Mushrooms
Peas
Poultry (chicken, turkey)
Spinach

These healing foods from chapter 2 are high in purines and should be *avoided* by those prone to gout:

Fish (herring, mackerel, sardines)
Mollusks (mussels)

Headaches

Seymour Diamond, M.D., has probably treated more headache sufferers than any other doctor. As founder of the Diamond Headache Clinic and the National Headache Foundation, he's discovered over the years that certain foods or food ingredients seem to crop up again and again as culprits in causing headaches.

These include caffeine, cured meats (like bacon and hot dogs), monosodium glutamate (MSG, found in many processed foods), chocolate, nuts, aged cheese, and salty foods. With the exception of nuts and cheese (which you should eat only in limited quantity anyway), none of these are listed as healing foods in chapter 2.

While certain foods are suspected of helping to trigger a headache, specialists throughout the United States report that most other foods are considered relatively safe for the headache prone.

If you suffer from headaches, feel free to eat these foods:

All low-fat meats, except pork
Apples
Apricots
Artichokes
Beans (snap)
Blueberries
Broccoli
Carrots
Celery
Cherries
Cottage cheese (low-fat)
Lemons and limes
Mushrooms
Oranges
Peas
Potatoes
Poultry (chicken, turkey)
Yogurt (low-fat)

Hearing Problems

Caution: Egg-salad sandwiches can make you deaf.

Yes, just as a diet high in saturated fat can block arteries of the heart, research suggests a fatty diet can block tiny arteries in the inner ear. The result: Ears "clogged" with dietary fat (from fatty cuts of meat, high-fat dairy products, and too many eggs) may be susceptible to noise-induced damage, because blood flow is stymied.

On the other side of the coin, "sound" eating habits can prevent nutrient deficiencies associated with hearing loss. A study done at Northwestern University, for example, found that hearing-impaired people benefited from zinc. Other studies suggest that calcium (by protecting the bones of the middle ear), vitamin A (possibly by revitalizing aging skin-membrane cells in the inner ear), and magnesium (by keeping the arteries of the ear healthy) may help preserve hearing. Look for foods high in these nutrients in the healing foods list in chapter 2. They include:

> All dark green and yellow fruits and vegetables, especially broccoli, brussels sprouts, carrots, kale, melons (cantaloupe), pumpkin, spinach, squash (winter)
> All low-fat meats
> Apricots
> Milk (low-fat)
> Poultry (chicken, turkey)
> Soybeans
> Tofu
> Wheat germ
> Yogurt (low-fat)

Heart Disease

You could probably fill a heart-shaped bathtub with the vast array of foods that have been shown to help nurture the heart. Unfortunately, you might be able to fill two bathtubs with the foods that have the ability to harm the heart.

When it comes to diet, stacks of research papers all report the same conclusion: Foods high in fat and cholesterol (and, unfortunately, high on many American shopping lists) are the biggest threats to a healthy heart. They leave deposits of these substances in the arteries, which eventually limits the flow of blood to the heart.

A high total blood-cholesterol count is considered by many experts to be the biggest risk factor for heart disease. And in a way that's good, because cholesterol is something each and every one of us can do something about. Plenty of research now shows that eating certain foods can help stop—and in some cases may even *reverse*—atherosclerosis, the cholesterol-powered buildup of artery-clogging plaque.

Taking their cue from these new medical discoveries, physicians are now advising their patients to eat more fruits and vegetables and cut back on high-fat meats, luncheon meats, whole dairy products, and processed foods. But they're also telling patients to eat more foods that have been found to have special cholesterol-lowering potential, like salmon and mackerel, beans and oats, and even certain oils.

What's so magical about those foods? For beans and oats, it's soluble fiber. For oils like olive and canola (but not regular polyunsaturated vegetable), it's monounsaturated fats. And certain fatty ocean fish contain omega-3 fatty acids. All these substances have been found to work in their own way to help lower cholesterol levels. For example:

Research by leading fiber researcher James W. Anderson, M.D., shows that adding soluble fiber to the diet can have a significant and immediate impact on high cholesterol. In one of his studies, Dr. Anderson found that men with fairly high cholesterol levels (around 260) lowered these levels an average of 60 points in just three weeks. In another study, cholesterol levels dropped 76 points from an average of 294 in six months. And all it took was a cup and a half of beans or a cup of oat bran added to the daily diet.

Research in favor of fish oil as a means of lowering cholesterol keeps accumulating. A review article published in the *Yale Journal of Biology and Medicine* reports that "the evidence shows that a diet rich in omega-3 fatty acids significantly reduces plasma cholesterol and triglycerides [a type of fat that increases the risk of heart disease]." The recommendation? Fish at least two or three times a week.

A study of 4,900 Italian men and women found that those with a high intake of olive oil had *lower* levels of cholesterol, while those with a high intake of butter (loaded with saturated fat) had *high* cholesterol levels.

And the good food news doesn't stop here. Pectin, a soluble fiber found in certain fruits such as apples, can bind with cholesterol and cholesterol-containing bile, causing them to be excreted. The result is less cholesterol circulating in the bloodstream.

Research indicates that eating onions and garlic on a regular basis may prevent heart attacks. Substances in the oils in these vegetables seem to render blood platelets less sticky, making it harder for blood to form clots, a principal trigger of heart attacks.

In perhaps the most dramatic study of all, people who ate a very-low-fat, vegetarian diet (along with other lifestyle changes) actually experienced *reversed* coronary blockages by an average of 10 percent.

Doctors say that cutting back on fat and cholesterol is the best way to start a heart-healthy diet. A low-cholesterol menu featuring the recipes in this book can be found on page 709. In fact, the ideal heart-saver diet combines an abundance of the healing foods listed in chapter 2. High on the list are:

All fruits, especially apples, figs, grapefruit, oranges, papayas
All vegetables
Beans (dried)
Bran (corn, oat, rice)
Fish (mackerel, salmon, tuna)
Garlic
Oats
Oil (canola, olive)
Onions
Soybeans

Hemorrhoids

"There's no question that more fiber in most people's diets could substantially lower their risk of developing hemorrhoids," says Lester Rosen, M.D., a specialist in bowel disease. "Fiber is also important for people with existing cases of hemorrhoids to help speed recovery."

As with constipation, the type of fiber that's most helpful is the insoluble kind. Insoluble fiber aids elimination of waste by giving stools more bulk and increasing their absorption of water, making them softer and less of a chore to pass. That puts less strain on the rectal tissues that erupt in hemorrhoids.

The following foods found in chapter 2 are among the best for avoiding hemorrhoid problems. Also, the menu plan designed for digestive problems on page 683 is helpful for those with hemorrhoids.

All grains
Apples
Artichokes
Beans (dried)
Blackberries
Bran, especially wheat
Figs
Nuts
Pomegranates
Prunes
Raspberries
Rice (brown)
Whole wheat flour

Hiatal Hernia

A hiatal hernia is an irritation caused when a small portion of the upper stomach slips through the hiatus, an opening in the diaphragm. It can result in belching, heartburn, and general discomfort, especially after a big meal. Alcohol, fatty foods, acidic foods, chocolate, coffee, spearmint, and peppermint can also aggravate it.

If you have a hiatal hernia, your doctor has probably already told you to avoid those foods and big meals. Several small meals instead of the typical three squares helps keep heartburn away.

If your doctor is up on his research, he may have also recommended that you go on a high-fiber, low-fat diet. Although there is little research showing that a high-fiber diet can benefit those with a hiatal hernia, research has found some interesting correlations, namely that hiatal hernias are most common in populations that suffer from other diseases linked to low fiber intake.

A menu plan designed for hiatal hernia using the recipes in this book can be found on page 717. And while you're grazing your way through the day, it might be helpful to reach for some of these high-fiber healing foods found in chapter 2:

All fruits
All grains
All vegetables

High Blood Pressure

Although there is as yet no single diet to prevent or treat high blood pressure, studies have proven one very important point: Nutrition plays an integral role in controlling this very serious (but usually symptomless) disease.

In fact, in one study, 39 percent of people with high blood pressure who changed their diets found they could control their hypertension without taking drugs. The methods used in the study included maintaining a low-sodium diet, reducing weight when necessary, and cutting back on alcohol. That shouldn't be all that surprising since overweight, salty foods, and drinking have been strongly linked with this disease.

But the dietary measures to help control high blood pressure—a leading risk factor in heart disease and stroke—are not just a list of have-nots. Studies have shown that certain nutrients can be beneficial. High on the list is potassium.

A number of studies have linked low intake of potassium with high blood pressure. In fact, one study from Temple University School of Medicine found that when potassium was reduced in the diets of people with normal pressure, their blood pressure went up. Researchers speculate that low potassium intake may somehow prompt the body to hoard sodium.

Perhaps even more important, research shows, is the ratio of sodium to potassium in the body. Obviously, you want less of the first and more of the second. And you can achieve that naturally by eating more fresh foods. "Whenever dietary sodium is reduced by eating fresh foods low in sodium, the relative intake of potassium will automatically increase because these two can't predominate in most foods," noted one research report. "The less of one, the more of the other."

High intakes of calcium are also linked to lower blood pressure. A study of 8,000 men found that those who drank no milk were almost twice as likely to have high blood pressure as those who drank a quart or more a day. Milk is a leading source of calcium. Increasing calcium in the diet, however, has had mixed results when it comes to helping to reduce high blood pressure. Some speculate that calcium works best for those who are salt sensitive.

And here's something else scientists have observed: Vegetarians tend to have lower blood pressures than meat eaters. One reason for this could be that many vegetables are chock-full of potassium. Also a vegetarian diet is naturally low in fat and high in fiber. Vegetarians tend to get a lot of vitamins C and E and the minerals calcium and magnesium. All these factors may help control blood pressure in various ways. Some scientists, for example, speculate that fiber may lower sodium absorption.

And there is some evidence that the fatty acids found in fish oil, which is believed to benefit the heart, may also have an effect on blood pressure in some people.

Because hypertension is so closely related to heart disease, doctors advise those with high blood pressure to follow the diet guidelines established for a healthy heart—namely a low-fat, low-sodium diet. (You can read more about this under Heart Disease on page 27.)

In addition, those with high blood pressure should look to the high-potassium, low-sodium, and high-calcium foods listed in chapter 2. Some of the best sources are listed below. A menu plan for better blood pressure can be found on page 726.

Apricots
Avocados
Bananas
Brussels sprouts

Cauliflower
Chestnuts
Fish
Milk (low-fat)
Mushrooms
Potatoes
Prunes
Spinach
Tofu

Impaired Immunity

If you want to load up your grocery cart with infection-fighting foods, make your way over to the produce aisle. Yellow, orange, and dark green vegetables are good sources of vitamin A, a key nutrient for better immunity.

"This nutrient is involved in protein synthesis," says Brian L. G. Morgan, Ph.D., assistant professor of human nutrition at Columbia University College of Physicians and Surgeons. "Cells are made of protein, so if you can't produce protein, you can't make the cells you need to kill bacteria."

Scientists have also studied the effects of vitamin E on the immune system. Compared with people treated with an inactive substance, patients supplemented with vitamin E showed significantly improved immune responses.

Other nutrients important to immunity include B vitamins, vitamin C, zinc, and iron.

Of course the best time to stock up on foods high in disease-fighting power is before you come down with an infection. Many of the healing foods listed in chapter 2 are high in immune-boosting nutrients. Some of the best are listed below. Also, a diet designed to boost the immune system can be found on page 735.

All dark green and yellow vegetables, especially carrots, pumpkin, spinach, squash (winter), sweet potatoes
Apricots
Beans (snap)
Bulgur
Citrus fruits (grapefruit, oranges, tangerines)
Fish
Kiwifruit
Mollusks (oysters)
Nectarines
Peppers (chili, sweet)
Poultry (chicken, turkey)

Irritable Bowel Syndrome

"Colonic motor dysfunction" sounds like something an auto-body mechanic would charge $600 or $700 to fix. It *is* a mechanical problem of sorts—but one that affects the human body. It's most commonly called irritable bowel syndrome or IBS, a collective term for abnormalities in the gastrointestinal system.

Symptoms of IBS often differ from one sufferer to another, but common complaints usually consist of stomach pain, bloating, constipation or diarrhea, or sometimes a combination of constipation and diarrhea. Because of this, it's often hard to diagnose. And it's only complicated by the fact that no one knows for sure what causes it, although stress is the leading suspect.

Food intolerance is another. Wheat, corn, dairy

36

products, coffee, tea, and citrus fruits can trigger attacks of IBS in sensitive people. Doctors who treat IBS advise patients to keep a detailed food diary for seven days, noting their symptoms, then to avoid any foods that seem to trigger colonic disturbances. Fatty foods and high-calorie meals are often culprits.

Eating foods high in fiber can also help regulate bowels, idling the diarrhea that runs amok in some IBS sufferers and loosening bowels paralyzed with constipation in others. Bran and other sources of insoluble fiber are especially helpful to those suffering primarily from constipation. But foods that tend to cause gas—like beans, lentils, and cabbage—should be avoided.

Researchers at the Bristol Royal Infirmary, in Great Britain, compared the effects of diets both high and low in wheat fiber on people with IBS. Those who ate wheat bran and whole wheat bread improved; people on a low-fiber diet did not.

The healing foods right for IBS sufferers can vary from person to person, depending on symptoms and food intolerances. The following foods found in chapter 2 are among those most commonly recommended by doctors. Also, the menu on page 683 using recipes from this book is designed to promote digestive serenity.

All vegetables
All whole grains
Apples
Bran
Citrus fruits (grapefruit, oranges)
Whole wheat flour

Kidney Stones

If you've ever had one, you know you don't ever want another. Yet painful kidney stones commonly recur within a year in 10 percent of those who develop them.

What causes all the trouble is small, brittle, yellow or brown chunks of mineral salts that form in the kidneys or in the tubes that link the kidneys to the bladder. Not enough water in the diet and high consumption of meat and dairy products are believed to contribute to the condition. (Those foods won't affect non-stone-formers, though.) So it stands to reason that cutting back on these antagonists might help prevent recurrences, notes Alan Wasserstein, M.D., director of the Stone Evaluation Center at the Hospital of the University of Pennsylvania.

Dr. Wasserstein advises his patients to drink lots of water, eat less meat, cut way back on salt, and keep a lid on high-calcium foods such as ice cream, milk, and cheese. He also recommends going easy on high-oxalate foods such as spinach, chocolate, tea, cola, rhubarb, parsley, peanuts, and citrus fruit. (Most stones are made up of calcium oxalate and calcium phosphate.) If a patient's stones contain uric acid, he advises avoiding alcohol, sardines, anchovies, herring, and organ meats such as liver.

So what should you eat? Dr. Wasserstein recommends a low-fat, low-salt diet, the kind prescribed for promoting heart health and reducing blood pressure. There are plenty of foods listed in chapter 2 that are healthful for those plagued with calcium kidney stones. They include:

38

All whole grains

Most fruits, except berries, citrus

Most vegetables, except asparagus, beets, chard, parsley, rhubarb, spinach

Pasta

Soybeans

Lactose Intolerance

If you're one of the 50 million Americans who have lactose intolerance, you probably think twice before drinking milk, regardless of its nutritional merit. One glass of milk or an ice cream cone can cause digestive distress that will leave you miserable with gas, bloating, and diarrhea.

Lactose intolerance means your body is unable to digest lactose, the sugar in milk and many other dairy products. So you'll probably be surprised to hear that *yogurt* just may be the answer to calming those troublesome symptoms. At least that's the latest bulletin from researchers on the front line. Their studies indicate that if you are lactose intolerant, eating yogurt every day can increase your ability to consume dairy products.

Yogurt contains bacteria that digest lactose in the small intestine, according to a study conducted by Naresh Jain, M.D., a gastroenterologist in Niagara Falls, New York. "Eating yogurt is a natural cure for lactose intolerance. At this time, it appears to be a novel and creative way of dealing with the problem." In his study, patients became more tolerant after eating yogurt twice a day for a week.

Another way to deal with the problem is to drink

lactase-treated milk products or those that contain milk substitutes, such as tofu-based desserts that are similar to ice cream.

If you have lactose intolerance, see the menu plan on page 744 and also put these healing foods on your list:

Soybeans
Tofu
Yogurt (low-fat)

Osteoporosis

Any woman concerned about her health knows that the biggest threat to aging bones is osteoporosis, a debilitating disease with a risk that goes up as estrogen levels go down.

But bone loss doesn't start with the onset of menopause. Menopause only accelerates it. And that's why women need to take preventive measures long before menopause begins.

By the late thirties, everyone (men are not excluded) gradually starts losing calcium from bones, partly because our bodies are less able to absorb calcium from food. Bones depend on calcium for strength, but the rest of the body needs calcium too. So when supplies are short, the bones are robbed of their valuable calcium. This becomes particularly critical during menopause, because reduced estrogen production interferes with the body's ability to use calcium efficiently.

But studies have proven that this doesn't have to happen. Osteoporosis, the bone-robbing disease, can be held at bay simply by making sure you get enough calcium in your diet. (Most women don't.)

The first solid study showing that extra dietary calcium may slow the bone loss of osteoporosis was completed in 1985 in Denmark. Researchers divided 36 women past menopause into three groups. During the two-year study, one group took estrogen (standard hormonal treatment), one took 2,000 milligrams of calcium a day, and one took inactive pills. Results: The women in the calcium group had less bone loss than those taking the placebo (inactive pill) but more bone loss than those taking estrogen.

Researchers at the University of Wisconsin later confirmed the Danish study, using 1,500 milligrams of calcium a day, with similar results. Because of that kind of research, many calcium experts recommend a daily intake of at least 1,200 milligrams of calcium for postmenopausal women at risk for osteoporosis who can't take estrogen. Risk factors for osteoporosis include early menopause, smoking, alcoholism, certain drug treatments, and a family history of fractures.

But how does the average postmenopausal woman get plenty of bone-protecting calcium in her diet without consuming a lot of high-cholesterol, high-fat milk and cheese, the best sources of calcium? By eating the low-fat varieties, of course. And by making sure to get vitamin D, too (no problem if you're drinking D-fortified milk). That's because vitamin D facilitates absorption of calcium.

And there's more good food news. How about dipping into some low-fat yogurt or minestrone, a meat-based vegetable soup? That's the advice from Tufts University professor Maury Massler, D.M.D. The calcium in yogurt is readily absorbed. And vegetable soup made with a beef bone also provides easy-to-digest, easy-to-absorb minerals, including calcium.

If calcium builds strong bones, then it's logical that bones themselves contain good amounts of calcium. Take advantage of this by eating canned fish with bones, such as salmon and sardines.

Even if you get enough calcium, though, your bones may lose significant amounts of the mineral if you consume too much salt, according to a report in the *American Journal of Clinical Nutrition*. So while you're helping yourself to calcium-rich, bone-protecting foods (listed below), curb your intake of pizza, chips, and other high-sodium food. The following foods are among the high-calcium items recommended in chapter 2. Also, a menu plan designed to help prevent osteoporosis and using the recipes in this book is on page 752.

Beans (dried)
Broccoli
Cheese (low-fat)
Fish, especially canned salmon, mackerel, sardines
Kale
Milk (low-fat)
Soybeans
Tofu
Yogurt (low-fat)

Overweight

Overweight is a problem that cannot be taken lightly. It is a contributing factor in a majority of diseases, most notably those that kill—like heart disease, high blood pressure, diabetes, and stroke.

Unfortunately, if losing weight were easy to do, 34 million Americans would not be classified as obese—20 percent above their ideal weight—and countless others would not be waging a battle every day with their scales.

But as the doctors at St. Bartholomew's Hospital in London found out, weight loss comes best to those who wait. They followed the diets of 108 obese women and found that sticking to a sound and sensible low-fat diet eventually produces the best results, even if at times the diet seems to be failing.

How does weight loss fit in with the healing foods listed in chapter 2? Quite nicely, thank you. Most of the foods featured in this book are naturals for a weight-loss plan because all are low in saturated fat, high in fiber, and loaded with nutrients to help keep you healthy if you are restricting calories. And many of the foods you'll find here have actually been shown to help enhance weight loss.

Apples and oranges, for instance, contain pectin, a type of fiber found mostly in fruits. It can help put the brakes on runaway appetites. Researchers at the University of Southern California found that adding 15 grams of concentrated pectin (the amount you'd find in eight pears, for example) to the meals of nine obese people prolonged the time required for food to leave their stomachs by 45 minutes. Apparently, pectin "plumps up" food as it's processed by the stomach, boosting feelings of fullness and dampening the appetite. By eating pectin-enriched meals, the people in the study decreased their food intake enough to lose an average of 6.6 pounds over a period of a month.

Another boon to weight loss is soup. Studies have illustrated that those who eat soup on a regular basis often lose weight. When dieters were studied, researchers found that those who ate the most soup lost the most weight. The soups used, of course, were clear, vegetable-based varieties.

Then there's the matter of fat. It shouldn't come as any surprise that the fat we eat is the fat we wear. That's because fat is the slowest substance for our bodies to digest. When your body's in need of energy, the first thing it reaches for is carbohydrates, then fat. If the body has all the calories it needs to burn, the fat is put into storage—and you know where.

Here's the hottest diet tip. Hot spices like chilies and mustard may also foster weight loss by "burning" calories, according to researchers from Oxford Polytechnic in England. Eating hot foods may boost the postmeal metabolic rate by as much as 25 percent, according to the scientists. And the effect may last 3 hours or longer.

But losing weight really doesn't require any tricks. Take a tip from the doctors in London and do it sensibly by using the low-fat, high-fiber foods in chapter 2. And if you need an assist, a menu plan (see page 761) using the recipes in this book is designed with weight loss in mind. Practically all the foods listed in chapter 2 can help you in your weight-loss efforts. Here are some of the best:

All fruits, especially apples, grapefruit, oranges, papayas, but not avocados
All vegetables
All whole grains
Beans (dried)
Bran
Cottage cheese (low-fat)
Crustaceans
Fish (low-fat varieties such as cod, flounder, haddock)
Herbs and spices (hot)
Pasta
Peppers (chili)
Popcorn
Poultry (chicken, turkey)
Tofu

Rheumatoid Arthritis
Preliminary research indicates that sufferers of this chronic joint condition may find comfort from eating a fish. Or, more precisely, a substance found in fish—fish oil.

In one of the studies, doctors at Albany Medical College gave either fish-oil capsules or placebos (inactive capsules) to 33 people with rheumatoid arthritis. After 14 weeks, the capsules were switched. The patients never knew which pill they were taking. Throughout the study, however, those who were given fish oil reported less pain, swelling, stiffness, weakness, fatigue, and tenderness in their joints.

Richard Sperling, M.D., a leading rheumatologist, found similar results in studies at Harvard University School of Medicine. He thinks fish oil works by blocking production of leukotriene B$_4$, an inflammatory substance in the blood. Still other research suggests that fish oil may work by squelching platelet-activating factor, yet another inflammatory chemical.

While scientists continue measuring the success of these substances, doctors feel rheumatoid-arthritis sufferers may benefit from eating fish often. Also, arthritis sufferers who take a lot of aspirin for their pain should make sure they eat plenty of foods with vitamin C. Large doses of aspirin rob the body of vitamin C. You'll find recipes containing these foods in the menus for rheumatoid arthritis on page 769. If you have the disease, look to these foods found in chapter 2:

Broccoli
Brussels sprouts
Citrus fruits, particularly grapefruit, oranges, tangerines
Fish (mackerel, salmon, tuna)
Melons (cantaloupe)

Skin Problems

It's been observed that fish-eating Greenland Eskimos have a below-average incidence of heart disease. And they have a below-average incidence of psoriasis.

Working on a hunch, researchers decided to find out what effect fish oil would have on people with psoriasis. After eight weeks of supplementation, they reported that 13 of their 18 patients improved. In another study, Danish researchers found that people with psoriasis improved on a low-fat diet supplemented with fish oil.

Psoriasis isn't the only skin problem that may respond to higher levels of fish oil in the diet. In a study conducted at the Baylor College of Medicine in Houston, mice developed fewer skin tumors, during exposure to high levels of ultraviolet light, when fed a diet high in fish oil than when they were on a fish-oil-free diet.

"The use of dietary oils in [skin] diseases seems to be a promising new approach," said dermatologist R. Rivkah Isserhoff, M.D., of the University of California, Davis, School of Medicine, in a review of scientific studies on the role of fish oil on skin problems.

Two other nutrients, vitamins A and C, are also beneficial to healthful skin. Vitamin A gets to the skin at the cellular level. It is essential to healthy tissues and membranes. In fact, Retin-A, a prescription drug that's supposed to have skin-enhancing qualities, is a chemical cousin of vitamin A. And vitamin C is important to the production of collagen, a protein that gives skin its strength.

Whether eating foods containing these nutrients will help your skin belie its years remains to be seen. But if you're looking for food to nourish the skin, try these healing foods from the list in chapter 2:

All dark green and yellow fruits and vegetables,
especially apricots, carrots, pumpkin, spinach, squash (winter), sweet potatoes
Citrus fruits (grapefruit, oranges, tangerines)
Fish (fatty varieties such as mackerel, salmon,
tuna)

Stroke

The older you get, the greater your chances of suffering a stroke, says James Halsey, M.D., director
of the Stroke Research Center at the University
of Alabama. If you're older *and* have high blood
pressure, consider yourself at greatest risk.

High blood pressure is the single most important cause of strokes. "The basic rule," says Dr.
Halsey, "is to reduce your overall consumption
of fat while replacing saturated with unsaturated
fats." And while you're at it, hide your saltshaker.
Sodium restriction alone could go a long way to
reducing your risk of stroke.

Preventing stroke isn't just a matter of avoiding certain foods, though. Studies show that
potassium-rich foods can cut your chances for
having a stroke, says Elizabeth Barrett-Connor,
M.D., professor and chair of the Department of
Community and Family Medicine at the University of California, San Diego. In a 12-year study,
Dr. Barrett-Connor divided 859 men and women
into three groups based on the amount of potassium in their diets—low, average, and high.
When the study concluded, the people in the
low-potassium group had the highest number of
stroke-associated deaths. And people who ate

high levels of potassium seemed to have no strokes at all, says Dr. Barrett-Connor. "By adding an extra serving of fruit or vegetables a day to their diet, people could protect themselves against having a stroke," she states.

Potassium helps to prevent strokes by protecting certain key cells from injury, explains Louis Tobian, M.D., of the University of Minnesota School of Medicine. In tests on laboratory animals, Dr. Tobian found that a diet high in potassium lowered the stroke rate by 91 percent.

"A high-potassium diet protects the endothelial cells, the cells that line the blood vessels, from the injury of high blood pressure," says Dr. Tobian. "By protecting these cells, it also helps to prevent thickening of the arteries, which is related to high blood pressure.

"By adding one baked potato, an 8-ounce glass of orange or grapefruit juice, half a melon, or a glass of skim milk to what you normally eat each day, you could help lower your stroke rate by 40 percent," says Dr. Tobian.

When you think of stroke prevention, think of high potassium. A menu plan for stroke prevention using the recipes in this book can be found on page 709. These are some of the high-potassium foods you'll find listed in chapter 2:

Apricots
Avocados
Bananas
Brussels sprouts
Cauliflower
Chestnuts

Fish
Milk (low-fat)
Mushrooms
Potatoes
Prunes
Spinach
Tofu

Urinary Tract Infections

An old folk remedy seems to be gaining some scientific backing. In research on both animals and humans, scientists have found there may be some merit to the belief that drinking cranberry juice can help prevent cystitis, a urinary tract infection that plagues many women. In one study, for example, drinking cranberry juice seemed to discourage recurring infections in 15 of 22 sufferers. How it helps, however, is up for debate.

On the other side of the ledger is a list of what *not* to eat if you're down with the disease. Certain foods can aggravate the burn of emptying the bladder. They include citrus fruits, spicy foods, coffee, alcohol, apples, apple juice, cantaloupe, carbonated drinks, chili peppers, grapes, peaches, pineapples, plums, strawberries, tea, tomatoes, and vinegar.

You should also watch out for avocados, bananas, cheese, lima beans, nuts, onions, prunes, rye bread, sour cream, soy sauce, and yogurt. They contain certain amino acids that have been found to be irritants.

Doctors advise patients troubled by cystitis to drink plenty of fluids. When increasing your fluid intake, you might want to include the juice of this healing food:

Cranberries

Wounds

Studies show that wounds such as surgical incisions heal best in people who consume a little more than the Recommended Dietary Allowance of vitamin C (60 milligrams). And a preliminary study from the University of Miami suggests that extra vitamin C can shorten the healing time for tooth extractions. The researchers speculate that vitamin C may work by stimulating the immune system and fostering scar-tissue growth, an important step in wound healing.

Vitamin-C-rich fruits, vegetables, and juices aren't the only foods that can help promote wound healing. Numerous studies show that vitamin A in the diet also stimulates wound healing, especially in people who are being treated with steroid drugs. (Steroids are often prescribed to control inflammation, but they also tend to make the skin heal more slowly.) But even without steroids, vitamin A deficiency can slow wound repair. So eating foods rich in vitamin A—like dark green and yellow vegetables—may help heal cuts or burns.

Then there's zinc. Studies have shown that people with low stores of zinc can help their wounds heal faster by increasing their supplies of this mineral. This is significant since mild zinc deficiency is not uncommon in the United States.

Fish oil may also help promote healing. But a

combination of all of these nutrients might even be better. At least that's what research at the Shriners Burns Institute in Cincinnati, Ohio, seems to indicate.

Doctors and nutritionists there tested the effects of nutrition therapy on 60 burn patients. A third of the patients were nourished with the standard tube-feeding formula for burns; the rest were prescribed formulas containing fish oil and extra zinc and vitamins A and C. Those on the special formula recovered faster and had significantly fewer infections.

If you're about to undergo surgery or are mending from a wound, consider the following foods listed in chapter 2. Also, a menu plan for wound healing using the recipes in this book can be found on page 777.

All dark green and yellow fruits and vegetables, especially apricots, carrots, pumpkin, spinach, squash (winter), sweet potatoes
Citrus fruits (grapefruit, oranges, tangerines)
Figs
Low-fat meats (beef, lamb, pork)
Mollusks (oysters)
Nuts (almonds, cashews)
Peppers (chili, sweet)
Poultry (chicken, turkey)
Salad greens
Waterfowl (duck)
Wheat germ

CHAPTER TWO

100 Foods for Health and Healing

The cornerstone of good health is a good diet—one packed with foods offering essential health-giving vitamins and minerals without being laden with fat and calories. And that's what the 100 foods highlighted in this chapter have to offer.

You won't be surprised to find that a lot of these foods are vegetables and fruits. As you discovered in chapter 1, that's because vegetables and fruits, more than any other foods, offer the most healing potential.

Broccoli, for instance, is a nutrient giant. As a cruciferous vegetable, it may decrease the risk of certain cancers. As a high-fiber, high-potassium, low-sodium food, it provides protection against heart disease high blood pressure, and stroke. And as a good source of calcium, it can help guard against osteoporosis.

Other produce is equally impressive. Carrots, cabbages, apples, pumpkins, potatoes, and winter squash earned their place on our list by being outstanding in a variety of healing nutrients.

Some of the foods on this list may surprise you. Beef, pork, and lamb, for example, have a reputation as dietary no-no's. But all are good sources of iron and can be part of a healing diet if you choose lean cuts and use them in moderation.

And you may wonder if such items as herbs and spices, celery, and mushrooms have enough nutrients to qualify as healing foods. The answer is that their strong point is exceptional *flavor*—enough to perk up a low-fat, low-salt diet so you can stay with it and reap its healthy benefits.

Certain foods on this list may be unfamiliar to you, but they're worth getting to know. For example, papayas, mangoes, and other tropical fruits have more than sun-drenched flavor; they're high in fiber and vitamins A and C for cancer protection. And kale is a tasty salad green that rivals the healing power of broccoli.

You'll also be introduced to a whole array of tasteful grains and their health benefits. Quinoa, an unusual grain once grown by the ancient Incas, is loaded with protein to help supplement a reduced-meat diet. Other oft-neglected grains such as buckwheat, bulgur, and millet are great ways to add a new dimension to your diet.

All of which brings up an important point: A *varied* diet supplies a wide range of nutrients and keeps you from getting bored with a few favorite foods. And variety is also what the list is all about.

If you make the foods in this chapter an integral part of your diet, you'll be using nature's best nutritional weapons against disease. Although its true that no specific diet can provide absolute protection from health problems, eating these foods may help increase your odds of living a slimmer, healthier, disease-free life.

Remember that a lifetime habit of healthy eating begins with meals that you truly enjoy. So use this list of 100 super foods—arranged in alphabetical order for your convenience—and the recipes that follow to serve yourself good health.

Apples: *One a day will do it.* An apple a day may indeed help keep the doctor away. That's because an apple delivers about 4.3 grams of dietary fiber—about as much as two slices of whole wheat bread. Most of it is in the insoluble form that prevents constipation and may protect against colon cancer. The rest is pectin, the fiber component that studies have shown can lower cholesterol levels.

Apples are a good source of potassium, which helps provide protection against strokes. And like most other fruits, they're also low in sodium (for better blood pressure), calories (for weight control), and fat (for lower cholesterol). As a bonus, apples are a great source of the mineral boron, which may help prevent the calcium losses from bone that may lead to osteoporosis.

Apricots: *A fruit brimming with beta-carotene.* These sweet-tart treats are packed with beta-carotene and fiber—all the better to fight cancer. Many studies have suggested that beta-carotene, the plant form of vitamin A, may have anticancer activity. Some studies suggest a protective effect in the stomach, colon, and cervix. And there's lots of evidence that colon cancer is less common in populations that eat a diet high in fiber.

Fresh apricots are practically calorie-free, containing only about 17 calories each. Dried apricots are a more concentrated source of calories, but $^1/_2$ cup still contains only about 150 calories and provides more than 90 percent of the Recommended Dietary Allowance (RDA) of vitamin A. In addition, apricots are high in potassium and low in sodium for blood pressure control and stroke protection.

Artichokes: *Dip into fiber.* More people should be on familiar terms with this unusual vegetable with the petal-shaped leaves. It contains amazing amounts of fiber, with one medium artichoke weighing in at 5.2 grams. That's more than you get in a whole bowl of oat-bran cereal, a rich fiber source. And that gives you a good head start on getting the 20 to 30 grams of fiber a day that the National Cancer Institute recommends for optimum health.

Although artichokes don't have large quantities of nutrients, they have enough vitamin A, vitamin C, folate, calcium, magnesium, and potassium to help combat diabetes, stroke, heart disease, and high blood pressure. And weight watchers should note that a whole medium 'choke has a mere 53 calories (as long as you forgo the hollandaise sauce). Also, eating an artichoke properly takes *time,* which can help overeaters control their appetites.

Asparagus: *Nutritional star of spring.* These elegant spears deserve a prominent place on your dinner table, especially in spring and early summer, when fresh stalks are plentiful. They're a dieter's dream, with 12 large spears having only 45 calories. Those same 12 stalks contain about

30 percent of the RDA of vitamin A and a generous amount of potassium to help prevent cancer, high blood pressure, and stroke.

In addition, asparagus contains no cholesterol and virtually no fat, making it an excellent food for those concerned about heart disease.

Avocados: *Rich in more ways than one.* You might wonder how a food with such a rich, silken, buttery texture can be *good* for you. Well, it can, thanks to its high content of heart-smart monounsaturated fat. That's the same fat predominant in olive oil, and it can actually help lower cholesterol levels in the body. In fact, in one study, men placed on an avocado-rich diet dropped their cholesterol levels anywhere from 9 to 43 percent. Since a 1 percent reduction in cholesterol causes a 2 percent drop in the risk of heart disease, that's *quite* significant.

Additionally, avocados are awesome sources of potassium and very low in sodium for double protection against high blood pressure and stroke. The avocado's only drawback is its high calorie count: 324 in a whole fruit. So whenever you plan to enjoy the avocado's health benefits, cut back calories elsewhere in your diet to make room.

Bananas: *Cure for many ills.* Banana peels may be for pratfalls, but the banana itself is no joke; a creamy-textured, medium-size banana has only 105 calories and the barest trace of fat.

What bananas *do* provide is lots of potassium for stroke protection. In fact, physicians often prescribe bananas as part of a regimen to lower blood pressure because this fruit is so high in potassium and magnesium.

Bananas have also been used to combat certain types of diarrhea. They not only restore lost potassium but also add valuable fiber to help end the problem. Ironically, bananas can also ease constipation, thanks to their generous fiber content.

Barley: *Down with cholesterol.* This healthy, high-fiber grain goes up against the best when it comes to cholesterol-lowering potential. According to researchers with the U.S. Department of Agriculture, two chemical compounds in barley lowered blood cholesterol levels by 40 percent in animals. In a study on people at Montana State University, seven volunteers ate barley fiber daily. After four weeks, the people with the highest cholesterol levels cut total cholesterol by 11 percent and harmful LDL cholesterol levels by 16 percent.

In addition, barley's high fiber content and low sodium count make it useful for helping to avoid certain types of cancer and also for managing high blood pressure.

The two most common forms of barley are Scotch and pearled. Scotch retains the bran and therefore has more fiber; soak it overnight before cooking. Pearled has had its bran layer removed.

Beans (dried): *Powerful protectors.* If you don't know beans about these health champs, make it your business to learn more. You can't get bored with these healthy legumes because there are so

58

many varieties available, including black beans, navy (or northern) beans, chick-peas, black-eyed peas, fava beans, limas, lentils, pinto beans, and soybeans. But regardless of their size and color, beans are an excellent source of complex carbohydrates, fiber, and protein. They boast healthy doses of anemia-fighting iron, nerve-soothing B vitamins, and bone-building calcium and phosphorus.

Perhaps their prime healing ingredient is soluble fiber. James W. Anderson, M.D., one of the country's leading cholesterol researchers advocates a diet high in dried beans for cholesterol control. In some studies, Dr. Anderson has seen cholesterol levels drop 60 points (in three weeks!) after adding pinto beans and navy beans to the diets of men with high cholesterol.

Besides soluble fiber, beans have a good helping of insoluble fiber to help prevent constipation and reduce the risk of diverticulosis and colon cancer. In addition, beans—as well as rice, potatoes, and seeds—contain compounds known as protease inhibitors, which may be potent anti-cancer weapons.

And beans are terrific girth-control devices. A study from Switzerland showed that beans can suppress the appetite for hours because they are digested very slowly. And since most beans average only 225 to 250 calories per cup, with very little fat, they're truly a lean choice for weight watchers.

Beans (snap): *Lightweight, iron strong.* Snap beans—as well as wax, Italian, and other fresh varieties—share most of the attributes of their dried counterparts. But since they're not as dense, they are lower in fiber and certain vitamins and minerals. Still, they are brimming with vitamins A and C, nutrients that are lacking in dried beans. That makes them ideal immunity boosters.

Fresh beans also have just enough iron—coupled with the vitamin C that enhances its absorption—to be a help against anemia. And these beans are a dieter's delight: A half cup of green or yellow snap beans has just 22 calories.

Beef (lean): *Keep it lean.* Yes, you can have your beef and heart health, too. Just make sure your beef is lean. In one Australian study, researchers pitted a vegetarian diet (that included milk and eggs) against an equal-fat diet containing lean meat. Both diets significantly lowered blood pressure, total cholesterol, and harmful LDL cholesterol.

Beef is dense in nutrients, so it packs a concentrated dose of vitamins and minerals. A 3-ounce serving of cooked lean beef contains about 17 percent of a woman's daily requirement for blood-building iron, and it's a very good source of zinc and B vitamins for better immunity.

The key to eating meat and staying healthy is to choose leaner cuts such as flank steak and skirt steak, whose fat is located around the outside for easy removal. For best economy, look for the new "select" variety, which is lower in fat than prime beef. At home, trim all visible fat *before* cooking. Studies show this results in leaner meat than trimming after cooking. When working with ground beef, buy the leanest available and microwave it. Experiments show that super-lean ground beef retains less fat when it is microwaved on paper towels than when it is roasted, broiled, or pan-fried in an electric skillet.

Beets: *A diet food that can't be beat.* Look to these red globes for a nice shot of no-fat, no-cholesterol, low-cal potassium to help lower blood pressure and protect against stroke. A whole cup of cooked sliced beets has only 52 calories—a figure low enough to warrant them a place of honor on your table. That same cup of beets has 3.4 grams of fiber, about the same as 1$^1/_2$ cups of cooked oatmeal.

Remember that although it's easier to peel cooked beets, you can peel and eat them raw. Raw beets have about twice the vitamin C as cooked ones for extra protection against cancer. Shred some into salads for a crunchy taste treat. And if you tire of the red color that bleeds onto your hands, look for one of the golden varieties on the market.

Blackberries: *Build strength with every bite.* It's worth your while to seek out these sweet little black beauties. With only 74 calories in a whole cupful, they're great snack food for dieters. And with fully half of your daily requirement for vitamin C in that cup, blackberries can help build immunity, speedçwound healing, and reduce the risk of some cancers.

The seeds in these little fruits provide an impressive amount of fiber. A cup of berries has 9 grams of dietary fiber—that's a sizable part of the 20 to 30 grams a day the National Cancer Institute recommends for possible protection against colorectal cancer. Further, blackberries' high-fiber, no-sodium, very-low-fat profile makes them ideal for diabetics. And their potassium content makes sense for stroke prevention.

Blueberries: *Diet delights.* Reach for a bit of blue heaven. For the 82 calories in a cup of blueberries, you get about one-third of the RDA for vitamin C and 3.4 grams of fiber. There's a tiny amount of sodium, a modest level of potassium, and just a trace of fat. All of which adds up to a berry wise choice at the produce counter.

Bran: *Full of fiber.* The bran news is good. All types of bran—wheat, oat, corn, soy, rice—are wonderful sources of both insoluble and soluble fiber. And each type of fiber has potent health-promoting strengths.

Insoluble fiber, the kind prominent in wheat bran, bulks up stool and speeds it through the colon. Experts theorize that cancer-causing agents are swept quickly away with the stool. It's also this bulking action that may help relieve constipation, hemorrhoids, and diverticular disease.

In addition, at least one study has shown that adding wheat bran to the diet may shrink precancerous polyps in the lower intestine, reducing the risk of colon and rectal cancers.

Soluble fiber—found in outstanding quantities

in oat, corn, and rice brans and soy fiber—is the hero when it comes to lowering cholesterol. Oat bran has gotten the most notice on this front, with numerous studies by Dr. James Anderson, a leading fiber researcher, and others showing impressive cholesterol-busting results. Likewise, studies with rice and corn brans indicate they have a similar effect on cholesterol.

Soy fiber may improve glucose tolerance and insulin response in people with adult-onset (type II) diabetes. And it seems to keep the bowels working at good speed, as wheat bran does. Another product, apple fiber, contains even more fiber than oat bran and may also be valuable for lowering cholesterol.

Broccoli: *Stalk trouble before it strikes.* Broccoli is one of the true superstars of the produce bin. It's a member in good standing of the crucifer family of vegetables, and studies have suggested that eating a diet rich in these veggies may decrease cancer risks. Broccoli is also packed with beta-carotene and vitamin C, two powerful cancer battlers. At least one study suggests that you can get the most anticancer power from broccoli by eating it raw, so cover all bases by enjoying it both cooked and au naturel.

Broccoli is rich in potassium, a mineral that's credited with a lowered incidence of high blood pressure and stroke. Its high fiber content also helps lower cholesterol, which—along with the green giant's low sodium and fat levels—lowers the risk of heart disease. Preliminary studies suggest that the vitamin C in produce such as broccoli may even head off heart disease before it starts by protecting against free radicals, unstable molecules thought to transform cholesterol into building blocks of artery-clogging plaque.

And broccoli is a great source of bone-building calcium, which can reduce your chances of developing osteoporosis. And it gives the overweight a diet boost by being both low in calories and high in hunger-satisfying fiber.

Brussels sprouts: *A package of potassium.* Meet another upstanding member of the crucifer clan. These "little cabbages" are almost as impressive in all areas of healing potential as broccoli. Although they have considerably less calcium than broccoli when cooked, the two are on par when raw. And cooked sprouts have as much vitamin C and iron as broccoli and almost *twice* as much stroke-preventing potassium as broccoli.

One tip: If you're one of those people who think they don't like brussels sprouts, try cooking the little vegetables until *just* tender. Over-cooking accounts for the characteristic strong flavor that many people object to.

Buckwheat: *Flour power—and kasha, too.* Pass the buckwheat, please! Generally thought of as a cereal grain, buckwheat is actually an herb whose seeds are eaten whole as groats or ground as flour. Unlike grains such as wheat and rye, buckwheat has no gluten, so people with celiac disease can use it freely.

Buckwheat is low in fat and calories, with $1/2$

cup of cooked roasted groats (kasha) containing about 97 calories. And it's high in fiber, which is so important for digestive health and possible cancer protection.

In addition, studies show that buckwheat is digested very slowly, which may give it the potential to prevent adult-onset (type II) diabetes and to improve glucose tolerance in those who already have the disease. And this slow digestion process means that you feel full longer, possibly curbing the urge to overeat later. Another plus is buckwheat's high-quality protein, which makes it beneficial for those cutting back on meat.

Many recipes call for coating the groats with beaten egg before cooking. If you're cutting back on cholesterol, use an equivalent amount of egg whites or egg substitute.

Bulgur: *A quick fiber option.* There's nothing vulgar about bulgur, a whole-grain product made from wheat kernels that have been steamed, dried, and crushed. This process lets you prepare bulgur very quickly as a substitute for long-cooking brown rice. Because only a small part of the bran is lost during processing, bulgur is nutritionally almost identical to whole wheat. That means it contains lots of dietary fiber for added protection against diverticular disease and certain types of cancer.

In addition, bulgur contains B vitamins and iron for increased immunity and a bit of potassium for better blood pressure and stroke protection.

Cabbage: *King of the anticancer clan.* When you think of the Big C—cancer—remember the Little C—cabbage. This wonderful cancer-fighting crucifer comes in so many varieties that you'll never tire of it. And that's good because some studies have suggested that consumption of the crucifers in general may reduce the risk of gastrointestinal and respiratory-tract cancers. Others indicate that the vitamin C in vegetables such as cabbage is protective against stomach and esophageal cancers. And there's lots of evidence that fiber (high in this vegetable) helps reduce the risk of colon cancer. Still further research suggests that cruciferous vegetables may slow cancer's spread once it has developed in the body.

Because the crucifers may work their wonders even better when raw, try to include lots of uncooked cabbage in your diet. Choose from regular green and red varieties plus savoy, bok choy, and napa (Chinese) cabbage. A half cup of shredded cabbage (perfect in a mixed green salad) contains a minuscule 8 calories. Dieters, take note.

Carrots: *Vitamin A plus.* What's up, doc? Cancer Protection. Carrots are chockablock with vitamin A and, perhaps more important, beta-carotene. This vegetable form of the vitamin is credited with activity against various cancers, including those of the larynx, esophagus, lung, colon, stomach, and cervix. Just half a cup of cooked carrots has almost four times the RDA for vitamin A. And although vitamin A is toxic in large doses, the beta-carotene form found in carrots and other vegetables is not.

What's down, doc? Cholesterol. Researchers from the U.S. Department of Agriculture say just two carrots a day can reduce cholesterol by as much as 20 percent, which can help lessen the threat of heart disease. And if you substitute crunchy, chewy carrots for less-nutritious snacks, your weight may go down. A whole large carrot has just 31 calories. Pretty good for rabbit food, eh?

Cauliflower: *Ahead in stroke protection.* Heads up when you pass this giant flower of the produce section. A tasty half cup of cooked florets has just 15 calories. And for those few calories you get lots of potassium and just a little sodium —the perfect formula for blood pressure and stroke control. What's more, that same half cup contains about 50 percent of your daily quota for vitamin C, a nutrient that helps build immunity, battle fatigue, and aid iron in countering anemia.

Then, too, cauliflower is another cancer-bashing cruciferous vegetable. In the years ahead, it may have even more power against cancer. Plant scientists are in the process of breeding a new, bright orange variety of cauliflower that would taste the same as white but pack *100 times* more cancer-blocking carotene into its lovely head.

Celery: *Versatile flavor enhancer.* This perennial favorite on the diet scene isn't all that high in specific nutrients (but that's to be expected from a food that's got only 6 calories in a whole stalk). Celery's strength lies in the big flavor it delivers with virtually no fat attached. And it's so versatile it can accent just about any dish—and you'll never tire of its taste. That makes it a boon to anyone on the kind of fat-restricted diet recommended for lowering cholesterol or dealing with conditions such as diabetes, hiatal hernia, or gallbladder problems, to name but a few.

Celery does contain a bit more sodium than many other vegetables, but that little taste of salt may be just enough to keep you from reaching for the saltshaker and doing greater damage. And celery has about $3^1/_2$ times more potassium than sodium, which helps the body prevent high blood pressure.

Cheese (low-fat): *Say calcium, please.* Here's good news for cheese lovers on a heart-healthy— or otherwise low-fat—diet: You *can* eat cheese, just make your selections wisely. A 1-ounce slice of even low-fat cheese can go a long way toward satisfying your daily protein requirement, especially if you're a vegetarian. And cheese is an excellent source of calcium to help guard against osteo-porosis. Further, studies seem to suggest a link between higher calcium intake and lower rates of intestinal cancer. And at least one study concluded that certain fatty acids in cheeses and milk may confer some degree of protection against cancer.

PUT THESE CHEESES ON YOUR MENUS

Cheese can be part of any healing diet, as long as you select those that are lowest in fat and calories. Sapsago, for example, is virtually fat-free, so you can use it liberally in your recipes. In fact, you'll find it in many of the recipes in this book. (If it's not available in your area, Parmesan is an acceptable substitute.) You will still need to practice a little discretion when it comes to those cheeses higher in calories—such as Cheddar, Colby, and Muenster—however, especially if weight loss is your goal. Generally, though, if you limit your selection to the cheeses listed in this table, you can consider yourself on the right side of health.

Cheese	Serving	Fat (g)	Calories
Yogurt cheese, nonfat	1 oz.	0	17
Pot cheese	1 oz.	0	25
Gammelost	1 oz.	0.1–0.3	52–60
Sapsago	1 tbsp.	0.4	12
Fromage blanc	1 oz.	0.5	18
Yogurt cheese, low-fat	1 oz.	0.6	30
Parmesan, grated	1 tbsp.	1.9	29
Monterey Jack, processed	1 oz.	2.0	50
Cheddar, processed	1 oz.	2.0–4.0	50–70
Swiss, processed	1 oz.	2.0–4.0	50–70
Muenster, processed	1 oz.	2.0–5.0	50–85
Swiss, lite	1 oz.	2.0–6.0	50–97
Cheddar, lite	1 oz.	3.0–6.0	65–90

Cheese	Serving	Fat (g)	Calories
Edam, reduced fat	1 oz.	3.1	65
String, lite	1 oz.	4.0–6.0	70–90
Mozzarella, part-skim	1 oz.	4.5	72
Scamorza, part-skim	1 oz.	5.0	70
Colby, low-fat	1 oz.	5.0	85
Muenster, lite	1 oz.	5.0	85
Farmer's	1 oz.	5.0–7.0	80–90
Feta	1 oz.	6.0	75
Monterey Jack, lite	1 oz.	6.0	80
Mozzarella, whole-milk	1 oz.	6.1	80
Neufchâtel	1 oz.	6.6	74

On other fronts, cheese may aid insomniacs because it contains tryptophan, an amino acid that helps the brain regulate sleep. And cheese may even benefit your teeth by remineralizing them and also by reducing acids that cause plaque and lead to cavities. Now that's something to smile about.

As the preceding chart shows, some cheeses that are lowest in fat include Sapsago (a skim-milk product from Switzerland suitable for grating), pot cheese (a drier form of cottage cheese), and yogurt cheese (drained yogurt with the texture of cream cheese).

Cherries: Get sweet on these treats. What sweet treats these are—even the sour varieties! They're low in calories (ten sweet cherries have only 49) and fat to benefit dieters, diabetics, and cholesterol watchers. They have almost no sodium but a decent amount of potassium to aid those with high blood pressure and those worried about stroke. And sour cherries have an impressive helping of vitamin A (close to 40 percent of the RDA in a cup of pitted fruit) and a nice amount of vitamin C (25 percent of the RDA)—all the better to wrestle cancer and bolster immunity.

For some gout sufferers, life is a bowl of cherries. Adding this fruit to their diet, they say, helps relieve their pain. Unscientific though they may be, believers claim that daily consumption of cherries brings them great relief. Considering cherries' other qualities, there's no reason not to enjoy them often.

Chestnuts: *Autumn's slim pickings.* If you're nuts about chestnuts, you've made a sane choice. These dark-shelled beauties are by far the slimmest relatives of the nut family. A large handful (eight or nine nuts) has less than 2 grams of fat clinging to its 175 calories. And that fat is largely of the beneficial monounsaturated and polyunsaturated varieties. At least one study found that linolenic acid, a type of polyunsaturate found in chestnuts, could lower blood pressure.

Speaking of blood pressure, chestnuts have an excellent sodium-to-potassium ratio. That means they're perfect for helping to control blood pressure and thereby prevent strokes.

Chestnuts also contain pectin, a water-soluble fiber that may be useful in treating overeating in obese people because it slows the digestive process. And shelling chestnuts one by one as you nibble certainly slows the *eating* process!

Chicken: *Lean to the light.* If your future's looking fowl, consider yourself lucky. Chicken is a very lean choice for frequent eating and is excellent for those on a heart-healthy diet. (See the chart below and opposite page.) Just be sure to follow a few simple tips: Don't eat the skin, which is composed largely of fat. Be aware that breast meat is inherently leaner than thigh meat. When you do serve thighs, remove as much visible fat as possible. If cooking a whole bird, get rid of those very large fat deposits just inside the cavity.

RATING THE BIRDS

Here's how various birds compare with one another in terms of calories, grams of fat, and percentage of calories from fat. In all cases, of course, the lower numbers are better. But all the numbers are quite acceptable for a healthy diet. Figures represent $3^1/_2$ ounces of uncooked boneless meat with both skin and any visible fat removed.

Poultry	Calories	Fat (g)	Calories from Fat (%)
Turkey, fryer-roaster, breast only	111	0.7	5
Capon, breast only	110	1.2	10
Cornish hen, breast only	110	1.2	10
Chicken, broiler or fryer, breast only	110	1.2	10

Poultry	Calories	Fat (g)	Calories from Fat (%)
Turkey, fryer-roaster, light and dark meat	110	1.6	13
Guinea fowl, light and dark meat	110	2.5	20
Turkey, fryer-roaster, dark meat only	111	2.7	21
Chicken, roaster, light and dark meat	111	2.7	21
Quail, breast meat	123	3.0	21
Pheasant, breast meat	133	3.3	22
Chicken, broiler or fryer, light and dark meat	119	3.1	23
Pheasant, light and dark meat	133	3.6	24
Chicken, roaster, dark meat	113	3.6	28
Quail, light and dark meat	134	4.5	30
Capon, dark meat	125	4.3	31
Chicken, broiler or fryer, dark meat	125	4.3	31
Cornish hen, dark meat	125	4.3	31
Duck, wild, breast meat	123	4.3	31

Do all that and you'll get the most benefit from chicken's nutrients: iron for anemia prevention, potassium for lower stroke risk, B vitamins for immunity, and zinc for wound healing. What's more, chicken contains selenium, a trace mineral that may help protect against some forms of cancer.

Corn: *Kernels in a healing battle.* There's nothing corny about this golden vegetable. It contributes B vitamins, vitamin C, potassium, and magnesium to help ward off fatigue. There's a decent amount of fiber for assistance against cancer as well as digestive problems. And it contains no gluten, so both fresh kernels and dried-corn products such as cornmeal, grits, and corn bran are suitable for those with celiac disease.

With a good amount of potassium and little sodium, corn is also on the menu for lowered blood pressure and stroke protection. Just be sure to check labels when buying canned or frozen corn for the presence of added sodium.

Although corn's not a particularly rich source of vitamin A, you should know that yellow varieties do contain the vitamin, while white ones do not.

Cottage cheese (low-fat): *More than diet food.* Low-fat cottage cheese deserves a separate listing from other cheeses because it's so versatile and because there may be confusion about the different types available. It's true that low-fat cottage cheese is not as concentrated a source of bone-building calcium as you'd expect from a milk product. But every bit counts if you're hoping to avoid osteoporosis and gastrointestinal cancer. Further, this cottage cheese is so low in fat, calories, and cholesterol that it warrants a place in the diets of weight watchers and those hoping to avoid heart disease. (See the chart on the next page.) And its high-quality protein is a boon to vegetarians.

A large part of cottage cheese's value is its ability to stand in for high-fat sour cream, cream cheese, and cheese spreads in many recipes. Just blender-ize it until smooth.

Cranberries: *Very versatile berries.* These tart little berries are low in calories—as long as you don't load them up with sugar. Pair them instead with naturally sweet fruits such as apples, oranges, or dried apricots. Like most fruits, cranberries have barely a speck of fat but do have modest amounts of stroke-fighting potassium and cancer-battling vitamin A. The raw berries also contain a nice amount of vitamin C: a cup of chopped fruit has almost 25 percent of the RDA. (And, yes, you can eat cranberries raw.) That same cupful has a respectable 4 grams of dietary fiber to help control cholesterol and ensure bowel health.

Scientists have also found that cranberry juice seems to prevent certain types of bacteria from clinging to the inside of the bladder and urinary tract, so it may help to ease bladder infections.

WHERE'S THE FAT?

Various types of cottage cheese and ricotta cheese may look alike, but they differ quite a bit in calories, cholesterol, and fat, including the percentage af calories that come from fat. Make it a point to use the lowest-fat product that satisfies your taste and desire for creaminess. All figures are for $^1/_2$ cup.

Cheese	Calories	Fat (g)	Calories from Fat (%)	Cholesterol (mg)
Cottage, dry curd	62	0.3	4	5
Cottage, 1% fat	82	1.2	13	5
Cottage, 2% fat	102	2.2	19	10
Cottage, creamed	109	4.7	39	16
Ricotta, part-skim	171	9.8	52	38
Ricotta, whole-milk	216	16.1	67	63

Crustaceans: *Vitamin sea.* You probably know these classy shellfish by their less-formal names: crab, shrimp, crayfish, and lobster. These denizens of the deep fit swimmingly into a health-conscious diet. They're nicely low in calories—as long as you deep-six the melted butter and tartar sauce. A serving (3 ounces) of cooked king crab has only 82 calories. Blue crab, shrimp, and lobster are about the same, and crayfish are just slightly higher.

Years ago, crustaceans were wrongly judged to have too much cholesterol for a heart-healthy diet. Today we know that although there is cholesterol in these seafoods—from 45 milligrams in king crab to 166 milligrams in shrimp—the amount is far less than originally thought. What's more important, perhaps, is the extra-skimpy amount of saturated fat in these foods. Doctors believe that saturated fat plays a larger role in the development of heart disease than does dietary cholesterol.

All of the above-mentioned crustaceans contain nice amounts of antistroke potassium to help counter their natural sodium levels. Crayfish are actually quite low in sodium, with only 58 milligrams per serving. The others range from 190 milligrams in shrimp up to a quite high 911 milligrams in king crab. So if you're on a sodium-restricted diet, choose your catch of the day with care.

Cucumbers: *Nothing but goodness.* Cukes are one of those foods that are valued more for what's *not* in them than for what is. There's basically no fat, no sodium, no cholesterol, and no calories (an entire $1/2$ cup has only 7!). That should make everyone happy—dieters, hypertensives, heart-smart eaters, and diabetics, to name a few.

Just make sure to enjoy these vegetables in their fresh state. Pickling them adds a lot of sodium.

Food for thought: Researchers have discovered that cucumber leaves carry an enzyme that alters cholesterol so it quickly passes through the digestive tract without being absorbed. They're working to convert this enzyme into an anticholesterol food additive. Until then, make cukes part of your own cholesterol-lowering diet.

Eggplant: *Mediterranean "medicine."* This deep purple dream is very low in calories, sodium, and fat. A whole cup of cooked cubes has a mere 27 calories, 3 milligrams of sodium, and a trace of fat. But it carries 4 grams of fiber (almost as much as a serving of oat bran) to help keep cancer and elevated cholesterol in their place. Some studies have suggested that eggplant itself actually can help lower cholesterol. And its 238 milligrams of potassium can contribute to putting the lid on high blood pressure. No wonder eggplant is such an indispensable part of the Mediterranean diets that doctors consider so healthy.

A word to the wise: At the stove, eggplant soaks up fat like a sponge. So if you're sautéing it, opt for good-for-you monounsaturated oils like olive and canola. But even then, try to keep quantities down.

Figs: *First fruit of fiber.* Figs are real fiber champs. Five of the dried fruits contain an impressive 8.7 grams of dietary fiber. That's more than you'd get in three bran muffins. Part of the fiber is in the insoluble form that combats constipation and reduces the risk of gastrointestinal and colon cancers. The rest is soluble to help lower cholesterol and reduce the risk of heart disease. Part of that soluble fiber is pectin, which may help curb a ravenous appetite by making you feel full longer.

But that's not all. Dried figs are a respectable

source of minerals, including iron (for anemia protection), potassium (to counter stroke), and zinc (to aid wound healing).

For a real taste treat, fill up on fresh figs in season. One medium fruit has only 37 calories to accompany its sweet, silken texture.

Fish: Striking nutritional oil. Holy mackerel! Who would've thought fish could be such fine food? All fish contain—to one degree or another —omega-3 fatty acids, special fats that can keep your heart healthy by lowering harmful cholesterol in the blood. And in one study, people who ate one or more fish meals a week had more flexible arteries, signaling a healthier cardiovascular system, than those who ate no fish.

FISHING FOR THE BEST

If you'd like to get maximum benefit per mouthful, pay heed to this fish chart. It lists the best sources of omega-3's, those beneficial fats that may help reduce the risk of blood clots that could lead to heart attacks or strokes. Although the jury is still out on just how much of the omega-3's you need for good health, many doctors believe that as few as two to four fish meals a week may help. All figures are for $3^1/_2$ ounces of uncooked seafood.

Seafood	Omega-3's (g)
Atlantic mackerel	2.6
Anchovies (canned)*	2.1
Atlantic herring	1.7
Atlantic salmon	1.7
Pink salmon (canned)	1.7
Sablefish	1.5
Chinook salmon	1.4
Whitefish	1.4
Sockeye salmon	1.3
Bluefin tuna	1.2
Coho salmon	1.0
Pink salmon	1.0

* Because of their high salt content, anchovies should not be eaten by those on a sodium-restricted diet.

Fish may also prevent strokes by preventing blood platelets from clumping and blocking arteries. Further, such diverse maladies as breast cancer, arthritis, asthma, diabetes, and psoriasis—all of which are thought to involve the immune system—may benefit from omega-3's.

The top sources of omega-3's? The "fattier" varieties of fish such as mackerel, herring, sablefish, bluefin tuna, and various types of salmon. And there's good news for those who like canned fish. The canning process does not deplete omega-3's. In fact, if you eat canned fish that contains bones—such as salmon, sardines, anchovies, and mackerel—you get an added benefit: an extra dose of calcium to help prevent osteoporosis and colon cancer and to lower high blood pressure. A side note: Tuna fish in solid white form has twice the omega-3's of chunk light varieties.

Many types of fish, including salmon, swordfish, and tuna, contain selenium. Some studies have linked this trace mineral with a lower risk of cancer, particularly those of the breast and colon.

The low-fat, milder types of fish, incKuding cod, haddock, flounder, and mahimahi, contain fewer omega-3's than their fatty oceanmates. But they're still superb dinner fare. They're a very lean, low-calorie alternative to red meat. Dieters have long turned to fish to help shed pounds. And although most fresh fish do contain sodium, they also have a hefty dose of potassium to help keep down blood pressure. So the story that fish is health food is one you can swallow hook, line, and sinker. Try to eat fish at least twice a week.

Game: *Beef-lover's alternative.* Are you game for a new taste sensation? Most game is naturally lower in fat than the usual cuts of red meat. And what they do have is mostly polyunsaturated. That makes them acceptable for meat eaters hoping to keep their risk of heart disease low.

Meat from the wild tends to be higher in protein and lower in calories than the well-marbled cuts in supermarkets. A $3^1/_2$-ounce serving of moose contains a mere 1.5 grams of fat; deer, 4 grams; and pheasant, 5.2. By comparison, the same portion of sirloin steak has 26.7 grams of fat.

More specifics: Domestic rabbit is even lower in cholesterol than chicken (57 milligrams in a serving versus 70 for chicken). Buffalo meat offers 50 percent less cholesterol, 70 percent less fat, and 30 percent more protein than beef. Texas antelope gets only 5 percent of its calories from fat. Pheasant meat is lean and very mild in taste. So make it your business to hunt for these healthy meats—either outdoors or at farmers' markets, specialty shops, and upscale supermarkets.

Garlic: Keep heart disease at bay. You can ward off more than vampires with garlic. Scientists are seriously examining the potential of this odoriferous bulb, so prominent in cuisines world-wide, to protect against heart disease. Studies have shown that garlic raises levels of beneficial cholesterol in the body while also lowering total cholesterol levels.

Garlic also thins the blood, reducing the chance of clotting. Blood clots are one of the most common causes of heart attack and stroke. And this herb lowers blood pressure and blood sugar levels.

A preliminary study from China suggests that allium family vegetables, which include garlic and onions, may reduce the risk of stomach cancer. The theory is that these vegetables have antibacterial and antifungal properties that may inhibit tumor growth.

Grapefruit: The secret's in its fiber. What dieter isn't on intimate terms with grapefruit? And with good reason—a whole cupful of juicy sections has only 74 slender calories. But nestled in among those calories is a fine amount of cholesterol-lowering pectin, a type of soluble fiber. In fact, when Florida researchers conducted cholesterol studies, they chose grapefruit pectin as their star ingredient. After eight weeks, test subjects showed a significant drop in cholesterol levels.

This golden fruit is a wonderful source of vitamin C, with a medium half containing 69 percent of the RDA. Vitamin C is known to fight fatigue, boost immunity, aid in wound healing, and help iron protect against anemia. It may also have anticancer properties.

A note to the colorblind: Pink and red grapefruit get their rich color from beta-carotene, which is believed to help prevent some forms of cancer. Pink varieties have *27 times* more carotene than white ones.

Grapes: *The vine healer.* These sweet little jewels are relatively low in calories—114 in a satisfying cupful. And they have some vitamin A and vitamin C to help ward off colds, flu, and other immunity problems. Further, they're high in potassium and very low in sodium, the perfect prescription for blood pressure control and possible antistroke benefit.

Grapes also contain boron, a little-known nutrient that could help safeguard calcium in the body and thereby help prevent osteoporosis.

Herbs and spices: *Kick the salt habit.* Herbs and spices do contain some vitamins and minerals, but most people don't eat them in large enough quantities for those nutrients to be significant. (In medicinal doses, many of them have healing qualities of their own.) When it comes to cooking, the real benefit of these aromatics is their ability to perk up the type of restrictive diets often recommended for blood pressure control, diabetes, diverticular disease, heart disease, gallbladder problems, gout, irritable bowel syndrome, lactose intolerance, overweight, ulcers, and more. No wonder these flavor enhancers are called the spice of life!

Kale: Carotene and calcium in every crunch. This attractive green packs a lot of punch for the crunch. It's another of the heavy-hitting crucifers that are considered so protective against cancer. And it's rich in vitamin A, potassium, calcium, and vitamin C. One cup of chopped raw leaves (enough for a lovely salad) has more than a day's requirement of both A and C but just 33 calories. That makes it a wise diet choice. And cooking doesn't destroy valuable carotene (the plant form of vitamin A). A cup of cooked kale has just a few more calories but *61 percent more* vitamin A—almost twice the RDA. That same cupful contains over 5 grams of fiber, more than a serving of oat-bran cereal.

Like certain other dark leafy greens, kale contains oxalic acid, which can bind with calcium in the body to keep it from being absorbed. But unlike spinach, for instance, kale has far more calcium than oxalic acid, so it's still considered a good source of this bone-strengthening mineral. One cup of cooked frozen kale has 179 milligrams of calcium—as much as 1 ounce of part-skim mozzarella.

At the market, be on the lookout for ornamental kales, which come in a gorgeous array of colors, so you won't become bored with this terrific vegetable.

Kiwifruit: *Key in vitamin C.* Also called the Chinese gooseberry, this fuzzy fruit is anything but silly. It's wonderfully low in calories—only 55 in a large fruit—and exotic enough to appease even the most jaded dieter. But more than that, it's a great source of vitamin C (with $1^1/_2$ times the RDA of 60 milligrams) to help bolster immunity and prevent breast cancer. And it's nicely high in potassium to benefit blood pressure and help provide stroke protection.

As a fiber source, the kiwi can hold its own against other fruits, including apples, strawberries, and even prunes—so much the better to counter diverticular disease, hemorrhoids, and constipation.

Lamb (lean): *Link to iron and zinc.* Be a lamb and include this meat in your diet. While it's always been promoted as a good source of iron to prevent anemia, lamb doesn't usually spring to mind when thinking about weight loss or heart health. Yet cuts of extra-lean lamb can qualify on both counts. A broiled, well-trimmed loin chop has just 92 calories and 3.7 grams of fat. That's not significantly more than a serving of dark-meat turkey. Three ounces of lean roasted leg has 158 calories and 6 grams of fat.

In addition, lamb is a good source of zinc, a mineral that's essential for wound healing and good immunity from a variety of infections. And people with hearing problems and taste-perception distortions have experienced improvement thanks to zinc.

A final note: Lamb is often an acceptable meat for those with food allergies and is frequently included in the type of rotation diet recommended for allergic people.

Lemons and limes: *Perk up taste without salt.* Don't be a sourpuss when it comes to these tropical delights. Weight watchers have long used these small-but-mighty fruits to perk up the taste of seafood salads, and vegetables in lieu of butter and fatty dressings. And the tart juice even seems to compensate for missing salt, so it can aid those on low-sodium diets.

And while few people will actually eat a whole lemon or lime, fresh-squeezed juice is a good source of vitamin C. Try it in sparkling mineral water as a low-cal pick-me-up.

Exciting news: A naturally occurring chemical in citrus fruit may have the power to prevent cancer. An animal study at the University of Minnesota showed that this bitter substance prevented stomach cancer from forming in a certain number of lab animals fed a potent cancer-causing substance. More research is planned in this area.

Mangoes: *The color of carotene.* Here's another native of the tropics with shining credentials. A cup of silky, juicy slices has a modest amount of calories but lots of vitamin A, in the form of beta-carotene, to help prevent cancer. And it's got plenty of vitamin C, fiber, and potassium. Mango even contains vitamin E, which some studies have linked to a reduced overall risk of cancer.

If you're not familiar with this sweet fruit, select underripe green fruit slightly blushed with rose, peach, or yellow. Let it ripen at room temperature for a few days until streaked with brighter color and slightly soft. Peel and core over a bowl to catch all the luscious juices. And don't expect the pit to come out easily; cut the flesh away with a sharp knife.

Melons: *Variety and vitamins.* Talk about an embarrassment of riches! There are more melons in the market these days than you can shake a stick at (if you were inclined to do such a thing). Besides the normal cantaloupe, honeydew, casaba, and watermelon, there's crenshaw, honeyloupe, pepino, persian, Santa Claus, yellow watermelon, and lots more. Although they may differ in taste and color, they're all low in calories, fat, and sodium.

Melons have valuable fiber and plenty of potassium. And they can be counted on to deliver a nice shot of vitamin C. As a bonus, the orange varieties such as cantaloupe are an excellent source of cancer-fighting beta-carotene. Even watermelon has enough vitamin A to make it a valuable addition to your diet.

Milk (low-fat): *Big benefits for bones.* Milk has been called the perfect food because it provides more elements to sustain life than almost anything else. It's our single best source of calcium; a cup of skim milk provides 38 percent of the RDA of 800 milligrams. (See the chart on pages 89–90.) The calcium in milk can fortify your bones against osteoporosis and may help prevent colon cancer as well as lower your blood pressure.

Milk is also a good source of antistress B vitamins, especially B_{12}, as well as vitamin A, potassium, and iodine. In addition, virtually all milk is enriched with vitamin D, which enhances calcium absorption. This "sunshine vitamin" may also help us hang on to calcium already stored in the bones, says a Tufts University study. That's especially important for older, fracture-prone women whose bones tend to lose calcium. And several preliminary studies have linked low levels of vitamin D with higher risk of colon cancer, so milk fortified with the vitamin may provide protection.

Research has shown that drinking skim milk may lower total cholesterol levels. In one study men who drank a quart of 2 percent milk a day increased the proportion of good cholesterol in their blood by 19.5 percent after three months and 31 percent after six months. Such a change is believed to be highly protective against heart disease.

Millet: *Easy on allergies.* If you're not used to eating grains, you might think millet's for the birds. And since it's a prime component of birdseed, you'd be partially right. But it's also a respectable food for all of us health-conscious humans.

Millet contains good amounts of B vitamins, iron, and potassium. And it contains protein that's as good as or better than that in rice, corn, and oats. With about 90 calories and very little fat in a cooked cup, it's perfect for weight watchers. And like other whole grains, it has a decent amount of fiber for digestive health and anticancer power.

Millet tends to be tolerated by people who are allergic to wheat or other grains. And it contains no gluten, so those with celiac disease should feel free to indulge.

IS YOUR MILK TOO FAT?

Here's how *your* favorite milk stocks up against the competition in terms of calories, fat, percentage of calories from fat, and milligrams of calcium. Don't be fooled by ads saying whole milk is only 4 percent fat. That's figured on a weight basis. The number of calories that come from fat—a more accurate assessment of health value—is considerably higher, tipping the scales at 49 percent. All figures below are for 1 cup of liquid milk.

Milk	Calories	Fat (g)	Calories from Fat (%)	Calcium (mg)
Evaporated skim, undiluted	198	0.5	2	738
Nonfat dry, reconstituted	81	0.2	2	279
Skim	86	0.4	5	302
Buttermilk	99	2.2	20	285
Low-fat (1%)	102	2.6	23	300
Low-fat (1%) with added calcium	102	3.0	26	500
Low-fat (2%)	121	4.7	35	297
Whole	158	8.2	49	291
Evaporated whole, undiluted	338	19.1	51	658

Mollusks: *Minerals galore.* Here's a pearl for seafood lovers: Mollusks—such as oysters, clams, scallops, and mussels—are considerably lower in cholesterol than once believed. And they contain virtually no saturated fat. When you take into consideration *both* cholesterol and saturated fat, these shellfish are a better dietary choice than even the leanest red meats. And mollusks also have those heart-healthy omega-3 fatty acids, with mussels and oysters containing more than scallops and clams.

But that's not all. Certain shellfish are virtual mineral depositories. Clams are so high in iron it's a wonder they don't rust! That makes them potent antianemia food. Mussels and oysters are also good sources of iron. Oysters contain plenty of zinc, a mineral needed for proper growth and development as well as wound healing and immunity to various infections. And oysters have their fair share of copper, which helps to regulate cholesterol metabolism and the heart. So eat hearty, mateys.

Mushrooms: *Weight-loss champions.* With new varieties cropping up in supermarkets like, well, mushrooms, these tasty little morsels are worth a second glance. They're ridiculously low in calories, with $1/2$ cup of raw pieces weighing in at 9 and $1/2$ cup of cooked just 21! Dieters can eat to their hearts' content, adding handfuls to salads, casseroles, and stews. And many varieties of mushrooms—shiitake, enoki, and porcini, just to name a few—have a meaty taste and texture, so they can help replace meat in many dishes.

Like many other vegetables, mushrooms are very high in potassium and correspondingly low in sodium, the perfect formula for better blood pressure and, hopefully, stroke control. In addition, mushrooms contain a decent amount of B vitamins, considering how few calories they have.

Nectarines: *Nutritiously well rounded.* Now here's a peach of a fruit! Like its fuzzy relative, the nectarine is refreshingly low in calories yet well supplied with cancer-fighting fiber and stroke-preventing potassium. And it's a nice source of vitamin A and vitamin C, for immune power and wound healing.

91

Nuts: *Mind your monos.* Health nuts love these crunchy little nuggets. It's a good thing because many nuts are high in monounsaturated fatty acids—those wonderful fats predominant in olive oil and other foods that have been shown to lower cholesterol. (See the chart on page 93.) Better yet, monounsaturated fats selectively lower "bad" cholesterol, leaving the protective kind intact. That translates to a reduced risk of heart disease.

But nuts have additional sterling qualities: They're high in fiber and contain decent amounts of various minerals. They're a good source of potassium and are quite low in sodium, as long as they're unsalted. Some—cashews and almonds in particular—are high in zinc, a trace mineral that's so necessary for cell growth.

A handful of nuts each day may help prevent heart attack, concluded a study on the eating habits of Seventh-Day Adventists. Those who regularly ate nuts had less than half the risk of heart attack of others who didn't eat nuts. Further, nuts contain vitamin E, which may delay the onset of atherosclerosis. And certain foods like Brazil nuts have a substance that researchers believe scavenges carcinogenic chemicals in the body and prevents normal cells from becoming cancerous.

The only drawback to nuts is their high calorie count. So eat them in place of other high-cal foods, not in addition to them. And limit yourself to a manageable small handful a day.

FAT IN A NUTSHELL

Here's how the most popular nuts rank in terms of monounsaturated fat. Macadamia nuts, those Hawaiian delicacies, lead the pack with 79 percent of their fat coming from beneficial monos. All values are for 1 ounce of nuts.

Nuts	Monounsaturated Fat %
Macadamia nuts	79
Hazelnuts, unblanched	78
Pistachio nuts	68
Almonds, unblanched	65
Pecans	62
Cashew nuts	59
Peanuts	50
Pine nuts	38
Brazil nuts, unblanched	35
English walnuts	23
Black walnuts	22

Oats: Workhorse for the heart. Feel your oats! Rolled oats are the base for that perennial breakfast favorite, cooked oatmeal. And although they're not quite as concentrated a source of cholesterol-lowering soluble fiber as oat bran, they're still high on the list of healing foods. Research has shown that eating 2 ounces of oats a day along with a diet low in saturated fat can lower blood-cholesterol levels in people with high levels of the blood fat.

And as the American Medical Association has pointed out, it's significantly cheaper to lower cholesterol with dietary changes (including oats and oat bran) than with drugs. Some doctors recommend aiming for at least 10 grams of fiber from oat products a day. A single serving of oatmeal gives you almost 3 grams.

In addition to having a modest number of calories (110 in a serving) and hardly any fat, oats contain cancer-battling selenium plus potassium, B vitamins, and iron.

Oil: *Olive and company strike it rich.* Health watchers have struck oil! Many of the most popular, flavorful oils on the market today are largely composed of beneficial monounsaturated or polyunsaturated fats. Monounsaturates—found in olive, canola, rice-bran, and other oils (see the chart on the opposite page)—are the emerging stars on the health scene. They help lower total cholesterol and bad-for-you LDL cholesterol without reducing protective HDLs.

CHECK YOUR OIL

How does your favorite oil stack up in health value? Oils with the most cholesterol-lowering monounsaturates should make regular appearances on your table. And remember that even the best oils are a mixture of monounsaturated, polyunsaturated, and saturated fats. So use them judiciously.

Oil	Mono-unsaturated Fats (%)	Poly-unsaturated Fats (%)
Hazelnut	78	10
Olive	74	8
Almond	70	17
Avocado	70	16
Apricot kernel	60	29
Canola (rapeseed)	56	33
Peanut	46	32
Sesame	40	42
Rice bran	39	35
Corn	24	59
Soybean	23	58
Walnut	23	63
Linseed	20	66
Sunflower	20	66
Grapeseed	16	70
Wheat germ	15	62
Safflower	12	75

Monounsaturated fats may also aid those with adult-onset (type II) diabetes, who have higher blood sugar and heart disease risks than other people. Scientists compared both a low-fat, high-carbohydrate diet—standard for diabetics—and a lower-carb, higher-mono diet. Glucose levels were actually lower on the mono diet. And although both diets lowered total cholesterol and harmful LDLs, the mono diet also lowered other undesirable blood fats while simultaneously raising good HDL.

Still other studies suggest that olive oil, and

possibly other monounsaturates, significantly lowers blood pressure. In one study, researchers found that the more monos consumed in a diet, the lower the blood pressure.

Although less impressive in healing potential, polyunsaturates also warrant a place in your diet. They too can lower cholesterol levels, but they may also lower HDL in the bargain.

No matter which healthy oils you use, be sure to *substitute* them for nasty saturated fats; don't simply add them to your total. And become acquainted with such aromatic oils as chili, hazelnut, walnut, and sesame. Their flavors are so prominent that you'll need just a small amount. As a bonus, their bold flavors will take the place of salt, thereby benefiting your blood pressure.

Onions: *A family with heart.* Don't cry—onions (along with leeks, scallions, shallots, and other members of the pungent allium family) are excellent health boosters. First off, they appear to share some of garlic's cholesterol-beating punch. It's theorized that onions may help offset the artery-clogging effects of a high-fat diet, which explains why they're so popular in the heart-smart Mediterranean diets. And white onions have been found to raise protective HDL cholesterol, to help forestall heart disease.

But that's not all. Certain substances in onions seem to inhibit the formation of blood clots, a principal trigger of most heart attacks. In addition, onions, scallions, garlic, and similar bulbous vegetables may guard against the development of stomach cancer. And a compound in onions may even help relieve asthma attacks. Not bad for peasant food.

Oranges: *Shining with vitamin C.* A day without an orange is like a day without 116 percent of the RDA of vitamin C. Citrus fruits are probably the best-known source of C, a key antioxidant that can help protect against cancer. The vitamin can also enhance your absorption of iron, so many tropical dishes that pair oranges with meat or beans have the right idea.

Oranges are also loaded with fiber, especially cholesterol-lowering pectin. And a few studies have noted that when vitamin C is added to a pectin-rich diet, cholesterol levels drop even lower. The orange provides terrific quantities of both. Pectin can also help diabetics keep their blood sugar and insulin levels normal and stable.

And another study found that people who get at least 300 milligrams of vitamin C a day in their diets (the equivalent of $2^{1}/_{2}$ glasses of orange juice) have a 30 percent lower rate of chronic respiratory problems than those who get only 100 milligrams.

Papayas: *Health gift from the tropics.* Here's another sunny tropical fruit that should grace your table often. Papaya overflows with supervitamins A and C. And it's very high in potassium for blood pressure and stroke control. And it's even got a portion of bone-building calcium wrapped up in its silky smooth flesh. A whole papaya contains just 117 calories and would form the basis for a delicious dieter's fruit salad.

Papayas are also rich in cholesterol-lowering pectin for a degree of protection from heart disease and bowel disease.

Parsley: Worth its weight in nutrients. Parsley is more than a throw-away garnish. It's a very low-cal source of vitamins A and C for cancer protection, potassium for healthy blood pressure, and even calcium for stronger bones. Throw $1/2$ cup of parsley into your mixed salad and you get almost half your day's supply of vitamin C and about a third of your vitamin A. With 10 tiny calories in that portion, parsley will certainly help trim your waistline while contributing hunger-satisfying fiber to your diet.

Parsnips: Sweet and nutty fiber food. Tired of the same old vegetables? Then look to this old-fashioned relative of the carrot for a special sweet, nutty flavor. A half cup of cooked slices has a respectable 63 calories but quite a bit of stroke-fighting potassium. There's even a little calcium and a tasty serving of vitamin C thrown in for good measure. And don't forget the fiber that's so important for cancer protection, cholesterol control, and digestive health.

Pasta: Oodles of benefits. Ah, pasta—the possibilities are limitless for this staple of heart-healthy diets. Once thought to be fattening fare, this international favorite has redeemed itself nicely. A 2-ounce serving (about 1 cup cooked) has virtually no fat, just 200 calories, a nice amount of protein, and enough potassium, calcium, iron, and niacin to make it a perfectly healthy food. And pasta retains most of its mineral content after being cooked, so all that goodness is right at your beck and call. Further, diabetics and dieters alike appreciate the high complex carbohydrate content of pasta that is responsible for its ability to stabilize blood sugar levels.

Pasta is available in an endless array of sizes, shapes, and colors—the result of using different grains and even vegetable-enriched flours. Whole wheat pasta is higher in fiber than white and therefore more filling. Pasta made from sweet lupin flour is higher in protein than normal varieties and contains considerably more fiber and calcium for enhanced cancer protection.

Noodles made from corn, buckwheat, rice, mung beans, and sweet potatoes are suitable for those with allergies to gluten or grain in general. And don't forget couscous, a pasta product from North Africa that's granular in texture and resembles bulgur. Like other pasta, it's very low in fat for heart health.

Peaches: *Sweet treat for dieters.* Peachy keen says it all. These sweet juicy fruits of summer are at the top of every dieter's hit parade. And with only 37 calories apiece, they're also nice sources of beta-carotene and fiber to help prevent cancer. Further, their sodium-to-potassium ratio is ideal for keeping high blood pressure under wraps.

Pears: *Boron for the bones.* In addition to the sterling healing qualities shared by many other fruits, pears also contain boron, a trace mineral that may affect calcium levels in the body.

In one study, people on a low-boron diet experienced decreased blood levels of calcium, the mineral needed for strong bones and cancer protection. And the diet also raised levels of a calcium-reducing hormone. The researchers involved theorize that boron may prevent the excretion of too much calcium. Although large doses of the mineral can be toxic, you can safely get all you need by eating a balanced diet containing pears, apples, nuts, grapes, and leafy vegetables—all good sources of boron.

Peas: *Nutrition in a snap.* Pass the peas, please. And don't forget the edible-pod varieties, such as snow peas and sugar snaps. All peas are wonderfully high in dietary fiber, with moderate amounts of potassium and even a nice shot of iron. The edible-pods are higher in vitamin C, especially if eaten raw. But the shelled peas have more vitamin A. So including both types in your diet covers you all the way around.

Peppers (chili): *Good for the blood.* Hot news on the nutrition front is the healing potential of chili peppers. And while these fiery wonders may be too spicy for some people's tastes, they're worth the heat. Just $1/4$ cup packs over 150 percent of the RDA for vitamin C and over 80 percent of the requirement for vitamin A.

But that's not all. These south-of-the-border favorites may help prevent heart disease. Hot peppers have been reported to increase the blood's ability to break up potentially dangerous clots. Capsaicin, an organic compound that gives hot peppers their punch, thins the blood, protecting against heart disease and stroke.

Chilies may also help "burn" calories. Hot spices may boost postmeal metabolism by as much as 25 percent, say scientists. And these foods may also help relieve congestion, whether due to bronchitis, asthma, allergies, or a cold. The amounts required for an effect are no greater than those typically found in Mexican or Indian foods eaten frequently. Olé!

Peppers (sweet): *Nutritious in any color.* These mild peppers used to come in just Christmas-colored green and red. Today, they run the gamut from yellow and orange to purple and brown. What they all have in common is a great nutritional profile. Red rates the most kudos, with staggering amounts of healing vitamins A and C. But the other colors are no slouches either. Basically similar, 1/2 cup of uncooked peppers still has more than a day's supply of vitamin C, a decent amount of A, and some fiber.

For those of you who always wondered: All peppers start out green. They turn other colors when ripe.

Persimmons: *So good Fuyu.* Whether you savor the buttery-soft Hachiya persimmon or the firmer Fuyu, you're getting a healthy helping of cancer-, cold-, and infection-stomping vitamin A. One fruit gives you nearly 75 percent of your daily quota. And although a persimmon–at 118 calories–isn't the lowest-cal fruit around, it fills the bill as a satisfying dessert. For those calories you get a fine amount of potassium and a bit each of vitamin C and calcium. Not to mention the pleasure of eating such a truly gorgeous fruit.

Pineapple: *It's sweet on the stomach—and more.* There's more to pineapple than slim calories, a fair amount of potassium, lots of vitamin C, a helping of fiber, and a nice amount of the trace mineral manganese (essential for protein and calorie metabolism). Scientists say it's an effective healing tool. That's because pineapple contains high amounts of bromelain, an enzyme that aids digestion, attacks bacteria, helps repair damaged skin, and dissolves blood clots. Makes you wonder how anything so powerful could taste so sweet.

Plums: *Full of potassium.* Why, shucks, these fruits are plum delicious. And plum nutritious. Weight watchers can eat them with impunity— after all, there are only 36 calories in each juicy fruit. For that matter, people concerned about blood pressure, stroke, and just plain fatigue will value plums' potassium. And there's a bit of vitamin A in each succulent plum to help immunity.

Don't worry about missing these luscious babies out of season. Canned varieties are just fine (but choose those packed in juice rather than in heavy syrup). A cup of canned plums has a really impressive amount of vitamin A.

Pomegranates: *Treasure trove of fiber.* The ancient Greeks considered pomegranates so irresistible that they couldn't even blame Persephone for eating the ruby red seeds when she shouldn't have, thereby inflicting us with winter.

Today this fruit is still a taste treat as well as a treasure trove of fiber, thanks to its scores of jewel-like seeds. What's more, it's got lots of potassium, barely any sodium, nary a trace of fat, and even a little vitamin C thrown in. Besides, it's a time-consuming proposition to break open a pomegranate and properly eat those little seeds, so weight watchers can munch away for a long time without actually consuming many calories.

Popcorn: *Super snack food.* Like pomegranates, popcorn is a good food for dieters. This crunchy finger food can keep a weight watcher happily amused without expanding the waistline. Prepared in an air popper, 1 cup has only 27 calories, a trace of fat, and almost no sodium.

In addition, the fiber in popcorn may actually help you *lose* weight. In one study, overweight women lost weight by adding just 6 grams of fiber a day to their diets. And they kept the weight off for at least a year. Six grams is about what you get in 5 or 6 cups of popped corn. That fiber may also have cancer-preventing properties. So when you've got a case of the munchies and need *something* to satisfy you, popcorn is a sure bet.

Pork (lean): *Lean toward the tenderloin.* You may be surprised to learn that pork does merit a place in the healing diet. As with beef and lamb, the cut is the key to healthy eating. Lean tenderloin gets only 26 percent of its calories from fat. That's almost as good as skinless chicken breast (at 20 percent). Center loin, pork leg, lean ham, and Canadian bacon (but not regular bacon) are also good choices.

No matter which cut you buy, however, make sure you choose the leanest version available. And then trim away all the visible fat. The reason for all this bother is that pork is an excellent source of healing B vitamins, zinc, protein, and iron. Your goal, then, is to enjoy pork as part of an overall healthy diet. Just don't go hog wild.

Potatoes: *Tops in potassium.* This spud's for you, and here's why: Potatoes are a fabulous source of potassium, making them top priority for those with high blood pressure. They are also high in vitamins C and B$_6$ for help in fighting fatigue and infections. They have lots of beneficial minerals, including iron and magnesium. And they contain virtually no fat. All of which means healing potential on many fronts, particularly heart disease and stroke. Even better, potatoes contain certain compounds called protease inhibitors that may be potent cancer fighters.

A large baked potato has about 220 calories and can form the centerpiece of any meal. Just top with some steamed vegetables and a little nonfat yogurt or salsa. You'll have a very satisfying, filling, fat-free meal.

Contrary to popular belief, most of a potato's vitamin C is *not* just under the skin. Researchers have determined that peeling spuds has almost no effect on their C content. So a large baker—with or without skin—supplies about 30 milligrams of the vitamin, half your daily requirement.

Prunes: *Nature's laxative.* When dried, many fruits become concentrated storehouses of fiber and minerals. And prunes are no exception. They're a great source of stroke-fighting potassium and blood-fortifying iron. In addition, they have an impressive amount of vitamin A, which pairs with the fiber for extra cancer power. And prunes have long enjoyed a reputation as nature's laxative, so they're tailor-made for digestive health. Their only drawback? A lot of calories in such little packages. Be sure to trim calories elsewhere in your diet to make way for these wrinkled wonders.

Pumpkin: *A leader in the cancer crusade.* Peter, Peter, pumpkin eater—he had the right idea about this Halloween favorite. Pumpkin is a veritable fountainhead of anticancer beta-carotene. In fact, a mere $1/2$ cup of canned pumpkin has over five times your daily quota for vitamin A. That means there's lots of extra A to knock out colds and other immunity disorders, benefit night vision, and keep the membranes of your body cells in tip-top condition.

That same serving has just 41 calories and a good amount of potassium for good blood pressure. And don't forget the helping of iron to defeat anemia and fatigue.

One note: If you cook your own pumpkin and mash it, you'll find it's a lot more watery than the canned variety. Just put it in a saucepan and stir over heat until suitably thick. That will concentrate the vitamins and minerals for better disease-fighting ability in a smaller amount of the vegetable.

Quinoa: *Protein pack from the Andes.* If you're not familiar with this grain-like food from the Andes, it's high time you gave it a try. This high-fiber food looks like canary feed, is cooked like rice, and has a squashlike taste with nutty overtones. Millions of Incans recognized it as a dietary staple—you should, too.

Quinoa (pronounced keen-wa) contains such an ideal balance of essential amino acids that the National Academy of Sciences has called it "one of the best vegetable sources of protein." That makes it essential for those people cutting back on meat and other traditional sources of complete protein.

In addition, it's got calcium, iron, vitamin E, and several of the B vitamins to help build bones, prevent anemia, battle cancer, and avoid fatigue. And it's essentially gluten-free for those with celiac disease.

Raisins: *Mineral mighty mites.* In recent years, the California Raisins have brought this food back into the limelight, and it's a good thing. Like prunes, raisins are a concentrated source of many minerals, including iron and potassium. With virtually no fat, they're excellent for those on a cholesterol-lowering diet. And although they're high in calories, a small handful of raisins has the power to appease a nagging sweet tooth, making dieters less likely to reach for a fattening snack.

Raspberries: *Multiple benefits in every bite.* Oh, what perfect little jewels! A whole cup of these lovely sweet-tart gems has only 61 calories but more than 6 grams of anticancer fiber. And that same cup has half of your daily requirement of immunity-building vitamin C, plus some potassium for better blood pressure. There's even a small helping of vitamin A and bone-strengthening calcium. So eat up when these berries are in season and don't forget to freeze some for winter.

Rice: *Universal staple of health.* More than half the world's population virtually lives on rice. *They* recognize this staple for the healing food it is. You should, too. Rice is an excellent complex-carbohydrate diet food that can satisfy hunger with just a moderate amount of calories —about 115 in a $1/2$-cup serving.

Rice is gluten-free and nonallergenic, so it's excellent for those with celiac disease and others allergic to gluten. Best of all, it's incredibly low in fat and sodium and has no cholesterol. And that's great news for hardy hearts and diabetics.

With its brownish bran intact, brown rice contains quite a bit of cancer-stomping fiber. And wild rice—which is actually the seed of an aquatic grass—has even more fiber than brown. So mix and match these grains to your heart's content.

More good news is that rice contains starch, which researchers think may have a positive effect on bowel cancer. And rice contains selenium, a trace element whose lack in the diet is asso-ciated with lung and skin cancers.

Rutabagas: *The cancer-fighting giants.* The next time you see one of these giant vegetables at the supermarket, don't pass it by. It's another member of the cancer-fighting crucifer family. It's high in potassium with good amounts of vitamin C and fiber. But it's so low in calories that a half cup of cooked cubes weighs in at a skinny 29. And the flavor of cooked rutabagas is very mild. Some folks like to mash them in with potatoes to give the spuds an interesting flavor and a creamy yellow color that only *looks* like there's lots of butter in the dish.

Salad greens: *Color is the key.* Salads are a dieter's mainstay (as long as he uses a low-cal dressing). But before you reach for the same old iceberg lettuce, realize that there are plenty of more nutritious greens waiting for a chance to tickle your taste buds. Dark green leafy vegetables—such as romaine lettuce, chicory, endive, arugula, dandelion, and turnip greens—are high in beneficial beta-carotene and vitamin C. Their vibrant color is the clue to their healing potential.

Greens tend to be so low in calories that you wonder how they can pack so many nutrients. Turnip greens, for instance, have just 7 calories in a $1/2$ cup but more than a quarter of the RDA for vitamin C and an impressive 43 percent of the RDA for vitamin A. Chicory and collards have even more of both nutrients. Many greens contain calcium and vitamin E to help prevent cancer. And naturally these garden greats have fiber to doubly assure them a place on your plate.

Seeds: Nutritional snack and topping. Many seeds, such as anise, dill, fennel, and caraway, rate a place in the healing diet because of the big flavor punch they deliver in a mere sprinkling. They enable dieters, diabetics, hypertensives, and those concerned about heart disease to season their foods without adding extra calories, salt, or fat. (Used medicinally, they can even have healing power of their own: Caraway seeds, for example, can help settle an upset stomach and relieve flatulence.)

Other seeds, such as sunflower, pumpkin, squash, and sesame, take a place in the healing diet because of their health-giving values. Although they contain a fair amount of calories and fat, their fat is largely unsaturated—to help prevent heart disease. And these seeds are high in fiber and minerals. Pumpkin seeds, for instance, have a nice helping of zinc for good immunity and wound healing. Sunflower seeds also contain selenium, plus vitamin E, and compounds known as protease inhibitors, to guard against cancer. Sesame seeds have lots of iron to help prevent anemia and a good helping of bone-building calcium.

Soybeans: *Vegetarian protein-plus.* Soybeans are an excellent source of protein for those on a vegetarian or limited-meat diet. They're high in blood-building iron, blood-pressure-regulating potassium, and bone-fortifying calcium. Like seeds, soybeans contain anticancer protease inhibitors. And in animal studies, soybeans slowed the progression of breast cancer.

As if that weren't enough, these legumes are loaded with pectin, which has been shown to help lower cholesterol and may even help over-eaters stay on their diets. A cup of cooked dried soybeans has 2.6 grams of pectin. In one study, 15 grams of pectin added to their meals helped overweight people feel satisfied more quickly. And their stomachs emptied more slowly, so they weren't hungry again too soon.

Spinach: *Leaves of plenty.* Popeye was no fool. A half cup of cooked spinach has only 21 calories. A half cup of raw spinach has just 6! With those meager calories, you get plenty of vitamin A (beta-carotene) to help reduce the risk of cancer. Spinach is also high in fiber and vitamin E for extra measure against cancer. And the beta-carotene may help you avoid macular degeneration, a deterioration of the retina that strikes many older folks.

Like most other vegetables, spinach has lots of potassium, for lower blood pressure, and no fat, for good heart health.

The only caution: Eating *excessive* amounts of spinach—$^1/_2$ pound a day—can block your absorption of calcium from both the spinach itself and other foods eaten at the same time. But researchers say that a cup of spinach eaten two or three times a week is just fine.

Sprouts: *Protein without calories.* Sprouts are seeds that have begun to, well, sprout. As they grow, their protein and vitamin contents increase. Most sprouts have 12 percent more protein than their original seeds. What's more, their B vitamins jump three to ten times, for protection against impaired immunity and fatigue. Best of all, sprouting actually creates vitamin C, even when the dry seeds don't have any.

Because the growing sprout uses up the starch in the seed, sprouts are very low in carbohydrates. They're also low in calories. A cup of alfalfa sprouts has only 10 calories. A cup of mung bean sprouts has just 32. Added raw to salads and sandwiches or lightly cooked in stir-fries, sprouts are a boon to the diet-weary.

And get this: Wheat sprouts have been shown to inhibit the genetic damage to cells caused by some cancer-causing agents. You couldn't ask more from a crunchy little food.

Squash (summer): *Diet fare for fair weather.* Good gosh, summer squash! When you're wondering what to do with all those zucchini, yellow crooknecks, pattypans, and other prolific garden favorites, we have a suggestion: Eat up and help yourself to good health. With negligible calories and a nice portion of filling fiber, they're perfect for dieters. In addition, these squash have potassium and barely any sodium—a winning combination in the war against high blood pressure. Thrown in are a smattering of magnesium for extra help with blood pressure, some vitamin A against cancer, and a little calcium for strong bones (every bit helps).

Squash (winter): *Powerhouse of healing.* Winter squash have even more healing potential than their warm-weather counterparts, thanks to the amazing amount of vitamin A some specimens carry. A half cup of baked butternut or hubbard squash contains considerably more than a full day's supply of this anticancer crusader. A helping of both vitamin C and fiber secures their position as cancer fighters.

A half cup of most varieties averages just 39 calories, with spaghetti squash weighing in at a light 23. All are good sources of potassium (with very little sodium) for help on the blood pressure and stroke fronts. And like summer varieties, they have a bit of calcium—plus some iron—thrown in for extra measure.

Strawberries: *Bursting with vitamin C.* Luscious, ripe, and warm from the sun—strawberries are a special treat, in more ways than one. A whole cupful has only 45 calories to help with weight control. And there's lots of potassium for blood pressure control. Of course, there's a nice helping of fiber and a big shot of vitamin C (140 percent of the RDA in that cup) to help prevent cancer.

But the big news with strawberries is that they contain a substance called ellagic acid, a chemical that scientists feel may fight three different cancer-causing agents in the body.

Sweet potatoes: *Leading cancer protector.* How sweet it is! These southern belles are powerhouses of vitamin A, so they're considered potent cancer fighters. With about five times the RDA of A in a single sweet, they're a safe bet to boost immunity to various ailments. Doctors say that their carotene can protect against tumor growth, possibly by boosting white blood cell activity. And diets high in the nutrient may lower the risk of cancers of the larynx, esophagus, lung, stomach, colon, and cervix.

Further, sweets also contain lots of fiber and vitamin C for added cancer protection. And the fiber does double duty to help keep cholesterol levels down and prevent digestive disorders. With a hefty amount of potassium—and hardly any sodium—sweet potatoes are good for your blood pressure. And with just 118 calories apiece and no fat to speak of, they're a food dieters should enjoy often.

Swiss chard: *Beet-family greens.* Swiss chard is a member of the beet family valued for its large green leaves and celery-like stalks. It's incredibly low in calories (18 in $1/2$ cup of cooked and just 3 in the same amount raw) but very high in protective vitamin A. It also contains enough fiber and vitamin E to be considered protective against cancer. And $1/2$ cup of cooked chard has a nice amount of iron, accompanied by a portion of vitamin C to enhance its absorption.

Tangerines: *The gift of healing.* Like other citrus fruits, these Christmas favorites are loaded with immunity-strengthening vitamin C. Just a cup of sections gives you a whole day's supply. And for only 86 calories, you get a generous amount of cancer-fighting vitamin A plus anti-stroke potassium and some fatigue-beating B vitamins. Tangerines are a present you can savor all winter.

Tofu: *Little bundles of soy.* This soy food from the Orient is ideal for anyone cutting back on dairy products. It's very high in good-quality protein. And it's got lots of calcium for strong bones, stable blood pressure, healthy bowels, and cancer protection. Unlike the dairy or meat products that it can easily replace, tofu has no cholesterol and contains mostly unsaturated fat. So it's very heart healthy. In fact, in one study, substituting tofu for cheese dropped cholesterol levels in a group of vegetarians in just three weeks.

Tofu is also very high in iron, for protection against anemia. And it's both high in potassium and low in sodium, which gives it an edge against strokes. And it even contains fiber—a surprise considering its silky-smooth, cheese-like texture. All in all, Americans would be well advised to eat more of this Far Eastern staple.

Tomatoes: *The joy of dieting.* Nothing beats a

vine-ripened tomato for summer-fresh flavor. But there's more than just good taste behind that lovely red (or yellow) facade. Tomatoes are so low in calories that you can eat one twice a day for the whole summer and never worry about gaining an ounce. A whole cup of chopped tomatoes has just 35 calories but lots of potassium, vitamin C, and vitamin A for helping to head off strokes, high blood pressure, cancer, and infections.

And don't feel too bad about having to eat canned tomatoes out of season. In addition to low calories and lots of potassium and vitamins A and C, these beauties contain a bit of calcium and even some iron. But if you're concerned about sodium intake, look for no-salt or low-salt brands.

Tropical fruits: *Tops in taste and nutrition.* When every calorie has to count, indulge in a taste of the tropics. These ambrosial fruits have luscious, creamy textures that seem rich and fattening but are really quite low in calories and fat. Further, they tend to be high in vitamins A and C as well as potassium and fiber.

Guavas, for instance, are so packed with vitamin C that a cup of chopped fruit has more than three times as much as an equal amount of orange segments. And that's *five times* the RDA of this cancer- and infection-fighting nutrient! Passion fruit have just a sprinkling of calories but lots of beneficial fiber, thanks to all their edible seeds. Starfruit have a nice portion of vitamin C plus a helping of vitamin A. And dates, like other dried fruits, are a concentrated source of many vitamins and minerals (but they're also high in calories, so take it easy).

Turkey: *Gobble without guilt.* Let's talk turkey. Roasted turkey breast (without skin) is lower in fat than any other commercially available meat. (See the chart on pages 72–73.) That makes it perfect for anyone dieting or trying to keep cholesterol levels nice and low. And it's a good source of iron, zinc, and B vitamins. Although the dark meat has more calories and fat, it does contain more iron for anyone worried about anemia.

As for ground turkey, be aware that fat content can vary from brand to brand. Read labels or ask your butcher about the meat's makeup. Some are composed entirely of ground breast, while others have a larger percentage of dark meat. Some brands even add fat. And many self-basting birds are injected with saturated fat that can send their fat content soaring.

Turnips: *Good for your heart.* For some reason, turnips don't get as much respect these days as they deserve. As cancer-fighting crucifers, they're good sources of fiber and vitamin C. And they're extremely low in calories, for a healthy heart and a trimmer profile.

If you grow your own turnips, be sure to eat the greens, too. They're loaded with vitamin A for extra cancer protection.

Veal (lean): *Better than beef.* Because veal comes from young cattle, it's lower in fat than most cuts of beef. The animals simply haven't had a chance to accumulate excess fat. But veal is still high in protein and a source of blood-building iron. And it's got plenty of potassium (and not too much sodium) to help blood pressure.

Watercress: *Swimming with goodness.* This sprightly green has a pungent flavor with a peppery snap. Its dark green leaves should be a clue to its nutrient value. For practically no calories, you get plenty of cancer-fighting beta-carotene and a little calcium, potassium, and vitamin C. Add handfuls to soups, salads, and sandwiches to help avoid obesity, high blood pressure, and stroke.

Waterfowl: *Soaring with iron.* Some of the best sources of iron on earth can be found flying high above it. Both duck and goose are high in the most absorbable type of iron to help prevent anemia. Goose is also rich in vitamin E as a hedge against cancer. And duck has a helping of zinc to aid wound healing and improve immune functions.

The trick when dealing with these fowl is to avoid the fat trap. Certain types of duck are lower in fat than others. Muscovy is a lean, meaty breed that's often available in farmers' markets and large supermarkets. To further lower fat in all waterfowl, trim away visible fat from the cavity and neck areas and remove the skin before eating. Prick the skin all over before roasting and place the bird on a raised rack above a drip pan for good fat drainage. (See the chart on pages 72–73.)

Wheat germ: *Nutritional gold.* It's easy to understand why this cereal food is considered nutritional gold. It's high in fiber for heart health, cancer protection, and good digestive function. But it's also a wonderful source of many vitamins and minerals. First, there's a good supply of B vitamins to maintain a healthy nervous system. Then there's vitamin E for blood health plus anemia-preventing iron and stroke-blocking potassium.

What's more, wheat germ is one of the best sources of zinc. All this with no cholesterol and a reasonable amount of calories and fat (almost all of which is the beneficial unsaturated type).

So enjoy wheat germ often. But don't relegate it to the breakfast table. Make it a healthy addition to baked goods, casseroles, salads, and meat loaves.

Whole wheat flour: *Foundation of health.* Whole wheat flour has an edge over white. It contains a nice portion of fiber-rich bran to help protect against colon cancer as well as prevent constipation, diverticular disease, and hemorrhoids. And it retains the nutrient-dense wheat germ (see above page) for added health benefits.

Wheat contributes B vitamins for enhanced immunity, vitamin E for possible cancer protection, iron for strong blood, potassium for stroke prevention, and zinc for wound healing. Whole grains such as wheat also contain selenium, which may confer some protection against lung cancer.

Whole wheat, which tends to be milled more coarsely than white flour, may have added benefits. Studies suggest that finely milled flour triggers a greater insulin surge and may increase the risk of such diseases as diabetes, gallstones, atherosclerosis, and obesity.

Yogurt (low-fat): *Cultured to cure.* You know that dairy products such as yogurt provide a healthy dose of bone-building calcium. (An 8-ounce serving of yogurt has more than half the RDA of calcium.) But a tantalizing trail of research suggests that this fermented-milk product may offer other benefits, including gastrointestinal relief, lower blood cholesterol, and cancer protection.

What's more, yogurt is a must for anyone with lactose intolerance. It's got certain digestive enzymes that allow for easy digestion, even if you normally have trouble with the lactose in milk and other dairy products. In fact, eating yogurt every day can help *eliminate* or reduce the symptoms of this uncomfortable disease.

Yogurt and other cultured milk products contain beneficial types of bacteria that help restore the digestive system to normal after antibiotic treatment. To get the most benefit, look for brands that contain "live cultures."

PART TWO

CHAPTER THREE

Great Beginnings

There's a festive aura about appetizers, hors d'oeuvres, and canapés. They evoke images of elegant dinners, intimate soirees, fun-filled parties. And if you feature savory high-health starters like the ones that follow, all your gatherings will be cause for celebration.

Red Pepper Canapés and Citrus-Marinated Carrots, for example, are overflowing with beta-carotene to help prevent cancer. Sole and Salmon Roulades and Tuna Tart with Basil have a nice helping of omega-3 fatty acids, which are so good for your heart. Onion Toast, Grilled Onion Brochettes, and Braised Leeks with Mustard Sauce put the cholesterol-lowering power of the onion family to tasty use. Spinach-Stuffed Mushrooms contain lots of potassium to help lower high blood pressure.

Low-fat, high-protein offerings like Stuffed Tofu Triangles or Fragrant Chicken in Bok Choy Leaves let you whet appetites as a first course or satisfy hungry guests at a cocktail party. For nutritious nibbles, provide plenty of crisp raw vegetables with yogurt-based dips like Sweet and Spicy Curry Dip or Roasted-Garlic Dip. And scatter bowls of low-fat, high-fiber popcorn wherever guests are likely to congregate. Pesto

Popcorn, Chili Popcorn, and Pumpkin-Seed Popcorn are sure winners.

Remember, good times and good health go hand in hand. Get all your special occasions off to the right start.

ARTICHOKE QUICHE

Healing Foods

Artichokes
Cottage cheese (low-fat)
Whole wheat flour

3 slices whole wheat bread
1 tablespoon olive oil
1 teaspoon dried thyme
$1/4$ teaspoon paprika

$1/2$ cup egg substitute
2 tablespoons grated Sapsago or Parmesan cheese
12 ounces cooked artichoke hearts
2 cups dry-curd cottage cheese

Pulverize the bread in a blender or food processor. Transfer to a medium bowl. Add the oil, thyme, and paprika. Press into the bottom and up the sides of a 9-inch pie plate. Bake at 400°F for 7 minutes.

In a food processor, puree the cottage cheese, egg substitute, and Sapsago or Parmesan. Transfer to a large bowl.

Pat the artichokes dry with paper towels. Cut the hearts into bite-size pieces. Stir into the cheese mixture. Pour into the pie shell.

Bake at 350°F for 30 minutes, or until a knife inserted in the center comes out clean. To serve, cut into thin slices.

Serves 8 to 12

CARROT STICKS WITH DILL PESTO

Healing Foods

Carrots
Garlic
Oil
Parsley

1 pound carrots
1/4 cup olive oil
3 cloves garlic, halved
1 tablespoon chopped lemon rind

1 3/4 cups chopped parsley
2 teaspoons lemon juice
1/3 cup chopped fresh dill

Cut the carrots into sticks about 3 inches long. Set aside.

In a food processor or blender, process the garlic and lemon rind until minced. Add the parsley and dill. Process until finely minced, stopping to scrape down the sides of the container as needed.

With the motor running, slowly add the oil and blend until a smooth paste is formed. Blend in the lemon juice. Spoon into a serving dish. Serve as a dip for the carrots.

Serves 8 to 12

MUSHROOMS STUFFED WITH CHEESE SOUFFLÉ

Healing Foods

Cottage cheese (low-fat)
Mushrooms
Onions

1 pound extra-large
  mushrooms, stems
  removed
$1/4$ teaspoon paprika
1 leek

$1/4$ cup dry-curd
  cottage cheese
1 teaspoon Dijon
  mustard
1 egg white

Blanch the mushrooms in boiling water for about 2 minutes. Remove from the water and drain, stem-side down, while you prepare the filling.

Remove tough green leaves from the leek. Trim the root end and slice the leek in half lengthwise. Rinse well to remove any grit from between the layers. Mince.

In a small bowl, mix the leeks, cottage cheese, and mustard.

In another small bowl, beat the egg white until stiff peaks form. Fold into the cottage cheese mixture.

Spoon the filling into the mushroom caps. Sprinkle with paprika.

Bake at 400°F until the filling is set, about 20 minutes.

Serves 6 to 8

SMOKY CUCUMBER DIP

Healing Foods

Cucumbers
Turkey
Yogurt (low-fat)

1 1/4 cups nonfat
   yogurt
1/2 cup finely chopped
   smoked turkey breast

1/2 cup minced
   cucumbers
1/8 teaspoon dillweed

In a small bowl, combine the yogurt, turkey, cucumbers, and dill.

Makes about 2 cups

RICE TIMBALES

Healing Foods

Milk (low-fat)
Rice

1 tablespoon
   canola oil
1 cup cooked
   wild rice
1/2 cup egg
   substitute

1 teaspoon coarse
   mustard
1 tablespoon flour
1 cup cooked rice
1 cup skim milk
2 scallions, minced

In a 2-quart saucepan over medium heat, whisk

127

together the oil and flour. Cook, stirring, for 2 minutes. Whisk in the milk, stirring well to prevent lumps. Cook, whisking constantly, until the sauce has thickened.

Remove from the heat and whisk in the egg substitute and mustard. Fold in the rice, wild rice, and scallions.

Coat 24 tiny muffin cups with nonstick spray. Spoon the rice mixture into the pans to almost fill the cups.

Place the muffin tins in a broiler pan. Add enough hot water to bring the water level two-thirds of the way up the outside of the tins. Bake at 400°F for about 20 minutes.

Remove the tins from water and let the timbales cool slightly. Run a knife around the edge of each to loosen.

Makes 24

GRILLED ONION BROCHETTES

Healing Food

Onions

1 pound small onions, unpeeled	2 teaspoons olive oil
1/4 cup lemon juice	1/2 teaspoon dried thyme

Boil the onions in water until just tender, about 10 minutes. Drain. Set aside until cool enough to handle.

Peel the onions, leaving the root end intact so

the layers will hold together. Trim off any root hairs.

In a large bowl, combine the onions, lemon juice, oil, and thyme. Allow to marinate for at least 1 hour.

Thread the onions onto metal skewers. Broil about 4 inches from the heat, turning the skewers often, until the onions are mahogany in color.

Serves 4 to 6

POPCORN: FLAVORED AND FAVORED

Popcorn's been basted with butter, sprinkled with salt, and slathered with sugar. But beneath all those coatings is a healing food crying to get out. A handful of air-popped popcorn has just 6 tiny little calories. And popcorn is nutritious, too, with a little iron to fight fatigue and some B vitamins to steady nerves.

To make sure your popcorn stays healthy, prepare it yourself. It's a breeze with an electric air popper. If you don't have one, simply use a heavy, deep saucepan. Although popcorn is usually popped over a layer of oil, you can pop it dry. Just place the kernels in the pan, cover with a lid and pop the corn over high heat. Shake the pan constantly, allowing heat to escape from time to time, until the popping stops.

Keep in mind that $1/3$ cup of uncooked kernels makes about 6 to 8 cups of popped corn.

Eat your popcorn plain or flavor it with just a sprinkle of oil and a generous shake of herbs or spices. Experiment on your own or try some of these combinations.

Pesto Popcorn

1 clove garlic, minced
1 tablespoon olive oil
$1/2$ teaspoon dried
  parsley

8 cups popped corn
2 tablespoons grated
  Parmesan cheese
$1/2$ teaspoon
  dried basil

In a 1-quart saucepan, cook the garlic in the oil for 1 minute (don't brown). Stir in the basil and parsley. Drizzle over the popcorn. Sprinkle with the cheese and mix well.

Makes 8 cups

Healing Foods

• Garlic   • Oil   • Popcorn

Curry Popcorn

2 teaspoons curry
  powder

8 cups popped corn
1 tablespoon
  canola oil

In a 1-quart saucepan, heat the curry powder in the oil until fragrant. Drizzle over the popcorn and mix well.

Makes 8 cups

Healing Foods

• Oil   • Popcorn

Pumpkin-Seed Popcorn

1/4 cup pumpkin
   seeds
1 tablespoon
   canola oil
1/4 teaspoon dried
   oregano

1/8 teaspoon chili
   powder
1/8 teaspoon ground
   cumin
8 cups popped corn

In a 1-quart saucepan over low heat, lightly toast the pumpkin seeds in the oil, stirring frequently. Stir in the oregano, chili powder and cumin. Drizzle over the popcorn and mix well.

Makes 8 cups

Healing Foods

• Oil • Popcorn • Seeds

Peanut Popcorn

8 cups popped corn
1 tablespoon
   canola oil
1/2 cup minced dates

3 tablespoons chopped
   peanuts
1/4 teaspoon ground
   cinnamon

Drizzle the popcorn with the oil. Mix in the dates, peanuts, and cinnamon.

Makes 8 cups

Healing Foods

• Nuts • Oil • Popcorn • Tropical fruits

Chili Popcorn

1 tablespoon
  tomato paste
1 teaspoon
  canola oil
2 tablespoons water

1 teaspoon chili
  powder
8 cups popped corn

In a 1-quart saucepan, combine the tomato paste and oil. Stir over medium heat for 1 minute. Add the water and chili powder. Cook for 2 minutes. Drizzle over the popcorn and mix well.

Makes 8 cups

Healing Food

• Popcorn

STUFFED TOFU TRIANGLES

Healing Foods

Crustaceans
Garlic
Tofu

MARINADE
$1/3$ cup stock
1 tablespoon low-
  sodium soy sauce
1 tablespoon vinegar
1 tablespoon peeled
  minced gingerroot

TOFU
3 ounces shelled,
  deveined shrimp
$1/2$ cup minced
  scallions
$1/4$ cup sliced
  water chestnuts

132

MARINADE
1 teaspoon sesame oil
1 clove garlic, minced

TOFU
1 tablespoon peeled
   minced gingerroot
1 clove garlic, chopped
$1^1/_2$ teaspoons
   cornstarch
$^1/_2$ teaspoon sesame oil
1 block (16 ounces)
   firm tofu
$^2/_3$ cup stock

To make the marinade: Combine the stock, soy sauce, vinegar, ginger, oil, and garlic in a shallow dish. Set aside.

To make the tofu: In a food processor, combine the shrimp, $^1/_3$ cup of the scallions, water chestnuts, ginger, garlic, cornstarch, and oil. Add 1 tablespoon of the marinade. Process with on/off turns until well mixed.

Cut the tofu into four equal triangles by slicing an "X" through the block. Cut each piece in half horizontally to make eight equal triangles.

Make a pocket in each triangle: Start at the point and make a horizontal incision that stops $^1/_2$ inch from the wide end.

Place the tofu in the marinade. Soak for 10 minutes; turn and soak another 10 minutes.

Divide the filling into eight portions. Gently stuff the triangles, smoothing the filled edges with your finger.

Coat a nonstick frying pan with nonstick spray. Place four of the triangles in the pan, standing them on their filled edges. (The filling will not come out.) Fry for 1 minute on each edge. Then fry for 1 minute on each flat side.

Add $1/3$ cup stock to the pan and simmer for 3 minutes. Flip the triangles and simmer for 3 minutes more. Remove to a serving platter. Repeat procedure with the remaining triangles and stock.

Add the marinade to the pan and boil it until reduced by half. To serve, pour the remaining marinade over the tofu. Sprinkle with the remaining scallions.

Serves 8

SPINACH-STUFFED MUSHROOMS

Healing Foods

Cottage cheese (low-fat)
Mushrooms
Spinach

10 ounces spinach
$1^1/2$ pounds extra-
  large mushrooms
$1/2$ cup minced onions
1 teaspoon olive oil
1 tablespoon low-
  sodium soy sauce

1 cup dry-curd
  cottage cheese
2 tablespoons grated
  Parmesan cheese
1 teaspoon dillweed
$1/4$ teaspoon
  ground pepper

Wash the spinach in plenty of cold water to remove any grit. Remove thick stems. Transfer the spinach to a large pot with just the water left clinging to the leaves. Cover and cook until wilted, about 5 minutes. Drain and let cool. Squeeze out excess moisture and chop finely.

Carefully separate the stems from the mushroom caps. Place the caps, stem-side up, in an oiled baking dish.

In a large nonstick frying pan, sauté the onions in the oil until soft.

Finely chop the mushroom stems and add to the pan with the onions. Sauté for 3 minutes. Remove from the heat and stir in the spinach, cottage cheese, Parmesan, dill, soy sauce, and pepper.

Divide the mixture among the mushroom caps, mounding it. Bake at 400°F for 20 minutes, or until the tops are lightly browned.

Serves 6 to 8

RED PEPPER CANAPÉS

Healing Foods

Carrots
Eggplant
Garlic
Peppers (sweet)

5 sweet red peppers, cut into $1/2$-inch strips
1 eggplant, cubed
$1/4$ cup stock
2 tablespoons olive oil
$1^1/2$ cups tomato sauce

1 stalk celery, finely chopped
1 cup sliced mushrooms
3 cloves garlic, minced
1 bay leaf

1 onion, sliced
1 carrot, finely
  chopped
1 tablespoon
  red-wine vinegar
1 loaf whole wheat
  French bread,
  thinly sliced

1/2 teaspoon dried
  oregano
1/2 teaspoon dried
  dried thyme
1 tablespoon
  lemon juice

In a 4-quart pot, sauté the peppers and eggplant in the stock and oil until tender, about 10 to 15 minutes. Set aside.

In a 2-quart saucepan, combine the tomato sauce, onions, carrots, celery, mushrooms, garlic, bay leaf, oregano, and thyme. Simmer over medium heat until the vegetables are tender, about 20 minutes.

Add the vinegar, lemon juice, and peppers and eggplant. Stir to combine. Chill. Discard the bay leaf.

Serve the spread on slices of French bread.

Serves 8

BRAISED LEEKS WITH MUSTARD SAUCE

Healing Food

Onions

1 pound thin leeks
1 cup chicken stock
1 bay leaf

1/4 teaspoon yellow
  mustard seeds
1 1/2 teaspoons Dijon
  mustard

Slice off the roots and tough green parts of the leeks. Then rinse the leeks carefully to remove all sand and grit. If the leeks are less than 1 inch in diameter, leave them whole. Otherwise, cut in half lengthwise, taking care not to disrupt the layers.

Combine the stock, mustard seeds, and bay leaf in a large frying pan. Add the leeks, cut side down. Bring to a simmer over medium heat. Then cover the pan and simmer for 8 minutes.

Remove the lid and set the pan in the refrigerator for about 30 minutes to chill.

When ready to serve, arrange the leeks on a serving platter. Strain and reserve the stock.

To make the mustard sauce, combine 3 tablespoons of the reserved stock with the Dijon mustard. Drizzle over the leeks.

Serves 4 to 6

MICRO METHOD:
Is Your Dishware Safe?

A microwave can be a great timesaver when cooking for a crowd. Hot dishes can be prepared in advance and arranged on their serving plates. Then it only takes a few minutes to zap them in the microwave and get them to the buffet table, still piping hot.

Glass, china, paper, pottery, and certain plastics commonly used for entertaining are also appropriate materials for the microwave. But check beforehand to make sure they are microwave safe. Look for labels that say "microwave oven safe" or "suitable for microwave." Make sure that dishes, teapots, and other items have no metal trim or screws in the handles or lids.

If you're unsure whether a piece of cookware is suitable for microwaving, perform this test:
* Fill a glass measuring cup with 1 cup of water.
* Place it in the microwave on or next to the dish you wish to test.
* Run the microwave for 1 minute an full power.
* If the dish becomes hot, don't use it for micro-waving. Only the water in the cup should heat up.

SOLE AND SALMON ROULADES

Healing Food

Fish

8 ounces salmon fillet
2 tablespoons egg
  substitute
1 teaspoon Dijon
  mustard
1/2 teaspoon minced
  fresh dill
1 pound thin
  sole fillets

Remove any skin and bones from the salmon. Cut the flesh into 1-inch chunks and place in the bowl of a food processor with the egg substitute, mustard, and dill. Process with on/off turns into a thick paste.

Cut each sole fillet in half lengthwise along its natural crease. Spread the salmon paste on the fillets. Roll up to enclose the filling, patting in the filling if it seeps out.

Bring about 1 inch of water to a boil in a large saucepan. Coat a steamer basket with nonstick spray. Place the fillets, seam-side down, in the basket. Add to the saucepan, cover, and steam for 4 minutes.

Makes about 12

VEGETABLES WITH CREAMY GARLIC SAUCE

Healing Foods

Artichokes
Beans (dried)
Beets
Carrots
Garlic
Potatoes
Yogurt (low-fat)

1 cup nonfat yogurt
6 cloves garlic, minced
1 tablespoon olive oil
1 large artichoke, cooked and cooled
1 cup cooked chick-peas

8 small potatoes, halved and steamed
1 cup carrot sticks, blanched
8 small beets, cooked and cooled

In a small bowl, fold together the yogurt, garlic, and olive oil. Transfer to a small serving bowl.

Arrange the artichoke, potatoes, carrots, beets, and chick-peas on a large platter.

Serve the vegetables with the sauce. (Eat the artichoke by tearing off leaves and dipping them into the sauce.)

Serves 4 to 6

FRAGRANT CHICKEN IN BOK CHOY LEAVES

Healing Foods

Cabbage
Chicken
Garlic

1 pound boneless, skinless chicken breast
1/4 cup minced scallions
1 tablespoon tahini (sesame-seed paste)
24 bok choy leaves

1 tablespoon low-sodium soy sauce
1 tablespoon peeled minced gingerroot
2 cloves garlic, minced
1 teaspoon lemon juice
1 teaspoon honey

Cut the chicken into 1-inch pieces. Transfer to a food processor and mince with on/off turns. Add the scallions, tahini, soy sauce, ginger, garlic, lemon juice, and honey. Process until just combined.

Place a rounded tablespoon of chicken mixture on the long edge of each bok choy leaf. Roll up, tucking in the corners as you go, to form cylindrical bundles.

Steam until the filling is cooked, about 10 minutes. (If necessary, steam in batches.)

Makes 24

COMPOTE OF RASPBERRIES AND ROASTED RED PEPPERS

Healing Foods

Peppers (sweet)
Raspberries
Salad greens

2 sweet red peppers
2 cups raspberries
1 tablespoon balsamic
   vinegar
1 loaf Whole Wheat
   French Bread, thinly
   sliced (page 284)

1 teaspoon olive oil
1 small head radicchio
   lettuce

Broil the red peppers until blackened on all sides. Allow to cool, then remove and discard the peel and seeds. Chop the peppers and place in a medium bowl.

Add the raspberries, vinegar, and oil. Toss to combine.

Separate the lettuce into individual cup-shaped leaves. Divide the compote among them. Serve with the bread.

Serves 8

SAUSAGE-STUFFED ZUCCHINI WHEELS

Healing Foods

Squash (summer)
Turkey
Whole wheat flour

3 medium zucchini
8 ounces lean Italian
   turkey sausage,
   casing removed
1/2 cup whole wheat
   bread crumbs
1 tablespoon chopped
   toasted pine nuts

1/4 cup shredded low-
   fat Swiss cheese
2 tablespoons minced
   fresh parsley
1/4 teaspoon grated
   nutmeg

Cut off 1/2 inch from each end of all zucchini. Using a small spoon or apple corer, remove the pulp and seeds, leaving a 1/4-inch shell (reserve the pulp). Roll a paper towel into a cylinder and insert it through each zucchini to absorb moisture. Chill while preparing the stuffing.

In a large frying pan, crumble the sausage and cook until browned. Drain on paper towels. Transfer the sausage to a food processor. Add the bread crumbs, cheese, parsley, pine nuts, nutmeg, and reserved pulp. Process until well mixed.

Remove the paper towels from the zucchini. Stuff with the sausage mixture, packing it in tightly. (If there is leftover stuffing, serve it on crackers or rolled in lettuce leaves.)

Chill the zucchini for 1 hour.

To serve, cut each zucchini into $^1/_4$-inch slices.

Serves 6

SAVORY STUFFED SNOW PEAS

Healing Foods

Garlic
Peas
Yogurt (low-fat)

4 cloves garlic
2 cups nonfat yogurt
1 teaspoon dillweed

1 teaspoon dried savory
36 snow peas

Boil the garlic for 2 minutes, then mash to a paste.

In a medium bowl, mix the garlic, yogurt, dill, and savory. Pour into a strainer lined with cheese-cloth. Cover with a piece of plastic, set over a bowl, and allow the yogurt to drain overnight. (Refrigerate in warm weather.)

Boil the snow peas for 2 minutes. Drain and cool. Open one long side of each pod.

Using a small spoon or a pastry bag fitted with a star tip, fill each pod with the yogurt mixture.

Serves 9 to 12

DILLED VEGETABLES

Healing Foods

Carrots
Corn
Squash (summer)

2 large carrots, julienned

2 thin yellow summer squash, julienned

12 ears canned baby corn, halved lengthwise

5 scallions, julienned

2 tablespoons vinegar

2 teaspoons Dijon mustard

1 teaspoon dillweed

1 clove garlic, minced

2 heads Belgian endive

Blanch the carrots in boiling water for 40 seconds. Drain, pat dry, and transfer to a large bowl.

Blanch the squash for 20 seconds. Drain, pat dry, and add to the bowl.

Add the corn and scallions.

In a small bowl, whisk together the vinegar, mustard, dill, and garlic. Pour over the vegetables and toss to coat well. Chill.

Separate the Belgian endive into petals. Use to line a large platter. Add the vegetables.

Serves 4 to 6

HORSERADISH DIP

Healing Food

Yogurt (low-fat)

1 1/2 cups nonfat
  yogurt
1/2 cup minced
  scallions

3 tablespoons
  prepared horseradish
2 tablespoons snipped
  chives

In a small bowl, combine the yogurt, scallions, horseradish, and chives.

Makes 2 cups

TUNA TART WITH BASIL

Healing Foods

Fish
Garlic
Parsley
Whole wheat flour

1 9-inch Whole Wheat
  Pie Shell, unbaked
  (page 272)
1 can (7 ounces)
  water-packed tuna,
  drained and flaked
2 tablespoons grated
  Sapsago or Parmesan
  cheese

3/4 cup stock
1/2 cup minced
  fresh parsley
1/4 cup egg substitute
3 cloves garlic, minced
1 teaspoon dried basil

145

Bake the pie shell at 400°F for 10 minutes. Set aside.

In a large bowl, mix the tuna, stock, parsley, egg substitute, garlic, and basil. Pour into the pie shell. Sprinkle with the cheese.

Bake at 350°F for 40 minutes, or until a knife inserted in the center comes out clean. To serve, cut into thin slices.

Serves 8 to 12

BETTER THAN CREAM CHEESE

Make your own lusciously smooth, creamy, low-fat alternative to cream cheese. It's called yogurt cheese, and it's got a lot going for it: just a fraction of cream cheese's calories and—if you use nonfat yogurt—none of its fat. Best of all, it's a snap to make.

Just line a large strainer with either cheesecloth, white paper towels, or a coffee filter. (Or use a special yogurt-cheese funnel.) Spoon in 4 cups of plain nonfat yogurt and let the whey drain out overnight. You'll end up with 1$\frac{1}{2}$ to 2 cups of nonfat yogurt cheese. Store your cheese covered in the refrigerator.

One note: Some brands of yogurt have gelatin or stabilizers in them that prevent the whey from draining off. Reading the label isn't always enough to tell you whether a particular yogurt is drainable. So try this test at home: Take a big spoonful of yogurt out of the container, leaving a depression. If the hole starts to fill with liquid within 10 minutes, you should have success making yogurt cheese.

Here are some ways to use your yogurt cheese for canapés on your hors d'oeuvre tray.

- Fold in chives and use to top baked potato slices or potato skins.
- Add fresh or dried herbs and use as a savory spread for toast or crackers.
- Mix with minced smoked turkey and use in place of cream cheese on bagel crisps.
- Stir in orange juice concentrate and minced fruit (such as strawberries) and use as a topping on cheese and crackers.
- Mix with Mexican salsa and use as a dip for crisp raw vegetables.

Sweet and Spicy Curry Dip

$^1/_4$ cup fruit chutney
1 tablespoon curry powder
1 cup yogurt cheese (see page 146)
$^1/_8$ teaspoon hot-pepper sauce

In a 1-quart saucepan, heat the chutney and curry powder for 1 minute, stirring frequently. Cool slightly.

In a small bowl, combine the yogurt cheese, curry mixture, and hot-pepper sauce.

Makes about 1 cup

Healing Food

- Yogurt (low-fat)

147

Roasted-Garlic Dip

8 cloves garlic,
  unpeeled
$1/3$ cup water
1 cup yogurt cheese
  (see page 146)

$1/8$ teaspoon ground
  red pepper
1 bay leaf

Place the garlic in a small ovenproof dish. Add the water and bay leaf. Bake at 350°F for 25 to 35 minutes, or until the garlic is tender. Discard the bay leaf.

Squeeze each clove of garlic out of its skin. Place in a small dish and mash well. Stir in the yogurt cheese and pepper.

Makes about 1 cup

Healing Foods

- Garlic
- Yogurt (low-fat)

Orange-Almond Cheese

1 cup yogurt cheese
  (see page 146)
3 tablespoons raisins,
  minced
1 tablespoon chopped
  almonds

$1^1/2$ teaspoons honey
$1^1/2$ teaspoons orange
  juice concentrate
$1/8$ teaspoon ground
  cinnamon

In a medium bowl, combine the yogurt cheese, raisins, almonds, honey, juice, and cinnamon.

Makes about 1 cup

Healing Foods

- Raisins
- Yogurt (low-fat)

148

Pesto Cheese

$^1/_2$ cup chopped
  fresh parsley
3 tablespoons
  sunflower seeds
1 tablespoon
  olive oil

1 teaspoon dried
  basil
1 cup yogurt cheese
  (see page 146)
1 teaspoon Dijon
  mustard

In a food processor, combine the parsley, sunflower seeds, oil, mustard, and basil. Process for 10 to 15 seconds, until a paste forms. Transfer to a medium bowl and stir in the yogurt cheese.

Makes about 1 cup

Healing Foods

• Parsley • Seeds • Yogurt (low-fat)

ONION TOAST

Healing Foods

Oil
Onions

1 tablespoon olive oil
1 teaspoon honey
1 teaspoon low-
  sodium soy sauce
$^1/_4$ cup apple-cider
  vinegar

$^1/_4$ teaspoon ground
  red pepper
$2^1/_2$ onions, thinly
  sliced
$^1/_2$ teaspoon dried
  thyme

1 loaf Whole Wheat
French bread, thinly
sliced (page 284)

In a large nonstick frying pan over medium heat,
combine the oil, honey, soy sauce, and pepper.

Add the onions and stir to combine. Cover the
pan and simmer over medium-low heat for 30
minutes, stirring occasionally.

Stir in the vinegar and thyme. Cover and simmer for about 20 minutes, stirring occasionally,
until the onions are very soft and thick, having
absorbed all the liquid.

While the onions are cooking, place the bread
slices in a single layer on cookie sheets. Bake at
350°F for about 10 minutes per side to toast
lightly.

Spread the slices with the warm onion mixture.

Serves 8 to 10

CHICKEN CANAPÉS
WITH BROCCOLI STUFFING

Healing Foods

Broccoli
Cheese (low-fat)
Chicken
Garlic
Nuts

1 pound boneless, skinless chicken breast
1 teaspoon Dijon mustard
2 ounces low-fat Swiss cheese, shredded
1 cup diced broccoli
2 cloves garlic, minced
1 tablespoon olive oil
3 tablespoons chopped almonds
$1/2$ teaspoon dried rosemary

Pound the chicken with a mallet until uniformly thin. Lay the pieces in a single layer on a flat surface and coat the top surface of the chicken lightly with the mustard. Sprinkle with the cheese.

In a large nonstick frying pan, sauté the broccoli and garlic in the oil for about 10 minutes. Add the almonds and rosemary. Remove from the heat.

Divide the filling mixture among the chicken pieces, positioning it along one edge of each piece. Roll the chicken to enclose the filling. Wrap each roll tightly in plastic wrap. Place in a steamer basket in a single layer.

Steam the chicken for about 10 minutes. Remove the rolls from the basket and refrigerate, still wrapped, for at least 2 hours.

To serve, unwrap the rolls and slice into thin disks. Keep chilled until ready to serve.

Serves 6 to 8

WATERCRESS CANAPÉS

Healing Foods

Cucumbers
Watercress
Yogurt (low-fat)

1 cup nonfat yogurt
2 scallions, minced
1 teaspoon dillweed
4 cups watercress
   sprigs

12 slices whole-grain
   bread
2 cups thinly sliced
   cucumbers
12 radishes, thinly
   sliced

Spoon the yogurt into a strainer lined with cheesecloth. Place over a bowl and allow to drain until thick, about 4 hours. Transfer to a small bowl and stir in the scallions and dill.

If desired, trim the crusts from the bread. Spread the bread with the yogurt mixture. Divide the cucumbers, watercress, and radishes among the slices and arrange them in attractive layers on the yogurt mixture.

Cut each slice into four squares or triangles.

Serves 12

ANTIPASTO WITH BAKED OYSTERS

Healing Foods

Broccoli
Figs
Fish
Kale
Mollusks

OYSTERS

16 oysters on the
  half shell
1 teaspoon Dijon
  mustard
1/2 teaspoon fennel
  seeds, crushed
1/2 cup minced
  tomatoes
3 tablespoons
  minced scallions

ANTIPASTO

16 kale leaves
1 cup steamed
  broccoli
6 ounces canned
  salmon, drained
  and chunked
1/2 cup dry-curd
  cottage cheese
1/2 teaspoon dried
  tarragon
8 dried figs
1 cup nonfat yogurt
1 teaspoon Dijon
  mustard
1 teaspoon fennel
  seeds, crushed

To make the oysters: Arrange the oysters in their
shells in a shallow baking dish. Combine the mustard and fennel. Brush over the oysters. Bake at
450°F for 10 minutes, or until the oysters have

153

turned from gray to whitish. Remove from the oven and sprinkle the tomatoes and scallions in the shells over the oysters.

To make the antipasto: Line a serving platter with the kale. Arrange the broccoli, salmon, and oyster shells on the kale.

In a cup, mix the cottage cheese and tarragon. Slit each fig with a sharp knife. Using a small spoon or a pastry bag fitted with a small tube, fill each fig with the mixture. Add to the platter.

In a small bowl, combine the yogurt, mustard, and fennel. Serve as a dressing. Use the kale leaves to scoop up the antipasto.

Serves 8

CITRUS-MARINATED CARROTS

Healing Food

Carrots

1 pound carrots	Juice of 1 lemon
1 onion, thinly sliced and separated into rings	Juice of 1 lime
	1 tablespoon low-sodium soy sauce
3 cups vinegar	2 teaspoons sesame oil
Juice of 1 orange	$1/2$ teaspoon black peppercorns

Cut the carrots into 3-inch sticks. Blanch in boiling water for 5 minutes, until crisp-tender. Drain and transfer to a large glass jar. Add the onions.

In a large bowl, combine the vinegar, orange juice, lemon juice, lime juice, soy sauce, oil, and peppercorns. Pour into the jar to cover the carrots. Cover and refrigerate for at least 4 hours.

To serve, drain off the liquid.

Serves 6 to 8

DILL-ZUCCHINI SPEARS

Healing Foods

Oil
Squash (summer)

2 tablespoons white-wine vinegar
2 cloves garlic, minced
1 teaspoon dillweed

$1/2$ teaspoon Dijon mustard
3 tablespoons canola oil
3 small zucchini, cut lengthwise into spears

In a small bowl, combine the vinegar, garlic, and mustard. Slowly whisk in the oil until thoroughly combined. Whisk in the dill.

Arrange the zucchini in a shallow dish. Pour the dressing over the zucchini. Cover and chill for at least 3 hours.

Serves 6 to 8

ROASTED EGGPLANT
HORS D'OEUVRES

Healing Foods

Eggplant
Garlic
Mushrooms
Peppers (sweet)
Whole wheat flour

1 eggplant, cut into 1-inch cubes

1 pound small mushrooms

1 loaf Whole Wheat French Bread (page 284)

2 sweet red peppers, sliced

10 cloves garlic

1 tablespoon olive oil

1 teaspoon dried thyme

Cook the eggplant in boiling water for about 4 minutes. Drain, then pat the pieces dry.

Combine the eggplant, mushrooms, peppers, garlic, oil, and thyme in a 9 x 13-inch baking dish. Bake at 450°F, stirring occasionally, for 25 minutes, or until the vegetables are tender and roasted.

Cut the bread into thin slices and toast lightly. Serve topped with the vegetable spread.

Serves 6 to 8

CURRIED YOGURT AND BROCCOLI

Healing Foods

Broccoli
Yogurt (low-fat)

2 cups nonfat yogurt
2 teaspoons curry
  powder
1 teaspoon ground
  cumin

2 teaspoons paprika
1 teaspoon ground
  coriander
1 pound broccoli
  florets

In a small bowl, combine the yogurt, curry powder, paprika, coriander, and cumin.

Blanch the broccoli in boiling water for 2 minutes. Drain and pat dry. Serve with the yogurt dip.

Serves 8

A COLORFUL ARRAY OF CRUDITÉS

What do you get when you give "rabbit food" a fancy French name? Crudités. These crisp raw vegetables, often served with dips and spreads, make excellent low-cal, low-fat, high-fiber alternatives to chips and crackers. And they're just right for between-meal snacks, elegant party fare, and festive-looking appetizers.

Select an array of colorful vegetables and cut

them in imaginative shapes and sizes, such as the ones suggested below. Keep a selection tightly wrapped in the fridge for impromptu noshing. And if you want to jazz them up with a tasty dip, choose a low-fat variety so you don't undermine their healing potential. (See "Better Than Cream Cheese" on page 146 for some healthy dip ideas.)

Vegetable	How to Cut
Broccoli	Cut into florets.
Carrots	Cut crosswise with a crinkle cutter or slice in quarters lengthwise.
Cauliflower	Cut into florets.
Celery	Cut stalks to 3 inches; cut fine slits halfway down each.
Cherry tomatoes	Leave whole.
Chinese cabbage (bok choy)	Serve ribs only.
Cucumbers	Cut into sticks and rounds. For rounds, peel cucumber if waxed; run tines of a fork down all sides, then slice thinly or cut into wedges lengthwise.
Green beans	Leave whole; snip off ends.
Peppers	Cut into strips or rings.
Scallions	Leave whole.
Sugar snap peas	Leave whole.
White mushrooms	Leave whole or cut off stems.
Zucchini	Cut into sticks and rounds or slice in wedges lengthwise.

CHAPTER FOUR

Soups and Chowders

Soup made a stir in the research lab a few years back when scientists discovered that eating it can help you lose weight. It's been a hot issue ever since.

In one study, for example, researchers at the Baylor College of Medicine and the Arkansas Department of Health asked dieters to eat soup with one or more meals a day. After one year, the soup group wound up considerably slimmer than another group of dieters who ate the same number of calories but without the daily soup requirement.

So what does soup have that makes it such choice diet fare? For starters, theorize researchers, soup tends to be eaten hot. That means you consume it slowly, giving your brain time to signal your appetite that it's satisfied before you can overeat. Also, soup is made up largely of water, and its bulk consists mainly of low-calorie vegetables plus fiber-rich grains and legumes—all of which work in your favor to fill you up.

Every recipe in this chapter was created with that mission in mind. And many—such as Apple-Barley Soup and Succotash Chowder, just to name two—are so hearty they can stand alone as a meal. You'll even find you can enjoy creamy

159

varieties without using high-fat butter, eggs, cream, or milk. "Getting Great Body" on page 170 tells you how.

Soup is a great way to savor the nutritive value of such great fillers as cholesterol-lowering beans and potassium-filled potatoes. And those who turn up their noses at fish for dinner often find they love it in soup or chowder. Salmon Bisque, Seafood Gazpacho, and Striper Chowder are perfect ways to have your fish and love it too.

EGGPLANT SOUP WITH TINY PASTA

Healing Food

Eggplant
Garlic
Pasta
Tomatoes

1 large onion, minced
1/2 cup minced celery
3 cloves garlic, minced
2 teaspoons olive oil
2 cups cubed eggplant
1/2 cup orzo or other tiny pasta, cooked

2 cups chopped tomatoes
1 3/4 cups chicken stock
1/8 teaspoon dried thyme
1/8 teaspoon crushed rosemary

In a 3-quart saucepan over medium heat, sauté the onions, celery, and garlic in the oil for 3 minutes.

Add the eggplant and tomatoes. Cover and simmer for 10 minutes.

Add the stock, thyme, and rosemary. Simmer for 20 minutes. Add the pasta and heat through.

Serves 4

STRIPER CHOWDER

Healing Foods

Fish
Parsley
Potatoes

12 ounces striped-bass fillets

$1/3$ cup thinly sliced scallions

1 tablespoon olive oil

1 teaspoon minced garlic

$1/2$ teaspoon low-sodium soy sauce

2 bay leaves

$1/8$ teaspoon red pepper

3 cups stock

1 cup chopped tomatoes

1 cup cubed potatoes

2 teaspoons prepared horseradish

1 teaspoon lemon juice

$1/2$ teaspoon dried thyme

$1/2$ cup minced fresh parsley

Cut the bass into $1/2$-inch chunbs and set aside.

In a 3-quart saucepan over medium heat, sauté

the scallions in the oil for 5 minutes. Add the garlic and sauté for 1 minute.

Add the stock, tomatoes, potatoes, horseradish, lemon juice, soy sauce, thyme, red pepper, and bay leaves.

Bring to a boil, then lower the heat and simmer for 10 minutes.

Add the fish and parsley. Simmer for 5 minutes. Discard the bay leaves.

Serves 4

DILLED CABBAGE SOUP

Healing Foods

Cabbage
Garlic
Onions
Potatoes

$^1/_2$ medium cabbage, chopped

2 large onions, chopped

1 teaspoon dill seeds

$1^1/_2$ cups tomato juice

$^1/_4$ cup minced fresh parsley

1 tablespoon olive oil

4 cloves garlic, minced

1 tablespoon vinegar

3 cups stock

1 large potato, diced

$^1/_2$ teaspoon caraway seeds

2 teaspoons low-sodium soy sauce

In a 3-quart saucepan, sauté the cabbage, onions, dill, and caraway in the oil, stirring occasionally, until the cabbage is translucent and wilted, about 10 minutes.

Add the garlic and vinegar. Cook for 1 minute. Add the stock, tomato juice, potatoes, and soy sauce.

Cover and simmer until the potatoes are tender, about 15 to 20 minutes. Add the parsley.

Serves 4

PUMPKIN SOUP

Healing Foods

Onions
Pumpkin
Seeds

1 large onion, minced
2 cups chicken stock
1 1/2 cups pureed cooked pumpkin
1/2 teaspoon dried oregano
1/4 teaspoon hot-pepper sauce
1/4 cup toasted pumpkin seeds

In a 2-quart saucepan, cook the onions in 2 tablespoons of the stock until limp.

Add the remaining stock, pumpkin, oregano, and hot-pepper sauce. Simmer for 15 minutes. Serve sprinkled with pumpkin seeds.

Serves 4

ESCAROLE SOUP

Healing Foods

Carrots
Onions
Parsnips
Salad greens

4 cups chicken stock
1 1/2 cups diced
  onions
1 cup diced celery
1/2 teaspoon curry
  powder
1 1/2 cups chopped
  escarole

1 cup thinly sliced
  carrots
1 cup thinly sliced
  parsnips
1/4 teaspoon ground
  fennel

In a 3-quart saucepan, combine the stock, onions, celery, carrots, parsnips, curry powder, and fennel. Bring to a boil, then reduce the heat and simmer until the vegetables are tender, about 30 minutes.

Add the escarole and cook for 10 minutes.

Serves 4

MICRO METHOD: Fresh-Tasting Soups

Microwaving enhances the flavor of vegetables, yielding soups that taste fresher than conventionally cooked potages. Use these guidelines to convert your favorite recipes to the microwave.

- Reduce the amount of liquid in your conventional recipe by one-fourth, since very little liquid evaporates during the short time it takes for microwaving soup. Exceptions are soups made with dried peas or beans. These need the full amount of liquid to rehydrate the legumes. (And some of the water *will* evaporate during the longer microwaving time needed for these types of soup.)
- Cut meat and vegetables into small, uniform pieces so they'll cook evenly and quickly.
- Microwave clear soups or brothy chicken-and-vegetable soups on high power.
- Use medium (50 percent) power and longer cooking times for soups based on less-tender cuts of meats, such as beef cubes. Start by cooking the beef in liquid to cover until tender. Then add vegetables and seasonings.
- For chicken stews, use broiler-fryers. They're younger and more tender than stewing hens. (You can microwave stewing hens, but they'll take nearly as long as with conventional cooking methods. Use medium power.)
- When making fish or shellfish soups, cook the rest of the ingredients first. Seafood begins to cook as soon as it's added to hot liquid. To avoid overcooking these delicate items, use 50 percent power and cook just until opaque. Allow a few minutes' standing time after microwaving to complete the cooking process.
- Soups or chowders made with milk can be microwaved on high. Choose a container that will hold double the volume of soup you are microwaving to avoid boilovers.

- When precooking vegetables for pureed soups, use high power and little or no liquid.
- Making very thick pureed soups is easy in the microwave. Conventional thick soups made on the stove must be cooked over low heat and stirred often to prevent sticking. Since sticking is not a problem with the micro-wave, such soups can be cooked on high and stirred only two or three times throughout cooking.

BUTTERNUT BISQUE

Healing Foods

Apples
Carrots
Milk (low-fat)
Potatoes
Squash (winter)

2 leeks
1 large butternut
  squash
3 cups stock
2 carrots, sliced
1 apple, chopped
1 potato, chopped
1 cup evaporated
  skim milk

1 large onion, chopped
$1/4$ cup chopped
  fresh parsley
2 cloves garlic
1 teaspoon dried
  oregano
$1/2$ teaspoon dried
  rosemary

Discard the tough green leaves and root end of the leeks. Halve the leeks lengthwise and wash well to remove any dirt from between the layers. Chop coarsely.

Peel, seed, and coarsely chop the squash.

In a 3-quart saucepan, combine the leeks, squash, stock, carrots, apples, potatoes, onions, parsley, garlic, oregano, and rosemary.

Cover and cook over medium heat until the vegetables are tender, about 30 minutes.

Puree in a food mill or blender, working in batches. Stir in the milk, adding more if the bisque is too thick.

Serves 4

SEAFOOD GAZPACHO

Healing Foods

Avocados
Mollusks
Parsley
Peppers (sweet)
Tomatoes
Yogurt (low-fat)

12 ounces bay
  scallops
1/2 cup minced
  fresh parsley
2 tablespoons
  lemon juice
3 cups peeled,
  seeded, and
  chopped tomatoes

1 1/2 cups tomato
  juice
1 avocado, chopped
1 cup chopped
  green peppers
1/2 cup chopped onions
1 tablespoon minced
  garlic

1 teaspoon hot- pepper sauce	1 cup nonfat yogurt

Blanch the scallops in boiling water for 1 minute. Drain and place in a large bowl. Add the parsley and lemon juice.

In a food processor, combine the tomatoes, tomato juice, avocados, peppers, onions, garlic, and hot-pepper sauce. Using on/off turns, process until coarsely chopped. Add to the bowl. Refrigerate for 2 hours, or until chilled.

To serve, ladle into shallow soup bowls. Top with dollops of yogurt.

Serves 4

PHEASANT AND MUSHROOM SOUP

Healing Foods

Carrots
Game
Mushrooms
Onions

1/4 cup dried porcini mushrooms	3 cups stock
1 cup minced fresh mushrooms	1 cup grated carrots
1 cup minced onions	2 tablespoons minced celery leaves
2 tablespoons olive oil	1 tablespoon red-wine vinegar

³/4 cup shredded   1 white truffle,
  cooked pheasant   minced (optional)

Soak the dried mushrooms in water to cover for about 20 minutes. Remove and discard any stems, mince the mushrooms, and reserve the liquid.

In a 3-quart saucepan, sauté the fresh mushrooms and onions in the oil until they turn a rich brown color, about 10 minutes.

Add the stock, carrots, celery, vinegar, dried mushrooms, and reserved soaking liquid. Bring to a boil, then reduce the heat and simmer for 15 minutes.

Add the pheasant and truffles (if used). Cook for 15 minutes.

Serves 4

CHUNKY TOMATO SOUP

Healing Foods

Onions
Parsley
Tomatoes

2 leeks   2 cups diced tomatoes
2 large onions, diced   ¹/2 cup minced
3 cloves garlic, minced   fresh parsley
1 tablespoon olive oil   ¹/2 teaspoon dried
3 cups chicken stock   thyme
1 bay leaf   2 teaspoons low-
2 teaspoons honey   sodium soy sauce

Remove and discard the tough green leaves and root end of the leeks. Cut the leeks in half lengthwise. Wash well to remove any dirt from between the layers, then chop coarsely.

In a 3-quart saucepan over medium heat, sauté the leeks, onions, and garlic in the oil until translucent, about 7 minutes.

Add the stock, tomatoes, parsley, thyme, and bay leaf. Cover and simmer for 20 to 30 minutes. Discard the bay leaf.

Stir in the soy sauce and honey.

Serves 4

GETTING GREAT BODY

Give your soups the rich, thick, satisfying texture you crave without resorting to butter, egg yolks, and cream. Simply puree part of the batch and add it back to the pot. Or stir in one or more of the following ingredients:

- Mashed potatoes
- Pureed vegetables, such as carrots, corn, or onions
- Evaporated skim milk
- Buttermilk
- Rice (whole or pureed)
- Beans (mash all or part of them)
- Pasta
- Bread cubes

ICED CANTALOUPE SOUP

Healing Foods

Melons
Milk (low-fat)
Yogurt (low-fat)

1 large cantaloupe
1 1/2 cups low-fat milk
2 tablespoons maple syrup
3/4 teaspoon ground cinnamon
3/4 teaspoon ground coriander
1/2 cup nonfat yogurt

Remove the seeds and rind from the cantaloupe. Cut the flesh into cubes.

In a blender, combine the cantaloupe, milk, maple syrup, cinnamon, and coriander. Blend well.

Transfer to a large bowl. Cover and chill for 1 hour.

While the soup is chilling, spoon the yogurt into a cheesecloth-lined sieve. Let drain over a bowl to thicken.

Whisk the yogurt into the soup.

Serves 4

CREAM OF CARROT SOUP

Healing Foods

Carrots
Onions
Potatoes

1 large onion, sliced
1 teaspoon canola oil
2 cups stock
3/4 cup skim milk

4 ounces carrots, sliced
1 large potato, cubed
1/2 teaspoon dried
  thyme

In a 2-quart saucepan, sauté the onions in the oil until softened, about 5 minutes.

Add the stock, cartots, potatoes, and thyme. Simmer until tender, about 25 minutes.

Puree in a food mill or blender. Stir in the milk.

Serves 4

TOMATO BISQUE

Healing Foods

Corn
Onions
Peppers (sweet)
Tomatoes

1 large onion,
  thinly sliced
1 tablespoon olive
  oil

5 cups chicken stock
2 sweet red peppers,
  diced
1 cup corn

4 large tomatoes,
  peeled, seeded,
  and chopped
2 tablespoons
  cornstarch

1 teaspoon dried
  basil
$^1/_4$ cup water
$^1/_4$ cup minced
  fresh parsley

In a 3-quart saucepan over medium-high heat, sauté the onions in oil until soft, about 3 to 5 minutes. Stir in the tomatoes. Let simmer for a few minutes.

Add the stock, peppers, corn, and basil. Bring to a boil, then reduce the heat and simmer for 1 hour.

In a cup, mix the water and cornstarch until smooth. Add to the soup and stir over heat until thickened. Let cool for about 5 minutes.

Puree in batches in a food processor or blender. Serve sprinkled with the parsley.

Serves 4 to 6

ICED LEEK AND ORANGE SOUP

Healing Foods

Onions
Oranges

5 leeks
4 cups stock
$1^1/_2$ cups orange juice
$^1/_2$ cup minced shallots

8 scallions, chopped
2 oranges, sectioned
1 bay leaf
1 tablespoon minced
  celery

173

Remove and discard the tough green leaves and root end of the leeks. Cut the leeks in half lengthwise. Wash well to remove any dirt from between the layers, then chop coarsely.

In a 3-quart saucepan, combine the leeks, stock, orange juice, shallots, scallions, oranges, bay leaf, and celery.

Bring to a boil. Reduce the heat and simmer until the vegetables are tender, about 30 minutes. Let cool 5 minutes.

Discard the bay leaf. In a blender, puree the soup in batches. Transfer to a large bowl. Chill before serving.

Serves 6

SOUTH AMERICAN SQUASH SOUP

Healing Foods

Beef (lean)
Tomatoes
Squash (winter)

4 ounces flank steak, trimmed of all visible fat
1 tablespoon olive oil
1 small butternut squash
1/4 teaspoon dried marjoram
1/4 teaspoon hot-pepper sauce

1 large onion, diced
2 1/2 cups beef stock
1 1/2 cups pureed tomatoes
2 teaspoons low-sodium soy sauce
1/4 teaspoon dried thyme

Cut the steak into $1/2$-inch cubes. In a 3-quart saucepan, brown the beef in the oil. Remove the beef from the pan.

Peel, seed, and cube the squash. Add to the pan, along with the onions. Cover and cook over medium-low heat for 15 minutes.

Add the beef, stock, tomatoes, soy sauce, marjoram, thyme, and hot-pepper sauce. Simmer until the squash is tender, about 15 minutes.

Serves 4 to 6

APPLE-BARLEY SOUP

Healing Foods

Apples
Barley
Carrots
Oil
Onions

2 large onions, thinly sliced
2 tablespoons canola oil
$3^1/2$ cups stock
$1^1/2$ cups apple juice
$1/3$ cup pearl barley
$1/4$ cup minced fresh parsley
2 large carrots, diced
$3/4$ teaspoon dried thyme
$1/4$ teaspoon dried marjoram
1 bay leaf
2 cups chopped apples
1 tablespoon lemon juice

In a 3-quart saucepan over medium heat, cook the onions in the oil, stirring constantly, for 5 minutes. Reduce the heat to medium-low, cover and cook, stirring frequently, for 20 to 25 minutes, or until the onions are golden brown and very soft.

Add the stock, apple juice, barley, carrots, thyme, marjoram, and bay leaf. Cover and cook for 1 hour, or until the barley is tender.

Add the apples, parsley, and lemon juice. Cook for 5 minutes, or until the apples are tender. Discard the bay leaf.

Serves 4

CAJUN SOUP

Healing Foods

Beans (dried)
Corn
Peppers (sweet)
Swiss chard

1 large onion, chopped
1 tablespoon olive oil
1 green pepper, diced
1/2 cup chopped celery
3 cloves garlic, minced
4 cups chicken stock
1 cup shredded Swiss chard
1/2 cup cooked black-eyed peas
1 large tomato, chopped
2 bay leaves
1/2 teaspoon dried rosemary
1/2 teaspoon dried oregano
1/2 teaspoon dried basil
4 cups corn
3/4 teaspoon paprika
1/4 teaspoon red pepper
1/4 teaspoon black pepper

In a 4-quart pot over medium heat, sauté the onions in the oil until light brown, 7 to 8 minutes. Add the green peppers, celery, and garlic. Cook for 5 minutes.

Add the stock, tomatoes, bay leaves, rosemary, oregano, and basil. Bring to a boil. Cover and simmer 15 minutes.

Add the corn, Swiss chard, black-eyed peas, paprika, and red and black pepper. Simmer for 5 minutes. Discard the bay leaves.

Serves 4

COOL PEACH SOUP

Healing Foods

Peaches
Raspberries

1 cup white
  grape juice
1 cup water
1/3 cup apple juice
  concentrate
1 teaspoon
  vanilla extract

1/4 teaspoon ground
  cinnamon
2 teaspoons
  lemon juice
4 large peaches
1 pint raspberries

In a 1-quart saucepan, bring the grape juice, water, apple juice concentrate, vanilla, and cinnamon to a boil. Simmer for 2 minutes.

Remove the pan from the heat and stir in the lemon juice.

Peel the peaches by immersing them in boiling

water for about 1 minute, then running them under cold water. The skins will easily slip off.

Chop two of the peaches and place in a blender or food processor. Add the liquid and process until smooth. Transfer to a large bowl.

Cut the remaining peaches into $1/2$-inch wedges. Add to the bowl, making sure the slices are covered with puree so they won't discolor.

Refrigerate the soup for at least 1 hour, or until well chilled.

Serve in shallow bowls topped with raspberries.

Serves 4

GARLIC AND POTATO SOUP

Healing Foods

Garlic
Milk (low-fat)
Onions
Potatoes

2 medium leeks
3 cups stock
1 pound potatoes, cubed
2 tablespoons crumbled feta cheese

4 cloves garlic, minced
1 cup evaporated skim milk
$1/4$ cup snipped chives

Remove and discard the tough green leaves and root end of the leeks. Cut the leeks in half lengthwise. Wash well to remove any dirt from between the layers, then slice thinly.

In a 3-quart saucepan, combine the leeks, stock, potatoes, and garlic. Bring to a boil. Reduce the heat to medium-low, cover loosely, and simmer until the potatoes are tender, about 15 minutes.

Stir in the milk and chives. Simmer just until heated through.

Place the cheese in a strainer. Rinse with cold water to remove excess salt. Pat dry. Sprinkle over the soup.

Serves 4

COLD ZUCCHINI SOUP

Healing Foods

Peppers (sweet)
Squash (summer)
Tomatoes

8 tomatoes, quartered
3 medium zucchini, chopped
3 stalks celery, chopped
1 green pepper, quartered
1/2 teaspoon grated lemon rind

1 large onion, quartered
2 tablespoons lemon juice
1/2 teaspoon dried basil
1/2 teaspoon ground cumin

In a food processor, combine the tomatoes, zucchini, celery, peppers, onions, lemon juice, basil, cumin, and lemon rind. Process with on/off turns until smooth. Served chilled.

Serves 6

Accent on Health: Sturdy Stock

A good stock is the foundation upon which full-bodied soups, stews, and sauces are built. In addition, it gives extra flavor to marinades and perks up vegetables lightly cooked in it, so you're not tempted to spruce them up with butter or a high-cal sauce.

In addition to its flavor contribution, a good homemade stock can have some health bonuses: It's low in calories. If made with little or no salt, it's low in sodium. If properly skimmed, it's nearly fat-free. And it's likely to contain some vitamins and minerals that leached out of the meat, bones, and vegetables that went into the stock.

For the best, most flavorful stocks, follow these basics:

- Include some bones (for all but vegetarian stocks). Bones—especially from veal—contain gelatin, which gives body to stock. For best results, hack or saw the bones into small pieces (or ask your butcher to do it).
- Save vegetable trimmings from other dishes and store them in the freezer until there are enough to make stock.
- Cut vegetables into large pieces so they won't fall apart during cooking and cloud the stock.
- Get rich, deep color by adding onion skins to the pot.

- For more nice color brown your bones and vegetables in the oven before adding them to the pot. About 30 minutes at 400°F should do it.
- To help draw valuable calcium from the bones, add an acidic ingredient to your stock. Tomatoes, vinegar, or lemon juice (even a lemon half) will do the trick.
- Simmer your stock over low heat for several hours to slowly extract its maximum flavor and nutrients.
- Strain the finished stock through cheesecloth or a clean kitchen towel. Then taste the stock carefully and boil it down to concentrate the flavor, if needed.
- Degrease the stock before using—that slashes its fat content. The easiest way is to refrigerate the stock overnight and lift off the congealed fat in the morning.

CHILLED BLUEBERRY SOUP

Healing Foods

Blueberries
Yogurt (low-fat)

2 cups blueberries
3/4 cup apple juice
1/4 cup orange juice
1 cup nonfat
  vanilla yogurt

1/4 teaspoon lemon
  extract
1/8 teaspoon grated
  nutmeg

In a 2-quart saucepan, combine the blueberries, apple juice, orange juice, lemon extract, and nutmeg. Bring to a boil over medium heat, stirring occasionally.

Reduce the heat and simmer for 1 minute.

Let cool for 5 minutes. Transfer to a blender and puree until smooth. Transfer to a large bowl. Chill for 1 hour.

While the soup is chilling, spoon the yogurt into cheesecloth-lined sieve. Let drain over a bowl to thicken.

To serve, ladle the soup into individual bowls. Top with dollops of yogurt.

Serves 4

SWEETHEART SOUP

Healing Food

Peppers (sweet)

8 sweet red peppers, chopped
1/2 cup minced celery
2 cloves garlic, minced
2 shallots, minced
1 tablespoon peeled minced gingerroot
1/8 teaspoon ground ginger
1 tablespoon olive oil
4 cups chicken stock
1 tablespoon lime juice
1/4 teaspoon ground coriander
1 tablespoon nonfat yogurt
1 tablespoon evaporated skim milk

In a 3-quart saucepan, sauté the peppers, celery,

garlic, shallots, and minced ginger in the oil for 5 minutes.

Add the stock, lime juice, coriander, and ground ginger. Simmer for 25 to 30 minutes, or until the peppers are tender. Let cool about 5 minutes.

In a blender, puree the soup in batches until smooth.

Pour into individual bowls.

To make the hearts, mix the yogurt and milk in a cup. Place a dot (about $1/4$ teaspoon) of the mixture on the surface of one bowl of soup. Place a toothpick in the soup about $1/4$ inch away from the dot and draw it through the dot, lifting it when the tail of the heart is about $1/2$ inch long. Wipe off the toothpick. Repeat to make several hearts in each bowl.

Serves 4

FRAGRANT BORSCHT

Healing Foods

Beets
Cabbage
Yogurt (low-fat)

4 cups beef stock
4 large beets, peeled
  and shredded
$1/2$ medium cabbage,
  shredded
$1^1/2$ cups nonfat yogurt

$1/4$ cup vinegar
2 tablespoons honey
2 teaspoons low-
  sodium soy sauce
$1/2$ cup tomato puree

In a 3-quart saucepan, combine the stock and beets. Cover and cook over medium heat until tender, about 20 to 25 minutes.

Add the cabbage, vinegar, honey, and soy sauce. Cover and cook until the cabbage begins to soften, about 7 to 10 minutes.

Add the tomato puree and cook 10 to 15 minutes.

To serve, ladle into soup bowls and top with a large spoonful of yogurt.

Serves 4

SUMMER-VEGETABLE SOUP

Healing Foods

Beans (snap)
Corn
Potatoes
Squash (summer)

1 cup chopped onions
1 teaspoon minced garlic
1 tablespoon olive oil
1 1/4 cups chicken stock
1 cup sliced celery
1 yellow squash, cubed

1 cup sliced green beans
1 cup cubed potatoes
1 bay leaf
1/2 teaspoon dried savory
1/4 teaspoon dried marjoram
2 cups corn

In a 3-quart saucepan, sauté the onions and garlic in the oil until soft, about 4 minutes. Add the stock, celery, beans, potatoes, bay leaf, savory, and marjoram. Cover and simmer over low heat for 15 minutes.

Add the squash and corn. Simmer for 10 to 15 minutes. Discard the bay leaf.

Serves 4

KOREAN HOT BEEF SOUP

Healing Foods

Beef (lean)
Cabbage
Tofu

4 ounces flank steak, trimmed of all visible fat

2 garlic cloves, minced

2 teaspoons low-sodium soy sauce

1 teaspoon peeled minced gingerroot

8 mushrooms, quartered

1 teaspoon dry mustard

1 teaspoon sesame oil

3 cups beef stock

2 cups shredded Chinese cabbage

10 scallions, thinly sliced

2 tablespoons vinegar

8 ounces tofu, cubed

Freeze the beef until firm enough to slice easily, about 30 minutes. Cut across the grain into paper-thin slices and then into 1-inch lengths.

In a pie plate, combine the garlic, soy sauce, ginger, mustard, and sesame oil. Add the beef and toss to coat. Set aside.

185

In a 3-quart saucepan, combine the stock, cabbage, scallions, mushrooms, and vinegar. Simmer for 10 minutes.

In a large nonstick frying pan over medium-high heat, sear the beef until no longer pink, about 5 minutes. Add to the soup, along with any pan juices. Add the tofu. Cook for 5 minutes to heat through.

Serves 4

SUCCOTASH CHOWDER

Healing Foods

Beans (snap)
Corn
Milk (low-fat)

1 large onion, chopped
1 stalk celery, diced
1 teaspoon dried sage
1 clove garlic, minced
1 tablespoon olive oil
1/4 cup minced parsley
1 teaspoon dry mustard

3 cups chicken stock
2 cups fresh baby lima beans
2 cups corn
3 tablespoons cornstarch
1 cup skim milk
1 teaspoon grated lemon rind
1/2 teaspoon dried tarragon

In a 3-quart saucepan over medium heat, sauté the onions, celery, sage, and garlic in the oil until tender, about 10 minutes.

Add the stock, limas, and corn. Simmer for 10 minutes.

Dissolve the cornstarch in the milk. Add to the soup. Add the parsley, lemon rind, mustard, and tarragon. Cook, stirring, until thick, about 5 to 10 minutes. Do not boil.

Serves 4

CREAMY BROCCOLI SOUP

Healing Foods

Beans (dried)
Broccoli
Onions

1 large onion, diced
1 tablespoon olive oil
2 cups stock
1 pound broccoli
  florets, chopped

1 cup cooked
  white beans
1 bay leaf
$1/4$ teaspoon ground
  allspice

In a 3-quart saucepan, sauté the onions in the oil until brown, about 15 minutes. Add the stock, broccoli, beans, bay leaf, and allspice. Bring to a boil.

Reduce the heat to a simmer, partially cover and simmer until the broccoli is tender, about 20 minutes.

Let cool for 5 minutes. Discard the bay leaf.

In a food processor or blender, puree the soup.

Serves 4

BROCCOLI-BUTTERMILK SOUP

Healing Foods

Broccoli
Garlic
Milk (low-fat)
Onions

1 pound broccoli
   florets
1 cup sliced onions

4 cloves garlic
2 cups buttermilk

Combine the broccoli, onions, and garlic in a steamer basket. Steam over boiling water until the broccoli is tender, about 12 minutes.

Transfer the vegetables to a food processor or blender and blend until pureed. Stir in the buttermilk.

Serves 4

SALMON BISQUE

Healing Foods

Fish
Milk (low-fat)
Onions

1 large onion, diced
1 tablespoon olive oil
2 tablespoons flour

$1^1/2$ cups tomato
   puree
$2^1/2$ cups stock

1 pound salmon fillet, cut into $1/2$-inch chunks	2 tablespoons minced fresh parsley
	2 cups evaporated skim milk

In a 3-quart saucepan, sauté the onions in the oil until translucent, about 5 minutes. Add the flour and cook until light brown, about 3 minutes.

Add the stock, tomato puree, salmon, and parsley. Simmer for 10 minutes.

Add the milk and heat through.

Serves 6

SAFETY FIRST

Bacteria love a good batch of stock as much as you do. They make themselves at home, prosper, and multiply. That's fine for them but potentially dangerous for you. So you need to handle your finished stock in a way that discourages bacterial growth. Here's how.

- Cool your finished stock quickly—and completely—before storing. Otherwise, warm stock at the center of the container will be just the right temperature for bacteria to thrive, even in the refrigerator.
- The easiest way to cool stock is to set the pot in a larger container of ice water. If the pot is very big, use your sink. (But be careful not to tip the stock pot or the ice water will dilute your perfectly seasoned stock.)

- Refrigerate only as much stock as you can use within a few days. Freeze the rest in pint or quart containers. (Be sure to label and date the containers and to use the stock within six months.)
- Before using your stock—whether frozen or refrigerated—bring it to a rolling boil as an extra precaution against bacteria.

EIGHT-VEGETABLE MILLET SOUP

Healing Foods

Beans (snap)
Carrots
Millet
Potatoes
Spinach
Squash (summer)

1 large onion, diced
1 tablespoon olive oil
3 cups chicken stock
2 carrots, diced
1 large potato, diced
1 stalk celery, diced
1/2 teaspoon
    dried basil
1 cup cooked millet
1 cup skim milk

1 zucchini, chopped
1 cup sliced
    green beans
1 tomato, diced
1 bay leaf
1/2 teaspoon
    dried thyme
1 cup shredded
    spinach

In a 3-quart saucepan, sauté the onions in the oil until translucent.

190

Add the stock, carrots, potatoes, celery, zucchini, beans, tomatoes, bay leaf, thyme, and basil.
Simmer for 30 minutes.

Stir in the spinach, millet, and milk. Simmer
for 5 minutes. Discard the bay leaf.

Serves 6

CLAM AND LOBSTER CHOWDER

Healing Foods

Crustaceans
Mollusks
Onions
Potatoes

4 cups chicken stock
2 large potatoes,
   quartered
2 cups sliced onions
1 tablespoon
   canola oil
3 cups water
1 cup evaporated
   skim milk

6 small red potatoes,
   cubed
$1/2$ cup sliced celery
1 teaspoon dried
   tarragon
2 cups shucked clams
8 ounces lobster meat,
   chopped
2 tablespoons minced
   fresh parsley

In a 4-quart pot, combine the stock and quartered
potatoes. Bring to a boil over medium-high heat.
Reduce the heat to low and simmer for 20 minutes.

In a large frying pan over medium heat, sauté
the onions in the oil for 8 to 10 minutes, or until
golden. Add to the potatoes.

191

Working in batches, puree the mixture in a blender. Transfer to a large bowl and set aside.

Using the same pot, combine the water, red potatoes, celery, and tarragon. Bring to a boil. Reduce the heat and simmer for 10 minutes. Add the clams and lobster. Simmer for 5 minutes.

Stir in the milk and pureed vegetables. Simmer for 5 minutes. Add the parsley.

Serves 6

CREAM OF MUSHROOM SOUP

Healing Foods

Milk (low-fat)
Mushrooms
Onions

8 ounces mushrooms, minced
1 cup minced onions
1 clove garlic, minced
1/8 teaspoon red pepper
1 tablespoon whole wheat flour

1 tablespoon minced fresh parsley
1/8 teaspoon grated nutmeg
2 tablespoons olive oil
2 cups stock
1 cup skim milk

In a 2-quart saucepan, sauté the mushrooms, onions, garlic, parsley, nutmeg, and pepper in the olive oil until the mushrooms soften and release their liquid. Sprinkle with the flour and cook, stirring, for 2 minutes.

Gradually stir in the stock. Bring to a boil, reduce the heat, cover, and simmer for 15 minutes.

Let cool for 5 minutes. In a blender, puree the soup in batches. Return it to the saucepan. Stir in the milk and heat through, but do not boil.

Serves 4

IRISH VICHYSSOISE

Healing Foods

Broccoli
Milk (low-fat)
Potatoes

3 large potatoes, diced
1 large bunch
broccoli, chopped
1 large onion,
sliced
1 teaspoon olive oil
1/2 teaspoon dried
thyme
1/4 teaspoon ground
rosemary
1/4 teaspoon
ground cumin
2 cups evaporated
skim milk
1 cup stock

Steam the potatoes and broccoli for 10 minutes, or until tender.

In a 3-quart saucepan, sauté the onions in the oil for 5 minutes. Add the thyme, rosemary, and cumin. Cook for 1 minute.

In a blender, working in batches, puree the potatoes, broccoli, and onions with the milk and stock. Return the soup to the saucepan and heat through.

Serves 4 to 6

CREAMY CORN CHOWDER

Healing Foods

Corn
Milk (low-fat)
Peppers (sweet)

1 sweet red pepper, diced

1/2 cup minced scallions

1 tablespoon olive oil

1 tablespoon whole wheat flour

2 cups corn

1 3/4 cups skim milk

1 teaspoon low-sodium soy sauce

1/8 teaspoon grated nutmeg

In a 2-quart saucepan over medium heat, sauté the peppers and scallions in the oil until crisp-tender, about 3 minutes.

Add the flour and cook 1 to 2 minutes more, stirring constantly. Remove from the heat.

In a blender, puree 1 cup of corn with 1 cup of milk. Add to the saucepan. Add the remaining corn and milk, soy sauce, and nutmeg.

Cook over medium heat, stirring frequently, until hot but not boiling. Reduce the heat and simmer for 5 minutes.

Serves 4

MAKING THINGS PERFECTLY CLEAR

When you need an absolutely clear stock, such as for consommé or aspic, clarify it in the following way.

- Make sure all the fat has been removed from the stock.
- In a small bowl, beat together two egg whites and 1 cup of cold stock.
- Bring the remaining stock to a boil in a clean pot.
- Whisk the egg white mixture into the boiling stock.
- Whisk until the mixture returns to a boil, then lower the heat and simmer *undisturbed* for 5 to 10 minutes.
- Do not stir the egg mass that rises to the top.
- Gently ladle the stock through a cheesecloth-lined sieve into a deep bowl. Do not allow the stock level to reach the strainer.
- After the stock has thoroughly drained, remove the strainer. Do not wring out the cheesecloth or press down on the egg mixture. Your stock should now be free of any cloudiness or sediment.

CHAPTER FIVE

The Super Salad Bowl

If your idea of a green salad is a wedge of iceberg lettuce, it's time to break out of the pale green rut. Just follow the green rule of thumb: The more colorful a salad ingredient, the more nutritious it is. Deep-green romaine lettuce, for example, has *eight times* more vitamin A than iceberg!

Other good choices include silky butterhead lettuce, deep-lobed oak leaf, fringed endive, emerald green spinach, arugula, watercress, hearty Swiss chard, and kale. And don't forget red radicchio! This ruby red jewel can add color and nutrients to salads.

Supermarkets, farmers' markets, and your own garden are excellent sources of healing greens. But don't stop with the lettuce bin—head for the cabbage patch. Cruciferous vegetables like broccoli, cauliflower, and bok choy (Chinese cabbage) help protect against certain kinds of cancer while adding texture to a salad, especially when eaten raw. (In fact, research from the University of Manitoba indicates that cruciferous vegetables may lose some of their anticancer properties when cooked.) That makes your favorite cole slaw a very wise choice.

But there's more to salads than bunny food.

They're a great way to work fish—so high in healthy omega-3's—into your weekly menu. Tired of regular tuna salad? Try Scallop Salad with Pineapple Relish or Avocado and Shrimp Salad (served on romaine lettuce).

Other salads in this section star flavorful, vitamin-packed roots like beets and carrots, pectin-rich apples, oranges, and other fruits, or cancer-fighting foods like raspberries and strawberries. High-fiber grains like rice and bulgur get into the act in recipes like East Indian Rice Salad.

EAST INDIAN RICE SALAD

Healing Foods

Carrots
Lemons and limes
Rice
Swiss chard

1 onion, minced
1 bay leaf
1 teaspoon canola oil
1 large carrot, julienned
2 cups cooked Basmati rice
1 tablespoon grated Parmesan cheese

2 cups shredded Swiss chard
2 tablespoons raisins
3 scallions, julienned
1/4 cup lemon juice
1/4 teaspoon grated nutmeg

197

In a large nonstick frying pan over medium heat, sauté the onions and bay leaf in the oil for 5 minutes.

Add the carrots and continue to cook until the onion is dark and fragrant and the carrots have softened, about 5 minutes.

Stir in the rice, Swiss chard, raisins, scallions, lemon juice, and nutmeg. Heat until the chard has wilted, about 2 minutes.

Remove the pan from the heat. Discard the bay leaf. Stir in the cheese.

Allow to cool to room temperature before serving.

Serves 4

MEXICAN CHICKEN SALAD

Healing Foods

Chicken
Garlic
Peppers (chili)
Salad greens
Seeds

1/2 cup lemon juice
2 jalapeño peppers, seeded and minced
2 tablespoons tomato paste
4 cloves garlic, minced

1 teaspoon ground cumin
1/4 teaspoon ground cinnamon
1 pound boneless, skinless chicken breasts

1 teaspoon dried
  oregano
2 tablespoons toasted
  sesame seeds

3 cups thinly sliced
  dark leafy greens

In a shallow glass dish, combine the lemon juice, peppers, tomato paste, garlic, oregano, cumin, and cinnamon.

Place the chicken between sheets of waxed paper or plastic wrap. Pound to an even thickness (about $1/3$ to $1/2$ inch) with a mallet. Place the chicken in the spice mixture and turn to coat all sides. Refrigerate for about 30 minutes, flipping the pieces midway.

Transfer the chicken to a lightly oiled broiler rack (reserve the marinade). Broil about 5 inches from the heat for 5 minutes per side, or until cooked through.

Place the marinade in a 1-quart saucepan. Bring to a boil and cook for about 30 seconds. Place the greens in a large bowl and pour the marinade over them. Toss to combine. Slice the chicken and serve on the greens. Sprinkle with the sesame seeds.

Serves 4

POTATO AND RASPBERRY SALAD

Healing Foods

Herbs and spices
Oil
Potatoes
Raspberries

1 pound small potatoes
1 1/2 cups raspberries
1/2 cup snipped chives
2 tablespoons canola
  oil
1/8 teaspoon grated
  nutmeg

1 tablespoon
  raspberry vinegar
1 tablespoon orange
  juice
1/4 teaspoon Dijon
  mustard

Steam the potatoes for 8 to 10 minutes, or until easily pierced with a fork. Set aside to cool, then cut into bite-size pieces.

In a large bowl, combine the potatoes, raspberries, and chives.

In a cup, whisk together the oil, vinegar, orange juice, mustard, and nutmeg. Pour over the potatoes and toss gently.

Serves 4

PEAR AND HAZELNUT SALAD

Healing Foods

Nuts
Oil
Pears
Salad greens
Watercress

1/3 cup stock
3 tablespoons
  canola oil
1 teaspoon minced
  shallots
1/2 teaspoon dried
  thyme

2 heads Belgian endive
1 bunch watercress
1 small head radicchio
2 pears, thinly sliced
1/4 cup chopped
  toasted hazelnuts
1 tablespoon crumbled
  blue cheese

In a small bowl, whisk together the stock, oil, shallots, and thyme.

Coarsely tear the endive, watercress, and radicchio. Place in a large salad bowl. Add the pears, hazelnuts, and cheese.

Pour the dressing over the salad. Toss gently. Serve immediately.

Serves 4 to 6

SALMON SALAD WITH ALMONDS AND BOK CHOY

Healing Foods

Cabbage
Fish
Nuts
Yogurt (low-fat)

8 ounces cooked
  salmon
2 cups sliced
  bok choy
1/4 cup sliced
  almonds

2 scallions, minced
1 cup nonfat yogurt
2 tablespoons
  crumbled blue
  cheese

Break the salmon into bite-size chunks. Place in a large bowl. Add the bok choy, almonds, and scallions.

In a small bowl, combine the yogurt and cheese. Combine with the salmon mixture.

Serves 4

MICRO METHOD: Marinated Salads

Creating colorful marinated vegetable salads is a snap using the microwave. You can cook your vegetables in one bowl, add dressing, and refrigerate the salad until dinnertime.

Just remember that foods keep cooking after they are removed from the microwave. So after you've cooked vegetables to just the right point, you may want to rinse them under cold water to stop the cooking process. Pat the veggies dry so dressing will adhere well, and sprinkle on your choice of dressing. Toss well to coat. Chill until serving time. The vegetables will taste "just-picked" fresh, and the colors will remain vibrant.

If you choose vegetables with similar textures, you can cook them together. For a salad that contains many different vegetables, cook the most dense varieties—such as carrots, winter squash, parsnips, or turnips—first. Cut them into uniform pieces and microwave for 2 or 3 minutes. Then add less-dense, quicker-cooking vegetables like cauliflower, celery, broccoli, or fresh asparagus. Cook them another 2 minutes.

Save the quickest cookers—mushrooms, zucchini, tomatoes, or scallions—for the end and zap them briefly, say 1 minute. Exact times will depend upon the sizes, shapes, and quantities of your vegetables. Just be careful not to overcook your selections. It's better for your salad to be crisp-tender than mushy.

To make a colorful presentation, choose contrasting garnishes. Try finely chopped red peppers on green or white vegetables. Or minced parsley and chives with yellow, orange, or white vegetables.

For an unusual marinated salad, shred red beets, rutabagas, or turnips and combine with a small amount of lemon juice. Microwave briefly, turning and tossing after every minute, until just tender. Rinse, as above, toss with vinaigrette, and refrigerate until ready to serve.

APPLES AND CELERIAC WITH HONEY-MUSTARD DRESSING

Healing Foods

Apples
Oil
Spinach

2 tablespoons
apple-cider vinegar
2 teaspoons coarse
mustard
2 teaspoons honey
1 shallot, chopped
1/4 cup diced red
onions
2 cups shredded
spinach

1/2 teaspoon black
pepper
1/4 cup canola oil
1 celeriac root
2 tablespoons
lemon juice
2 green apples,
shredded
1/3 cup nonfat yogurt
1 cup radish slices

Place the vinegar, mustard, honey, shallots, and pepper in a blender container. Process on high speed until well mixed. With the blender running, slowly pour in the oil to form an emulsion.

Trim and wash the celeriac. Cut into a fine julienne and place in a large bowl. Add the lemon juice and combine well to keep the celeriac from discoloring. Mix in the apples, yogurt, onions, and dressing.

Serve on a bed of spinach with the radishes.

Serves 4

ROTINI WITH ROSEMARY VINAIGRETTE

Healing Foods

Onions
Pasta
Spinach

2¹/₂ cups cooked rotini

2 cups shredded spinach

¹/₂ cup minced scallions

1 clove garlic, minced

3 tablespoons lemon juice

2 tablespoons olive oil

1 teaspoon Dijon mustard

1 teaspoon dried rosemary

In a large bowl, combine the rotini, spinach, and scallions.

In a small bowl, whisk together the lemon juice, oil, mustard, garlic, and rosemary.

Pour the dressing over the rotini. Toss well to combine. Serve at room temperature or very slightly chilled.

Serves 4

GARLIC AND EGGPLANT SALAD

Healing Foods

Eggplant
Garlic
Peppers (sweet)
Salad greens

1 eggplant
1 whole garlic bulb
2 onions, thinly
  sliced
2 sweet red peppers,
  sliced
2 tablespoons olive oil

1 tablespoon dried
  thyme
12 slices whole-
  grain bread
2 cups shredded
  collard greens

Peel the eggplant and cut into 1-inch chunks. Blanch in boiling water until just tender, about 4 minutes. Drain and pat dry.

Separate the garlic bulb into cloves and peel each.

In a 9 x 13-inch glass baking dish, combine the eggplant, garlic, onions, peppers, oil, and thyme. Stir to coat the vegetables with the oil.

Bake uncovered at 450°F until the vegetables are brown, about 25 minutes (stir a few times during cooking). Remove from the oven.

Place the bread on a baking sheet and bake until crisp, about 4 minutes per side. Cut each slice into quarters.

Serve the vegetables warm or at room temperature on a bed of collards. Eat with the bread croutons.

Serves 4

BULGUR AND SWEET-PEPPER SALAD

Healing Foods

Bulgur
Garlic
Peppers (sweet)
Tomatoes

$1/2$ cup stock
$1/2$ cup bulgur
3 cloves garlic,
　minced
4 plum tomatoes,
　chopped
1 teaspoon
　snipped chives

2 sweet red peppers,
　julienned
$1/4$ cup apple-cider
　vinegar
1 tablespoon olive oil
$1/2$ teaspoon dried
　thyme

In a 1-quart saucepan, bring the stock to a boil. Add the bulgur and garlic. Cover, remove from the heat, and let stand for 20 minutes, or until the liquid has been absorbed. Fluff with a fork and place in a large bowl.

Add the tomatoes and peppers. Toss to combine.

In a cup, whisk together the vinegar, oil, thyme, and chives. Pour over the bulgur. Toss to combine.

Serves 4

LEAN BEEF
WITH GREENS AND FETA

Healing Foods

Beans (snap)
Beef (lean)
Oil
Salad greens

8 ounces lean
top round
1 tablespoon coarse
mustard
4 cups torn chicory
2 cups sliced
green beans
1 tablespoon beef
stock

1 sweet red pepper,
julienned
2 scallions, minced
3 tablespoons
red-wine vinegar
2 tablespoons olive oil
1 teaspoon dried
oregano
1 tablespoon
crumbled feta cheese

Rub the beef on both sides with the mustard. Broil or grill about 5 inches from the heat until cooked the way you like it, about 7 minutes on each side for medium rare. Let stand for 5 minutes, then slice thinly across the grain.

In a large bowl, combine the chicory, beans, peppers, and scallions.

In a small bowl whisk together the vinegar, oil, stock, and oregano. Pour over the greens and toss to combine.

Arrange the greens on individual serving plates. Top with the beef. Sprinkle with the cheese.

Serves 4

ORANGES WITH RADISHES AND DATES

Healing Foods

Oranges
Salad greens
Tropical fruits

4 large navel oranges
2 tablespoons
lemon juice
1 tablespoon honey
2 tablespoons
chopped walnuts
$1/2$ teaspoon ground
cinnamon
2 heads Boston lettuce
10 red radishes,
thinly sliced
$1/2$ cup pitted dates

With a small sharp knife, remove the peel and white pith from the oranges. Slice the oranges crosswise into $1/4$-inch rounds. Place on a large platter.

In a cup, whisk together the lemon juice, honey, and cinnamon. Pour over the oranges. Cover and chill for 30 minutes.

Tear the lettuce into small pieces and place in a large bowl. Add the radishes and walnuts. Drain the dressing from the oranges and pour over the lettuce. Toss well. Add the oranges and dates. Toss to combine.

Serves 6

Accent on Health: A Splash of Vinegar

Vinegar is one of the oldest known ingredients used in cooking. The name comes from the French words for sour wine: *vin aigre*. But vinegar is much more than fermented wine. It's a low-calorie, no-fat, sodium-free boon to salads, cooked vegetables, and even fruits.

While many varieties are made from wine—champagne, sherry, white wine, red wine, rice wine, or fruit wine—others come from ale (malt vinegar), apples (apple-cider vinegar), grains (distilled vinegar), or unfermented grapes (balsamic vinegar).

Wine vinegars vary in quality and taste. Rice-wine vinegar, for instance, is less acidic than many other types, so you can use more of it in a vinaigrette with a given amount of oil. That reduces both the grams of fat and the calories per serving.

The finest vinegars start with good wine. It's fermented in a way that changes the alcohol to acetic acid. In the old Orleans process, barrels of three parts wine and two parts vinegar are inoculated with a starter culture and simply left open to the air. The vinegar added to the wine prevents the growth of unwanted organisms and encourages the growth of the vinegar bacteria. In this process, the bacteria slowly turn the alcohol to acid without destroying the fine flavors of the wine.

In the town of Modena in Northern Italy, a wine vinegar known as balsamic vinegar is produced. Made from special grapes that are cooked over a fire and aged in wooden casks, the vinegar is matured for years. This results in a richly colored, aromatic vinegar. Because this process is so time-consuming, balsamic and other naturally made vinegars can be expensive. But just a small amount makes a delicious difference in salads.

You can make your own flavored vinegars for home use or to give as healthful gifts. Start with plain apple-cider vinegar, white-wine vinegar or a mixture of both. For gift giving, seek out beautiful, unusual bottles. Or simply reuse the bottle the plain vinegar came in. Remove the original label and tie a ribbon around the cap.

- *Herb vinegar.* Rinse and pat dry whole herb sprigs—try tarragon, thyme, rosemary, savory, basil, oregano, marjoram, or dill. Place a few sprigs in a sterile pint jar. Heat 2 cups of plain vinegar to a simmer in a small stainless steel or ceramic saucepan. Use a funnel to pour the hot vinegar into the bottle, allow to cool, and then cap tightly. Let stand for a week before using. Store at room temperature.
- *Garlic vinegar.* Skewer a peeled garlic clove and place in a sterile pint jar, alone or with herbs. Add 2 cups hot vinegar as in herb vinegar recipe, but remove the garlic after one or two days to prevent the development of botulism.
- *Berry vinegar.* Heat 2 cups of plain vinegar to a simmer as in herb vinegar recipe. Add $1/2$ cup rinsed and dried berries, 1 tablespoon honey, and a twist of orange or lemon rind. Cool to room temperature, cover the pan, and allow to steep in a cool place for two to three days.

When ready to bottle, reheat the vinegar to the simmering point, then strain into a pint jar.

CORN SALAD WITH LEMON-DILL DRESSING

Healing Foods

Beans (dried)
Corn
Salad greens

3 cups corn
1 cup cooked
  lima beans
1/2 cup diced
  tomatoes
1/4 cup diced
  celery
1/4 cup diced
  sweet red peppers
2 tablespoons minced
  scallions

3 tablespoons
  lemon juice
1 teaspoon Dijon
  mustard
1/2 teaspoon dillweed
1/4 teaspoon hot-
  pepper sauce
1 head romaine
  lettuce

In a large bowl, combine the corn, limas, tomatoes, celery, peppers, and scallions.

In a small bowl, whisk together the lemon juice, mustard, dill, and hot-pepper sauce. Pour over the corn mixture and toss. Chill thoroughly.

Tear the lettuce into bite-size pieces. Place on a serving platter. Top with the salad.

Serves 4

CARROT SALAD

Healing Foods

Carrots
Garlic
Oil
Watercress

1 pound carrots,
  thinly sliced
4 cloves garlic, minced
3 tablespoons lemon
  juice
2 tablespoons olive
  oil

$1/2$ teaspoon ground
  cumin
$1/4$ teaspoon ground
  allspice
$1/4$ teaspoon red pepper
$1^1/2$ cups watercress
  leaves

In a 2-quart saucepan, cook the carrots and garlic in water to cover until the carrots are crisp-tender, about 10 minutes. Drain and transfer to a large bowl.

In a cup, whisk together the lemon juice, oil, cumin, allspice, and pepper. Pour over the warm carrots. Allow to cool. Toss with the watercress.

Serves 4

SPROUTS AND CHEESE

Healing Foods

Apples
Beans (dried)
Carrots
Cucumbers
Peppers (sweet)
Sprouts

2 apples, cubed
1 1/2 cups sliced
   carrots
1 cup chopped
   green peppers
1 cup sliced
   cucumbers
1 cup cooked
   chick-peas
1 tablespoon light
   mayonnaise

1 cup alfalfa sprouts
2/3 cup cubed low-
   fat Cheddar cheese
1/4 cup raisins
3 tablespoons apple-
   cider vinegar
2 tablespoons
   canola oil
1/4 teaspoon dried
   thyme
1/4 teaspoon
   dried oregano

In a large bowl, combine the apples, carrots, peppers, cucumbers, chick-peas, sprouts, cheese, and raisins.

In a cup, whisk together the vinegar, oil, mayonnaise, thyme, and oregano. Pour over the salad and toss to combine.

Serves 4

SPICY SHRIMP SALAD WITH COOL MANGO DRESSING

Healing Foods

Crustaceans
Kale
Mangoes
Pineapple

1 mango
2 tablespoons lemon juice
1 pound large shrimp, peeled and deveined
1 tablespoon chicken stock
1 cup chopped tomatoes
1 teaspoon chili powder
$^1/_4$ teaspoon hot-pepper sauce
$1^1/_2$ cups chopped pineapple
1 red onion, thinly sliced
2 cups torn kale leaves

Peel the mango and cut the flesh away from the pit. In a blender or food processor, puree the mango and lemon juice.

In a large nonstick frying pan over medium-high heat, combine the shrimp, stock, chili powder, and hot-pepper sauce. Stir until the shrimp are well coated with the seasonings and cooked through, about 3 minutes.

Remove from the heat. Add the pineapple, tomatoes, and onions.

Line a large platter with the kale. Spoon the salad onto the greens. Drizzle with the mango puree.

Serves 4

SMOKED TURKEY AND GRAPES

Healing Food

Grapes
Salad greens
Turkey

2 tablespoons
white-wine vinegar
1 teaspoon Dijon
mustard
2 tablespoons
olive oil
1 tablespoon minced
fresh parsley
1 pound smoked
turkey breast,
sliced

1 tablespoon
snipped chives
$1/4$ teaspoon
dried chervil
$1/4$ teaspoon
dried tarragon
1 small head
curly endive
3 cups seedless
green grapes

In a small bowl, whisk together the vinegar and mustard. Slowly whisk in the oil and continue until thoroughly emulsified. Stir in the parsley, chives, chervil, and tarragon.

Arrange the endive on a large platter. Top with the turkey and grapes. Drizzle with the dressing.

Serves 4 to 6

CURRIED POTATO SALAD

Healing Foods

Nuts
Potatoes
Raisins

1 pound potatoes	3 tablespoons
1/4 cup raisins	sliced almonds
2 scallions, minced	1/2 cup nonfat yogurt
2 tablespoons chutney	1 teaspoon curry
	powder

Cut the potatoes into 1-inch chunks. Steam until tender, about 12 minutes. Transfer to a large bowl. Stir in the raisins, scallions, and almonds.

In a small bowl, whisk together the yogurt, chutney, and curry powder. Pour over the potatoes and combine well. Serve warm.

Serves 4

OIL'S WELL WITH OLIVE OIL

Olive oil has been highly esteemed throughout history. The Etruscans, and the Romans who succeeded them, revered it as sacred. They valued the golden oil as a healing balm and used it to massage and soothe the muscles of athletes before and after their vigorous games. In more modern times, olive oil is again regarded as a natural restorer. This monounsaturated oil shows evidence of controlling cholesterol, a major factor in heart disease.

Careful handling at home will safeguard olive oil's best qualities. Because the oil can easily pick up foreign odors and flavors, either buy it in small quantities or decant large amounts into smaller containers. Keep the bottles tightly capped or corked. Heat can cause the oil to turn rancid, so store it in a cool place. You can store large quantities in the refrigerator. Although chilling solidifies the oil, it has no effect on flavor and quality. Simply let the oil warm to room temperature for ease of pouring.

There are four major classifications of olive oil, plus another that's new.

- *Extra-virgin* is extracted from the highest-quality, undamaged olives. This first pressing yields a green, slightly cloudy oil with a strong fruity taste. The opacity of the extra-virgin oil indicates its high quality and low acid content.

  This type, which may be referred to as "fruity," is best used where its intense flavor can be appreciated without masking other flavors, such as in green salads.
- *Virgin oil* is obtained from the second pressing of the olive paste. The olives used might not have been as ripe or unblemished. Virgin oil ranges in color from medium green to dark yellow and in flavor from lightly fruity to sweet and nutty. More economical than extra-virgin oil, virgin olive oil is also excellent for use in salad dressings and marinades.
- *Pure* is a mixture of lower-quality virgin oil and additional oil extracted from the olive paste with an infusion of hot water. Pure olive oil is

further refined, reducing the amount of acid, color and odor present in the final product. Usually a clear gold color with only the faint oily taste of olives, it is most often used in cooking, where it adds its own subtle flavor and aroma and enhances other foods.

- *Fine* olive oil is the last to be extracted from the olive pulp. Water and other solvents may be used to obtain this final, lower-quality extraction, which is generally not recommended for home use.
- *Light* olive oil, the newest variety, is named not for its caloric content but for its flavor. Light is pure olive oil made with very little virgin oil. It's aimed at consumers who want to use olive oil at the stove or in salads with only a hint of the olive taste.

PEAR AND POTATO SALAD

Healing Foods

Herbs and spices
Oil
Pears
Potatoes

12 small red potatoes
2 pears, thinly sliced
2 tablespoons minced scallions
2 tablespoons raisins

$1/3$ cup chicken stock
3 tablespoons canola oil
1 tablespoon vinegar
2 teaspoons orange juice concentrate

2 tablespoons chopped toasted peanuts
1 tablespoon chopped red onions
1/8 teaspoon ground allspice
1/8 teaspoon ground cinnamon
1/8 teaspoon peeled minced gingerroot
1/8 teaspoon ground red pepper

Steam the potatoes 8 to 10 minutes, or until easily pierced with a fork. Cut into halves or quarters and place in a large bowl. Add the pears, scallions, raisins, peanuts, and onions.

In a small bowl, whisk together the stock, oil, vinegar, orange juice concentrate, cinnamon, ginger, allspice, and red pepper. Pour over the salad and toss gently to combine.

Serves 4

AVOCADO AND SHRIMP SALAD

Healing Foods

Avocados
Crustaceans
Salad greens

3 avocados, peeled and cubed
1 cup cooked shrimp
2 scallions, minced
1 tablespoon olive oil
1 head romaine lettuce
2 tablespoons minced fresh coriander
2 tablespoons lemon juice
1 clove garlic, minced

In a large bowl, combine the avocados, shrimp, scallions, and coriander.

In a small bowl, whisk together the lemon juice, oil, and garlic. Pour over the avocado mixture and toss well.

Separate the head of lettuce into individual petals. Arrange on a serving plate. Spoon on the avocado mixture. Serve at room temperature.

Serves 4

SCALLOP SALAD WITH PINEAPPLE RELISH

Healing Foods

Avocados
Lemons and limes
Mollusks
Peppers (chili)
Peppers (sweet)
Pineapple

1 pineapple, peeled, cored, and coarsely chopped
1 red onion, diced
1 small chili pepper, minced
1 sweet red pepper, julienned
1 clove garlic, minced

$1/2$ cup minced fresh coriander
2 tablespoons minced fresh parsley
1 tablespoon vinegar
$1^1/4$ pounds bay scallops
$1/2$ cup lime juice
1 avocado

In a large bowl, combine the pineapple, onions, chili peppers, coriander, parsley, and vinegar. Chill for several hours.

In a 2-quart saucepan, poach the scallops in boiling water for 45 seconds, or until opaque. Drain and rinse with cool water.

In a medium bowl, combine the scallops, red peppers, lime juice, and garlic. Toss well. Cover and refrigerate for 1 to 2 hours.

Peel and dice the avocado. Add to the scallops just before serving. Serve with the pineapple relish.

Serves 4

DON'T SABOTAGE YOUR SALAD

Salads are "good, healthy diet food" only when you make the right mix-and-match selections. The wrong choices can garner you as much fat and calories as a steak dinner. When you decide to toss together a full-meal salad, double-check this list. It can help you chart a safe course through potentially troubled waters.

Choose freely from the "full speed ahead" foods. They're low in fat and calories and high in healing potential.

Practice moderation with the "go easy" foods. Although these items are not inherently bad, they may pose drawbacks for some people. Avocados, nuts, and certain oils, for instance, are great sources of beneficial monounsaturated oils, but they may have more calories than you bargained for. Other items, such as pickles, are low in calories but may be high in sodium. Low-fat cheeses can run the gamut from a respectable 2 grams of fat per ounce up to 8 or 9 grams—almost as much as regular cheese. Pick and choose carefully according to your dietary concerns.

As for the "steer clear" items, they have a lot going against them—including empty calories and large deposits of saturated fat, cholesterol, or sodium. You're best off giving them wide berth.

Full Speed Ahead

- Baked potatoes
- Cabbage, kale, and other cruciferous greens
- Cooked beans
- Cooked shrimp, fish, and other seafood
- Fresh fruit
- Hard-cooked egg whites
- Herbs and spices
- Lettuce, spinach, and other leafy greens
- Low-cal dressings
- Low-fat cottage cheese
- Plain pasta
- Poached chicken and turkey
- Raw vegetables
- Rice
- Roasted red peppers
- Sprouts
- Steamed vegetables
- Tofu
- Vinegar lemon juice
- Water chestnuts
- Water-packed tuna

- Yogurt
- Yogurt cheese

Go Easy

- Avocados
- Lean roast beef
- Low-fat cheese
- Margarine
- Marinated vegetables
- Nuts
- Oil
- Oil-packed tuna
- Olives
- Pickles
- Regular cottage cheese
- Sunflower and other seeds

Steer Clear

- Bacon
- Butter
- Chow mein noodles
- Cream cheese
- Croutons
- Fried onion rings
- Fried potato skins
- Full-fat cheese
- Full-fat dressings
- Hard-cooked egg yolks
- Mayonnaise-based salads
- Salami, pepperoni, and other lunch meats
- Sour cream
- Syrup-packed fruit

DANDELION GREENS WITH BEANS

Healing Foods

Beans (dried)
Beans (snap)
Oil
Salad greens

4 cups torn
  dandelion leaves
1 cup steamed
  green beans
1 cup cooked
  white beans
2 tablespoons
  minced red onions

1 tablespoon
  chopped walnuts
1 tablespoon
  crumbled feta cheese
2 tablespoons olive oil
1 tablespoon
  white vinegar
$1/4$ teaspoon dry
  mustard

In a large bowl, mix the dandelion leaves, green beans, white beans, onions, walnuts, and cheese.

In a small bowl, whisk together the oil, vinegar, and mustard. Pour over the salad and toss well to coat. Serve at room temperature or slightly chilled.

Serves 4

MONKFISH SALAD
WITH TOMATO CHUTNEY

Healing Foods

Cabbage
Cucumbers
Fish
Oil
Tomatoes

TOMATO CHUTNEY

3 cups chopped
  tomatoes
1 medium onion,
  chopped
1 green pepper,
  chopped
$1/2$ cup apple-
  cider vinegar
2 tablespoons honey
1 teaspoon
  ground ginger
1 clove garlic, minced
1 teaspoon mustard
  seeds
$1/4$ teaspoon red
  pepper

YOGURT SAUCE

3 tablespoons
  apple-cider vinegar
1 teaspoon Dijon
  mustard
$3/4$ cup nonfat yogurt
3 tablespoons
  snipped chives

SALAD

1 pound monkfish
  fillets
2 tablespoons lemon
  lemon juice
1 bay leaf
$1/4$ cup olive oil
2 tablespoons apple-
  cider vinegar
$1 1/2$ cups shredded
  cabbage
1 cucumber, thinly
  sliced

To make the tomato chutney: In a 2-quart sauce-pan, combine the tomatoes, onions, peppers, vinegar, honey, ginger, garlic, mustard seeds, and red pepper. Bring to a boil, then lower the heat and simmer uncovered for 1 hour, stirring frequently. Allow to cool.

To make the yogurt sauce: In a small bowl, whisk together the vinegar and mustard. Stir in the yogurt and chives. Chill until ready to use.

To make the salad: Rinse the fish in cold water. If necessary, remove any membranes. Place the fish in a large frying pan. Add the lemon juice, bay leaf, and cold water to cover.

Bring to a boil, reduce the heat to medium, cover the pan, and simmer the fish until it flakes when tested with a fork, about 8 to 10 minutes. Discard the bay leaf.

Cool slightly, then remove the fish with a slotted spoon. Separate it into large chunks, place in a large bowl and chill for 1 hour.

In a cup, whisk together the oil and vinegar. Drizzle half over the monkfish. Toss to combine.

In a large bowl, combine the cabbage and cucumbers. Toss with the remaining dressing. Divide the mixture among serving plates. Top with the fish. Serve with the tomato chutney and the yogurt sauce.

Serves 4

WILD-RICE SALAD

Healing Foods

Peppers (sweet)
Rice
Salad greens

4 cups water
1 cup wild rice, rinsed
2 tablespoons pine
  nuts
1 green pepper,
  julienned
1 sweet yellow
  pepper, julienned
2 scallions, minced
$^1/_4$ teaspoon dry
  mustard

1 clove garlic, minced
1 teaspoon dried basil
$^1/_2$ teaspoon
  dried thyme
2 tablespoons
  red-wine vinegar
1 tablespoon
  lemon iuice
1 tablespoon olive oil
1 head Boston lettuce
2 tablespoons
  crumbled feta cheese

In a 2-quart saucepan, bring the water to a boil.
Add the rice and boil uncovered for 35 minutes,
or until the rice is tender but still a bit chewy.
Drain well and set aside.

Heat a nonstick frying pan over medium heat.
Add the pine nuts and shake the pan over heat
for 2 or 3 minutes to toast the nuts. Transfer to
a large bowl. Add the rice, green peppers, yellow
peppers, scallions, garlic, basil, and thyme.

In a cup, whisk together the vinegar, lemon
juice, oil, and mustard. Pour over the rice mixture
and toss well to combine.

Serve on a bed of lettuce. Sprinkle with the cheese.

Serves 4

SPICY BEET SALAD

Healing Foods

Beets
Carrots
Oil

2 pounds beets
2 tablespoons
  tarragon vinegar
2 tablespoons
  olive oil
2 teaspoons low-
  sodium soy sauce
2 tablespoons minced
  fresh parsley

$1/4$ teaspoon dry
  mustard
$1/4$ teaspoon
  ground ginger
1 cup shredded
  carrots
2 tablespoons
  sliced scallions

In a 3-quart saucepan, cook the beets in water to cover until tender, about 45 minutes. Drain and rinse under cold water. Slice off the tops and squeeze the beets to remove the skins. Cut the beets into $1/2$-inch slices and place in a large bowl.

In a small bowl, whisk together the vinegar, oil, soy sauce, mustard, and ginger. Pour over the beets and toss to combine.

Arrange the beets on a platter. Sprinkle with the carrots, scallions, and parsley.

Serves 4

BERRIES AND GREENS

Healing Foods

Onions
Salad greens
Strawberries
Watercress

1^1/$_2$ cups watercress
leaves
1^1/$_2$ cups torn
arugula
1^1/$_2$ cups sliced
strawberries
^{1}/$_2$ cup fiddlehead
ferns

2 tablespoons apple-
cider vinegar
1 tablespoon olive oil
^{1}/$_4$ teaspoon grated
orange rind
1 red onion,
thinly sliced

In a large bowl, combine the watercress, arugula, strawberries, onions, and ferns. Sprinkle with the vinegar, oil, and orange rind. Toss to combine.

Serves 4

Accent on Health: Dress for Success

Salad dressing can make or break a salad, especially one composed largely of health-rendering greens and vegetables. The right dressing enhances the flavor of the basic ingredients without overwhelming them or undermining their health qualities. The wrong dressing can smother a nutritious food under a blanket of fat and calories.

Here are some ways to dress a salad that make good sense.

Remember that no matter what type of dressing you choose, you should use only enough to lightly coat the salad. One way to do that is to mix your salad in an oversized bowl, large enough to toss the ingredients freely and to thoroughly distribute a modest amount of dressing. To add more flavor to your salad, rub the inside of the bowl with a cut clove of garlic before adding the salad.

Watercress Dressing

$1/2$ cup nonfat yogurt
$1/2$ cup packed
   watercress leaves
2 tablespoons olive oil
2 tablespoons vinegar

2 scallions, thinly
   sliced
1 clove garlic, minced
$1/2$ teaspoon dried
   tarragon

In a blender, combine the yogurt, watercress, oil, vinegar, scallions, garlic, and tarragon. Process until smooth.

Makes 1 cup

Healing Foods

- Watercress
- Yogurt (low-fat)

Creamy Raspberry Dressing

1 cup nonfat yogurt
1 cup raspberries
1/4 teaspoon dried grated orange rind

1/4 teaspoon grated lime rind
1/4 teaspoon dried basil

Line a strainer with cheesecloth. Add the yogurt and allow to drain over a bowl for 30 minutes. Transfer to a medium bowl.

Puree the raspberries in a food processor. Fold into the yogurt. Add the orange rind, lime rind, and basil. Combine well.

Makes 1 cup

Healing Foods

• Raspberries   • Yogurt (low-fat)

Green-Herb Dressing

1 cup low-fat cottage cheese
1 cup nonfat yogurt
3 tablespoons grated Sapsago or Parmesan cheese
2 tablespoons lemon juice

1 tablespoon honey
2 teaspoons Dijon mustard
2 teaspoons minced shallots
1 teaspoon dried basil
1/4 teaspoon black pepper

In a blender or food processor process the cottage cheese until very smooth. Transfer to a medium bowl.

Whisk in the yogurt, Sapsago or Parmesan,

lemon juice, honey, mustard, shallots, basil, and pepper.

Makes about 2^1/$_2$ cups

Healing Foods

   Cottage cheese (low-fat) • Yogurt (low-fat)

Tangy Horseradish Dressing

1 cup low-fat cottage cheese	2 tablespoons prepared horseradish
1 cup nonfat yogurt	3 tablespoons snipped chives

In a blender or food processor, process the cottage cheese until very smooth. Transfer to a medium bowl.

Whisk in the yogurt, chives, and horseradish.

Makes about 1^1/$_3$ cups

Healing Foods

   • Cottage cheese (low-fat) • Yogurt (low-fat)

Honey-Lime Dressing

^{1}/$_4$ cup lime juice	^{1}/$_4$ teaspoon grated lime rind
^{1}/$_4$ cup egg substitute	^{1}/$_8$ teaspoon paprika
1 tablespoon honey	^{1}/$_8$ teaspoon ground coriander
1 tablespoon white-wine vinegar	
^{1}/$_2$ teaspoon dry mustard	^{1}/$_4$ cup water
	^{1}/$_4$ cup canola oil

In a blender combine the lime juice, egg substitute, honey, vinegar, mustard, lime rind, paprika, and coriander. Process on low speed until well mixed.

With the blender running, add the water. Then add the oil in a slow, steady stream.

Makes 1 cup

Healing Foods

- Lemons and limes
- Oil

TROPICAL CHICKEN SALAD

Healing Foods

Chicken
Mangoes
Oil
Swiss chard
Tomatoes
Yogurt (low-fat)

3 cups chicken stock
1 pound boneless, skinless chicken breasts
4 tomatoes, chopped
2 mangoes, chopped
2 tablespoons peeled minced gingerroot

1/4 cup olive oil
3 tablespoons lemon juice
1 cup nonfat yogurt
2 tablespoons light mayonnaise
3 cups shredded Swiss chard

In a large frying pan over medium heat, bring the stock to a boil. Add the chicken. Cover and cook until tender, about 15 minutes. Remove from the pan and let cool 5 minutes. Shred or cut the meat into bite-size pieces.

In a large bowl, combine the chicken, tomatoes, and mangoes.

In a small bowl, whisk together the oil and lemon juice. Pour over the chicken and toss to combine.

In a small bowl, combine the yogurt, mayonnaise, and ginger.

Divide the Swiss chard among salad plates. Top with the chicken. Serve the yogurt dressing on the side.

Serves 4

EQUINOX SALAD

Healing Foods

Oil
Peas
Spinach

2 cups spinach leaves
1 cup cooked peas
1 cup coarsely
   shredded daikon
   radishes
3 tablespoons
   olive oil
1 teaspoon Dijon
   mustard

12 red radishes,
   thinly sliced
8 scallions, julienned
$1/4$ cup enoki
   mushrooms
2 tablespoons vinegar
$1/8$ teaspoon grated
   nutmeg

In a large bowl, combine the spinach, peas, daikon radishes, red radishes, scallions, and mushrooms.

In a small bowl, whisk together the oil, vinegar, mustard, and nutmeg. Pour over the vegetables and toss to combine.

Serves 4

SEA KABOB SALAD WITH CURRY VINAIGRETTE

Healing Foods

Crustaceans
Fish
Garlic
Peppers (sweet)

SALAD
1/4 cup vinegar
2 cloves garlic, minced
3 bay leaves
6 ounces jumbo shrimp, peeled and deveined
6 ounces large sea scallops
6 ounces shark, cut into 1-inch chunks
3 yellow peppers, julienned

VINAIGRETTE
2 tablespoons vinegar
1 teaspoon Dijon mustard
1 teaspoon coarse mustard
1 teaspoon curry powder
2 cloves garlic, minced
1 teaspoon rinsed capers
1/4 teaspoon black pepper

To make the salad: In a 9 x 13-inch baking dish, combine the vinegar, garlic, and bay leaves. Add the shrimp, scallops, and shark. Toss to coat. Cover and allow to marinate for 1 hour.

Thread the seafood onto skewers. Broil about 4 inches from the heat for 3 to 4 minutes per side. Allow to cool for a few minutes, then transfer to a large bowl. Add the peppers.

To make the vinaigrette: In a small bowl, whisk together the vinegar, Dijon mustard, coarse mustard, curry powder, garlic, capers, and pepper. Pour over the seafood mixture. Toss to coat. Serve immediately.

Serves 4

SQUASH SALAD WITH BUTTERMILK DRESSING

Healing Foods

Broccoli
Cabbage
Squash (summer)
Tomatoes

8 ounces yellow summer squash, julienned

2 tomatoes, cut into wedges

$1/2$ teaspoon dried basil

2 cups shredded red cabbage

$1/3$ cup broccoli stems, julienned

$1/4$ cup buttermilk

1 teaspoon Dijon mustard

$1/8$ teaspoon curry powder

237

Steam the squash until tender, about 12 minutes.

Transfer to a large bowl. Add the tomatoes and broccoli.

In a small bowl, whisk together the buttermilk, mustard, basil, and curry powder. Pour over the squash mixture and toss well to combine.

Place the cabbage on a serving platter. Spoon on the squash mixture. Serve warm.

Serves 4

ASPARAGUS AND SHELLFISH SALAD

Healing Foods

Asparagus
Kale
Mollusks
Peppers (sweet)

1 pound asparagus
  spears
1/4 cup minced
  shallots
1 tablespoon olive oil
1/2 cup stock
1 tablespoon vinegar
2 tablespoons minced
  parsley

12 clams in their
  shells, scrubbed
12 mussels in their
  shells, scrubbed
  and debearded
2 tablespoons minced
  sweet red peppers
2 cups torn kale
1 sweet yellow pepper,
  thinly sliced

In a large pot of boiling water, blanch the asparagus for 2 minutes. Drain and set aside.

In a 4-quart pot, sauté the shallots in the oil for 4 minutes. Add the stock and vinegar; heat to boiling. Add the clams; cover and cook for 1 minute. Add the mussels; cover and cook for 3 to 5 minutes, or until all the shells open.

Remove and discard the shells; also discard any unopened shells. Place the clams and mussels in a large bowl. Sprinkle with the red peppers and parsley.

Pour the cooking liquid over the shellfish, being careful not to transfer any sediment or sand at the very bottom of the pot.

Divide the asparagus, kale, and yellow peppers among individual dinner plates. Spoon on the shellfish mixture. Serve warm or at room temperature.

Serves 4

GREENS AND TANGERINES

Healing Foods

Apples
Grapes
Salad greens
Tangerines

2 cups torn red
  lettuce
2 tablespoons olive oil

2 cups tangerine
  sections
1 cup red grapes,
  halved

1 tart apple, diced
2 tablespoons
  lemon juice

1 teaspoon minced
  fresh tarragon
$1/4$ teaspoon dried
  mint

Place the lettuce in a large serving bowl. Toss with the oil until coated.

Add the tangerines, grapes, and apples. Sprinkle with the lemon juice, tarragon, and mint. Toss to combine.

Serves 4

THE MANY VERSIONS OF VINAIGRETTE

Vinaigrette is *the* traditional French salad dressing. A simple combination of olive oil, wine vinegar, mustard, and a dash of freshly ground pepper, it may be seasoned to suit your taste.

Because this dressing is so easy to prepare and to vary, it will expand your creative options while enhancing your health. The monounsaturated olive oil that forms its base can help to lower cholesterol levels. (If pure olive oil is too strong for your taste, replace part of it with canola oil, another heart-healthy monounsaturate.) The pungent vinegar adds zip to distract your taste buds from a craving for salt.

Always dress and toss a green-lettuce salad at the last minute. Rinse and thoroughly dry the greens so the dressing can cling to the leaves.

With salads that improve from marinating—such as bean, cooked-vegetable, or grated-vegetable salads—add the dressing ahead of time, toss, and chill until needed. Store vinaigrette in a tightly sealed glass container in the refrigerator.

Here's a basic vinaigrette and a bowlful of variations.

- *Basic vinaigrette.* Combine $1/2$ cup olive oil, 3 to 4 tablespoons red- or white-wine vinegar, $1/2$ teaspoon Dijon mustard, and a dash of freshly ground pepper. Stir well before spooning a small amount over salad.
- *Garlic vinaigrette.* Add 1 garlic clove (minced) to the basic recipe.
- *Balsamic vinaigrette.* Substitute balsamic vinegar for the wine vinegar in the basic recipe.
- *Cider vinaigrette.* Substitute 2 tablespoons apple-cider vinegar for the wine vinegar in the basic recipe (apple-cider vinegar is stronger in flavor so you need less).
- *Tomato vinaigrette.* Add 2 to 3 tablespoons tomato juice to the basic recipe.
- *Shallot vinaigrette.* Add 1 tablespoon finely minced shallots to the basic recipe.
- *Three-mustard vinaigrette.* Reduce the Dijon mustard in the basic recipe to $1/4$ teaspoon. Add $1/4$ teaspoon tarragon or green-pepper mustard and $1/2$ teaspoon coarse mustard.
- *Parsley vinaigrette.* Add 1 tablespoon minced fresh parsley to the basic recipe. Add garlic, if desired.
- *Lemon vinaigrette.* Substitute lemon juice for all or part of the vinegar and add a dash of freshly grated lemon rind to the basic recipe.

- *Lean vinaigrette.* Reduce the oil to $1/3$ cup and use $1/4$ cup rice-wine vinegar. Season as desired.
- *Creamy vinaigrette.* Add $1/2$ cup nonfat yogurt to the basic recipe.
- *Calico vinaigrette.* Add 1 tablespoon minced sweet red peppers and 1 tablespoon minced scallion tops to the basic recipe. (Great on vegetable salads.)
- *Hot 'n' spicy vinaigrette.* Add 1 garlic clove (minced), $1/2$ small hot green chili pepper (seeded and minced), $1/4$ teaspoon dried oregano, and a dash of red-pepper flakes to the basic recipe. (Goes well with south-of-the-border bean salads.)

WARM SALMON SALAD

Healing Foods

Fish
Kale
Oil
Peppers (sweet)

2 tablespoons low-sodium soy sauce

2 teaspoons peeled minced gingerroot

1 teaspoon honey

2 cloves garlic, minced

$1/8$ teaspoon red pepper

8 ounces salmon fillet

2 tablespoons olive oil

2 tablespoons balsamic vinegar

2 tablespoons minced shallots

1 tablespoon lemon iuice

1 pound kale, torn   2 green peppers,
   into bite-size pieces   julienned
1/3 cup stock

In a 9 x 13-inch baking dish, whisk together
the soy sauce, ginger, honey, garlic, and red
pepper.

Cutting on the bias, slice the salmon into
10 to 12 thin pieces. Add to the soy mixture,
turning to coat each piece on both sides. Let
stand 15 minutes.

In a small bowl, whisk together the oil, vinegar,
shallots, and lemon juice.

Divide the kale among salad plates. Top with
the peppers.

In a large nonstick frying pan over medium-
high heat, heat the stock. Add the salmon and
cook about 10 to 15 seconds per side. Add
to the salad plates. Drizzle with the oil and
vinegar dressing. Serve warm.

Serves 4

CHAPTER SIX

Breads and Breakfasts

Breads, muffins, scones, waffles, pancakes—all these and more can be yours from a healthy bakery. Made with high-fiber, low-fat grains, these goodies are just right for weight watchers, the cholesterol conscious, and those with diabetes or high blood pressure. Many get sweetness from added fruit or a savory tang from vegetaboes and herbs. Both types serve as a gentle reminder that baked goods can greatly enhance a nutritious diet.

If yeast breads are your passion, you'll love the Potato-Cheese Bread, Dilled Carrot Bread, Whole Wheat French Bread, and other selections in this chapter. For something just a bit different, try the Pineapple Focaccia, a variation on a traditional Italian flat bread.

When time is at a premium, opt for muffins or quick breads. One-Hour Oat Bread has lots of cholesterol-lowering oats and oat bran plus raisins for a hint of sweetness. Cranberry Bread is a welcome treat all year round (freeze some cranberries for summer enjoyment). As for muffins, we've got a basketful, including pecan-oat, bran-flake, orange, carrot, and cornmeal-cheese.

Don't forget that batter-based pancakes, crêpes, waffles, and blinis can also be healthy breakfast, brunch, and dessert fare. Egg whites or egg substitute keeps cholesterol low, and canola or olive oil adds beneficial monounsaturates to a heart-smart diet. Serve these special goodies with plenty of fresh fruit or high-fiber "preserves," such as Carrot Spread, Prune Butter, or Savory Pear Spread. You'll relish their natural sweetness.

RICE-WAFFLE STACK

Healing Foods

Cottage cheese (low-fat)
Milk (low-fat)
Rice
Strawberries
Whole wheat flour

12 ounces frozen unsweetened strawberries
2 teaspoons cornstarch
$1/2$ teaspoon lemon juice
1 tablespoon honey
2 tablespoons canola oil
$1^1/4$ cups low-fat cottage cheese

2 cups whole wheat flour
2 teaspoons baking powder
$1/2$ teaspoon baking soda
$1^2/3$ cups buttermilk
$1/4$ cup egg substitute
1 cup cooked brown rice

Thaw the berries, reserving the liquid.
In a 1-quart saucepan, mix 1 tablespoon of the

liquid with the cornstarch until smooth. Add the remaining liquid, lemon juice, and berries. Bring to a boil, stirring constantly. Cook until thick. Stir in the honey. Set aside.

In a large bowl, stir together the flour, baking powder, and baking soda.

In a medium bowl, beat together the buttermilk, egg substitute, and oil until smooth.

Pour the liquid ingredients into the dry ingredients and mix well. Stir in the rice.

Heat a waffle iron, and lightly brush the grids with oil. Pour in enough batter to just fill. Close and cook until the steaming stops and the waffles are crisp.

Press the cottage cheese through a fine sieve to break up the curds.

Place one large waffle (do not separate the individual waffles) on a serving plate. Spread on a layer of cottage cheese. Top with another waffle. Spread on a layer of the strawberry mixture. Continue stacking, ending with strawberry mixture. Top with a dollop of cottage cheese. Slice into wedges to serve.

Serves 4 to 6

BUCKWHEAT BLINI

Healing Foods

Buckwheat
Cottage cheese (low-fat)
Grapes
Milk (low-fat)
Oil
Peaches

BLINI
1^1/$_2$ cups warm
  water (110°F)
1 tablespoon
  active dry yeast
1^1/$_2$ cups unbleached
  flour
1^1/$_2$ cups skim milk
1^1/$_2$ cups buckwheat
  flour
^{1}/$_2$ cup egg substitute
^{1}/$_4$ cup canola oil
1 tablespoon honey
3 egg whites

TOPPING
2 cups dry-curd
  cottage cheese
2 tablespoons
  maple syrup
^{1}/$_2$ teaspoon
  grated lemon rind
^{1}/$_4$ teaspoon vanilla
  extract
3 cups sliced peaches
1 cup halved
  seedless grapes

To make the blini: In a large bowl, combine the water and yeast. Set aside to proof for 15 minutes (the yeast will become foamy).

Stir in the unbleached flour. Cover and let the batter rise for 1 hour.

Whisk in the milk, buckwheat flour, egg substitute, oil, and honey. Cover and let rise for 1 hour.

In a clean bowl with clean beaters, beat the egg whites until stiff. Fold into the batter.

Coat a nonstick frying pan or griddle with nonstick spray. Heat over medium-high heat. Drop tablespoon-size mounds of batter into the pan. Cook until browned underneath and nearly dry on the top. Turn and cook briefly on the other side.

To make the topping: In a food processor, blend the cottage cheese, maple syrup, lemon rind, and vanilla until smooth. Transfer to a small bowl.

Serve over the blini with the peaches and grapes.

Serves 8

CORN-BRAN BREAD

Healing Foods

Bran
Milk (low-fat)

1 cup corn bran
1 cup unbleached
  flour
2 teaspoons
  baking powder
1 tablespoon
  canola oil

$^1/_2$ teaspoon baking
  soda
1 cup buttermilk
1 egg white
2 tablespoons
  maple syrup

In a large bowl, mix the corn bran, flour, baking powder, and baking soda.

In a medium bowl, combine the buttermilk, egg white, maple syrup, and oil.

Pour the liquid ingredients over the flour mixture. Stir to combine, but don't overmix.

Coat an $8^1/2$ x $4^1/2$-inch loaf pan with non-stick spray. Add the batter to the pan. Level out the top and bake at 425°F for 18 minutes, or until a cake tester inserted in the center comes out clean. Let cool before slicing.

Makes 1 loaf

BRAN-FLAKE MUFFINS

Healing Foods

Apricots
Bran
Milk (low-fat)
Oats
Whole wheat flour

$1^1/2$ cups ready-to-eat oat-bran flakes
1 cup whole wheat flour
$1/2$ cup rolled oats
$1/2$ cup oat bran
$2^1/2$ teaspoons baking powder
3 egg whites
$1/2$ teaspoon grated nutmeg
$1/2$ cup chopped dried apricots
1 tablespoon grated orange rind
1 cup buttermilk
$1/4$ cup honey
1 tablespoon canola oil

In a large bowl, mix the oat flakes, flour, oats, oat

bran, baking powder, and nutmeg. Stir in the apricots and orange rind.

In a medium bowl, blend the buttermilk, egg whites, honey, and oil.

Pour the liquid ingredients over the flour mixture. Stir to combine, but don't overmix.

Line 12 muffin cups with cupcake papers. Divide the batter among them, filling each cup almost to the top. Bake at 375°F for 18 to 20 minutes, or until the muffins are lightly browned.

Makes 12

APPLE SQUARES

Healing Foods

Apples
Rice

4 apples, coarsely shredded

2 cups cold cooked rice

1/2 cup unbleached flour

1/4 cup raisins

2 tablespoons maple syrup

1/4 cup whole wheat flour

1 tablespoon baking powder

1 teaspoon ground cinnamon

1/2 cup egg substitute

1 tablespoon vanilla extract

Spoon the apples into a strainer. Press with a spoon to extract excess liquid. Set the apples aside.

In a large bowl, mix the rice, unbleached flour,

whole wheat flour, baking powder, and cinnamon. Stir in the raisins.

In a medium bowl, combine the egg substitute, maple syrup, and vanilla.

Pour the liquid ingredients over the flour mixture. Add the apples. Mix well.

Coat a 9 x 9-inch baking dish with nonstick spray. Spread the apple mixture evenly in the pan.

Bake at 325°F for 40 to 45 minutes.

Serves 6

Accent on Health: High-Fiber Spreads

Keep your whole-grain breads, muffins, and scones naturally healthy with fiber-rich spreads instead of high-fat butter. Here are three fiber champs.

Carrot Spread

2 cups shredded carrots	2 tablespoons lemon juice
2 cups apple juice	1 tablespoon grated lemon rind
2 tablespoons honey	

In a 2-quart saucepan, combine the carrots, apple juice, honey, lemon juice, and lemon rind. Simmer over medium heat, stirring frequently, until thick, about 30 to 45 minutes.

Store in a tightly closed container in the refrigerator.

Makes about 1¹/₂ cups

Healing Food

• Carrots

Prune Butter

2 cups pitted prunes
1³/₄ cups apple
  juice
8 dried figs,
  stems removed

1 teaspoon vanilla
  extract
1 teaspoon grated
  orange rind

In a 2-quart saucepan, combine the prunes, apple juice, figs, vanilla, and orange rind. Bring to a simmer and cook over low heat, stirring frequently, for 30 minutes.

Let the mixture cool slightly. Transfer to a food processor or blender. Process until smooth (if mixture becomes too thick, thin with additional apple juice).

Store in a tightly closed container in the refrigerator.

Makes about 2 cups

Healing Foods

• Figs • Prunes

Savory Pear Spread

5 ripe pears, chopped
2 tablespoons
  lemon juice
2 tablespoons honey
1 tablespoon peeled
  grated gingerroot

1 tablespoon apple-
  cider vinegar
$1/2$ teaspoon ground
  cinnamon
$1/4$ teaspoon ground
  allspice
$1/4$ teaspoon
  grated nutmeg

In a 2-quart saucepan, combine the pears, lemon juice, honey, ginger, vinegar, cinnamon, allspice, and nutmeg. Cook over low heat for 30 to 40 minutes, or until the pears are very tender.

In a food processor or blender, process the mixture until chunky. If the mixture is not thick, return it to the saucepan and stir over medium heat until desired thickness is reached.

Store in a tightly closed container in the refrigerator.

Makes about 2 cups

Healing Foods

• Herbs and spices   • Pears

FRENCH TOAST
WITH TOMATO SALSA

Healing Foods

Oil
Peppers (sweet)
Tomatoes
Whole wheat flour

2 egg whites
8 slices whole wheat
  or whole-grain bread
2 tablespoons olive oil
1 scallion, minced
1/8 teaspoon hot-
  pepper sauce

1 cup chopped
  tomatoes
1 green pepper,
  chopped
2 teaspoons lemon
  juice

Place the egg whites in a pie plate. Whisk with a fork until foamy. Dip both sides of the bread slices into the whites.

Heat a large nonstick frying pan on medium-high heat. Add 1 tablespoon of the oil and swirl the pan to coat the bottom evenly. Add half of the bread slices and cook for about 2 minutes per side, or until mottled with brown.

Repeat with the remaining oil and bread.

While the bread is browning, combine the tomatoes, peppers, scallions, lemon juice, and hot-pepper sauce in a small saucepan. Heat until warm and fragrant, about 3 minutes.

Place the toast on individual serving plates. Spoon the salsa on top.

Serves 4

PINEAPPLE FOCACCIA

Healing Foods

Pineapple
Seeds
Whole wheat flour

$^{1}/_{2}$ cup warm
  water (110°F)
1 tablespoon active
  dry yeast
2 teaspoons honey
$^{3}/_{4}$ cup dried
  pineapple,
  thinly sliced

1 tablespoon
  canola oil
1 cup unbleached
  flour
$^{1}/_{2}$ cup whole wheat
  flour
2 tablespoons
  sesame seeds

In a large bowl, mix the water, yeast, honey, and 2 teaspoons of the oil. Let stand for about 2 minutes, or until the yeast is dissolved.

Sift together the unbleached flour and whole wheat flour. Add to the yeast mixture. Stir well.

Turn the dough out onto a floured surface and knead until elastic, about 5 or 6 minutes. Let stand 5 minutes.

Coat two 9-inch round cake pans with nonstick spray. Roll the dough into two circles and place in the pans. Divide the pineapple between the pans and press it into the dough. Brush lightly with the remaining oil. Sprinkle with the sesame seeds.

Bake at 500°F for 7 minutes. Cover with foil to prevent the fruit from burning. Bake another 5 to 8 minutes.

Remove from the pans and cut with kitchen shears or a pizza cutter. Serve warm.

Serves 4

WHAT'S WRONG WITH THIS LOAF?

When your breads turn out flawed, use this checklist to determine what went wrong and how to avoid problems the next time around.

Poor Rising
For yeast breads:
- Check the temperature of the liquid. Liquids should be 105° to 115°F.
- Check the expiration date on the yeast package. Yeast should be stored in the refrigerator for best results.
- Increase the rising time.
- Move the dough to a warmer place to rise.
For quick breads:
- Check the temperature of the liquid. Liquids should be at room temperature.
- Blend the ingredients thoroughly, but don't overmix them.

Too Dark or Crusty
- Use less sweetener.
- Reduce the oven temperature.
- Shorten the baking period.

Pale Color
- Use a higher oven temperature.
- Use more sweetener.
- Lengthen the baking period.

Dry

- Reduce the oven temperature.
- Shorten the baking period.
- Use more sweetener.
- For yeast breads, use less yeast.

Hard

- Reduce the oven temperature.
- Shorten the baking period.
- Check the quantity or type of flour.
- Use more liquid.
- For yeast breads, use less yeast.

Tough or Chewy

- Check the quantity of flour.
- Increase the rising time.
- Use less liquid.
- Shorten the baking period if tough.
- Lengthen the baking period if chewy.

Still Damp after Baking

- Check the quantity of flour.
- Lengthen the baking period.
- Remove the bread from the pan and put it back in the oven for a few minutes with the oven turned off.

Filled with Air Bubbles

For yeast breads:
- Allow the dough to rise more slowly by moving it to a cooler spot.
- Shorten the rising time.
- Use less yeast.

Flat Rather than Rounded Loaves
- Check the quantity of flour.
- Place the pans farther apart in the oven while baking.

APPLE BREAKFAST BREAD

Healing Foods

Apples
Bran
Nuts
Whole wheat flour
Yogurt (low-fat)

2 apples
1 cup whole
  wheat flour
1 cup unbleached
  flour
1/2 cup oat bran
1 teaspoon baking
  powder
1 teaspoon baking
  soda
1/4 cup apricot
  all-fruit preserves

1 teaspoon ground
  cinnamon
1/3 cup coarsely
  chopped almonds
3 egg whites
3/4 cup nonfat yogurt
1/3 cup maple syrup
1 tablespoon canola oil
1 teaspoon
  vanilla extract
1 tablespoon
  orange juice

Coat a 9-inch tube pan with nonstick spray.

Cut 1 apple into slices and arrange them around the bottom of the pan. Chop the other apple and set aside.

In a large bowl, mix the whole wheat flour, unbleached flour, oat bran, baking powder, baking soda, and cinnamon. Stir in the chopped apples and almonds.

In a medium bowl, combine the egg whites, yogurt, maple syrup, oil, and vanilla.

Pour the liquid ingredients over the flour mixture. Stir to combine, but don't overmix.

Add the batter to the prepared pan and level out the top. Bake at 375°F for 25 minutes.

Let cool for 5 minutes on a wire rack. Run a knife between the bread and the sides of the pan to loosen the bread. Let stand for 10 minutes before unmolding. Cool completely before serving.

Combine the preserves and orange juice in a 1-quart saucepan. Heat briefly to melt the preserves. Drizzle over the bread.

Makes 1 loaf

SWEET POTATO SCONES

Healing Foods

Bran
Sweet potatoes
Whole wheat flour

1/2 cup whole
  wheat flour
1/2 cup unbleached
  flour
1/4 cup corn bran

1/8 teaspoon ground
  cinnamon
1/8 teaspoon grated
  nutmeg

1 teaspoon
  cream of tarter
1/2 teaspoon
  baking soda
2 tablespoons canola
  oil

3/4 cup shredded
  sweet potatoes
1/4 cup raisins,
  chopped
1/3 cup buttermilk

In a large bowl, mix the whole wheat flour, un-bleached flour, corn bran, cream of tartar, baking soda, cinnamon, and nutmeg. Stir in the sweet potatoes and raisins.

Add the buttermilk and oil. With floured hands, knead the mixture for about 2 minutes.

On a lightly floured surface, roll out the dough to a generous 1/4 inch thick. Cut out 2 1/2-inch rounds. Transfer to a lightly oiled baking sheet. Use all the dough by rerolling leftovers.

Bake at 475°F for 6 to 8 minutes. Serve warm.

Makes about 18

CORNMEAL-CHEESE MUFFINS

Healing Foods

Cheese (low-fat)
Corn
Milk (low-fat)

1 1/2 cups cornmeal
1/2 cup whole
  wheat flour
2 1/2 teaspoons
  baking powder

3/4 cup skim milk
1/4 cup egg substitute
2 tablespoons olive oil
2 tablespoons honey
1 cup corn

¾ cup shredded
  low-fat Monterey
  Jack cheese

In a large bowl, combine the cornmeal, flour, and baking powder.

In a medium bowl, combine the milk, egg substitute, oil, and honey.

Stir the liquid ingredients into the dry ingredients until just blended, but don't overmix. Fold in the corn and cheese.

Coat 12 muffin cups with nonstick spray. Fill about three-quarters full with the batter. Bake at 375°F for 15 minutes.

Makes 12

ONE-HOUR OAT BREAD

Healing Foods

Bran
Milk (low-fat)
Oats
Whole wheat flour

2 cups whole
  wheat flour
1 cup oat bran
1 cup rolled oats

1 tablespoon baking
  powder
2 cups buttermilk
¼ cup raisins

In a large bowl, combine the flour, oat bran, oats, raisins, and baking powder.

Pour in the buttermilk and use a large rubber

261

spatula to combine well. If the dough becomes too stiff to stir, flour your hands and finish mixing by hand.

Shape the dough into a round loaf 7 inches in diameter. Smooth the top and sides.

Line a baking sheet with parchment paper and set the loaf on it. Use a sharp knife to slash an "X" about 1/4 inch deep in the top. If any raisins are visible, poke them into the dough with your finger so they won't burn.

Sprinkle the loaf with a bit of flour. Bake at 425°F for about 45 minutes, or until the bottom of the loaf sounds hollow when tapped.

Let cool completely before slicing.

Makes 1 loaf

GOLDEN FRENCH TOAST

Healing Foods

Bananas
Oil
Raspberries
Whole wheat flour
Yogurt (low-fat)

1/2 cup egg substitute
1/2 cup apple juice
1/2 cup water
1 teaspoon vanilla
  extract
8 slices whole wheat
  or whole-grain bread

1 cup nonfat yogurt
1 tablespoon honey
1/4 teaspoon almond
  extract
2 tablespoons canola oil
2 cups raspberries
1 banana, thinly sliced

In a small bowl, beat together the egg substitute, apple juice, water, and vanilla with a fork until just combined. Pour into a 9 x 13-inch baking dish. Add the bread and turn to coat both sides. Allow to soak until most of liquid has been absorbed.

In a small bowl, combine the yogurt, honey, and almond extract. Set aside.

In a large frying pan over medium heat, heat 1 tablespoon of the oil. Add half of the bread and cook for several minutes, until browned on both sides. Repeat with remaining oil and bread.

Serve topped with the yogurt mixture, raspberries, and bananas.

Serves 4

CRANBERRY MUFFINS

Healing Foods

Cranberries
Milk (low-fat)
Oil
Wheat germ
Whole wheat flour

1 1/3 cups whole
  wheat flour
1/3 cup wheat germ
1 tablespoon
  baking powder

3/4 cup skim milk
1/3 cup honey
1/4 cup egg substitute
2 tablespoons canola oil
1 cup coarsely
  chopped cranberries

In a large bowl, combine the flour, wheat germ, and baking powder.

In a medium bowl, combine the milk, honey, egg substitute, and oil.

Stir the liquid ingredients into the dry ingredients until just blended, but don't overmix. Fold in the cranberries.

Coat 12 muffin cups with nonstick spray. Fill about three-quarters full with the batter. Bake at 375°F for 20 to 25 minutes.

Makes 12

MICRO METHOD: Muffin Magic

To adopt your favorite muffin recipes for the microwave:
- Add 1 tablespoon of extra oil to the recipe for each cup of flour.
- Use a ring-shaped microwave-muffin pan. (Or use custard cups arranged in a circle.)
- Use two cupcake liners for each muffin to absorb any excess moisture.
- Fill the liners one-third to one-half full to allow for higher rising.
- Because the muffins will not brown attractively, sprinkle on one of the following toppings before baking: wheat germ, oatmeal, cornmeal, herbs, seeds (try poppy, sesame or caraway), or chopped nuts.
- Microwave the muffins on full power until the tops spring back when touched. Rotate the pan after half the cooking time. Full cooking times are approximately:

- One muffin—15 to 45 seconds
- Two muffins—30 seconds to 2 minutes
- Four muffins—1 to $2^1/_2$ minutes
- Six muffins—2 to $4^1/_2$ minutes

Bring Back Freshness

Muffins are best right from the oven (be it a microwave or conventional oven). They're hot, moist, tender, and *fresh*. To recapture that just-baked taste and texture in days-old muffins:

- Wet a microwave-safe white paper towel.
- Wring out the excess moisture.
- Wrap the towel around one or two muffins (split if desired).
- Microwave an full power far about 40 seconds for one muffin (1 minute for two). Voilà—oven-fresh delights!

FRUIT AND NUT BREAD

Healing Foods

Apricots
Carrots
Milk (low-fat)
Nuts
Oil
Whole wheat flour

2 cups thinly sliced carrots
1 cup buttermilk

1 cup unbleached flour

1/2 cup egg substitute
1/2 cup canola oil
1/3 cup honey
2 cups whole
  wheat flour
1/2 teaspoon
  grated nutmeg
1/4 cup chopped
  almonds

2 teaspoons
  baking soda
1 teaspoon
  baking powder
1/2 teaspoon
  ground ginger
1 cup chopped apricots
1/3 cup chopped
  pitted dates

Place the carrots in a 1-quart saucepan. Add cold water to cover. Bring to a boil and cook until the carrots are tender, about 15 minutes. Drain and puree in a food mill or food processor. Measure out 1 1/4 cups of puree and place in a large bowl. (Reserve any remaining puree for another use.)

Add the buttermilk, egg substitute, oil, and honey. Combine well.

Sift together the whole wheat flour, unbleached flour, baking soda, baking powder, ginger, and nutmeg. Stir into the carrot mixture.

Fold in the apricots, dates, and almonds.

Coat two 8 1/2 x 4 1/2-inch loaf pans with non-stick spray and lightly flour them. Divide the dough between the pans.

Bake at 350°F for 45 to 60 minutes, or until a tester inserted in the center comes out clean. Cool in the pans 10 minutes. Then remove and cool on wire racks before slicing.

Makes 2 loaves

ORANGE MUFFINS

Healing Foods

Bran
Raisins
Whole wheat flour

1¹/₂ cups whole wheat flour
¹/₂ cup bran
¹/₂ cup raisins
1¹/₂ teaspoons baking soda
³/₄ cup orange juice
¹/₄ cup egg substitute
¹/₄ cup honey
2 tablespoons canola oil
Grated rind of 1 orange

In a large bowl, combine the flour, bran, raisins, and baking soda.

In a medium bowl, mix the orange juice, egg substitute, honey, oil, and orange rind.

Stir the liquid ingredients into the dry ingredients until just blended, but don't overmix.

Coat 12 muffin cups with nonstick spray. Fill about three-quarters full with the batter. Bake at 375°F for 15 minutes.

Makes 12

CINNAMON-SCENTED FRENCH TOAST

Healing Foods

Oil
Peaches
Raspberries
Whole wheat flour

$1/2$ cup evaporated
  skim milk
2 egg whites
$1/8$ teaspoon ground
  cinnamon
1 cup raspberries

8 slices whole wheat
  or whole-grain bread
2 tablespoons canola oil
3 peaches, sliced
$1/8$ teaspoon
  grated nutmeg

In a small bowl, whisk together the milk, egg whites, cinnamon, and nutmeg. Pour into a 9 x 13-inch baking dish.

Cut the bread in half for easier handling. Briefly soak the bread in the milk mixture, flipping the pieces to coat both sides.

Coat a large nonstick frying pan with nonstick spray. Heat the pan over medium-high heat. Pour in 1 tablespoon of the oil. Add half of the bread and brown the pieces on both sides, about $2^{1}/2$ minutes per side.

Repeat with the remaining oil and bread. Serve warm, topped with the peaches and raspberries.

Serves 4

PERFECT CRÊPES

Despite their French name and gourmet mystique, crêpes are really just thin pancakes. They're so adaptable, they can be served at almost any meal. Begin with properly made crêpes, such as the buckwheat or whole wheat ones below. Then add whatever fillings or toppings suit your fancy (see the suggestions that follow).

Because they are much thinner and made from a lighter batter, crêpes are cooked a little differently than pancakes. Here's how.

- Coat a heavy frying pan or crêpe pan with nonstick spray (or brush it lightly with canola oil).
- Heat until hot, then take the pan off the stove. Pour in a few tablespoons of batter and swirl the pan to distribute the batter evenly. If there's too much batter, pour the excess back into the bowl.
- Cook the crêpe over medium heat for about 1 minute, then loosen the edges gently with a spatula. It should be golden brown on the bottom and dry on the top.
- Turn the crêpe over and cook it until the other side is spotty brown, about 30 seconds.
- Turn finished crêpes out onto a wire rack to cool for a few minutes, then stack them. They won't stick together if they're cold.
- Recoat the pan with nonstick spray or canola oil as needed.

Whole Wheat Crêpes

1¹/₂ cups skim milk 1 cup whole wheat
¹/₂ cup egg substitute flour
¹/₂ teaspoon ground
  cinnamon

Place the milk, egg substitute, and cinnamon in a blender container. Blend for 5 seconds.

Add the flour and process on low to medium speed until the batter is smooth, stopping once or twice to scrape down the sides of the container.

Place the blender container in the refrigerator for 30 minutes. Blend again briefly before cooking.

Follow the basic cooking directions above.

Makes about 12 crêpes

Healing Foods

• Milk (low-fat) • Whole wheat flour

Buckwheat Crêpes

1¹/₃ cups skim milk ¹/₄ cup unbleached
¹/₂ cup egg substitute flour
¹/₄ teaspoon vanilla 1 teaspoon ground
  extract cinnamon
³/₄ cup buckwheat
  flour

In a blender, combine the milk, egg substitute, and vanilla. Blend for 5 seconds.

Add the buckwheat flour, unbleached flour,

and cinnamon. Process on low to medium speed until the batter is smooth, stopping once or twice to scrape down the sides of the container.

Place the blender container in the refrigerator far 30 minutes. Blend again briefly before cooking.

Follow the basic cooking directions an opposite page.

Makes 12 to 14 crêpes

Healing Foods

- Buckwheat
- Milk (low-fat)

Fillings
- Cooked fish, shellfish, or poultry
- Cooked vegetables
- Scrambled egg substitute with herbs
- Shredded low-fat cheese
- Pureed low-fat cottage cheese
- Stewed dried fruit
- Chopped fresh fruit
- Apple-prune butter
- Applesauce

Toppings
- Nonfat plain or flavored yogurt
- Tomato sauce
- Chopped fish or poultry in a low-fat white sauce
- Sautéed mushrooms or onions
- Pureed fresh fruit
- Chopped fresh fruit
- Finely grated lemon or orange rind

HEART-HEALTHY PIECRUST

If you love yummy quiches and savory pies but don't want to load up on the saturated fat most pastry crusts supply, you'll be delighted to try this whole wheat version. Olive oil lends some valuable monounsaturated oil to the crust. If you're making a crust for dessert, replace the olive oil with canola oil, another monounsaturate but without the bite.

This recipe makes a standard 9-inch single-crust shell. To make an 8-inch shell, reduce the ingredients to $1\frac{1}{2}$ cups flour and $\frac{1}{4}$ cup oil. Use just enough water to hold the crust together.

Whole Wheat Pie Shell

2 cups whole wheat pastry flour	$\frac{1}{3}$ cup olive oil $\frac{1}{4}$ cup ice water

Place the flour in a medium bowl. Drizzle with the oil. Use a pastry blender to evenly distribute the oil and produce a mixture that's the consistency of coarse cornmeal.

Sprinkle on the water, 1 tablespoon at a time, and continue mixing until you can gather the dough into a ball.

Roll the dough into an 11-inch circle on a pastry cloth. Patch any cracks that may form, but otherwise try not to handle the dough more than necessary. Transfer the dough to a 9-inch glass pie plate. Trim the dough, leaving a 1-inch overhang. Crimp the overhanging dough into a decorative edge.

Chill the crust for 20 minutes. Fill and bake according to your pie or quiche recipe. For an unfilled crust, prick the shell all over with a fork. Bake it at 350°F for 18 minutes (if making an 8-inch crust, bake it for 14 minutes). Let cool before filling.

Makes 1 crust

Healing Foods

- Oil   • Whole wheat flour

WHOLE-GRAIN AND SEED BREAD

Healing Foods

Bran
Bulgur
Oil
Seeds
Whole wheat flour

2^1/$_2$ cups water
^{1}/$_2$ cup bulgur
1 tablespoon active
  dry yeast
^{1}/$_4$ cup honey
^{1}/$_4$ cup sesame seeds

^{1}/$_4$ cup olive oil
3^1/$_2$ cups whole
  wheat flour
1 cup bran
1 cup oat bran
^{1}/$_4$ cup sunflower seeds

In a 1-quart saucepan, bring 1 cup of the water to a boil. Add the bulgur. Cover and set aside for 15 minutes.

Heat the remaining $1\frac{1}{2}$ cups of water to luke-warm (about 110°F). Transfer to a large bowl. Stir in the yeast, honey, and oil. Set aside for about 5 minutes to proof (the yeast will become foamy).

Stir in the flour, bran, oat bran, sesame seeds, sunflower seeds, and bulgur. Mix well by hand or in a food processor (process until the dough forms a ball; work in batches, if necessary).

Place in a lightly oiled bowl, turning to coat the dough on all sides. Cover and set in a warm, draft-free place until doubled in bulk, about 1 hour.

Punch down the dough and knead on a lightly floured surface for a few minutes. Divide in half and shape each piece into a loaf.

Coat two 9 x 5-inch loaf pans with nonstick spray. Place the dough in the pans. Allow to rise in a warm place until doubled in bulk, about 1 hour.

Bake at 350°F for 45 to 50 minutes, or until the loaves sound hollow when tapped on the bottom. Cool before slicing.

Makes 2 loaves

RICE-BRAN SCONES

Healing Foods

Bran
Milk (low-fat)
Raisins

1 cup rice bran
1 cup unbleached
   flour
2 teaspoons
   baking powder
1 teaspoon
   vanilla extract

$1/2$ teaspoon ground
   cinnamon
$1/2$ cup raisins
$2/3$ cup buttermilk
$1/3$ cup maple syrup
1 egg white

In a medium bowl, mix the rice bran, flour, baking powder, and cinnamon. Stir in the raisins.

In a small bowl, blend the buttermilk, maple syrup, vanilla, and egg white.

Pour the liquid ingredients over the flour mixture. Stir to combine well, but don't overmix.

Turn the dough out onto a floured counter. With floured hands, divide into two balls. Pat into 6-inch circles about $3/4$-inch thick. Cut each circle into four wedges.

Line a baking sheet with parchment paper. Transfer the wedges to the sheet.

Bake the scones at 400°F for 15 minutes, or until light brown.

Makes 8

PECAN-OAT MUFFINS

Healing Foods

Bran
Milk (low-fat)
Nuts
Oats
Raisins

275

1 cup oat bran
2/3 cup rolled oats
1/3 cup whole
   wheat flour
1/3 cup unbleached
   flour
1/4 cup chopped
   pecans

3 tablespoons raisins
1 tablespoon
   baking powder
1/4 cup egg substitute
1 1/4 cups buttermilk
1/4 cup maple syrup
1 tablespoon canola oil
1 1/2 teaspoons
   vanilla extract

In a large bowl, mix the oat bran, oats, whole wheat flour, unbleached flour, pecans, raisins, and baking powder.

In a medium bowl, whisk together the egg substitute, buttermilk, maple syrup, oil, and vanilla.

Pour the liquid ingredients over the dry ingredients. Mix until just combined, about 10 or 15 strokes, but don't overmix.

Lightly coat 12 muffin cups with nonstick spray. Spoon the batter into the cups. Bake at 400°F for about 20 minutes, or until the tops are lightly golden and rounded.

Makes 12

RISE AND SHINE

The success of yeast-risen breads and rolls depends, quite logically, on yeast. The single-celled fungi that make up yeast convert starches in dough into carbon dioxide, which inflates the dough into a nice plump bread shape. If you're confused about the various types of yeast available, here's a short primer:

- *Active dry yeast* is the most commonly used form. This granular yeast comes in individual packets or bulk form. Kept under refrigeration, it lasts for months. (It's said that dry yeast found in Egyptian tombs was still viable after centuries.) But for best results, heed the expiration date on the package. If using bulk yeast, transfer it to a jar with a tight-fitting lid and mark the date on the jar. If the yeast is more than a year old, proof it before using. Use $2^1/_2$ to 3 teaspoons of bulk yeast to equal one individual packet.
- *Rapid-rise yeast* is a type of dry yeast that allows bread to rise much faster than regular yeast. It comes in individual packets.
- *Compressed cake yeast* comes in little foil-wrapped blocks. A $^2/_3$ ounce cake equals one packet of dry yeast. When fresh, compressed yeast is crumbly and falls apart easily. It is much more perishable than dry yeast and stays fresh for only two weeks under refrigeration. For longer storage, you may freeze the yeast. Wrap it tightly, then freeze it in a container filled with flour. The flour insulation helps the yeast to freeze slowly. It keeps for three to six months. Thaw at room temperature.

CARAWAY PANCAKES

Healing Foods

Apples
Milk (low-fat)
Seeds
Whole wheat flour
Yogurt (low-fat)

PANCAKES

1/2 cup whole
   wheat flour
1/2 cup unbleached
   flour
1 teaspoon
   baking powder
1/2 teaspoon ground
   caraway seeds
1/2 teaspoon
   ground cinnamon
1/3 cup golden raisins
1 apple, minced
1/2 cup buttermilk
1/2 cup nonfat yogurt
1/4 cup egg substitute
2 tablespoons maple syrup

TOPPING

2 cups chunky
   applesauce
1 cup nonfat
   vanilla yogurt
1/4 teaspoon
   ground cinnamon

To make the pancakes: In a medium bowl, sift together the whole wheat flour, unbleached flour, baking powder, caraway, and cinnamon. Stir in the raisins and apples.

In a small bowl, combine the buttermilk, yogurt, egg substitute, and maple syrup.

Pour the liquid ingredients into the dry ingredients. Stir to combine.

Coat a nonstick frying pan with nonstick spray. Heat on medium-high. Drop tablespoon-size mounds of batter into the pan. Cook 2 to 3 minutes, then flip and continue cooking until richly browned and puffed.

To make the topping: In a small bowl, mix the applesauce, yogurt, and cinnamon. Serve over the pancakes.

Serves 4 to 6

POTATO WAFFLES WITH PEACH SAUCE

Healing Foods

Milk (low-fat)
Nuts
Peaches
Potatoes
Whole wheat flour
Yogurt (low-fat)

WAFFLES
1/2 cup whole
   wheat flour
1/2 cup unbleached
   flour
2 teaspoons
   baking powder

PEACH SAUCE
1 1/4 cups nonfat yogurt
2 peaches, chopped
2 tablespoons
   maple syrup
1/8 teaspoon
   grated nutmeg

WAFFLES (cont'd)
$1/4$ teaspoon
  ground allspice
1 cup skim milk
$1/2$ cup egg substitute
1 tablespoon honey
1 tablespoon canola oil
2 cups mashed potatoes
$1/4$ cup chopped hazelnuts
3 egg whites

To make the waffles: Sift the whole wheat flour, unbleached flour, baking powder, and allspice into a large bowl.

In a medium bowl, combine the milk, egg substitute, honey, and oil. Stir in the potatoes and hazelnuts.

Pour the liquid ingredients into the dry ingredients and mix well.

In a clean bowl with clean beaters, beat the egg whites until stiff. Fold into the batter.

Heat a waffle iron and lightly brush the grids with oil. Pour in enough batter to just fill. Close and cook until the steaming stops and the waffles are crisp. (Because of the moisture in the potatoes, these waffles will take longer to bake than other waffles.)

To make the peach sauce: In a small howl, combine the yogurt, peaches, maple syrup, and nutmeg. Serve over the waffles.

Serves 4 to 6

MICRO METHOD: Raising Yeast Bread

Made traditionally, yeast breads take hours to rise in the legendary "warm place." That's fine if you're not in a hurry and have time to hang around the house. But when time or patience is in short supply, you can get an assist from your microwave. The only catch: You need a full-size microwave with multipower settings.

Here's how to tell if your particular oven is suitable for the task.

- Place 2 tablespoons of cold stick margarine in a small cup. Position the cup in the center of the oven.
- Select 10 percent power (low) and run the microwave for 4 minutes. If the margarine melts completely, your microwave is unsuitable to raise yeast breads.

To raise yeast bread:
- Shape the dough into a ball and place in a lightly oiled bowl. Turn the dough to coat all sides with the oil.
- Cover the bowl loosely with waxed paper. Set aside.
- Fill a 4-cup glass measuring cup with 3 cups of water. Heat the water on full power for 6 to 8 minutes, or until boiling.
- Add the bowl of dough to the microwave next to the water.
- Run the microwave on low (10 percent) for about 15 minutes, or until the dough has doubled in size.

- Punch the dough down and divide it in half. Cover, let rest 10 minutes, then shape each half into a loaf.
- Place each loaf in a lightly oiled $8^1/2 \times 4^1/2$-inch ceramic or glass loaf pan. Set aside.
- Again heat the 3 cups of water until boiling (about 4 to 5 minutes this time).
- Add the loaf pans to the microwave beside the water. Cover loosely with waxed paper.
- Heat on low (10 percent) for about 7 minutes, or until the dough nearly doubles in size.
- Bake the dough in a conventional oven according to your recipe.

DILLED CARROT BREAD

Healing Foods

Carrots
Cottage cheese (low-fat)
Whole wheat flour

$1/4$ cup lukewarm water

2 teaspoons honey

1 tablespoon active dry yeast

$1^1/4$ cups shredded carrots

$3/4$ cup dry-curd cottage cheese

$1^3/4$ cups whole wheat flour

$1/4$ cup egg substitute

$1/4$ cup grated Parmesan cheese

1 tablespoon olive oil

1 teaspoon dill seeds

$1/2$ teaspoon caraway seeds

$1/2$ teaspoon salt (optional)

$1^1/4$ cups unbleached flour

In a large bowl, combine the water and honey. Sprinkle on the yeast and stir to combine. Set aside for 10 minutes to proof (the yeast will become foamy).

Add the carrots, cottage cheese, egg substitute, Parmesan, oil, dill, caraway, and salt (if used).

Stir in the whole wheat flour, using a wooden spoon. Add enough of the unbleached flour to form a sticky dough that comes away from the sides of the bowl.

Coat a large bowl with nonstick spray. Add the dough and turn to coat all sides. Cover with plastic wrap and towels. Place in a warm, draft-free spot and let rise until doubled in bulk, about 1 hour.

Stir down the dough with an oiled spoon.

Coat a 9 x 5-inch loaf pan or $1^1/_2$-quart casserole dish with non-stick spray. Flour your hands lightly, transfer the dough to the pan and pat it in evenly. Cover with a towel. Let rise in a warm place until doubled in bulk, about 45 minutes.

Bake at 375°F for 40 to 45 minutes, or until the bread sounds hollow when tapped.

Cool in the pan for 10 minutes. Turn out onto a wire rack. Cool completely before slicing.

Makes 1 loaf

FRENCH BREAD WITH A BONUS

We've taken the traditional French bread recipe and enriched it with olive oil and skim milk for added health benefits and substituted whole wheat in place of white for more fiber. The result is a tasty, crusty, and attractive loaf that's one up on health.

Whole Wheat French Bread

$1/2$ cup skim milk	1 teaspoon salt
1 cup boiling water	(optional)
1 package active	$3^3/4$ cups sifted
dry yeast	whole wheat flour
$1/4$ cup warm water	1 egg white
(85°F)	1 teaspoon water
$1^1/2$ tablespoons	$1/4$ cup poppy seeds
olive oil	1 tablespoon honey

In a 1 quart saucepan, heat milk to just under the boiling point. Add the boiling water. Set aside to cool to lukewarm.

In a large bowl, dissolve the yeast in the warm water. Stir in the oil, honey, and salt (if used). Set aside for 10 minutes to proof (the yeast will become foamy).

Add the milk mixture to the yeast and stir with a wire whisk to combine well. Add the flour 1 cup at a time, stirring with a wooden spoon after each addition. Form the dough into a ball. Do not knead. The dough will be soft but not silky smooth.

Leave the dough in the bowl and cover with a damp cloth. Set in a warm, draft-free place to rise until dough is doubled in bulk (about 2 hours).

Punch down the dough. Place on a lightly floured board and roll into a 10 x 14-inch rectangle about $1/2$ inch thick. Cut lengthwise into six strips. Using three strips of dough at a time, braid the dough into two loaves.

Coat a double-welled French-bread pan with nonstick spray. (Or use a large baking sheet.) Place the dough in the pan and set in a warm place to rise until doubled in bulk (about 45 minutes).

In a cup, whisk the egg white and 1 teaspoon water until foamy. Brush over the top of each loaf. Sprinkle with poppy seeds.

Bake at 400°F for 10 minutes. Then lower the oven temperature to 350°F and bake for 10 minutes longer, or until the crust is golden brown.

Remove the bread from the oven and set on a wire rack to cool for 20 minutes before slicing.

Makes 2 loaves

Healing Foods

- Milk (low-fat)
- Seeds
- Oil
- Whole wheat flour

BANANA PANCAKES

Healing Foods

Bananas
Barley
Oranges
Whole wheat flour

1⅓ cups whole wheat flour
1½ teaspoons baking powder
¾ cup cooked barley
½ cup skim milk
2 bananas, sliced
2 cups orange segments
½ cup mashed bananas
2 egg whites
2 tablespoons maple syrup
1 tablespoon canola oil
2 tablespoons all-fruit preserves

In a medium bowl, sift together the flour and baking powder. Stir in the barley.

In a small bowl, whisk together the milk, mashed bananas, egg whites, and maple syrup.

Pour the milk mixture into the flour. Stir to combine, but do not overmix.

Coat a well-seasoned cast-iron or nonstick frying pan with non-stick spray. Heat over medium-high heat. Add half of the oil.

Spoon in ¼ cup of the batter for each pancake. Cook until bubbles form on the top. Then flip and cook the other side for another minute. Transfer to a platter and keep warm.

Repeat with the remaining oil and batter. Transfer to the platter.

Add the preserves to the frying pan. Stir to melt. Add the bananas and oranges. Heat for 2 to 3 minutes, occasionally flipping the pieces with a spatula. Serve over the pancakes.

Serves 4

POTATO-CHEESE BREAD

Healing Foods

Cheese (low-fat)
Potatoes
Whole wheat flour

$2^{1}/4$ cups chicken
  stock
$^{1}/3$ cup grated
  Sapsago or
  Parmesan cheese
2 tablespoons olive oil
2 tablespoons honey
$2^{3}/4$ cups whole
  wheat flour

1 teaspoon
  dried thyme
1 teaspoon dillweed
2 tablespoons active
  dry yeast
$1^{1}/2$ cups mashed
  potatoes
$2^{3}/4$ cups unbleached
  flour

In a 3-quart saucepan, heat the stock to luke-warm. Remove from the heat. Add the cheese, oil, honey, thyme, and dill. Gently stir in the yeast. Stir in the mashed potatoes. Set aside for 10 minutes to proof (the yeast will become foamy).

In a large bowl, mix the whole wheat flour and unbleached flour. Gradually stir 4 cups of flour into the potato mixture.

Turn the dough onto a floured surface and knead in the remaining flour. Knead for about 10 minutes, or until the dough is smooth and elastic.

Lightly oil a large bowl. Add the dough and turn to coat all sides. Allow to rise in a warm, draft-free place for 30 to 40 minutes, or until doubled in bulk.

Punch down the dough and knead for 1 minute. Divide into two portions and form into loaves.

Coat two 8$^{1}/_{2}$ x 4$^{1}/_{2}$-inch loaf pans with non-stick spray. Add the dough, cover, and let rise for 30 minutes, or until doubled in bulk.

Bake at 350°F for 30 to 35 minutes, or until the loaves sound hollow when tapped.

Allow the loaves to cool on wire racks for 30 minutes.

Makes 2 loaves

PECAN WAFFLES WITH STRAWBERRY SAUCE

Healing Foods

Nuts
Oil
Strawberries
Whole wheat flour

WAFFLES
$^{3}/_{4}$ cup whole
    wheat flour
$^{3}/_{4}$ cup unbleached
    flour
1$^{1}/_{2}$ teaspoons
    baking powder
$^{1}/_{2}$ cup chopped pecans
1$^{1}/_{4}$ cups apricot nectar
$^{1}/_{2}$ cup egg substitute
$^{1}/_{4}$ cup maple syrup
2 tablespoons canola oil

SAUCE
2 cups sliced
    strawberries
$^{1}/_{2}$ cup apricot nectar
2 tablespoons maple
    syrup

288

To make the waffles: In a large bowl, sift together the whole wheat flour, unbleached flour, and baking powder. Stir in the pecans.

In a medium bowl, whisk together the nectar, egg substitute, maple syrup, and oil.

Pour the liquid ingredients over the flour mixture. Stir to combine, but don't overmix.

Heat a waffle iron, and lightly brush the grids with oil. Pour in enough batter to cover two-thirds of the bottom grids. Bake according to the manufacturer's directions, but start checking for doneness after 3 minutes.

Repeat until the batter is used up; occasionally brush the grids with oil to prevent sticking.

To make the sauce: Place the strawberries, nectar, and maple syrup in a food processor. Process with on/off turns until smooth.

Drizzle the sauce over the waffles.

Serves 4 to 6

RAISIN-OAT BREAD

Healing Foods

Oats
Potatoes
Raisins
Whole wheat flour

1 large potato
2 tablespoons honey
1 cup whole
  wheat flour

1 cup unbleached
  flour
$2^1/2$ teaspoons
  baking soda

| 1 teaspoon | 3/4 cup rolled oats |
| cream of tartar | 1/2 cup raisins |

Peel and slice the potato. Place in a 1-quart sauce-pan with water to cover and cook until tender. Drain, reserving 3/4 cup of the potato water. Mash the potato.

In a small bowl, combine 1/2 cup mashed potato, honey, and the reserved potato water.

Sift the whole wheat flour, unbleached flour, baking soda, and cream of tartar into a large bowl. Stir in the oats and raisins.

Make a well in the center of the dry ingredients and pour in the potato mixture. Stir until a stiff dough forms. Turn out onto a floured board and knead 1 minute with floured hands. Shape into a ball.

Coat an 8-inch round cake pan with nonstick spray. Add the dough and flatten slightly. With a sharp knife, make a cross slash in the top of the loaf.

Bake at 375°F for 25 to 35 minutes, or until the loaf sounds hollow when tapped. Cool completely before serving.

Makes 1 loaf

PRUNE MUFFINS

Healing Foods

Bran
Milk (low-fat)
Prunes
Whole wheat flour

1 cup ready-to-eat 100% bran cereal
1 1/2 cups buttermilk
2 egg whites
1/4 cup molasses
1/2 cup oat bran
1 cup chopped prunes

2 tablespoons canola oil
1 teaspoon vanilla extract
1 cup whole wheat flour
1 tablespoon baking powder

In a medium bowl, combine the bran cereal and buttermilk. Let stand until the cereal is soft, about 10 minutes.

Add the egg whites, molasses, oil, and vanilla. Combine well.

In a large bowl, combine the flour, oat bran, and baking powder. Stir in the prunes.

Pour the milk mixture into the flour mixture. Stir to combine, but don't overmix.

Line 12 muffin cups with cupcake papers. Spoon the batter into the cups. Bake at 400°F for about 18 minutes.

Makes 12

CARROT MUFFINS

Healing Foods

Carrots
Milk (low-fat)
Raisins
Whole wheat flour

2 cups whole
wheat flour
2/3 cup ready-to-eat
bran flakes
2 teaspoons
baking powder
1 teaspoon ground
cinnamon
2 tablespoons
canola oil

$^1/_4$ teaspoon grated
nutmeg
$1^1/_2$ cups skim milk
$1^1/_2$ cups shredded
carrots
$^1/_2$ cup raisins
$^1/_4$ cup egg substitute
$^1/_4$ cup honey
2 tablespoons molasses

In a large bowl, combine the flour, bran flakes, baking powder, cinnamon, and nutmeg.

In a medium bowl, combine the milk, carrots, raisins, egg substitute, honey, oil, and molasses.

Stir the liquid ingredients into the dry ingredients until just blended, but don't overmix.

Coat 12 muffin cups with nonstick spray. Fill about three-quarters full with the batter. Bake at 375°F for 20 to 25 minutes.

Makes 12

CRANBERRY BREAD

Healing Foods

Corn
Cranberries
Whole wheat flour
Yogurt (low-fat)

2 cups unbleached flour

1 1/2 cups whole wheat flour

1/2 cup cornmeal

1 tablespoon baking powder

1/2 teaspoon ground cinnamon

1/2 teaspoon grated nutmeg

3/4 cup finely chopped cranberries

1 teaspoon anise seeds

1 1/2 cups nonfat yogurt

1/4 cup buttermilk

1/4 cup egg substitute

1 tablespoon honey

Sift the unbleached flour, whole wheat flour, cornmeal, baking powder, cinnamon, and nutmeg into a large bowl. Add the cranberries and anise seeds.

In a medium bowl, combine the yogurt, buttermilk, egg substitute, and honey.

Pour the liquid ingredients into the flour bowl. Mix well, using a large rubber spatula.

Turn the dough out onto a floured counter. With floured hands, shape into a 7-inch mound, smoothing out any cracks as you go.

Coat a baking sheet with nonstick spray. Place the dough on the sheet. Use a sharp knife to slash an "X" in the top, about 1/2 inch deep (to help keep the loaf from splitting raggedly

as it rises). Sprinkle the top with a bit of unbleached flour.

Bake at 450°F for about 30 minutes, or until
the bottom of the bread sounds hollow when
tapped. Remove from the oven and let stand
about 20 minutes before slicing. Best served
warm.

Makes 1 loaf

CINNAMON BUNS

Healing Foods

Bran
Milk (low-fat)
Nuts
Oats

DOUGH
3/4 cup buttermilk
1 tablespoon
active dry yeast
2 tablespoons maple
syrup
2 tablespoons
canola oil
3/4 cup whole
wheat flour
3/4 cup unbleached
flour
1/2 cup oat bran
1/4 cup rolled oats
1 tablespoon skim milk

FILLING
3 tablespoons maple
syrup
2 teaspoons ground
cinnamon
1/3 cup raisins, chopped
2 tablespoons
chopped almonds
1 egg white,
lightly beaten

To make the dough: Heat the buttermilk in a small saucepan until warm (110°F). Pour $1/4$ cup into a large bowl. Stir in the yeast, maple syrup, and oil. Set aside for about 5 minutes to proof (the yeast will become foamy).

Stir in the whole wheat flour, unbleached flour, oat bran, and oats. When the dough gets too stiff to stir, add enough of the remaining buttermilk to make a workable dough.

Turn the dough out onto a lightly floured surface. Knead for about 5 minutes. Transfer to a lightly oiled bowl, turn to coat the dough on all sides, and cover the bowl with plastic.

Set the bowl in a warm, draft-free spot until the dough is doubled in bulk, about 30 to 50 minutes.

Punch the dough down and let rise for a second time until doubled again, about 30 to 50 minutes.

Turn the dough out onto a lightly floured surface. Roll into a 9-inch square. Brush with the skim milk.

To make the filling: In a cup, combine the maple syrup and cinnamon. Brush on the dough. Sprinkle with the raisins and almonds.

Starting at one edge, roll up the dough to enclose the filling. With a sharp knife, cut the roll into nine slices.

Line a baking sheet with parchment paper. Lay the rolls flat on the sheet $1/4$ inch apart. Brush the tops and sides with egg white. Set in a warm, draft-free place to rise for about 30 minutes.

Bake at 400°F for 25 minutes, or until lightly browned.

Serves 9

CHAPTER SEVEN

The Great Grains

Grains truly are the staff of life. With lots of fiber and hunger-satisfying carbohydrates, whole grains form a very solid base for a healthy diet. Some, such as barley and oats, have been proven to help lower cholesterol. Others, like millet and the increasingly popular quinoa, are very high in protein, making them invaluable for those who don't eat much meat. Rice is a good source of cancer-fighting starch, and buckwheat may help improve glucose tolerance in diabetics.

The recipes in this chapter showcase these grains—and others—in dishes for every meal of the day. Start your morning with fruit-filled Oat-Bran Muesli or Apricot-Quinoa Cereal. Have a light lunch of Bulgur-Stuffed Yellow Peppers or Cabbage and Kasha. For a satisfying dinner, look to Skillet Barley and Beef or Spinach Risotto.

Don't forget that pasta and its Moroccan cousin couscous are also grain products. Couscous with Chicken and Vegetables is an entire meal by itself. Try Pasta with Salmon and Sun-Dried Tomatoes or Buckwheat Noodles with Grilled Tuna when entertaining. And remember that you can keep pasta low in calories with the right sauce. Spicy Aurora Sauce and Green-Pepper Pesto prove the point.

As side dishes, Couscous with Sweet Corn, Wild-Rice Pilaf, Chestnut Stuffing, and Pineapple-Rice Stuffing shine. So no matter how you like your grains—sweet or savory—there's always a place for these hearty staples in the healing diet.

CABBAGE AND KASHA

Healing Foods

Buckwheat
Cabbage
Carrots

1 cup roasted buckwheat groats (kasha)
1 cup sliced mushrooms
3 cloves garlic, minced
2 tablespoons olive oil
1 1/2 teaspoons caraway seeds
1 cup tomato juice

2 cups stock
2 teaspoons low-sodium soy sauce
1 onion, diced
4 cups shredded cabbage
1 large carrot, diced
1 sweet red pepper, diced
1/4 teaspoon black pepper

In a large frying pan over medium-high heat, toast the buckwheat for 5 to 7 minutes, stirring frequently. Transfer to a bowl and set aside.

In the same frying pan, sauté the mushrooms and half of the garlic in 1 tablespoon oil for 10 minutes, or until the mushrooms are brown and no liquid is left. Add the stock, soy sauce, and buckwheat. Cover and simmer for 15 minutes, or until the buckwheat is tender. Set aside.

In another large frying pan, sauté the onions and remaining garlic in the remaining 1 tablespoon oil for 3 to 4 minutes.

Add the cabbage, carrots, peppers, caraway, and black pepper. Sauté for 5 minutes. Add the tomato juice and simmer for 15 minutes.

Arrange the buckwheat and cabbage on a large platter.

Serves 6

CABBAGE NOODLES

Healing Foods

Cabbage
Oil
Pasta
Seeds
Yogurt (low-fat)

1 head green cabbage
2 tablespoons caraway
  seeds, crushed
1 1/2 cups nonfat
  yogurt

1/4 teaspoon ground
  black pepper
3 tablespoons olive oil
1/4 cup stock
8 ounces broad noodles

Chop or coarsely shred the cabbage.

In a large frying pan over medium-high heat, sauté the cabbage, caraway, and pepper in the oil for 10 minutes.

Add the stock. Reduce the heat to medium, cover, and cook, stirring occasionally, for 30 minutes, or until browned.

In a large pot of boiling water, cook the noodles until tender. Drain and add to the cabbage. Brown for 5 minutes. Serve with the yogurt.

Serves 4

JAPANESE NOODLES WITH SPINACH RIBBONS

Healing Foods

Garlic
Onions
Pasta
Spinach

2$^1/_2$ ounces thin rice-stick noodles	3 cloves garlic, minced
1$^1/_2$ cups chicken stock	3 cups shredded spinach leaves
1$^1/_2$ teaspoons dried sage	1 cup minced scallions
	1 teaspoon low-sodium soy sauce

In a large pot of boiling water, cook the noodles for 4 minutes. Drain and set aside.

In a large nonstick frying pan, combine the stock, sage, soy sauce, and garlic. Bring the mixture to a simmer.

Add the noodles. Do not stir or the noodles will tangle; instead gently move them around using chopsticks or tongs. When the noodles are heated, add the spinach and scallions. Simmer about 20 seconds, or until the spinach is wilted. Serve in shallow bowls.

Serves 4

NOODLES WITH NUT SAUCE

Healing Foods

Garlic
Nuts
Pasta

$1/2$ cup chopped broccoli rabe
1 tablespoon olive oil
2 cloves garlic
1 teaspoon dried basil
$1/2$ teaspoon dried thyme

$1/3$ cup pecans
$1/4$ cup low-fat milk
2 tablespoons low-fat cottage cheese
8 ounces angel-hair pasta

In a large nonstick frying pan over medium heat, combine the broccoli rabe, oil, garlic, basil, and thyme. Sauté until the greens wilt, about 3 minutes.

Transfer the mixture to the bowl of a food processor. Add the pecans, milk, and cottage cheese. Process with on/off turns until almost smooth.

In a large pot of boiling water, cook the pasta according to package directions until tender. Do not overcook. Drain and return to the pot. Add the sauce and toss to combine.

Serves 4

BROCCOLI
AND CHEESE PASTA

Healing Foods

Broccoli
Cheese (low-fat)
Oil
Pasta

4 cups broccoli florets
2 tablespoons olive oil
1 cup chicken stock
2 ounces Neufchâtel cheese, cubed
2 tablespoons Sapsago Parmesan cheese
$^1/_2$ teaspoon dried thyme
$^1/_2$ teaspoon black pepper
8 ounces angel-hair pasta

In a large nonstick frying pan, stir-fry the broccoli in the oil until crisp-tender. Transfer to a plate and set aside.

Add the stock, Neufchâtel, thyme, and pepper to the pan. Whisk until creamy. Return the broccoli to the pan, stir to coat, and remove from the heat. Sprinkle with the Sapsago or Parmesan.

In a large pot of boiling water, cook the pasta until tender. Drain and add to the broccoli mixure. Toss to combine.

Serves 4

LINGUINE
WITH SWEET PEPPERS

Healing Foods

Garlic
Onions
Pasta
Peppers (sweet)

1 large onion, sliced
1 bay leaf
1 tablespoon olive oil
2/3 cup chicken stock
3 sweet red peppers, thinly sliced
1/2 teaspoon dried oregano
1 cup sliced mushrooms
4 cloves garlic, minced
1/4 cup minced fresh parsley
1 teaspoon dried basil
1/2 teaspoon dried thyme
4 ounces linguine

In a large nonstick frying pan, sauté the onions and bay leaf in the oil about 5 minutes.

Add the stock, peppers, mushrooms, garlic, parsley, basil, thyme, and oregano. Simmer uncovered for 5 to 7 minutes, or until the peppers are soft and the liquid has reduced somewhat. Remove the bay leaf.

In a large pot of boiling water, cook the linguine until just tender. Drain and add to the pan with the vegetables. Toss to combine.

Serves 4

PASTA WITH SALMON AND SUN-DRIED TOMATOES

Healing Foods

Cottage cheese (low-fat)
Pasta
Salmon
Tomatoes

1 cup water
1 tablespoon vinegar
1 bay leaf
8 ounces salmon fillet
1 cup low-fat
   cottage cheese
1 tablespoon grated
   Romano cheese

2 tablespoons skim milk
$1/8$ teaspoon
   grated nutmeg
8 ounces
   spinach fettuccine
$2/3$ cup sliced
   sun-dried tomatoes

In a large frying pan, combine the water, vinegar, and bay leaf. Bring to a boil. Reduce the heat to low and add the salmon. Cover and cook for 4 to 6 minutes, or until opaque. Discard the bay leaf.

Remove the salmon with a slotted spoon and let cool. Break into 1-inch chunks. Set aside.

In a blender or food processor, combine the cottage cheese, milk, and nutmeg. Process until smooth.

In a large pot of boiling water, cook the fettuccine until just tender. Drain and transfer to a large serving bowl. Add the tomatoes, Romano, and half of the cottage-cheese mixture. Toss to combine. Add the salmon and remaining cheese mixture. Toss gently.

Serves 4

PEAS AND PASTA

Healing Foods

Cheese (low-fat)
Pasta
Peas

8 ounces vermicelli
1 cup peas
1 cup sugar snap peas
1/4 cup shredded low-fat Swiss cheese
1/4 teaspoon grated nutmeg

1/4 cup shredded part-skim mozzarella cheese
3 tablespoons grated minced fresh basil

In a large pot of boiling water, cook the vermicelli until tender. Drain and transfer to a large serving bowl.

Steam the peas and snap peas for about 4 minutes, or until crisp-tender. Add to the pasta with the Swiss, mozzarella, basil, and nutmeg. Toss to combine.

Serves 4

SKILLET BARLEY AND BEEF

Healing Foods

Barley
Beef (lean)
Carrots
Mushrooms

6 ounces flank steak,
    trimmed of all
    visible fat
1 cup barley
4 cups water
1 bay leaf
1 tablespoon olive oil

1 onion, chopped
2 cloves garlic, minced
2 carrots, thinly sliced
12 mushrooms, sliced
$1^1/_2$ cups beef stock
$1^1/_2$ teaspoons dried
    thyme

Partially freeze the beef (about 1 hour) to make slicing easier. Cut it lengthwise into 2-inch strips. Then slice paper thin across the grain.

In a 2-quart saucepan, combine the barley, water, and bay leaf. Bring to a boil, lower the heat, and simmer uncovered for 20 minutes.

In a large nonstick frying pan over medium heat, stir-fry the beef in the oil until cooked through, about 3 minutes. Remove from the pan and keep warm.

Add the onions and garlic to the pan. Cook until limp, about 5 minutes. Add the carrots and mushrooms; cook for 2 minutes.

Drain the barley and discard the water. Add the barley to the frying pan. Stir in the stock and thyme. Cover and simmer for 15 to 20 minutes, or until the barley is just tender.

Add the beef and warm through. Discard the bay leaf.

Serves 4

FETTUCCINE WITH GRAPES

Healing Foods

Cottage cheese (low-fat)
Grapes
Onions
Pasta

8 scallions, julienned
1/4 cup chicken stock
2 cups red seedless
  grapes, halved
1/4 teaspoon dried
  thyme
1/4 teaspoon grated
  nutmeg

1 1/4 cups low-fat
  cottage cheese
1/4 cup skim milk
2 tablespoons grated
  Sapsago or
  Parmesan cheese
12 ounces fettuccine
1/4 cup minced
  fresh parsley

In a large nonstick frying pan, sauté the scallions in the stock for 3 minutes. Add the grapes and thyme. Heat for 2 minutes. Set aside.

In a food processor or blender, puree the cottage cheese, milk, Sapsago or Parmesan, and nutmeg until smooth.

In a large pot of boiling water, cook the fettuccine until tender. Drain and place in a large serving bowl. Add the cheese mixture and grapes. Toss gently to combine. Sprinkle with the parsley.

Serves 4

SPAGHETTI WITH SPINACH CHIFFONADE

Healing Foods

Cottage cheese (low-fat)
Pasta
Raspberries
Spinach

12 ounces spaghetti
3 cups finely
  shredded spinach
2 tablespoons minced
  scallions
1 tablespoon olive oil
1 cup raspberries

1/2 cup low-fat
  cottage cheese
2 tablespoons grated
  Parmesan cheese
1/8 teaspoon grated
  nutmeg

In a large pot of boiling water, cook the spaghetti until just tender. Drain and place in a large serving bowl. Keep warm.

In a large nonstick frying pan, sauté the spinach and scallions in the oil until the spinach is wilted, about 2 minutes. Add to the spaghetti and toss lightly to combine.

In a food processor, blend the cottage cheese, Parmesan, and nutmeg until smooth. Add to the frying pan and heat briefly, stirring constantly. Pour over the pasta. Add the raspberries and toss to combine.

Serves 4

RICE IS NICE
FOR A LOW-FAT CRUST

When you need a super-fast, no-fuss crust for quiches or other savory pies, whip up this rice shell. It's very low in fat and has a nice crunchy texture. Use any type of cooked rice you wish.

Rice Crust

$1/4$ cup egg substitute
1 egg white, lightly
    beaten

3 cups cold cooked
    rice

In a medium bowl, whisk together the egg substitute and egg white. Add the rice and combine well.

Coat a 9-inch glass pie plate with nonstick spray. Transfer the rice to the plate. Cover it with a piece of waxed paper and use your hand to flatten the rice into a firm crust extending up the sides of the plate. Discard the paper.

Bake at 350°F for 20 to 25 minutes, or until the crust is dry to the touch. (If you will be baking the crust after you add a filling, reduce the initial baking time to 15 minutes. Add the filling, then cover the edges of the crust with foil to prevent them from turning rock-hard as the pie bakes.)

Makes 1 crust

Accent on Health: The Right Stuffings

Stuffings have a bad reputation that is, in part, deserved. Although the base of most stuffings is wholesome grains, such as bread and rice, the addition of high-fat extras offsets this great beginning. Standard recipes call for butter, eggs, cream, sausage, or bacon. None of them are appropriate for a health-promoting diet.

Fortunately, you can enjoy great stuffings that are good for you. Let stock act as a moistener in place of fat. Use egg substitute as a binder. Get flavor from a variety of aromatics, such as onions, garlic, celery, herbs, and spices. And for extra measure when roasting whole poultry, bake the stuffing in a separate casserole. That way it won't absorb any fat that drips from the bird as it cooks.

For variety, use stuffings rolled up in fish fillets or boneless chicken breasts. Or use them in vegetables, such as sweet peppers, winter squash, or hollowed-out large onions.

Chestnut Stuffing

1 pound chestnuts
1 large onion, chopped
2 stalks celery, sliced
4 ounces mushrooms, sliced
1 tablespoon olive oil
1 cup chicken stock
1/4 cup minced fresh parsley
1/4 cup egg substitute
1/2 teaspoon dried sage
1/4 teaspoon black pepper
1/8 teaspoon celery seed
3 cups whole wheat bread cubes
1 tablespoon low-sodium soy sauce

With a sharp knife, carve an "X" on the flat side of each chestnut. Place in a 3-quart saucepan with just enough water to cover. Cover the pan and simmer for 20 minutes, or until tender. Drain and set aside until just cool enough to handle. Peel while still warm. Quarter and set aside.

In a large frying pan, sauté the onions, celery, and mushrooms in the oil until almost soft, about 7 minutes.

Add the stock, parsley, soy sauce, pepper, and celery seed. Simmer for 3 minutes. Add the bread, chestnuts, and egg substitute. Mix well.

Coat a $1^1/2$-quart casserole with nonstick spray. Add the stuffing. Cover and bake at 350°F for 40 minutes. Remove the cover and bake 15 minutes to brown the top.

Serves 4

Healing Foods

• Chestnuts   • Onions   • Whole wheat flour

Wild-Rice Stuffing

1 cup diced onions
4 cloves garlic, minced
1 tablespoon olive oil
1 cup wild rice, rinsed
$3^1/2$ cups chicken stock
$1/4$ teaspoon ground allspice
$1/2$ cup raisins
$1/8$ teaspoon red-pepper flakes
1 cup long-grain white rice
$1/2$ cup chopped dried apricots
$1/2$ cup minced fresh parsley
$1/2$ teaspoon dried basil

310

In a 3-quart ovenproof casserole over medium heat, sauté the onions and garlic in the oil until golden, about 3 or 4 minutes. Add the wild rice and stir to coat. Sauté for 3 or 4 minutes, or until the rice is lightly toasted.

Add the stock, allspice, and red pepper. Bring to a boil. Reduce the heat to medium-low. Cover the casserole and simmer for 20 minutes.

Stir in the white rice, apricots, raisins, parsley, and basil. Cover and bake at 350°F for 10 minutes.

Remove the cover and bake for 10 to 15 minutes, or until all liquid has been absorbed and the rice is tender.

Serves 8

Healing Foods

• Apricots • Garlic • Parsley • Raisins • Rice

Pineapple-Rice Stuffing

2 1/2 cups cooked rice

1 cup chopped pineapple

1/2 cup raisins

1/4 cup minced shallots

1/4 teaspoon freshly ground allspice

1/3 cup chopped toasted almonds

In a large bowl, combine the rice, pineapple, raisins, almonds, shallots, and allspice.

Makes about 4 1/2 cups

Healing Foods

• Nuts   • Pineapple   • Raisins   • Rice

311

BUCKWHEAT NOODLES WITH GRILLED TUNA

Healing Foods

**Buckwheat
Fish
Garlic
Salad greens**

2 tablespoons
lemon juice
1 tablespoon olive oil
1 pound tuna steaks
1 sweet red
pepper, chopped
1 tomato, peeled,
seeded, and chopped
3 cups shredded
red lettuce

1 cup tomato juice
2 tablespoons vinegar
3 cloves garlic, minced
$1/4$ cup minced
fresh parsley
12 ounces
buckwheat noodles
1 tablespoon toasted
sesame seeds

In a cup, combine the lemon juice and oil. Brush on both sides of each piece of tuna. Place in a baking dish, cover and refrigerate for 1 hour.

Broil the tuna about 6 inches from the heat for about 5 minutes per side, or until cooked through.

In a blender, puree the peppers, tomatoes, tomato juice, vinegar, and garlic. Transfer to a small bowl and stir in the parsley.

In a large pot of boiling water, cook the noodles according to package directions until tender. Drain and place in a large bowl. Toss with the sesame seeds and half of the tomato mixture.

To serve, divide the lettuce among four dinner plates. Top with the noodles and tuna. Drizzle the fish with the remaining tomato mixture.

Serves 4

CHINESE VEGETABLE PASTA

Healing Foods

Broccoli
Carrots
Pasta
Peppers (sweet)

1 tablespoon canola oil
1 large onion,
  thinly sliced
2 carrots, julienned
1 sweet red
  pepper, julienned
2 cups cooked
  vermicelli

1 cup broccoli florets
1 clove garlic,
  thinly sliced
2 tablespoons low-
  sodium soy sauce
1 tablespoon vinegar

In a large nonstick frying pan or wok, heat the oil. Add the onions and stir-fry for 2 minutes.

Add the carrots, peppers, broccoli, and garlic. Stir-fry for 2 minutes.

In a small bowl, stir together the soy sauce and vinegar. Pour over the vegetables. Add the vermicelli and toss well to combine.

Serves 4

CABBAGE-STUFFED SHELLS

Healing Foods

Cabbage
Cottage cheese (low-fat)
Cucumbers
Pasta
Yogurt (low-fat)

1 onion, minced
1 clove garlic, minced
1 tablespoon canola oil
2$^1/_2$ cups finely
  chopped cabbage
1 large cucumber,
  shredded

1 cup low-fat
  cottage cheese
$^1/_2$ teaspoon dillweed
16 jumbo shells
1 cup nonfat yogurt
1 teaspoon low-
  sodium soy sauce

In a large nonstick frying pan, sauté the onions and garlic in the oil until soft, about 4 minutes.

Add the cabbage. Cover and cook over low heat 5 to 6 minutes, or until the cabbage is tender. Let cool for about 15 minutes.

Stir in the cottage cheese and dill.

In a large pot of boiling water, cook the shells until just tender. Drain.

Stuff the shells with the cabbage mixture.

In a small bowl, combine the yogurt, cucumbers, and soy sauce.

Serve the shells at room temperature with the cucumber sauce.

Serves 4

BULGUR-STUFFED YELLOW PEPPERS

Healing Foods

Bulgur
Peppers (sweet)

$1/2$ cup stock
$1/2$ cup bulgur
4 sweet yellow
  peppers
$1/2$ cup minced onion
1 tablespoon olive oil
$1^1/2$ cups warm
  tomato sauce

2 cloves garlic, minced
$1/2$ teaspoon
  dried thyme
$1/2$ cup low-fat
  cottage cheese
$1/4$ cup egg substitute

In a 2-quart saucepan, bring the stock to a boil. Add the bulgur. Cover and remove from the heat. Set aside until the bulgur has absorbed the stock, about 20 minutes.

Slice the tops off the peppers. Remove the seeds and inner membranes. Blanch the peppers in boiling water until just tender, about 4 minutes. Set aside to cool.

In a large nonstick frying pan, combine the onions, oil, garlic, and thyme. Sauté over medium heat until the onions are tender, about 5 minutes. Add to the pan with the bulgur.

In a food processor or blender, puree the cottage cheese and egg substitute until smooth. Add to the pan with the bulgur. Combine all the ingredients well.

315

Divide the filling among the peppers.

Place the filled peppers in a 9 x 9-inch baking dish. Bake at 350°F for 25 minutes, or until the stuffing is firm and cooked through. Serve with the tomato sauce.

Serves 4

OAT-BRAN MUESLI

Healing Foods

Bran
Kiwifruit
Oats
Oranges
Seeds
Yogurt (low-fat)

2 cups nonfat yogurt
2 cups rolled oats
1 cup oat bran
1/4 cup pumpkin
    seeds

1 banana, sliced
1 orange, sectioned
    and chopped
2 kiwifruit, chopped

In a large bowl, combine the yogurt, oats, and oat bran. Cover and refrigerate overnight.

Mix in the pumpkin seeds, bananas, oranges, and kiwis.

Serves 4

WILD-RICE PILAF

Healing Foods

Nuts
Onions
Rice

1 tablespoon olive oil
1 cup minced onions
1 stalk celery, minced
4 ounces wild rice
2 tablespoons
   toasted pine nuts

1 teaspoon minced
   garlic
$1/4$ teaspoon red
   pepper
2 cups chicken stock
1 bay leaf

In a 2-quart saucepan over medium heat, heat the oil. Add the onions, celery, garlic, and pepper. Cook for 2 minutes, until lightly browned and soft.

Add the stock, wild rice, bay leaf, and pine nuts. Bring to a boil, cover, and lower the heat so the liquid simmers. Continue cooking for 55 minutes. Uncover and cook until all the liquid has been absorbed. Discard the bay leaf.

Serves 4

WILD RICE AND RASPBERRIES

Healing Foods

Raspberries
Rice

1 1/2 cups chicken
   stock
3/4 cup wild rice
2 teaspoons
   canola oil

1/8 teaspoon dried
   marjoram
1 cup raspberries
2 tablespoons
   minced parsley

In a 1-quart saucepan, bring the stock to a boil. Transfer to the top of a double boiler. Add the wild rice, oil, and marjoram.

Cover and cook over boiling water for 1 to 1 1/2 hours, or until the liquid has been absorbed and the rice is tender.

Transfer to a serving bowl. Fold in the raspberries and parsley.

Serves 4

SOWING THE SEEDS OF SUCCESS

Strictly speaking, most seeds are not grains. No matter. We're including them in this chapter because they have the same earthy quality as grains. And they're an excellent, crunchy addition to most other foods. Just be aware that all seeds are not identical in nutrient profile.

Herb seeds, such as caraway, dill, anise, fennel, and coriander, pack big flavor in their small packages. Because their pronounced flavor goes a long way, you need very little in any given dish. And they add virtually no fat or calories to your diet.

Sesame and sunflower seeds, on the other hand, are much higher in fat and calories. But that's to be expected, since these seeds are often pressed to extract cooking oil. What's more, their mild flavors make it easy to consume them by the handful. Poppy seeds are similarly rich in oil. Use all these seeds as flavor accents.

Pumpkin and squash seeds fall somewhere in the middle. They're lower in fat and calories than the oily seeds but not low enough for absent-minded snacking. A few tablespoons per serving won't hurt an otherwise low-fat diet.

Here are some savory ways to use seeds.

Breads
- Combine caraway, dill, and poppy seeds. Knead into whole wheat or rye dough before letting it rise.
- Add cumin and pumpkin seeds to cornbread batter before baking.

Fish
- Toss fennel and mustard seeds into the liquid when poaching fish.
- When grilling whole fish, sprinkle the cavities with fennel and dill seeds.

Chicken
- Combine fenugreek, cumin, coriander, and fennel seeds. Pulverize and add to yogurt-based marinades.

Vegetables
- Toss cooked green beans with poppy and dill seeds.
- Sprinkle thick tomato slices with dill seeds. Broil until heated through.

- Toss cooked sweet potato chunks with toasted pumpkin seeds.

Dessert
- Add anise seeds to the liquid when poaching fruit.
- Add sesame seeds to pie crusts before baking.

COUSCOUS WITH CHICKEN AND VEGETABLES

Healing Foods

Beans (dried)
Carrots
Chicken
Pasta
Peppers (sweet)
Pumpkin
Turnip

CHICKEN
2$^1/_2$ pounds
  chicken thighs
1 large onion,
  coarsely chopped
1 tablespoon olive oil
2$^1/_2$ cups water
1 tomato, coarsely
  chopped
$^1/_4$ cup minced
  parsley

VEGETABLES
1 pound carrots, cut
  into 1-inch pieces
1 pound small
  turnips, quartered
2 cups cubed
  peeled pumpkin
2 cups water
2 green peppers, cut
  into 1-inch pieces

CHICKEN (cont'd)

$1/2$ teaspoon ground
  ginger
$1/2$ teaspoon ground
  cinnamon
$1/8$ teaspoon
  black pepper

VEGETABLES (cont'd)

2 cups cooked
  chick-peas

COUSCOUS

1 pound couscous

SAUCE

2 tablespoons
  lemon juice
$1/4$ teaspoon red
  pepper
$1/4$ teaspoon ground
  cumin
$1/4$ teaspoon paprika

To make the chicken: Remove and discard the skin and all visible fat from the chicken. Pat dry with paper towels.

In a 6-quart pot or Dutch oven over medium-high heat, brown the chicken and onions in the oil, turning frequently, for 5 to 10 minutes. Add the water, tomatoes, parsley, ginger, cinnamon, and pepper.

Bring to a boil, reduce the heat, cover, and cook for 30 minutes, or until the chicken is tender.

Remove the chicken from the pan, cover and keep warm. Keep the pan with the cooking liquid on the stove.

To make the vegetables: Add the carrots, turnips, pumpkin, and water to the pan. Bring to a boil, reduce the beat, and simmer for 10 minutes.

Add the peppers, chick-peas, and cooked chicken. Simmer for 5 minutes. Keep warm.

To make the couscous: Strain 2 cups of stock from the vegetables. In a 1-quart saucepan, bring the stock to a boil. Remove from heat and add the couscous. Cover and let stand for 5 minutes, or until all the liquid has been absorbed. Fluff with a fork. Transfer to a serving platter and keep warm.

To make the sauce: Strain 1 cup of stock from the vegetables. Place in the 1-quart saucepan. Add the lemon juice, red pepper, cumin, and paprika. Bring to a boil. Transfer to a small serving bowl.

Use a slotted spoon to place the vegetables and chicken atop the couscous. Moisten with some of the remaining vegetable liquid. Serve with the sauce.

Serves 6

CORN PASTA WITH AVOCADO SAUCE

Healing Foods

Avocados
Lemons and limes
Pasta

1 large avocado
1/4 cup lime juice
1 teaspoon minced garlic
1/2 teaspoon chili powder

1/4 teaspoon dried oregano
8 ounces corn-pasta ribbons

Peel and pit the avocado. Cut the flesh into chunks and place in a food processor or blender. Add the lime juice, garlic, chili powder, and oregano. Process until smooth.

Bring a large pot of water to a boil. Add the pasta and cook according to package directions until just tender. Drain and place in a large bowl. Toss with the avocado sauce.

Serves 4

SPINACH RISOTTO

Healing Foods

Onions
Spinach
Rice

5 cups stock
1 tablespoon olive oil
1 1/2 cups arborio
   or other short-
   grain rice
2 tablespoons grated
   Parmesan cheese

1/2 teaspoon
   curry powder
1 1/2 cups chopped
   spinach
1/2 cup minced
   scallions
2 leeks, chopped

In a 2-quart saucepan, bring the stock to a boil. Keep warm.

In a large nonstick frying pan over medium heat, heat the oil. Add the rice, leeks, and curry powder. Sauté for about 3 minutes.

Ladle in enough stock to just cover the rice. Simmer gently, stirring frequently, until the rice has absorbed all the stock.

Repeat, adding about 1 cup of stock at a time, until all the stock is used and the rice is tender. Do not rush the process; total cooking time should be about 25 minutes.

Stir in the spinach, scallions, and cheese. Combine well.

Serves 4

FUSILLI WITH FRESH TOMATO SAUCE

Healing Foods

Lemons and limes
Oil
Pasta
Tomatoes

5 tomatoes, peeled, seeded, and chopped

1/4 cup chopped fresh basil

1/4 cup lemon juice

2 shallots

2 tablespoons olive oil

8 ounces fusilli

2 tablespoons grated Sapsago or Parmesan cheese

In a food processor or blender, process the tomatoes, basil, lemon juice, shallots, and oil until a chunky paste forms. Set aside for about 2 hours to let the flavors blend.

Cook the fusilli according to package directions until just tender. Drain well and place in a large bowl. Add the cheese and tomato sauce.

Serves 4

MICRO METHOD: Pasta Encores

Does pasta belong in the microwave? Sometimes. Although you can cook dried pasta in a microwave, it's not terribly practical. You can prepare only small amounts, and it takes just as long as—if not longer than—on the stove. What you can do successfully is heat or reheat dishes containing already-cooked pasta.

The power level you should use depends on whether you can stir the food or not. Something like macaroni and cheese or spaghetti and sauce can be stirred during reheating, so you can use a higher power level. When you stir the food, you move the hot food from the edges of the container to the center and thereby evenly distribute the heat.

Foods that cannot be stirred, such as lasagna, benefit from a lower power level (from 50 percent to 70 percent). That prevents the outer edges from drying out before the center is sufficiently hot.

One way to tell if your pasta dish is heated through is to carefully feel the bottom of the plate or casserole. If the container is warm, the food probably is, too. But do be careful—dishes can become quite hot in a short period of time. Always use a pot holder to lift the dish and touch the bottom gingerly.

If making casseroles, remember that food continues to cook after it's removed from the microwave. You're better off undercooking your pasta dish and letting it stand a few minutes to finish itself off. If it needs additional time in the oven after that, you can easily return it to the micro-wave. But it's hard to salvage a dish that's been overcooked.

COMPONATA WITH RIGATONI

Healing Foods

Eggplant
Herbs and spices
Oil
Onions
Pasta
Peppers (sweet)
Squash (summer)
Tomatoes

3 tablespoons olive oil
2 cups thinly
  sliced onions
4 cloves garlic, minced
2 cups cubed
  eggplant
1¹/₂ cups chopped
  tomatoes
1¹/₂ cups thinly
  sliced zucchini
1 large sweet red
  pepper, thinly sliced
8 ounces rigatoni
¹/₃ cup grated
  Sapsago or
  Parmesan cheese

1 cup thinly sliced
  mushrooms
¹/₄ cup minced
  fresh parsley
1 teaspoon dried
  basil
¹/₂ teaspoon dried
  oregano
¹/₄ teaspoon
  dried sage
¹/₄ teaspoon
  dried thyme
¹/₄ teaspoon
  hot-pepper sauce

In a 6-quart pot over medium heat, heat the oil. Add the onions and cook until soft, stirring often, about 10 minutes.

Add the garlic. Cook for 1 minute.

Add the eggplant, tomatoes, zucchini, peppers, mushrooms, parsley, basil, oregano, sage, thyme, and hot-pepper sauce. Cover and cook over medium-low heat for about 10 minutes, or until the vegetables have released their natural juices.

Raise the heat to medium and cook, uncovered, for 15 to 20 minutes, or until the vegetables are soft.

In a large pot of boiling water, cook the rigatoni until tender. Drain and transfer to a large serving platter.

Top with the vegetables and sprinkle with the cheese.

Serves 4

MILLET-STUFFED APPLES

Healing Foods

Apples
Cottage cheese (low-fat)
Millet

1/2 cup millet
1 cup boiling water
4 large apples
1 1/4 cups low-fat
  cottage cheese

1/4 teaspoon ground
  cinnamon
1/8 teaspoon grated
  nutmeg
1/2 cup water

| 3 tablespoons chopped raisins | 1/4 cup apple juice |
| | 2 tablespoons shredded low-fat Muenster cheese |

In a 1-quart saucepan over medium heat, toast the millet by stirring with a wooden spoon for a few minutes. Add the boiling water, cover, and simmer for 20 minutes, or until all water has been absorbed. Set aside.

Cut approximately 1/2 inch from the top of each apple. Remove the cores. Hollow the apples with a spoon or melon scoop, leaving sturdy shells. Finely chop 1 cup of apple pulp and set aside. (Reserve the tops and remaining pulp for another use.)

In a food processor, puree the cottage cheese until smooth. Transfer to a medium bowl. Add the chopped apples, raisins, Muenster, cinnamon, and nutmeg. Stir in the millet.

Coat an 9 x 9-inch baking dish with nonstick spray. Divide the millet mixture among the apples. Spread any remaining mixture in the bottom of the dish. Top with the apples. Add the water and apple juice to the dish. Bake at 350°F for 30 to 35 minutes, or until the apples are soft.

Serves 4

APPLES AND OAT CEREAL

Healing Foods

Apples
Bran
Milk (low-fat)
Raisins

4 cups water
1^1/$_3$ cups oat bran
^{1}/$_2$ cup raisins
1 apple, shredded
1 tablespoon
  maple syrup

^{1}/$_2$ teaspoon ground
  caraway seeds
^{1}/$_2$ teaspoon
  ground cinnamon
1–2 cups skim milk

In a 2-quart saucepan, bring the water and oat bran to a vigorous boil, stirring constantly. Reduce the heat to low and cook for 2 minutes, stirring frequently, until thick.

Remove from the heat and stir in the raisins, apples, maple syrup, caraway, and cinnamon. Let stand 5 minutes. Spoon into bowls and serve with the milk.

Serves 4

SAVORY RICE PILAF

Healing Foods

Garlic
Onions
Rice

2 cups long-grain white rice	$1/2$ cup apple juice
1 tablespoon olive oil	1 large onion, diced
4 cups stock	2 cloves garlic, minced
$1/2$ teaspoon dried thyme	2 teaspoons lemon juice

In a 2-quart saucepan, combine the rice and oil. Stir over medium heat until the rice is golden brown, about 5 minutes.

Add the stock, apple juice, onion, garlic, lemon juice, and thyme. Bring to a boil. Reduce the heat to low, cover the pan, and simmer until all the liquid has been absorbed and the rice is tender, about 20 minutes.

Fluff with a fork before serving.

Serves 6

DO THEE, RIGATONI, TAKE THIS SAUCE . . .

Some pasta lovers will confess that their idea of "wedded bliss" is the joining of their favorite pasta with the perfect sauce. For some, fettuccine and white clam sauce is the consummate match. Others grow delirious over vermicelli and seafood. The tradition-minded never get tired of spaghetti and tomato sauce. With 600 different shapes and sizes of pasta and endless possibilities for sauce, you could eat pasta every day for a year and not repeat the same combination.

Here are a few matchmaking guidelines.

• Light creamy or oil-based sauces go well with

long, thin pasta like vermicelli—they keep the strands separate and slippery, so they don't clump together.
- Chunky sauces containing meat, vegetables, or seafood go nicely with medium-size shaped pasta—shells, tubes, or grooved pasta, like penne and rigatoni. The openings and ridges in the pasta trap bits of sauce and fill in those tubes and grooves.
- Thick, smooth sauces cling best on flat ribbon noodles, like fettuccine.

For more specific applications, follow these suggestions:
- *Baked casseroles.* The best shapes for baked casseroles are elbow macaroni, egg noodles, ziti, rigatoni, large shells, manicotti, cannelloni, and, of course, lasagna. Their thick walls stand up to baking without falling apart.
- *Salads.* Pasta shapes appropriate for salads include elbows, rotini (spirals), ditalini, ziti, cut fusilli, radiatore, shells, and farfalle (bow ties). Their nooks and crannies provide plenty of places to collect dressing and seasonings.
- *Soups.* Tiny, delicate pastas—like pastina, tubetti, orzo, and alphabets—and fine egg noodles are best for clear soups, like chicken broth. Slightly larger and sturdier shapes—like small shells or elbows, ditalini, and radiatare, along with broken vermicelli or capellini—are best for more robust, hearty soups, like minestrone, where they can hold their own against beans, potatoes, vegetables, or other ingredients.

331

COUSCOUS WITH SWEET CORN

Healing Foods

Corn
Garlic
Pasta

1$^1/_2$ cups chicken
stock
1 cup couscous
1$^1/_2$ cups corn
1 cup chopped
Italian tomatoes
1 tablespoon
lemon juice

2 cloves garlic, minced
1 teaspoon
chili powder
$^1/_4$ teaspoon
ground cinnamon
2 tablespoons
snipped chives

In a 2-quart saucepan, bring the stock to a boil. Add the couscous. Cover the pan, remove it from the heat, and let stand for about 5 minutes, or until all the liquid has been absorbed. Fluff with a fork.

In a large nonstick frying pan over medium heat, combine the corn, tomatoes, garlic, chili powder, and cinnamon. Cook until the liquid from the tomatoes evaporates, about 5 minutes. Stir in the chives and lemon juice.

Add the couscous and stir to combine.

Serves 4

BARLEY PILAF WITH GRILLED APPLES

Healing Foods

Apples
Barley

PILAF

1 cup barley
2 teaspoons
  canola oil
1 teaspoon vanilla
  extract
$1/8$ teaspoon
  ground cinnamon
$1/8$ teaspoon
  grated nutmeg
$1/8$ teaspoon
  ground cardamom
$1^1/2$ cups apple juice
$1^1/2$ cups water

APPLES

2 baking apples
2 tablespoons
  apple juice
$1/4$ teaspoon
  ground cinnamon

To make the pilaf: In a 2-quart saucepan, combine the barley, oil, vanilla, cinnamon, nutmeg, and cardamom. Sauté until fragrant, about 2 minutes.

Add the apple juice and water. Bring to a boil, reduce the heat, cover, and simmer for 45 to 60 minutes, or until the barley is tender and all the liquid has been absorbed.

To make the apples: Core the apples and cut crosswise into thin rounds. Place on a baking sheet. Sprinkle with 1 tablespoon apple juice and

$1/_8$ teaspoon cinnamon. Broil about 4 inches from the heat for about 3 minutes.

Flip the slices and sprinkle with the remaining juice and cinnamon. Grill for 2 minutes. Serve hot with the pilaf.

Serves 6

APRICOT-QUINOA CEREAL

Healing Foods

Apricots
Millet
Quinoa

$1^1/_2$ cups water
1 cup apricot nectar
1 cup chopped
   dried apricots
$1/_2$ cup millet
$1/_4$ cup low-fat
   cottage cheese

$1/_2$ teaspoon
   ground cinnamon
$1/_4$ teaspoon
   ground mace
$1/_2$ cup quinoa
2 tablespoons
   maple syrup

In a 2-quart saucepan, bring the water, apricot nectar, apricots, cinnamon, and mace to a boil.

Rinse the quinoa according to the package instructions. Add the quinoa and millet to the saucepan. Reduce the heat to a simmer. Partially cover the pan and cook until the liquid is absorbed and the grains are tender, 15 to 20 minutes.

Press the cottage cheese through a sieve into a small bowl. Stir in the maple syrup. Stir the mixture into the cereal. Serve warm.

Serves 4

TARRAGON CHICKEN
WITH LINGUINE

Healing Foods

Carrots
Chicken
Onions
Pasta

1 pound boneless,
  skinless chicken
  breasts
6 ounces linguine
$1/4$ cup minced
  fresh parsley

1 cup stock
8 mushrooms, sliced
2 carrots, julienned
1 large onion,
  thinly sliced
$1/2$ teaspoon
  dried tarragon

Cut the chicken into strips 3 inches long by $1/2$ inch wide. Set aside.

Bring a large pot of water to a boil. Add the linguine and cook according to package directions until just tender. Drain and set aside.

In a large frying pan over medium heat, bring the stock to a simmer. Add the chicken and cook for 7 minutes, stirring frequently.

Add the mushrooms, carrots, onions, parsley, and tarragon. Cook until the chicken is tender, about 5 minutes.

Add the linguine to the pan. Toss to combine. Heat until the linguine is hot.

Serves 4

CHILI CON KASHA

Healing Foods

Beef (lean)
Buckwheat
Onions
Peppers (sweet)
Tomatoes

8 ounces extra-lean ground beef
1 large onion, minced
1 green pepper, diced
1 clove garlic, minced
1 tablespoon chili powder

1 cup roasted buckwheat groats (kasha)
1 can (28 ounces) stewed tomatoes
1 cup tomato sauce
1 cup nonfat yogurt
1/2 cup chopped scallions

In a large nonstick frying pan over medium-low heat, brown the beef, stirring frequently. Drain off any accumulated fat and pat the beef with a paper towel to absorb any remaining fat.

Add the onions, peppers, and garlic. Sauté until the onions are limp, about 5 minutes.

Add the buckwheat, tomatoes, tomato sauce, and chili powder. Cover and cook 20 minutes, or until the buckwheat is tender. Serve topped with the yogurt and scallions.

Serves 4

PASTA PORTION GUIDE

Just how much pasta do you need to cook for tonight's spaghetti dinner or macaroni casserole? The general rule is that 2 ounces of dry pasta equal one serving. But unless you have a kitchen scale, it can be difficult to gauge just how much 2 ounces of a particular variety is without cooking the whole box, measuring the yield and doing some long division.

So we did some of the weighing, measuring, and cooking for you to come up with portion guidelines for a handful of different pastas. This chart shows how much of each variety to measure out before cooking to serve two or four people. In most instances, 2 ounces of dry pasta turned into 1 cup cooked.

Pasta	For 2	For 4
Bow ties	2 cups	4 cups
Corn ribbons	3 cups	6 cups
Egg noodles	3 cups	6 cups
Elbow macaroni	1 cup	2 cups
Manicotti tubes	4	8
Rigatoni	2 cups	4 cups
Shells, jumbo	8	16
Shells, medium	2 cups	4 cups
Spaghetti	1-inch bunch	$1^1/_2$-inch bunch
Spirals	$1^1/_2$ cups	3 cups
Ziti	$1^1/_2$ cups	3 cups

Accent on Health: Sauce Sorcery

There are just two things you *never* want to do to pasta. The first is to overcook it. The second is to undermine its healing potential with a fat-heavy sauce. The wrong sauce can turn a respectable 200-calorie plate of pasta into a 700-calorie diet disaster with more fat than you should eat in an entire day.

When making homemade sauce, especially cream versions, keep these tips in mind.

- Replace heavy cream with a white sauce made of low-fat or skim milk thickened with flour.
- Enrich white sauces with a little egg substitute instead of egg yolk. You'll get the same golden color and velvety texture without all the yolk's cholesterol.
- Cut back on saturated fat and cholesterol by using olive oil, canola oil, or margarine in place of butter. But remember that these fats are not lower in calories than butter, so use them judiciously.
- If making meat sauce, brown the meat first in a separate frying pan. Drain it on paper towels, and then pat it dry with more towels to draw off as much fat as possible.
- Use the lowest-fat cheeses you can find, and even then be a little stingy with them.
- Puree cooked vegetables, such as peppers, onions, or cauliflower as low-cal thickeners for thin sauces.
- Get creamy body from well-blended low-fat or dry-curd cottage cheese. But be careful not to

338

overheat a cottage-cheese sauce or it might curdle. Just barely warm it on the stove. Then mix with hot cooked pasta to heat it further.

- Add just enough sauce to your pasta to lightly coat it, not to smother it.

Mushroom-Cheese Sauce

1 cup low-fat cottage cheese	4 ounces mushrooms, thinly sliced
1/3 cup chicken stock	1 tablespoon olive oil
1 teaspoon Worcestershire sauce	1 clove garlic, minced
	1 onion, minced

In a blender or food processor blend the cottage cheese, stock, and Worcestershire until smooth. Set aside.

In a large nonstick frying pan over medium heat, sauté the onions and mushrooms in the oil until soft. Add the garlic and stir for 1 minute. Remove the pan from the heat. Stir in the cheese mixture. Warm over medium-low heat.

Makes 2 cups

Healing Foods

- Cottage cheese (low-fat)
- Mushrooms   • Onions

Spicy Aurora Sauce

1 onion, chopped	2 cloves garlic, chopped
1 sweet red pepper, chopped	1 teaspoon dried oregano

1 tablespoon canola oil

4 cups chopped tomatoes

1 jalapeño pepper, seeded and minced

1 cup dry-curd cottage cheese

3 tablespoons grated Sapsago or Parmesan cheese

In a large nonstick frying pan over medium heat, sauté the onions and red peppers in the oil for 5 minutes, or until soft. Add the tomatoes, jalapeño peppers, garlic, and oregano.

Cover and cook for 5 minutes, or until the tomatoes are soft and juicy. Remove the cover and cook, stirring occasionally, for 15 minutes.

Transfer to a food processor. Add the cottage cheese and puree for 2 minutes, or until the mixture is pink and no longer looks curdled.

Return the mixture to the frying pan, add the Sapsago or Parmesan and reheat briefly. Serve immediately. (To reheat leftovers, use either very low heat or a double boiler.)

Makes 3 cups

Healing Foods

- Cottage cheese (low-fat) • Peppers (sweet)
- Tomatoes

Herbed Pepper Sauce

2 large sweet red peppers, chopped

1 large onion, chopped

1 tablespoon olive oil

1 clove garlic, minced

1 cup chicken stock

1 teaspoon dried oregano

$1/2$ teaspoon dried basil

$1/2$ teaspoon dried savory

In a large nonstick frying pan over medium heat, cook the peppers and onions in the oil for about 10 minutes, or until soft and lightly browned. Add the garlic and stir for 1 minute.

Add the stock, oregano, basil, and savory. Cover and simmer for 10 minutes. Using a slotted spoon, transfer the vegetables to a blender or food processor. Add enough liquid to facilitate blending. Puree to desired consistency.

Makes $2^1/2$ cups

Healing Foods

- Onions
- Peppers (sweet)

Green-Pepper Pesto

2 green peppers, chopped
1 cup fresh basil
$1/2$ cup pumpkin seeds

$1/4$ cup grated Parmesan cheese
$1/4$ cup olive oil
4 cloves garlic, minced

Blanch the peppers in boiling water for 5 minutes. Drain and transfer to a food processor.

Add the basil, pumpkin seeds, cheese, oil, and garlic. Process until smooth.

Makes about $1^1/4$ cups

Healing Foods

- Garlic
- Oil
- Peppers (sweet)
- Seeds

341

SPAGHETTI WITH GUACAMOLE

Healing Foods

Avocados
Oil
Pasta

1 large very ripe
avocado
1 onion, minced
2 teaspoons
lemon juice
1 tomato, chopped

$^1/_4$ teaspoon hot-
pepper sauce
8 ounces spaghetti
1 tablespoon
olive oil

Peel and pit the avocado. Mash with a fork and place in a small bowl. Stir in the onions, lemon juice, and hot-pepper sauce.

In a large pot of boiling water, cook the spaghetti until just tender. Drain and transfer to a warm serving bowl. Toss with the oil. Spoon the avocado mixture and tomatoes on top.

Serves 4

ASPARAGUS AND BULGUR

Healing Foods

Asparagus
Bulgur

1/2 cup water
1/3 cup bulgur
1/3 cup thinly
  sliced pimientos
1/4 cup vinegar
12 stalks asparagus,
  trimmed

2 tablespoons olive oil
1 tablespoon
  snipped chives
1 teaspoon
  dried thyme

In a l-quart saucepan, bring the water to a boil. Add the bulgur. Cover and let stand for 15 minutes, or until the liquid has been absorbed. Fluff with a fork.

In a large bowl, combine the pimientos, vinegar, oil, chives, and thyme. Add the bulgur.

Blanch the asparagus in boiling water for 4 minutes. Slice diagonally into 2-inch sections. Add to the bulgur mixture. Combine well.

Serves 4

CHAPTER EIGHT

Beans and Legumes

Want a first-class ticket to heart health? Make friends with the lowly legumes. Dried beans are such an important healing food they deserve a chapter of their own. When fiber researcher James W. Anderson, M.D., conducted his landmark cholesterol studies at the University of Kentucky, his subjects consumed the amount of fiber in *1¹/2 cups* of beans every day. Cholesterol levels averaging a dangerously high 294 fell by 76 points in six months.

If you're among the lucky few not worried about cholesterol, beans still have your number. They're rich in iron, B vitamins, and calcium, and they're amazingly low in fat and sodium. With constipation-preventing fiber and no cholesterol, beans offer something for everybody.

There are literally dozens of types to choose from, so you can have infinite variety when planning meals. The recipes in this chapter take advantage of that bounty, with dishes ranging from Lentil Tacos and New Orleans Red Beans to White-Bean Gumbo and Moroccan Chicken with Chick-Peas. For those who love to nibble, we have a tasty selection of lean bean dips to pair with raw vegetables.

Considering beans' sterling credentials, it's not

hard to understand why they're a mainstay of almost every cuisine on the globe. You can give an international flavor to your menus with Nachos (from Mexico), Falafel Pockets (from the Middle East), and Caribbean Bean Casserole (from the West Indies), among others. With such a wide variety of beans and bean recipes to choose from, you'll have no trouble eating the 3 to 5 cups of beans a week often recommended for optimum health.

WHITE-BEAN GUMBO

Healing Foods

Beans (dried)
Garlic
Onions
Peppers (sweet)
Rice
Tomatoes

$^1/_3$ cup whole wheat flour
$3^2/_3$ cups stock
1 green pepper, finely chopped
1 stalk celery, finely chopped
1 teaspoon dried thyme
2 cups cooked pea beans
1 large onion, finely chopped
2 cups chopped tomatoes
3 cloves garlic, minced
2 bay leaves
$^1/_2$ teaspoon hot-pepper sauce
2 cups hot cooked rice

lace the flour in a nonstick frying pan. Cook over medium-high heat, stirring constantly, until the flour is medium brown in color, about 7 minutes. Remove the pan from the heat, and pour in $2/3$ cup of the stock. Whisk until smooth.

In a 3-quart saucepan, bring the remaining stock to a boil. Whisk the flour mixture into the stock. Add the peppers, celery, onions, tomatoes, garlic, bay leaves, and thyme.

Bring to a boil, then reduce the heat to a simmer. Cover the pan loosely. Simmer the gumbo, stirring occasionally, for 15 minutes. Add the drained beans and hot-pepper sauce.

Simmer until the vegetables are tender, about 15 minutes. Discard the bay leaves.

Serve over the rice.

Serves 4 to 6

HERBED BEAN SALAD

Healing Foods

Beans (snap)
Soybeans
Tomatoes

1 cup fresh (green) soybeans	2 tablespoons lime juice
1 cup fresh cranberry beans	2 tablespoons minced fresh mint
1 clove garlic, minced	1 large tomato, cut into 4 thick slices

Cook the soybeans and cranberry beans in boiling water to cover for 5 minutes. Drain and place in a large bowl.

Add the lime juice, mint, and garlic. Chill.

Divide the tomatoes among individual salad plates. Top with the beans.

Serves 4

MEXICAN BEAN PIE

Healing Foods

Beans (dried)
Peppers (sweet)
Tomatoes

4 corn tortillas
$1/2$ cup sliced scallions
2 green peppers, diced
2 cloves garlic, minced
1 tablespoon olive oil
$1/4$ cup shredded low-fat Monterey Jack cheese

2 cups cooked pinto beans, mashed
2 tomatoes, chopped
2 teaspoons chili powder
1 teaspoon ground coriander
$3/4$ cup egg substitute

Heat the tortillas at 350°F for 5 to 8 minutes, or until crispy. Break into pieces, then pulverize in a blender.

Coat four 5-inch pie pans with nonstick spray. Coat with the tortilla crumbs. Reserve any extra.

In a large nonstick frying pan, sauté the scallions, peppers, and garlic in the oil until tender, about 5 minutes.

Add the beans, tomatoes, chili powder, and coriander. Sauté for 5 minutes.

Remove from the heat and stir in the egg substitute. Divide among the prepared pans. Sprinkle with reserved crumbs.

Bake at 375°F for 20 minutes.

Top with the cheese.

Serves 4

BLACK BEANS AND RICE

Healing Foods

Beans (dried)
Garlic
Onions
Peppers (sweet)
Rice

1 tablespoon olive oil

2 sweet red peppers, finely chopped

1 large onion, finely chopped

1 stalk celery, finely chopped

2 cups hot cooked rice

2 cloves garlic, minced

$1/4$ teaspoon dried thyme

2 cups cooked black beans

2 tablespoons apple-cider vinegar

1 cup nonfat yogurt

Heat the oil in a large nonstick frying pan. Add the peppers, onions, celery, garlic, and thyme. Sauté over medium heat until the vegetables are fragrant and tender, about 10 minutes.

Add the beans and vinegar. Cook until the beans are hot, about 3 minutes.

To serve, divide the rice among shallow bowls. Top with the beans and yogurt.

Serves 4

LENTIL LOAF

Healing Foods

Beans (dried)
Onions

2 tablespoons
chopped walnuts
1 large onion,
finely chopped
2 tablespoons minced
green pepper
2 teaspoons canola oil
2 cups cooked lentils
$1/2$ cup stock
2 teaspoons red-
wine vinegar

$1/2$ cup whole wheat
bread crumbs
2 tablespoons flour
$1/2$ teaspoon
dried sage
$1/2$ teaspoon
dried thyme
$1/4$ cup egg substitute
1 egg white
2 teaspoons
Worcestershire sauce

In a large nonstick frying pan over medium heat, toast the walnuts until lightly browned and aromatic, stirring constantly. Remove and set aside.

In the same pan, sauté the onions and peppers in the oil until the onions are just beginning to brown, about 5 minutes. Remove from the heat and stir in the lentils, bread crumbs, flour, sage, thyme, and walnuts.

In a small bowl, beat together the egg substitute and egg white. Whisk in the stock, vinegar, and Worcestershire sauce. Add to the lentil mixture.

Coat an $8^1/_2$ x $4^1/_2$-inch loaf pan with non-stick spray. Add the lentil mixture. Bake at 350°F for 40 to 45 minutes, or until a knife inserted in the center comes out clean.

Serves 4 to 6

MICRO METHOD: No More All-Nighters

Here's an easy way to soak beans that doesn't take all night. Rinse 1 pound of dried beans. Place in a 5-quart micro-safe casserole with 6 or 7 cups of cold water. Microwave on full power for 8 to 10 minutes, or until the water boils. Boil for 2 minutes. Let the beans stand for 1 hour before proceeding with your recipe.

Because dried beans must slowly absorb water to become tender, they won't cook any more quickly in the microwave than atop the stove.

One thing to keep in mind when buying dried beans and other legumes, such as lentils: Look for bright colors and uniform size. Dullness indicates long storage, which will markedly prolong cooking time no matter what method you use. And beans of different sizes won't cook at the same speed, leaving you with some that are either overcooked or still tough.

BREAD STUFFED WITH LENTILS

Healing Foods

Beans (dried)
Carrots
Cheese (low-fat)
Parsley

1 (9-inch round) crusty loaf of whole-grain bread
2 cups apple cider
1 cup dried lentils
2 carrots, finely chopped
1 bay leaf
2 stalks celery, finely chopped
1/4 cup egg substitute
1 large onion, finely chopped
1 green pepper, finely chopped
2 cloves garlic, minced
1 tablespoon olive oil
1/2 cup shredded low-fat Cheddar cheese
1/2 cup minced fresh parsley
1 teaspoon dried thyme

Using a serrated knife, horizontally cut the top quarter from the bread. Wrap the top in foil and set aside.

Scoop out the soft interior of the bread, leaving a 3/4-inch to 1-inch shell. Do not puncture the sides or bottom of the loaf. Reserve the removed crumbs for another use. Set aside the hollow loaf.

In a 3-quart saucepan, combine the cider, lentils, carrots, and bay leaf. Bring to a boil. Reduce the heat and simmer, partially covered, for 35 to 40 minutes, or until the lentils are tender and all the liquid has been absorbed. Stir occasionally to prevent sticking. Discard the bay leaf.

In a large nonstick frying pan, sauté the celery, onions, peppers and garlic in the oil until softened, about 5 minutes. Add to the lentil mixture. Stir in the cheese, parsley, egg substitute, and thyme.

Spoon the lentils into the hollow loaf. Wrap the loaf in foil and place on a baking sheet. Bake at 350°F for 1 hour. Add the foil-wrapped top to the oven and bake another 5 minutes.

Unwrap the filled loaf and place it on a large serving platter. Unwrap the top and put it in place. To serve, scoop out the lentil mixture. Then cut the bread with a serrated knife and serve with the lentils.

Serves 6 to 8

NEW ORLEANS RED BEANS

Healing Foods

Beans (dried)
Garlic
Onions
Peppers (chili)
Peppers (sweet)
Rice

1 pound dried red
  beans, soaked
  overnight
6 cups water
1 large onion, chopped

1 small hot chili
  pepper, seeded
  and minced
1/2 teaspoon crushed
  red-pepper flakes

1 green pepper,
  chopped
1/4 cup minced
  fresh parsley
4 garlic cloves,
  minced
2 bay leaves

1/8 teaspoon ground
  red pepper
1 teaspoon
  dried thyme
1 teaspoon dried basil
3 cups hot cooked
  rice

Drain the beans. In a 4-quart pot, combine the beans, water, onions, green peppers, parsley, garlic, chili peppers, pepper flakes, ground pepper, bay leaves, thyme, and basil.

Cover and bring to boil over medium heat. Reduce the heat to low and cook for 3 to 4 hours, or until the beans are tender. Stir occasionally as the beans cook. Most of the water will be absorbed; if necessary, add a little more water during cooking to keep the mixture from sticking. Discard the bay leaves.

Serve over the rice.

Serves 6

FALAFEL POCKETS

Healing Foods

Beans (dried)
Garlic
Oil
Sprouts
Whole wheat flour
Yogurt (low-fat)

1/2 cup chick-peas, soaked overnight

4 cups water

2/3 cup stock

1/3 cup uncooked bulgur

3 cloves garlic, minced

1/8 teaspoon ground cinnamon

1/8 teaspoon red pepper

2 tablespoons whole wheat flour

1 cup diced tomatoes

1 cup nonfat yogurt

2 cups whole wheat bread crumbs

2 tablespoons minced fresh coriander

2 tablespoons tahini (sesame-seed paste)

1 tablespoon lemon juice

1 teaspoon ground cumin

1/4 cup egg substitute

1 tablespoon water

3 tablespoons olive oil

6 pitas, split and warmed

4 ounces alfalfa sprouts

Drain the chick-peas. Place in a 2-quart saucepan with the water. Bring to a boil, cover, and cook over medium heat for $1^{1}/_{2}$ to 2 hours, or until very tender. Drain. Puree with a food mill or food processor. Transfer to a large bowl.

In a 1-quart saucepan, bring $^{1}/_{3}$ cup of the stock to a boil. Add the bulgur, garlic, cinnamon, and red pepper. Cover, remove from the heat and let stand for 20 minutes, or until the liquid has been absorbed. Fluff with a fork. Add to the chick-peas.

In the same saucepan, whisk together the flour and the remaining $^{1}/_{3}$ cup stock. Cook, whisking constantly, until the sauce comes to a boil and becomes very thick. Add to the bowl with the chick-peas.

Add $^{1}/_{2}$ cup of the bread crumbs, the coriander, tahini, lemon juice, and cumin. Mix well. Cover and refrigerate 1 hour, or until cold and thick.

Form the mixture into 12 patties about $1/2$ inch thick.

In a shallow bowl, lightly beat the egg substitute and water with a fork. Dip the patties into the mixture and then into the remaining bread crumbs to coat completely.

In a large nonstick frying pan, sauté the patties in the oil until golden on both sides.

Serve in the pita pockets topped with the tomatoes, yogurt, and sprouts.

Serves 4

TASTE EXTENDERS

Add zest and flavor to dried beans while they cook by making some simple additions or substitutions for plain water when simmering.

- Cook beans with chicken, beef, or vegetable stock.
- If adding the beans to fish soups, cook them in a mixture of half water and half clam juice.
- Add onion, garlic, and finely grated lemon rind to the cooking water for extra flavor.
- Don't add lemon juice, tomato juice, or other acidic ingredients to the cooking liquid until the beans are tender. Acids tend to toughen beans as they cook.
- Season beans with herbs and spices. If using fresh herbs, add them near the end of the

cooking period so their delicate flavors aren't lost. The following flavor groups work especially well: garlic, ginger, and low-sodium soy sauce; rosemary and finely grated orange rind; cumin seeds, chili powder, and oregano; caraway seeds, paprika, and dry mustard.

- Add crunch to cooked beans with raw vegetables, toasted seeds, diced fresh fruit, or chopped nuts.
- Marinate cooked beans in a mixture of herb vinegar and a splash of olive oil. Toss into vegetable or green salads.

CHICK-PEA CHILI

Healing Foods

Beans (dried)
Onions
Peppers (sweet)
Rice
Salad greens
Tomatoes
Yogurt (low-fat)

1 large onion, minced
2 cloves garlic, minced
1 tablespoon olive oil
2 cups cooked chick-peas
1 1/2 cups tomato sauce
1 teaspoon ground cumin
1/2 teaspoon dried oregano
1/8 teaspoon red pepper
2 cups hot cooked rice

1 tablespoon
  chili powder
1 cup nonfat yogurt
1 cup diced tomatoes

1 cup diced
  green peppers
1 cup shredded
  lettuce

In a 2-quart saucepan over medium heat, cook the onions and garlic in the oil until translucent. Stir in the chick-peas, tomato sauce, chili powder, cumin, oregano, and red pepper. Simmer, uncovered, about 30 minutes.

Serve over the rice topped with the yogurt, peppers, tomatoes, and lettuce.

Serves 4

GREAT NORTHERN SOUP

Healing Foods

Beans (dried)
Carrots
Herbs and spices
Peppers (sweet)

1 cup dried Great
  Northern beans,
  soaked overnight
1 large onion,
  chopped
1 green pepper,
  chopped
1 stalk celery,
  chopped
2 tablespoons
  lemon juice

1 carrot, chopped
2 cloves garlic,
  chopped
1 tablespoon canola oil
2 cups chicken stock
$1/2$ cup orange juice
1 teaspoon low-
  sodium soy sauce
$1/4$ teaspoon
  ground cumin
$1/4$ cup snipped chives

Drain the beans. Place in a 4-quart saucepan with water to cover. Cover the pan and simmer until the beans are almost tender, about $1^1/_2$ hours. Drain and transfer to a bowl.

In the same pan, sauté the onions, peppers, celery, carrots, and garlic in the oil until tender.

Add the beans, stock, orange juice, soy sauce, and cumin. Cover and simmer until the beans are tender, about 45 to 60 minutes. Remove from the heat and cool slightly.

Working in batches, puree the soup in a blender or food processor. Return it to the pan. Add the lemon juice and heat briefly. Serve sprinkled with the chives.

Serves 4 to 6

MUSHROOM AND LENTIL SOUP

Healing Foods

Beans (dried)
Carrots
Mushrooms
Onions

1 large onion, chopped	1 carrot, diced
1 tablespoon olive oil	$^1/_2$ cup dried lentils
5 cups stock	1 teaspoon dried rosemary
8 ounces mushrooms, sliced	1 bay leaf

In a 3-quart saucepan over medium heat, sauté

the onions in the oil until lightly browned, about 12 to 15 minutes.

Add the stock, mushrooms, carrots, lentils, rosemary, and bay leaf. Bring to a boil. Reduce the heat, cover loosely, and let simmer until the lentils are tender, about 30 minutes.

Discard the bay leaf.

Serves 6

MOROCCAN CHICKEN WITH CHICK-PEAS

Healing Foods

Beans (dried)
Bulgur
Chicken
Garlic
Nuts
Onions

$1^1/_2$ cup chick-peas, soaked overnight

4 cups water

1 cup finely chopped onions

2 tablespoons olive oil

$^1/_2$ cup almonds

3 cloves garlic, minced

$2^1/_2$ cups stock

3 tablespoons lemon juice

$^1/_2$ teaspoon ground cinnamon

$^1/_2$ teaspoon ground ginger

$^1/_8$ teaspoon turmeric

$^1/_8$ teaspoon saffron

1 cup thinly sliced onions

1 chicken (3 pounds)

$^1/_2$ teaspoon paprika

$1^1/_2$ cups uncooked bulgur

Drain the chick-peas. Place in a 2-quart saucepan with the water. Cover and cook over medium heat for 1 hour. Drain.

In a large nonstick frying pan, sauté the chopped onions in the oil until wilted, about 5 minutes. Add the almonds and garlic. Sauté for 3 minutes. Do not let the garlic brown.

Stir in the cinnamon, ginger, turmeric, and saffron.

Coat a 5-quart casserole dish with nonstick spray. Add the onion mixture. Top with the chick-peas and cover with the sliced onions.

Add 1 cup of stock and the lemon juice. Bring to a simmer on top of the stove.

Remove the skin and all visible fat from the chicken, especially the neck and cavity areas. Split the chicken in half along the breast and backbone. Lay the pieces over the onions, skin side up. Sprinkle with the paprika.

Cover and bake at 350°F for 1 to $1^1/_2$ hours or until the chicken is tender.

In a 1-quart saucepan, bring the remaining $1^1/_2$ cups stock to a boil. Add the bulgur, cover, remove from the heat, and let stand for 20 to 30 minutes, or until soft.

Fluff the bulgur with a fork and transfer to a large serving platter.

Using a slotted spoon, cover the bulgur with the chick-pea and almond mixture, adding enough liquid to moisten the bulgur. Lay the chicken over the top.

Serves 4

FAVA BEANS: A HEALTH TREAT FROM THE MEDITERRANEAN

The fava bean is a native of the Mediterranean that's been enjoyed in Europe and the Middle East for ages. In fact, its ancestry is said to go all the way back to the Bronze Age. With a meaty texture that's earned it the name *il carne del povero* (the meat of the poor), it deserves a more prominent place on American tables.

Favas pleasantly blend the taste of lima beans and peas, and they contain comparable amounts of iron, potassium, and protein. Like other beans, they're low in fat and high in complex carbohydrates.

Also known as broad beans, favas grow in curved pods with thick, bulging seeds that resemble round limas. They're sometimes picked immature and eaten in the pod like snow peas. Young beans are excellent simmered, steamed, or stir-fried. When buying fresh favas, select plump pods that are free of decay or shriveling. Use within a few days.

Older beans have a skin that needs to be removed and are good for stewing. The best way to skin the fresh beans is to boil them for 10 minutes and then chill them for a few hours. That helps you slip off the skin more easily. Favas are also sold dried. Soak and cook them like other beans.

During summer in Italy, mature young fava beans are traditionally served at the end of a meal as a replacement for dessert. The beans are shelled by each person at the table and eaten out of hand. In the Middle East, the cooked dried beans are mashed into a paste, laced with lemon juice and garlic, and eaten with pita bread.

SAVORY LIMA BEANS

Healing Foods

Beans (snap)
Oil
Onions
Tomatoes

3 cups lima beans
1 cup minced
   red onions
1 cup halved
   cherry tomatoes
$1/2$ teaspoon dried
   savory

$1/4$ cup apple-cider
   vinegar
2 tablespoons olive oil
1 clove garlic, minced
1 teaspoon Dijon
   mustard
$1/4$ teaspoon
   black pepper

Blanch the lima beans in boiling water for 5 minutes. Drain and transfer to a large bowl. Add the onions and tomatoes. Toss to combine.

In a cup, whisk together the vinegar, oil, garlic, mustard, savory, and pepper.

Pour over the vegetables and toss to combine. Allow to marinate for 30 minutes.

Serves 6

FAVAS WITH TINY PASTA

Healing Foods

Beans (dried)
Carrots
Herbs and spices
Oil
Pasta

3 carrots, thinly sliced
2 cups cooked
    fava beans
1 cup cooked acini
    di pepe or other
    tiny pasta

$1/4$ cup snipped chives
3 tablespoons
    red-wine vinegar
2 tablespoons olive oil
1 teaspoon dried basil
$1/2$ teaspoon dry
    mustard

Blanch the carrots in boiling water for 3 minutes. Drain and place in a large bowl. Add the drained favas, pasta, and chives.

In a cup, whisk together the vinegar, oil, basil, and mustard. Pour over the salad. Toss well to combine.

Allow to marinate at least 2 hours before serving. Serve at room temperature.

Serves 4

NACHOS

Healing Foods

Beans (dried)
Cheese (low-fat)
Peppers (sweet)

12 corn tortillas
1 1/2 cups cooked
   pinto beans
1/2 cup shredded
   low-fat Monterey
   Jack cheese

1 cup salsa
1 cup minced
   sweet red peppers

Cut the tortillas into quarters. Place the pieces on a baking sheet and bake at 400°F until crisp but not brown, about 5 minutes. Let cool for a few minutes. Coarsely mash the beans. Spread the beans on the tortillas and return the wedges to the baking sheet. Dot with the salsa. Sprinkle with the peppers and cheese.

Bake until the cheese has melted, about 3 minutes. Serve warm.

Serves 4

Variation:
Before the second baking, sprinkle the tortillas with minced jalapeño peppers, minced sweet red peppers, or minced black olives.

GOOD-LUCK PEAS

Healing Foods

Beans (dried)
Carrots
Kale
Oil
Onions

2 cups cooked
  black-eyed peas
2 cups shredded
  carrots
1 cup shredded kale
1 cup minced leeks
$1/2$ teaspoon dried
  sage

2 tablespoons
  lemon juice
2 tablespoons
  red-wine vinegar
2 tablespoons olive oil
1 teaspoon dried basil
$1/4$ teaspoon dry
  mustard

In a large bowl, combine the peas, carrots, kale, and leeks.

In a small bowl, whisk together the lemon juice, vinegar, oil, basil, sage, and mustard. Pour over the peas and toss to combine.

Serves 4

VEGETABLE CHILI

Healing Foods

Beans (dried)
Carrots
Garlic
Onions
Tomatoes

2 tablespoons olive oil
2 cups finely
  chopped onions
2 cups diced celery
2 cups diced carrots
1 sweet red
  pepper, diced
4 cloves garlic,
  minced
1 1/2 cups stock

2 tablespoons whole
  wheat flour
1 tablespoon
  chili powder
4 cups crushed
  tomatoes
1 cup dried adzuki
  beans, soaked over-
  night

In a 4-quart pot, heat the oil. Add the onions, celery, carrots, peppers, garlic. Sauté for 5 to 10 minutes, or until tender. Stir in the flour and chili powder.

Add the tomatoes, stock, and drained beans.

Cover and simmer for 30 minutes. Remove the lid and simmer 30 minutes, or until the vegetables and beans are tender and the liquid has thickened.

Serves 4 to 6

CASPIAN SPLIT PEAS

Healing Foods

Barley
Beans (dried)
Cabbage
Carrots
Garlic
Tomatoes

4 cups stock
2 large tomatoes, diced
2 carrots, thinly sliced
2 cloves garlic, minced

1 cup shredded cabbage
$1/2$ cup green split peas
$1/2$ cup barley
$1/4$ cup minced fresh parsley

In a 4-quart pot, combine the stock, tomatoes, carrots, cabbage, split peas, barley, and garlic.

Bring to a boil, reduce the heat to medium-low, cover and simmer for about $1^1/4$ hours, or until the barley is tender.

Stir in the parsley.

Serves 6

PINTO-BEAN STEW

Healing Foods

Beans (dried)
Corn
Peppers (sweet)
Pumpkin
Tomatoes

1 large onion,
thinly sliced

1 clove garlic, minced

1 tablespoon
dried oregano

1 tablespoon
chili powder

2 teaspoons canola oil

1 cup corn

2 cups chopped
tomatoes

3 cups stock

1 cup dried pinto beans,
soaked overnight

1 green pepper, diced

$1^1/_2$ cups cubed
pumpkin

In a large nonstick frying pan, sauté the onions, garlic, oregano, and chili powder in the oil for 3 to 4 minutes. Add the tomatoes and cook for 5 minutes.

Transfer to a 3-quart casserole dish. Add the stock and drained beans. Cover and bake at 375°F for $1^1/_2$ hours.

Add the peppers, pumpkin, and corn. Bake for 1 hour, or until the beans and vegetables are tender.

Lightly mash about half of the beans before serving to help thicken the stew.

Serves 4 to 6

MAIN-DISH ANTIPASTO

Healing Foods

Asparagus
Beans (dried)
Broccoli
Carrots
Cheese (low-fat)
Fish
Oil
Peppers (sweet)

MARINADE

$1/3$ cup olive oil
2 tablespoons
rice-wine vinegar
2 tablespoons herb
vinegar
1 tablespoon minced
fresh parsley
$1/2$ teaspoon dry
mustard
$1/2$ teaspoon dried
oregano
$1/4$ teaspoon paprika
$1/8$ teaspoon
black pepper

ANTIPASTO

1 cup cooked chick-
peas or kidney beans
1 onion slice
1 clove garlic, halved
1 sweet red pepper
24 green beans,
trimmed
2 large carrots,
julienned
12 mushrooms
2 large stalks broccoli
12 asparagus spears
8 cubes part-skim
mozzarella cheese
4 black olives
1 can ($7^1/2$ ounces)
water-packed tuna

To make the marinade: In a small bowl, whisk together the oil, rice-wine vinegar, herb vinegar,

369

parsley, mustard, oregano, paprika, and pepper.

To make the antipasto: Place the chick-peas or kidney beans in a small bowl. Add 3 to 4 tablespoons of marinade and toss to coat. Top with the onion and garlic. Cover and refrigerate until needed.

Broil the pepper 3 to 4 inches from the heat until charred on all sides. Wrap the pepper in a damp dish towel and set aside for 5 minutes. Peel off the blackened skin and discard the seeds. Cut the flesh into thin strips. Set aside.

Arrange the beans in half of a large steaming basket. Arrange the carrots in the other half. Cover and steam over 1 inch of boiling water for 4 to 5 minutes, or until crisp-tender. Rinse under cold water to stop the cooking, pat dry, and set aside.

Steam the mushrooms for 8 to 10 minutes, or until cooked through. Pat dry and set aside.

Peel the tough skin away from the broccoli stems. Cut the broccoli into florets, leaving 2 inches of stem intact. Steam for 2 to 3 minutes, or until crisp-tender. Rinse under cold water, pat dry, and set aside.

Trim the woody ends from the asparagus. With a vegetable peeler, remove the scales from the spears. Steam the asparagus for 3 to 5 minutes, or until crisp-tender. Run under cold water, pat dry, and set aside.

When ready to serve, remove and discard the onion and garlic from the beans. Toss the beans with their dressing, then drain and save the marinade.

For a decorative presentation, arrange the vegetables on a large serving platter in this order: broccoli, mushrooms, carrots, green beans, peppers, asparagus. Spoon the marinade from the beans over the vegetables. Whisk the remaining marinade and drizzle over the platter. Add the cheese, olives, and chick-peas or kidney beans.

Open the can of tuna and press out excess liquid with the can lid. Invert the can and turn the tuna out onto the platter in one piece.

Serve the antipasto at room temperature.

Serves 4

DILLED SPLIT PEAS

Healing Foods

Beans (dried)
Carrots
Onions
Yogurt (low-fat)

4 cups stock
3 cups water
2 cups yellow
  split peas
1 large onion, minced
2 carrots, diced

2 stalks celery,
  chopped
1 tablespoon low-
  sodium soy sauce
2 teaspoons dillweed
1 1/2 cups non-fat
  yogurt

In a 4-quart pot, combine the stock, water, and split peas. Bring to a boil, reduce the heat, partially cover, and simmer for 30 minutes.

371

Add the onions, carrots, celery, soy sauce, and dill. Cook over medium-low heat, stirring occasionally, for 30 minutes, or until the peas and vegetables are tender.

Puree the soup in batches in a blender on low speed. Reheat, if necessary, before serving.

To serve, ladle into individual bowls. Top with spoonfuls of the yogurt.

Serves 6 to 8

CARIBBEAN BEAN CASSEROLE

Healing Foods

Beans (dried)
Cheese (low-fat)
Oil
Peppers (sweet)
Rice

1 onion, minced	2 tablespoons olive oil
2 sweet red peppers, diced	1 cup stock
1 red chili pepper, minced	1 cup kidney beans, soaked overnight
2 cloves garlic, minced	1 bay leaf
2 ounces part-skim mozzarella cheese, thinly sliced	2 cups hot cooked rice
	$1/2$ cup minced fresh coriander
	$1/4$ cup tomato juice

In a large nonstick frying pan, sauté the onions, red peppers, chili peppers, and garlic in the oil for 5 minutes.

Add the stock, drained beans, and bay leaf. Cover and simmer over low heat for 1 1/2 hours, or until the beans are tender. If necessary, add a little more liquid. Discard the bay leaf.

Coat a 2-quart casserole dish with nonstick spray. Spread the rice in the dish. Pour the tomato juice over the rice. Top with the beans. Sprinkle with the coriander. Cover with the cheese.

Broil about 5 inches from the heat until the cheese is melted and lightly browned.

Serves 4

HUMMUS WITH PUMPKIN AND POMEGRANATE

Healing Foods

Beans (dried)
Garlic
Pomegranates
Pumpkin

1 cup cooked
  chick-peas
1 cup mashed
  cooked pumpkin
3 cloves garlic,
  minced

1/3 cup tahini
  (sesame-seed paste)
1/4 cup minced
  fresh parsley
2 pomegranates
8 pitas, split and
  warmed

In a food processor, puree the chick-peas, pumpkin, tahini, parsley, and garlic until smooth.

Transfer to a serving plate.

Break open the pomegranates and separate the seeds from the inner membranes. Sprinkle the seeds over the hummus. Serve chilled or at room temperature with the pitas.

Serves 4

CHILI BEANS RANCHERO

Healing Foods

Beans (dried)
Bulgur
Carrots
Garlic
Herbs and spices
Onions
Peppers (chili)
Tomatoes

1 pound dried kidney beans, soaked overnight
6 cups water
2 cups tomato sauce
4 scallions, thinly sliced
2 stalks celery, finely chopped
2 carrots, finely chopped
2 onions, diced
1 tomato, diced

1 sweet red pepper, diced
2 small chili peppers, seeded and minced
$1/4$ cup minced fresh parsley
5 garlic cloves, minced
1 tablespoon chili powder
2 teaspoons paprika
$1^1/2$ teaspoons dried oregano

1 teaspoon dried
  marjoram
1/4 teaspoon ground
  red pepper
4–5 cups hot
  cooked bulgur

1 teaspoon
  ground cumin
1/2 cup shredded
  low-fat Cheddar
  cheese
2 bay leaves

Drain the beans and place in 4-quart pot. Add the water. Cover and bring to a simmer over medium heat. Turn the heat to low and cook for 1 hour.

Add the tomato sauce, scallions, celery, carrots, onions, tomatoes, red peppers, chili peppers, parsley, garlic, chili powder, paprika, oregano, marjoram, cumin, ground red pepper, and bay leaves. Cover and simmer for 1 hour. Discard the bay leaves.

Serve over the bulgur. Sprinkle with the cheese.

Serves 8 to 10

COUSCOUS AND CHICK-PEA STEW

Healing Foods

Beans (dried)
Pasta
Peppers (chili)
Raisins
Squash (winter)
Turnips

375

1 large onion, diced
1 tablespoon olive oil
1 teaspoon
  ground ginger
$1/2$ teaspoon turmeric
$1/2$ teaspoon ground
  cinnamon
$1/2$ teaspoon black
  pepper
$1/3$ cup raisins
1 jalapeño pepper,
  seeded and minced
1 cup couscous

2 cups stock
1 large butternut
  squash, peeled
  and cubed
3 small turnips,
  sliced into $1/2$-
  inch wedges
$1 1/2$ cups cooked
  chick-peas
$1/4$ cup minced fresh
  coriander
$1 1/2$ cups water

In a 4-quart pot, sauté the onions in the oil until tender, about 5 minutes. Add the ginger, turmeric, cinnamon, and pepper. Cook for 1 minute.

Add the stock, squash, turnips, drained chickpeas, raisins, coriander, and peppers.

Bring to a boil, lower the heat, cover and simmer for 35 minutes, or until the vegetables are tender.

In a 1-quart saucepan, bring the water to a boil. Add the couscous. Cover, remove from the heat and let stand for 15 minutes, or until the water has been absorbed. Fluff with a fork.

Place the couscous on a serving platter. Top with the vegetables.

Serves 4

BLACK-EYED PEAS
WITH SPINACH

Healing Foods

Beans (dried)
Spinach

2 tablespoons vinegar
1 tablespoon olive oil
1 teaspoon
  Dijon mustard
1 clove garlic, minced
$1/4$ teaspoon
  dried oregano
2 plum tomatoes,
  chopped

$1/4$ teaspoon
  dried basil
$1/8$ teaspoon
  grated nutmeg
2 cups shredded
  spinach
$1^1/2$ cups cooked
  black-eyed peas
1 small onion,
  thinly sliced

In the small bowl, whisk together the vinegar, oil, and mustard. Stir in garlic, oregano, basil, and nutmeg.

In a large bowl, combine the spinach, peas, tomatoes, and onions. Pour on the dressing and toss well to combine.

Serves 4

NAVY-BEAN SOUP

Healing Foods

Beans (dried)
Garlic
Onions
Parsnips
Peppers (sweet)

$3/4$ cup dried navy beans, soaked overnight

6 cups beef stock

1 cup chopped tomatoes

3 parsnips, diced

$1/2$ teaspoon caraway seeds

2 onions, coarsely chopped

2 yellow frying peppers, diced

5 cloves garlic, minced

1 teaspoon dried thyme

2 tablespoons red-wine vinegar

Drain the beans. Place in a 4-quart pot with the stock. Simmer for 25 minutes.

Add the tomatoes, parsnips, onions, peppers, garlic, thyme, and caraway.

Cover and simmer until the beans are tender, about 20 minutes. Crush some of the beans with a potato masher to thicken the soup.

Stir in the vinegar.

Serves 6 to 8

DIP INTO SOMETHING HEALTHY

Beans make a great alternative to cheese spreads and sour cream dips for those on a heart-healthy diet. In addition to being low in fat, their high fiber content will help make a little go a long way when it comes to appeasing your appetite. That means bean dips are perfect for the weight watcher, too!

The basic directions are the same for all the dips that follow.

- If cooking your own beans, make sure they're very soft so you can mash them easily. Drain the beans but save at least $1/2$ cup of the liquid.
- If using canned beans, drain them and reserve the liquid. Place the beans themselves in a strainer and rinse under cold water to remove excess sodium.
- Transfer the beans to a blender or food processor. Process them until smooth, adding only enough liquid to facilitate blending.
- Stir in the listed condiments and spices. (If you want to try combinations of your own, use approximately 2 teaspoons of seasoning plus 2 tablespoons of condiments or chopped vegetables for each cup of beans.)
- Serve your spreads on toasted pita chips, whole-grain crackers, corn tortillas (cut into sixths and toasted), or crudités (bite-size broccoli, cauliflower, carrots, mushrooms, celery, or other cut fresh vegetables).

Chili Bean Dip

1 cup cooked
pink beans
1 teaspoon chili
powder
1 teaspoon onion
powder

1 teaspoon chopped
green chili peppers
$1/4$ teaspoon red
pepper

Makes about 1 cup

Healing Food

- Beans (dried)

Creole Bean Dip

1 cup cooked red
beans
2 tablespoons
finely chopped
green peppers

2 tablespoons
minced tomatoes
5 drops hot-pepper
sauce

Makes about 1 cup

Healing Food

- Beans (dried)

Coriander-Bean Dip

1 cup cooked red
beans
1 teaspoon
ground coriander

1 teaspoon
ground cumin

Makes about 1 cup

Healing Food

- Beans (dried)

Red-Pepper Bean Spread

1 cup cooked Great
   Northern beans
3 tablespoons finely
   chopped sweet red
   peppers

1 tablespoon finely
   chopped scallions

Makes about 1 cup

Healing Food

- Beans (dried)

Beans Florentine

1 cup Great Northern
   beans
2 tablespoons chopped
   cooked spinach
   (squeezed dry)

$1/2$ teaspoon dried
   thyme
$1/2$ teaspoon onion
   powder

Makes about 1 cup

Healing Food

- Beans (dried)

Curried Pea Spread

1 cup cooked peas

$1/2$–1 teaspoon
   curry powder

Makes about 1 cup

Healing Food

- Peas

Hummus Bi Tahini

1 cup cooked
chick-peas
2 tablespoons tahini
(sesame-seed paste)
2 teaspoons lemon
juice

2 teaspoons minced
fresh parsley
$1/2$ clove garlic,
minced

Makes about 1 cup

Healing Food

- Beans (dried)

Fiesta Bean Dip

1 cup cooked
black beans
2 tablespoons finely
chopped sweet
red peppers
1 tablespoon finely
chopped scallions

1 tablespoon minced
tomatoes
2 teaspoons minced
fresh parsley
$1/8$ teaspoon white
pepper
1 tablespoon finely
chopped celery

Makes about 1 cup

Healing Food

- Beans (dried)

LENTIL TACOS

Beans (dried)
Lettuce
Onions
Peppers (sweet)
Tomatoes

1 1/2 cups minced
  onions
1 cup minced sweet
  red peppers
2 cloves garlic,
  minced
1 tablespoon olive oil
1 1/2 cups chopped
  tomatoes
1 cup dried lentils
1 cup tomato juice
1/4 teaspoon
  red pepper
8 corn tortillas
1/2 cup shredded
  low-fat cheese

1 cup stock
1/2 cup minced
  fresh parsley
2 tablespoons
  chili powder
2 tablespoons
  chopped raisins
1 tablespoon molasses
1 tablespoon low-
  sodium soy sauce
1/2 teaspoon
  ground cumin
1 bay leaf
2 cups shredded
  lettuce

In a large nonstick frying pan over low heat, cook the onions, peppers, and garlic in the oil until the onions are wilted, about 10 minutes.

Add 1 cup of the tomatoes, the lentils, tomato juice, stock, parsley, chili powder, raisins, molasses, soy sauce, cumin, red pepper, and bay leaf. Cook over low heat for 1 hour, stirring frequently.

Uncover and continue cooking, stirring frequently, until the mixture is thick. Discard the bay leaf.

Heat the tortillas at 350°F for 5 to 8 minutes or until crisp. Fill with the lentil mixture. Top with the lettuce, cheese, and remaining tomatoes.

Serves 4

CUBAN BEAN STEW

Healing Foods

Beans (dried)
Garlic
Onions
Peppers (chili)

1/2 cup dried black
  beans, soaked
  overnight
4 cups chicken stock
1 large onion,
  chopped
1 stalk celery,
  thinly sliced
4 cloves garlic,
  minced
1 bay leaf

2 hot chili peppers,
  seeded and minced
1/4 cup minced
  fresh parsley
1 tablespoon peeled
  minced gingerroot
1 tablespoon low-
  sodium soy sauce
1 teaspoon
  dried thyme

Drain the beans. Place in a 3-quart casserole dish. Add the stock, onions, celery, peppers, parsley, ginger, soy sauce, garlic, thyme, and bay leaf.

Bring to a simmer on top of the stove.

Transfer to the oven and bake at 375°F for 2 hours, or until the beans are tender. Discard the bay leaf.

Serves 4

GRILLED TILEFISH WITH BEAN SALSA

Healing Foods

Beans (dried)
Fish
Garlic
Tomatoes

2 cups cooked
    black beans
2 large tomatoes,
    diced
1 large onion, diced
1/2 cup minced
    fresh coriander
2 cloves garlic,
    minced

3 tablespoons vinegar
1 tablespoon minced
    chili peppers
1/4 cup stock
2 tablespoons lime juice
1 tablespoon olive oil
1 teaspoon black
    pepper
1 pound tilefish fillets

In a 2-quart saucepan, combine the beans, tomatoes, onions, coriander, vinegar, and peppers. Cover and let stand about 30 minutes.

In a small bowl, whisk together the stock, lime juice, oil, black pepper, and garlic.

Place the fish in a shallow baking dish. Pour the oil mixture over it. Cover, refrigerate, and marinate for 30 minutes.

Coat a broiler rack with nonstick spray. Transfer the fish directly to the rack. Broil about 4 inches from the heat for 5 to 7 minutes per side, or until cooked through. Transfer to serving plates.

While the fish is cooking, heat the bean mixture for a few minutes, until just warm. Serve with the fish.

Serves 4

RED BEANS IN EDIBLE CUPS

Healing Foods

Beans (dried)
Beans (snap)
Cabbage
Oil
Tomatoes

2 cups cooked
  kidney beans
2 cups cooked
  yellow beans, cut
  into 1-inch pieces
2 large tomatoes,
  diced
2 tablespoons olive oil

2 shallots, minced
1 tablespoon
  snipped chives
1 teaspoon
  dried basil
2 tablespoons vinegar
12 small purple
  cabbage leaves

In a large bowl, combine the drained kidney beans, yellow beans, tomatoes, shallots, chives, and basil.

In a cup, whisk together the vinegar and oil.

Pour over the bean mixture. Toss well to combine.

To serve, place the cabbage leaves on individual plates. Divide the beans among them.

Serves 4

CHAPTER NINE

Vegetarian Main Meals

Want to live longer? Become a vegetarian. Long-term studies of Seventh-Day Adventists who advocate vegetarianism show that their death rate from heart disease is half that of the national average. And one study, which followed 25,000 Adventists over a 21-year period, found that those men who did eat meat had the highest death rate of all. As meat consumption rose, so too did their risk of developing diabetes and possibly certain forms of cancer.

The fact that Adventists also shun cigarettes and alcohol no doubt plays a part in their better-than-average heart disease rate. But their no-meat—meaning low-fat—lifestyle definitely works greatly in their favor, according to David Snowdon, Ph.D., of the University of Minnesota School of Public Health, who reported the study.

This doesn't mean that *you* have to shun meat forever to garner similar health benefits. But you could eat meat less often. After all, any healing diet should contain a fair share of vegetarian dishes. Why? Because fruits and vegetables, especially the rich green and yellow varieties, are storehouses of valuable nutrients that fight heart disease and cancer. They also provide the beneficial fiber so important to digestive health.

Many of the dishes in this chapter emphasize grains, which provide protein often lacking in a meatless regimen. What's more, these recipes are filling and hearty. Lentils, other legumes, and tofu, found in such dishes as Lentil and Leek Burritos, Corn Crêpes with Bean Filling, and Indonesian Stir-Fry, are also protein-rich. All contain enough fiber and protein for satisfying fill-me-up power.

SPINACH AND FETA PIE

Healing Foods

Garlic
Nuts
Spinach
Wheat germ

1 pound spinach	2 garlic cloves, minced
1 cup egg substitute	1 teaspoon
$1/2$ cup nonfat yogurt	dried oregano
$1/4$ cup crumbled	$1/2$ teaspoon
feta cheese	ground cinnamon
$1/4$ cup wheat germ	3 tablespoons
	ground pecans

Wash the spinach in cold water to remove any grit. Cook in a large pot with just the water left clinging to the leaves until wilted. Let cool and squeeze all liquid from the leaves. Transfer to a food processor. Chop with on/off turns.

389

Add the egg substitute, yogurt, cheese, garlic, oregano, and cinnamon.

In a cup, combine the wheat germ and pecans.

Coat a 9-inch pie plate with nonstick spray. Add the wheat germ mixture and distribute evenly in the bottom and up the sides.

Pour the spinach mixture into the pan. Bake at 400°F for 30 to 40 minutes, or until a knife inserted in the center comes out clean.

Serves 4

ONION AND PESTO PIE

Healing Foods

Cottage cheese (low-fat)
Garlic
Nuts
Oil
Onions

2 cups thinly
  sliced onions
3 tablespoons olive oil
3 cups low-fat
  cheese cheese
1/4 cup walnuts
3 cloves garlic,
  chopped
1/4 teaspoon
  grated nutmeg

2 tablespoons minced
  fresh parsley
1 teaspoon
  dried basil
2 tablespoons
  lemon juice
1/2 cup egg substitute
1/4 cup grated Sapsago
  or Parmesan cheese
1/8 teaspoon
  black pepper

In a large nonstick frying pan over medium heat, sauté the onions in 1 tablespoon of the oil until soft, about 10 minutes. Cool.

In a food processor, blend the cottage cheese, walnuts, garlic, parsley, and basil with on/off turns until well combined. With the motor running, gradually add the lemon juice and the remaining 2 tablespoons oil. Mix until thick. Transfer to a large bowl.

Add the onions, egg substitute, cheese, nutmeg, and pepper. Mix well.

Coat a 9-inch springform pan with nonstick spray. Pour in the onion mixture. Bake at 350°F for 45 to 60 minutes, or until a knife inserted in the center comes out clean. Let cool on a wire rack for 20 minutes. Remove the sides of the pan.

Serves 6

GREEK SPINACH AND RICE

Healing Foods

Cottage cheese (low-fat)
Onions
Rice
Spinach

1 cup minced onions
2 tablespoons stock
1 pound spinach, chopped
3 cups cold cooked rice

1 cup low-fat cottage cheese
$1/4$ cup shredded low-fat Cheddar cheese
$1/4$ cup egg substitute

| 1 1/2 teaspoons dillweed | 3 tablespoons minced fresh parsley |

In a large nonstick frying pan, cook the onions in the stock until soft. Add the spinach and cook over low heat, stirring constantly, until wilted. Cook until all liquid has evaporated.

In a large bowl, combine the rice, cottage cheese, Cheddar, egg substitute, parsley, and dill. Fold in the spinach mixture.

Coat a 1 1/2-quart casserole with nonstick spray. Add the rice mixture. Bake at 375°F for 20 to 25 minutes, or until heated through and light brown on top.

Serves 4

BREAKFAST SCRAMBLE WITH OVEN FRIES

Healing Foods

Oil
Potatoes
Tofu

1 1/2 pounds baking potatoes	1 cup soft tofu (squeezed of excess water)
2 tablespoons olive oil	8 egg whites
1 teaspoon paprika	1 cup egg substitute
1 teaspoon Dijon mustard	1 teaspoon dillweed

Cut the potatoes into $1/2$-inch cubes. Pat dry. Toss with 1 tablespoon of the oil and the paprika.

Coat a jelly-roll pan with nonstick spray. Add the potatoes in a single layer. Bake at 425°F until browned and just crusty, about 25 minutes.

In a blender, combine the tofu, egg whites, egg substitute, mustard, and dill. Process until smooth, about 10 seconds.

In a large nonstick frying pan on medium heat, warm the remaining oil. Add the egg mixture. Use a spatula to move the egg mixture around until cooked through. Serve with the potatoes.

Serves 4

CONFETTI SPAGHETTI SQUASH

Healing Foods

Peppers (sweet)
Squash (winter)

1 large spaghetti
  squash
$1/2$ cup diced
  green peppers
$1/2$ cup diced
  sweet red peppers
$1/4$ cup diced onions
1 clove garlic,
  minced

$1/4$ cup minced
  fresh coriander
$1/4$ cup chicken stock
1 tablespoon olive oil
1 teaspoon red-wine
  vinegar
$1/4$ teaspoon
  ground cumin

Place the squash in a very large pot. Add water

393

to cover. Bring to a boil and cook, uncovered, for 30 to 60 minutes, or until easily pierced with a fork. Drain, halve, and set aside until cool enough to handle. Discard the seeds. With a fork, separate the flesh into strands and place in a large bowl.

In a large frying pan, combine the green peppers, red peppers, onions, coriander, stock, oil, vinegar, cumin, and garlic. Cover and cook over medium heat for 5 minutes.

Add the squash and toss to conibine. Cover and cook for 2 minutes to heat through.

Serves 4

MICRO METHOD:
Spaghetti Squash in a Flash

Spaghetti squash is a vegetable wonder that combines the best of two good foods. It's a low-fat, low-calorie *vegetable* with all the fun and sensory pleasure of *pasta*. As a bonus, spaghetti squash has its own delightful taste and fabulous texture. It can be served solo as a vegetable, but it is most versatile as a nutritious pasta substitute.

Stove-top preparation requires boiling a whole spaghetti squash for as much as 45 minutes. A microwave turns spaghetti squash into a spur-of-the-moment pleasure. Here's how.

- Select a small-to-medium spaghetti squash, about $1^1/2$ to 2 pounds, to serve four people.
- Cut the squash in half and remove the seeds.

- Place each half, cut side dawn, on a separate plate. The squash is moist enough to cook without any added liquid.
- Microwave each half separately on full power for 6 to 8 minutes, or until the flesh is tender and can be easily pulled from the shell in strands.
- Remove the squash strands from the shell gently, using a fork.
- Top with any sauce suitable for pasta, including pesto. Do not stir with a spoon. Instead lift the strands with forks and toss with the topping until the sauce is well distributed.

ACORN SQUASH STUFFED WITH CORNBREAD

Healing Foods

Corn
Nuts
Oil
Squash (winter)

CORNBREAD
$3/4$ cup yellow
  cornmeal
$1/2$ cup whole
  wheat flour
$1^{1}/2$ teaspoons
  baking powder
$1/2$ cup skim milk
$1/4$ cup egg substitute
$1/4$ cup chopped pecans

SQUASH
2 large acorn squash
2 tablespoons olive
  oil
1 teaspoon
  dried basil
1 teaspoon grated
  nutmeg
$1/2$ cup apple juice
1 tablespoon honey

To make the cornbread: In a large bowl, mix the cornmeal, flour, and baking powder. In a small bowl, mix the milk, egg substitute, and honey. Pour the liquid ingredients into the flour mixture and stir lightly. Fold in the pecans until all the flour is moistened. Do not overmix.

Coat a 9 x 5-inch loaf pan with nonstick spray. Add the batter. Bake at 350°F for 15 minutes. Allow the bread to cool.

To make the squash: Cut the squash in half lengthwise. Scoop out and discard the seeds. Coat a 9 x 13-inch baking dish with nonstick spray. Add the squash, cut side down. Add a small amount of water to the pan so the squash won't stick during baking.

Bake at 350°F for 45 to 60 minutes, or until just tender. Do not overbake or the squash will collapse.

Allow the squash to cool slightly. Scoop out the flesh, leaving a $1/2$-inch shell. Transfer the pulp to a large bowl.

Crumble the cornbread and add to the bowl. Add the oil, basil, and nutmeg. Toss lightly to mix. Add the apple juice and mash lightly with a potato masher. Do not overmix; stuffing should be slightly lumpy. If necessary, add a bit more juice to make a moist mixture.

Mound the stuffing in the squash shells. Bake at 350°F for 15 minutes, or until heated through.

Serves 4

CORN CRÊPES WITH BEAN FILLING

Healing Foods

Beans (dried)
Broccoli

CRÊPES

1/4 cup cornmeal
1/4 cup unbleached flour
1/4 teaspoon turmeric
1/2 cup skim milk
1/2 cup pureed corn
1/4 cup egg substitute
2 teaspoons canola oil
1 tablespoon snipped chives

FILLING

1 cup cooked pinto beans
1/4 cup minced fresh parsley
1 clove garlic, chopped
1 tablespoon lemon iuice
1 teaspoon Dijon mustard
10 stalks broccoli, steamed
1/4 cup shredded low-fat Monterey Jack cheese
1 cup chopped tomatoes

To make the crêpes: In a large bowl, mix the cornmeal, flour, and turmeric. Whisk in the milk, corn, egg substitute, oil, and chives. Let stand for 20 minutes. The batter should be the consistency of heavy cream. If it isn't, thin with additional milk.

Coat a nonstick crêpe pan with nonstick spray. Heat over medium heat until hot. Add 2 tablespoons of the batter and swirl to coat the bottom completely. Cook until the top surface is dry and the underside is light brown. Flip and cook the underside briefly. Cool on a wire rack. Repeat with the remaining batter.

To make the filling: In a food processor, puree the beans, parsley, garlic, lemon juice, and mustard until smooth.

Divide the filling among the crêpes. Lay a broccoli stalk atop the filling along one edge. Roll to enclose the broccoli. Arrange, seam side down, on an ovenproof platter.

Sprinkle with the Monterey Jack. Broil for several minutes to warm the crêpes and melt the cheese. Sprinkle with the tomatoes.

Serves 3 to 4

POTATO CURRY

Healing Foods

Garlic
Herbs and spices
Oil
Onions
Peas
Potatoes
Yogurt (low-fat)

2 pounds potatoes, cut into $1/2$-inch cubes

2 cups peas

1 large onion, diced

3 cloves garlic, minced

1 tablespoon peeled minced gingerroot

$1/4$ cup minced fresh coriander

2 tablespoons olive oil

1 tablespoon ground coriander

$3/4$ teaspoon ground cumin

$3/4$ teaspoon turmeric

$1/2$ teaspoon red pepper

1 cup nonfat yogurt

2 tablespoons lemon juice

Steam the potatoes for 5 minutes. Add the peas to the steamer basket and steam another 5 minutes, or until the potatoes are tender. Set aside.

In a large nonstick frying pan over medium heat, sauté the onions, garlic, and ginger in the oil until wilted. Add the ground coriander, cumin, turmeric, and red pepper. Cook, stirring, for 2 minutes.

Reduce the heat to low and add the potatoes and peas. Toss well to coat with spices. Cover and heat through.

Remove from the heat and gently fold in the yogurt. Sprinkle with the fresh coriander and lemon juice.

Serves 4

ZUCCHINI-RICOTTA PUFFS

Healing Foods

Cottage cheese (low-fat)
Squash (summer)
Wheat germ

1 cup low-fat
   cottage cheese
1 cup shredded
   zucchini
1/4 cup minced
   parsley
4 egg whites

1 teaspoon paprika
1 teaspoon
   dried oregano
1 teaspoon dry
   mustard
3/4 cup egg substitute
1/2 cup wheat germ

In a large bowl, combine the cottage cheese, zucchini, parsley, paprika, oregano, and mustard. Beat in the egg substitute.

In a large bowl with clean beaters, beat the egg whites until stiff. Fold into the zucchini mixture.

Coat four 5-inch pie plates with nonstick spray. Add 1 tablespoon of the wheat germ to each pan and distribute evenly. Add the zucchini mixture. Sprinkle with the remaining wheat germ.

Bake at 400°F for 15 to 18 minutes, or until the tops are puffy and golden.

Serves 4

SAVORY POTATO CRUST

This easy potato-based crust is suitable for almost any type of entrée filling. It's much quicker to make than a standard crust and contains far fewer calories.

For variety, add 2 tablespoons minced onion or 2 teaspoons dried herbs—such as oregano, marjoram, or basil—to the potatoes. Or replace the oil with $1/4$ cup shredded low-fat cheese.

Potato Pie Shell

3 medium potatoes, finely shredded
$1/4$ cup egg substitute

1 tablespoon canola oil
1 tablespoon flour

Coat a 9-inch pie plate with nonstick spray. Add the potatoes.

In a small bowl, combine the egg substitute, oil, and flour. Pour over the potatoes and pat the mixture in the bottom of the pan and up the sides to form a crust.

Broil about 8 inches from the heat for 15 minutes, or until bronze.

Makes 1 crust

Healing Foods

• Oil • Potatoes

INDONESIAN STIR-FRY

Healing Foods

Garlic
Nuts
Onions
Peppers (chili)
Rice
Tofu

3 hot green chili peppers, seeded and minced

2 tablespoons peeled minced gingerroot

4 cloves garlic, minced

1 tablespoon canola oil

1 tablespoon lemon juice

2 cups cubed tofu

3–4 cups hot cooked rice

1 cup diced sweet red peppers

1 cup thinly sliced scallions

2 cups stock

1/2–3/4 cup peanut butter

2 tablespoons low-sodium soy sauce

1 teaspoon honey

1/2 teaspoon red-pepper flakes

In a large nonstick frying pan over medium heat, sauté the chili peppers, ginger, and garlic in the oil for 5 minutes. Add the red peppers and scallions. Stir for 1 to 2 minutes, or until the scallions are limp.

Add the stock, stirring to loosen any bits of seasonings from the bottom of the pan. Add the peanut butter, soy sauce, lemon juice, honey, and pepper flakes. Cook over medium heat, stirring constantly, until the sauce thickens and begins to simmer.

Add the tofu. Cover the pan and reduce the heat to low. Cook for 10 minutes, or until the peppers are just tender. Serve over the rice.

Serves 6 to 8

GREEK GARDEN KABOBS

Healing Foods

Eggplant
Garlic
Tomatoes
Yogurt (low-fat)

1 cup nonfat yogurt
1/4 cup minced
   fresh mint
4 cloves garlic,
   minced

1/2 teaspoon
   dried oregano
1 large eggplant, cut
   into 1 1/2-inch chunks
20 cherry tomatoes

In a shallow baking dish, combine 1/2 cup yogurt, 2 tablespoons mint, half of the garlic, and a pinch of oregano.

Add the eggplant and toss to coat well. Cover and allow to marinate for 30 minutes.

Thread the eggplant and tomatoes onto skewers. Broil or grill about 4 inches from the heat for about 2 minutes on each side.

In a small bowl, combine the remaining yogurt, mint, garlic, and oregano. Use as a dipping sauce for the kabobs.

Serves 4

403

EGGS WITH CHILI SAUCE

Healing Foods

Avocados
Garlic
Peppers (chili)
Salad greens
Sprouts
Tomatoes
Yogurt (low-fat)

1 large onion, minced
3 cloves garlic,
   minced
1 tablespoon olive oil
1 1/2 cups shredded
   romaine lettuce
4 flour tortillas
1 avocado,
   thinly sliced
1 cup alfalfa sprouts

3 hot or mild chili
   peppers, chopped
1/4 cup chopped
   fresh coriander
1/2 teaspoon
   dried oregano
1 1/2 cups egg substitute
1 cup nonfat yogurt
1 cup diced tomatoes

In a large nonstick frying pan, cook the onion and garlic in the oil until limp. Add the lettuce, chili peppers, coriander, and oregano. Cook for about 3 minutes, or until the lettuce has wilted. Transfer to a large bowl.

Clean the frying pan and coat with nonstick spray. Add the egg substitute and cook over low heat until lightly scrambled.

Divide among the tortillas. Top with the chili mixture. Do not roll the tortillas. Serve flat topped with the avocados, yogurt, sprouts, and tomatoes.

Serves 4

CORN-PONE PIE

Healing Foods

Apples
Corn
Milk (low-fat)
Oil
Tomatoes

TOMATO CHUTNEY
4 tomatoes, chopped
$1/2$ cup minced onions
$1/2$ cup minced celery
1 bay leaf
1 tablespoon apple juice
1 apple, chopped
$1/4$ cup apple-cider vinegar
$1/2$ teaspoon ground cinnamon
$1/4$ teaspoon ground allspice

PIE
$1^1/2$ cups yellow cornmeal
1 cup unbleached flour
1 tablespoon baking powder
$1/2$ teaspoon turmeric
$1/4$ teaspoon ground allspice
$1/2$ cup corn
$1/4$ cup minced scallions
$1/4$ cup minced fresh parsley
$1^1/2$ cups buttermilk
$1/4$ cup honey
$1/4$ cup egg substitute
2 tablespoons canola oil

To make the tomato chutney: In a 2-quart saucepan, combine the tomatoes, onions, celery, bay leaf, and apple juice. Simmer for 5 minutes.

405

Add the apples, vinegar, cinnamon, and all-spice. Partially cover and simmer, stirring frequently, for 40 minutes, or until thick. Discard the bay leaf.

To make the pie: In a large bowl, sift together the cornmeal, flour, baking powder, turmeric, and allspice. Add the corn, scallions, and parsley and mix until combined.

In a medium bowl, whisk together the buttermilk, honey, egg substitute, and oil. Pour into the flour bowl. Using a large rubber spatula, quickly combine the mixtures.

Coat a 9-inch pie plate with nonstick spray. Add the batter. Level the top. Bake at 375°F for about 25 minutes, or until a knife inserted in the center comes out clean.

Serve topped with the chutney.

Serves 4

VEGETARIAN SAUSAGE LINKS

Healing Foods

Beans (dried)
Garlic
Oil
Rice
Salad greens

1 small onion, minced
3 tablespoons olive oil
1 cup minced
  collard greens

3 cloves garlic,
  minced
2 cups cold
  cooked rice

2 tablespoons grated
  Parmesan cheese
1 teaspoon
  dried oregano
1 teaspoon
  dried sage
1 cup warm
  tomato sauce

1 cup cooked
  kidney beans
$1/4$ cup egg substitute
1 teaspoon
  dried thyme
$1/2$ cup dry
  bread crumbs

In a large nonstick frying pan, sauté the onions in 1 tablespoon of the oil until soft, about 5 minutes.

Add the collard greens, cheese, and garlic. Sauté until the greens wilt, about 3 minutes.

In a large bowl combine the rice, beans, egg substitute, thyme, oregano, and sage. Stir in the onion mixture.

Transfer to a food processor. Process just until the mixture is a solid mass but not pureed, about 6 seconds.

Divide into eight parts. Form each part into a sausage shape. Roll in the bread crumbs.

Coat a baking sheet with nonstick spray. Set the sausages on the sheet and brush with the remaining oil. Broil until mottled brown on all sides, about 5 or 6 minutes.

Serve with the tomato sauce.

Serves 4

THE 20-MINUTE PIZZA

This homemade pizza is more than delicious. It's wholesome, healthy, and ready in less time than it takes to have a pie home delivered.

Whole Wheat Pizza

$^1/_2$ cup lukewarm
  water (about 110°F)
1 tablespoon canola
  oil
1 teaspoon quick-rise
  active dry yeast
$^1/_2$ teaspoon honey
$1^1/_4$ cups whole
  wheat flour

$^1/_4$ teaspoon garlic
  powder
$^1/_4$ teaspoon
  onion powder
$^1/_2$ cup thick tomato
  sauce
1 cup shredded
  part-skim mozzarella
  cheese

In a large bowl, combine the water, oil, yeast, and honey. Stir to dissolve the yeast. Add the flour, garlic powder, and onion powder. Mix thoroughly.

Let the dough rest for 5 minutes.

Coat a 12-inch pizza pan with nonstick spray. Place the dough on it and shape into an 11-inch round. Spread on the sauce, leaving a $^1/_2$-inch border. Sprinkle with the cheese.

Bake at 475°F for 12 minutes.

Serves 2

Healing Foods

- Cheese (low-fat)   • Whole wheat flour

Variations:
- Make a Hawaiian pizza by topping the tomato sauce with unsweetened pineapple (crushed and drained), halved seedless grapes, and raisins.
- Replace the tomato sauce in the basic recipe with Mexican salsa. Top with sliced hot peppers and shredded low-fat Monterey Jack cheese.

- For a dessert pizza, omit the tomato sauce and top the crust with sliced fruit, chopped nuts, and a mild cheese, such as low-fat Muenster or Havarti.

BROCCOLI QUESADILLA

Healing Foods

Avocados
Broccoli
Cheese (low-fat)
Garlic
Peppers (chili)
Yogurt (low-fat)

1 head broccoli, broken into large florets
1 tablespoon olive oil
1 red onion, finely chopped
2 garlic cloves, minced
$1/2$ teaspoon ground cumin
$1/4$ teaspoon chili powder
1 cup salsa
1 cup nonfat yogurt
$1/8$ teaspoon ground cinnamon
2 jalapeño peppers, seeded and minced
6 cherry tomatoes, quartered
1 tablespoon minced fresh coriander
6 flour tortillas
$1/2$ cup shredded part-skim mozzarella cheese
1 avocado, sliced

Steam the broccoli until crisp-tender. Chop coarsely and set aside.

In a large nonstick frying pan, heat 1 teaspoon

of the oil. Add the onions and sauté over medium heat for 3 to 4 minutes to soften. Add the garlic, cumin, chili powder, and cinnamon. Cook for 1 minute.

Add the broccoli, peppers, tomatoes, and coriander. Stir well and sauté another 3 to 4 minutes. Transfer to a bowl and set aside.

Clean the frying pan. Brush lightly with some of the remaining oil and heat over medium-high heat.

Divide the broccoli mixture among the tortillas. Sprinkle with the cheese. Fold in half.

Working in batches, fry each tortilla for 2 to 3 minutes per side, pressing with a spatula to flatten it a bit. Brush the pan with more oil as necessary.

To serve, top each tortilla with salsa, yogurt, and avocados.

Serves 6

SPICY VEGETABLES WITH TOFU

Healing Foods

Broccoli
Cauliflower
Garlic
Rice
Tofu

1 onion, thinly
sliced
1 sweet red pepper,
cut into 2-inch
strips
2 stalks celery, thinly
sliced diagonally
4 cloves garlic, minced
1 tablespoon peeled
minced gingerroot
$1/4$ cup stock
2 cups hot
cooked rice

1 tablespoon minced
chili pepper
1 tablespoon canola oil
$1/4$ cup thinly
sliced mushrooms
$3/4$ cup broccoli florets
$3/4$ cup sliced cauli-
flower florets
$1/4$ cup peas
1 cup cubed tofu
1 tablespoon low-
sodium soy sauce

In a large frying pan over medium heat, sauté the
onions, red peppers, celery, garlic, ginger, and
chili peppers in the oil for 5 minutes. Add the
mushrooms, broccoli, cauliflower, and peas. Stir
to combine.

Add the tofu, stock, and soy sauce. Cover and
cook for 3 to 4 minutes, or until the vegetables
are crisp-tender.

Serve over the rice.

Serves 4

ITALIAN-STYLE FRIED RICE

Healing Foods

Artichokes
Cheese (low-fat)
Oil
Onions
Rice
Spinach

8 artichoke hearts, chopped
1 cup thinly sliced onions
2 cloves garlic, minced
1 shallot, minced
3 tablespoons olive oil

2 cups shredded spinach
4 cups cold cooked rice
3 tablespoons grated Sapsago or Parmesan cheese

In a large nonstick frying pan, sauté the artichokes, onions, garlic, and shallots in 1 tablespoon of the oil until tender, about 4 minutes.

Add the spinach and sauté until the spinach wilts. Transfer to a large bowl.

Sauté the rice in the remaining oil until heated through. Stir in the spinach mixture. Sprinkle with the cheese.

Serves 4

SPICY STUFFED PEPPERS

Healing Foods

Beans (dried)
Corn
Peppers (chili)
Peppers (sweet)
Tomatoes

1/3 cup minced
scallions
1 clove garlic, minced
1 tablespoon olive oil
2 tomatoes, chopped
1 jalapeño pepper,
seeded and
thinly sliced
1 cup cooked
black beans

2 tablespoons minced
fresh parsley
1 teaspoon
dried oregano
1 teaspoon
ground cumin
1 bay leaf
2 cups corn
4 large sweet
red peppers

In a large frying pan, cook the scallions and garlic in the oil until soft, about 4 minutes. Add the tomatoes, jalapeno peppers, parsley, oregano, cumin, and bay leaf. Bring to a boil and cook, stirring frequently, until the tomatoes are soft and the mixture has thickened, about 10 minutes.

Add the corn, partially cover, and simmer about 8 minutes. Discard the bay leaf. Stir in the beans. Keep warm over very low heat.

Cut about 1/2 inch off the top of each pepper. Discard the seeds. Steam the whole peppers until tender.

Divide the stuffing among the peppers.

Serves 4

413

POTATO BAKE WITH MUSHROOM STROGANOFF

Healing Foods

Mushrooms
Onions
Potatoes
Yogurt (low-fat)

4 large baking potatoes
1 1/2 cups nonfat yogurt
1 teaspoon Dijon mustard
1 large onion, diced
1/2 teaspoon dried thyme
2 cloves garlic, minced
1 tablespoon olive oil
1 1/2 pounds small mushrooms, quartered
1/2 teaspoon dillweed
1/8 teaspoon grated nutmeg

Bake the potatoes at 375°F for 1 hour, or until easily pierced with a fork.

While the potatoes are baking, line a strainer with cheesecloth and set it over a bowl. Add the yogurt and set it aside to drain for about 15 minutes. Transfer to a small bowl. Whisk in the mustard and set aside.

In a large nonstick frying pan over medium-high heat, sauté the onions and garlic in the oil until the onions wilt, about 5 minutes.

Add the mushrooms, dill, thyme, and nutmeg. Sauté until the mushrooms are brown and fragrant, about 10 minutes. Remove from the heat.

Stir in the yogurt mixture.

Serve over the potatoes.

Serves 4

MEXICAN CORN CASSEROLE

Healing Foods

Cheese (low-fat)
Corn
Garlic
Oil
Onions
Peppers (chili)
Tomatoes

1 cup minced onions
$1/2$ cup minced
 green peppers
3 cloves garlic, minced
2 tablespoons water
2 cups chopped
 tomatoes
$1/2$ cup minced
 fresh coriander
2 cups corn
$1/2$ cup chopped
 mild chili peppers

$3/4$ teaspoon
 dried oregano
$1/2$ teaspoon
 ground cumin
2 teaspoons red-
 wine vinegar
$2^1/2$ cups stock
1 cup cornmeal
$1/4$ cup olive oil
1 cup shredded low-fat
 Monterey Jack cheese
$1/2$ cup minced
 scallions

In a large frying pan, sauté the onions, green peppers, and garlic in water until tender, about 5 minutes. Add the tomatoes, coriander, oregano, and cumin. Bring to a boil. Cover, reduce the heat and simmer 10 minutes. Remove the lid and cook, stirring, until thick. Stir in the vinegar.

Place the stock in a 2-quart saucepan. Whisk in the cornmeal and oil. Cook over medium heat, stirring constantly, until the mixture bubbles and becomes very thick, about 15 minutes. Stir in the corn.

Coat a 9-inch pie plate with nonstick spray. Spread half of the corn filling in the plate. Sprinkle with the cheese, chili peppers, and scallions. Cover with the remaining corn mixture. Top with the tomato mixture.

Bake at 350°F for 40 minutes.

Serves 4

POLENTA: CORNMEAL BY ANOTHER NAME

Polenta is a hearty peasant dish made from cornmeal. The Italians have relished it for centuries. Today, it's making a comeback as a filling, complex-carbohydrate dish that's a refreshing change from potatoes, rice, and noodles.

Basically, polenta is cornmeal that's cooked until thick, cooled until firm, cut into slices, and topped with a sauce. Depending on the topping, it can serve as an appetizer, main course, or side dish.

Although making the polenta itself takes a bit of time, you can do that part at your leisure. For that matter, you can prepare the topping ahead of time, too. Then it's a simple matter of reheating the two for dinner in a flash.

Polenta

1 cup yellow
  cornmeal
1 cup water
2^1/$_2$ cups stock

3 tablespoons olive oil
^{1}/$_2$ cup shredded
  low-fat cheese

In a large bowl, whisk together the cornmeal and water.

In a 3-quart saucepan, bring the stock and oil to a boil. Whisk in the cornmeal and stir until the mixture thickens, about 3 or 4 minutes. That will keep the polenta smooth and free of lumps.

Cook over medium heat, stirring constantly with a wooden spoon, for 25 minutes.

Add the cheese. Mix well. Cover the pot and leave it on the heat for 3 minutes, without stirring. Shake the pot a little to allow some steam to get under the polenta so it will unmold from the pot easily.

Coat an 8^1/$_2$ x 4^1/$_2$-inch loaf pan with nonstick spray. Add the polenta and allow to set until quite firm.

Unmold it onto a cutting board or countertop. Cut into ^{3}/$_4$ to 1-inch slices.

Sauté, broil, or bake the slices until hot, then add your choice of topping.

Serves 4

Healing Foods

• Cheese (low-fat) • Corn • Oil

417

Mediterranean Topping

1 cup sliced onions
1 tablespoon olive oil
2 cups broccoli florets
1 1/2 cups sliced
  mushrooms
1 cup sliced yellow
  summer squash
1/4 teaspoon hot-
  pepper sauce

1 cup crushed tomatoes
1/4 cup minced
  fresh coriander
1/2 teaspoon
  dried savory
1/4 teaspoon
  dried thyme

In a large frying pan over medium heat, sauté the onions in the oil until soft, about 5 minutes. Add the broccoli, mushrooms, and squash. Sauté for 5 minutes.

Add the tomatoes, coriander, savory, thyme, and hot-pepper sauce.

Cover and cook 20 minutes, or until the vegetables are tender.

Serves 4

Healing Foods

- Broccoli
- Squash (summer)
- Mushrooms
- Tomatoes
- Onions

Primavera Sauce

1 cup julienned
carrots
1 cup julienned
zucchini
1/2 cup julienned
scallions
3 tablespoons
unbleached flour

1 1/2 cups skim milk
1 teaspoon Dijon
mustard
1 teaspoon dillweed
3 tablespoons grated
Sapsago or
Parmesan cheese
3 tablespoons olive oil

Steam the carrots, zucchini, and scallions until tender, about 4 minutes.

In a 2-quart saucepan, combine the flour and oil. Stir over medium heat for 3 minutes. Whisk in the milk. Cook, whisking constantly, until the sauce thickens and comes to a boil. Whisk in the mustard and dill. Remove from the heat. Stir in the vegetables and cheese.

Serves 4

Healing Foods

- Carrots   • Milk (low-fat)   • Oil
- Squash (summer)

Asparagus Topping

2 cups sliced
asparagus
1 cup sliced
mushrooms
1/2 cup minced
shallots
2 tablespoons stock

2 teaspoons
snipped chives
1/2 teaspoon dried
tarragon
1/4 cup shredded
low-fat Colby cheese
1 teaspoon olive oil

Steam the asparagus until tender, about 5 to 7 minutes.

In a large frying pan, combine the mushrooms, shallots, stock, and oil. Cook over medium heat until the mushrooms are tender. Stir in the chives, tarragon, and asparagus. Heat through. Sprinkle with the cheese.

Serves 4

Healing Foods

- Asparagus   • Mushrooms

RUSSIAN VEGETABLE PIE

Healing Foods

Cabbage
Cottage cheese (low-fat)
Mushrooms
Oil
Onions
Whole wheat flour

3 cups thinly
shredded cabbage
2 tablespoons olive oil
1 teaspoon dillweed
$1\frac{1}{2}$ cups thinly
sliced mushrooms
1 large onion,
thinly sliced
1 9-inch Whole Wheat
Pie Shell, unbaked
(page 272)

$\frac{1}{2}$ teaspoon
dried tarragon
$\frac{1}{2}$ teaspoon
dried basil
1 cup low-fat
cottage cheese
$\frac{1}{4}$ cup egg substitute
$\frac{1}{4}$ cup grated
Parmesan cheese
2 hard-cooked eggs

In a large nonstick frying pan over medium heat, sauté the cabbage in 1 tablespoon of the oil until wilted, about 7 minutes. Do not overcook. Add the dill and transfer to a large bowl.

In the same frying pan, sauté the mushrooms and onions in the remaining 1 tablespoon of oil until the onions are tender and any liquid released by the mushrooms has evaporated. Stir in the tarragon and basil. Remove from the heat.

In a food processor, blend the cottage cheese, egg substitute, and 2 tablespoons of the Parmesan until smooth, about 3 minutes.

Spread the cabbage in the pie shell.

Thinly slice the eggs crosswise. If you are limiting cholesterol, discard the yolks. Layer the eggs on top of the cabbage.

Top with the mushroom mixture. Pour the cottage cheese mixture over all. Sprinkle with the remaining 2 tablespoons Parmesan.

Bake at 350°F for 30 minutes, or until the top is set and golden brown.

Serves 4

SPAGHETTI SQUASH WITH TOMATO SAUCE

Healing Foods

Onions
Tomatoes
Squash (winter)

1 large spaghetti squash	5 plum tomatoes, chopped
1 large onion, diced	$1/2$ cup tomato puree
2 cloves garlic, minced	1 teaspoon dried oregano
$1/2$ teaspoon black pepper	3 tablespoons grated Parmesan cheese

Place the squash in a very large pot. Add water to cover. Bring to a boil and cook, uncovered, for 30 to 60 minutes, or until easily pierced with a fork. Drain, halve, and set aside until cool enough to handle.

Coat a 2-quart saucepan with nonstick spray. Add the onions and sauté over medium heat until translucent, about 5 minutes. Add the garlic and sauté 1 minute.

Add the tomatoes, tomato puree, oregano, and pepper. Simmer for 20 minutes.

Discard the seeds from the squash. Using a fork, separate the flesh into spaghetti-like strands. Reheat briefly in a large frying pan. Serve topped with the sauce and sprinkled with the cheese.

Serves 4

ENCHILADAS WITH CHEESE AND KALE

Healing Foods

Cheese (low-fat)
Kale
Oil

2 cups shredded kale
1/2 cup minced
   scallions
2 tablespoons olive oil
1 cup salsa

8 corn tortillas
1 cup shredded low-
   fat Monterey Jack
   cheese

In a large nonstick frying pan over medium heat, sauté the kale and scallions in 1 tablespoon of the oil until tender, about 5 minutes.

Divide the mixture among the tortillas. Top with the cheese. Roll up each tortilla to enclose the filling.

Clean the frying pan and warm it over medium heat. Add the remaining 1 tablespoon oil. Place the enchiladas, seam-side down, in the pan. Let brown for several minutes on each side.

Add the salsa. Cover the pan, reduce the heat and simmer for about 5 minutes, basting frequently.

Serves 4

VEGETABLE PAELLA

Healing Foods

Peppers (sweet)
Rice
Squash (summer)
Tomatoes

1/4 cup stock
1 teaspoon turmeric
1 sweet red pepper, thinly sliced
4 Italian tomatoes, diced
2 medium zucchini, thinly sliced

3 cups cold cooked rice
1 tablespoon olive oil
2 tablespoons grated Sapsago or Parmesan cheese
2 tablespoons minced fresh parsley

In a large nonstick frying pan, combine the stock and turmeric. Add peppers, tomatoes, and zucchini. Cook until the vegetables are crisp-tender, about 5 minutes. Transfer to a large bowl.

Add the rice and oil to the pan. Stir-fry over medium-high heat for 5 minutes. Add the vegetables and stir to combine. Sprinkle with the cheese and parsley.

Serves 4

CORN ENCHILADAS

Healing Foods

Corn
Oranges
Peppers (chili)
Rice
Yogurt (low-fat)

1 large dried chili
  pepper
  (preferably ancho)
2 teaspoons canola oil
1 cup corn
1/2 cup minced
  sweet red peppers
2 scallions, minced
2 cloves garlic,
  minced
4 flour tortillas
2 tablespoons
  lime juice
1/4 fresh minced
  coriander

1 1/2 cups cold
  cooked rice
1/2 teaspoon
  dried oregano
1/2 teaspoon
  hot-pepper sauce
1/4 teaspoon
  ground cinnamon
1/3 cup shredded
  low-fat cheese
1 cup nonfat
  yogurt
2 cups orange
  sections

Place the chili pepper in a small bowl and cover with boiling water. Let stand until softened, about 15 minutes. Discard the stem and seeds. Mince the pepper; reserve the soaking water.

In a large nonstick frying pan, heat the oil. Add the chili peppers, corn, red peppers, scallions, and garlic. Sauté about 5 minutes.

Add the rice, oregano, hot-pepper sauce, and cinnamon. Sauté for several minutes, until heated through. Remove from the heat and stir in the cheese.

Reserve about $1/2$ cup of filling. Divide the remainder among the tortillas. Roll up each tortilla to enclose the filling.

In the same frying pan, heat the lime juice and $1/2$ cup of the reserved soaking liquid. Place the tortillas in the pan, seam-side down. Cover and simmer until the liquid has been absorbed and the enchiladas are heated through, about 5 minutes.

In a small bowl, combine the yogurt and coriander.

Serve the enchiladas topped with reserved filling, yogurt, and orange sections.

Serves 4

TOO HOT TO HANDLE

Has this ever happened to you: You're chopping hot peppers and you absentmindedly rub your eye. Or touch your lips. Or scratch your nose. Aye Chihuahua! It feels like the fire gods of the Aztecs are seeking revenge on your face! Congratulations, you've just had a rude introduction to capsaicin, the fiery oil that gives chili peppers their characteristic bite and zing (as well as their healing quality). And as you found out, capsaicin can inflame more than your taste buds.

To keep the heat where it belongs:

- Always wear rubber gloves when peeling, seeding, chopping, or otherwise working with hot peppers.
- If you don't have suitable gloves, pull on plastic sandwich bags.
- In any case, remember *never* to touch or rub your face until you've washed your hands thoroughly with warm soapy water.
- For that matter don't touch your children or pets until you're sure there's no capsaicin left on your hands.
- Remember that the area under your nails is very tender and susceptible to capsaicin's bite. So are open cuts.
- Carefully wash all utensils, including the chopping block, with hot soapy water to avoid transferring the irritating oil to other foods.

As for your taste buds, you've probably already discovered that even a tall glass of water won't douse the pain. That's because capsaicin is soluble in oil but not water. Apparently the oil floats the capsaicin away. Milk products, including yogurt, are traditionally used to cool down overheated mouths. Rice and bread also seem effective for putting out the fire.

Some Hot Ideas

With all that in mind, here are some pointers and cooking ideas for using hot chili peppers.
- Most of a chili's fire is concentrated in its seeds and inner ribs. So if you'd like just a little heat in your food, discard those portions.
- Although there's no sure way to predict a

chili's heat, generally the smallest ones are the hottest.

- Roasting fresh chilies removes any bitterness. To do so, skewer one on a utility fork and hold it over a gas flame until burnt on all sides. Or broil the pepper about 4 inches from the heat until charred all over. Wrap in a tea towel until cool, then scrape away the skin.
- Soaking fresh chili peppers in water for a hour or so can help tame their flavor.
- For adding spice to roast beef or pork, slice a chili into slivers. Then use a sharp knife to make slits in the roast. Poke a sliver of chili into each slit. Roast as usual.

LENTIL AND LEEK BURRITOS

Healing Foods

Beans (dried)
Onions
Tomatoes

2 leeks
3/4 teaspoon
   dried oregano
3/4 teaspoon
   chili powder
1/2 teaspoon paprika
1/2 teaspoon hot-
   pepper sauce
1 tablespoon lime
   juice

1/4 teaspoon
   ground cumin
2 cups cooked lentils
4 flour tortillas
1/4 cup shredded
   low-fat cheese
1 tablespoon canola oil
4 tomatoes, quartered
2 scallions,
   finely chopped

428

Cut the leeks in half lengthwise. Rinse well to remove any grit from between the layers. Chop finely.

Coat a large nonstick frying pan with nonstick spray. Add the leeks, oregano, chili powder, paprika, hot-pepper sauce, and cumin. Sauté over medium heat until the mixture is fragrant and the leeks are tender, 5 to 6 minutes. Mix in the lentils.

Divide the mixture among the tortillas. Sprinkle with the cheese. Roll up the tortillas to enclose the filling.

Clean the frying pan. Add the oil and heat briefly on medium high. Add the burritos, seam-side down, and heat until the bottoms are just brown, about 2 minutes.

In a food processor or blender, combine the tomatoes and lime juice. Process briefly with on/off turns until coarsely chopped.

Flip the burritos and cover with the tomatoes. Partially cover the pan and simmer until the tomatoes are heated through, about 4 minutes. Sprinkle with the scallions.

Serves 4

EGGS: THE REAL THING?

You may notice that most of the recipes in this book call for egg whites or egg substitute rather than whole eggs. That's because most people on a healing diet would prefer to limit their cholesterol intake. And egg yolks are particularly rich in cholesterol—the usual estimate is 250 to 275 milligrams in a single large yolk. For people on a strict cholesterol-lowering diet, that's almost twice their cholesterol quota for an entire day.

Egg whites, on the other hand, are composed almost entirely of low-cal, high-quality protein. So you can eat all you want. Egg substitutes are made mostly of egg whites and contain no cholesterol and fewer calories than whole eggs. Some brands have no fat at all; others weigh in at about half of what's in an egg. Read the labels.

Here are some tips for using egg substitutes and egg whites.

- Thaw egg substitute before using and store leftovers in the refrigerator. Use the excess within a week.
- For casseroles and most baked goods, replace each whole egg with 2 egg whites or $1/4$ cup egg substitute.
- In dishes where only egg yolks are required, use $1/4$ cup egg substitute for each yolk. But be aware that recipes calling for more than 2 yolks may not turn out well if made with egg sub.
- When making cakes, get nice volume by increasing the egg substitute to $1/3$ cup in place of each whole egg.
- If making a cake that calls for three or four eggs, reduce the amount of liquid (usually milk) by 2 tablespoons to compensate for the extra egg liquid.
- Because egg substitute is pasteurized, it's suitable for uncooked salad dressings and mayonnaise.

- Egg substitutes do contain real egg, so treat foods you prepare with them just as you would egg dishes. Refrigerate custards, mayonnaise-based salads, and other foods as usual.
- You can make omelets, frittatas, and scrambled eggs with all whites. Add a little mustard for egg-yolk color.
- For reduced-cholesterol egg dishes, pair one yolk with two, three, or four whites.

CHAPTER TEN

Fish and Seafood

Until a few years ago, fish was considered "health food" because of what it didn't have—lots of fat and calories. Dieters ordered fish as a lean alternative to steak, chops, and other red meats. Then scientists stumbled across an intriguing phenomenon: Heart disease was rare among Greenland Eskimos, despite their high consumption of animal fats (including whale blubber). But the Eskimos also ate a lot of fatty fish like mackerel, and therein lies the clue to this dietary paradox.

Mackerel happens to be the richest source of special polyunsaturated fats called omega-3 fatty acids. These fatty acids, also found in other deep-water fish like salmon, herring, sablefish, and tuna, may help lower blood levels of cholesterol and triglycerides. In some studies, they inhibited the formation of plaque on artery walls, fending off heart disease and stroke.

What's more, shellfish—mollusks and crustaceans such as shrimp, crab, oysters, and clams—also contain omega-3's. And seafood in general tends to be high in important nutrients like magnesium, potassium, zinc, and iron. Clams, for example, are a tremendous source of blood-building iron, and oysters are loaded with zinc for fighting off infections.

432

The only catch? To benefit from the healing powers of fish, you should probably eat two or three sea meals a week. But with recipes like the ones in this chapter, that shouldn't be too hard to swallow! Dark-fleshed fish like salmon, mackerel, and bluefish are your best bets, but even milder varieties contribute omega-3's. For a rundown of the top omega-3 sources, see "Fishing for the Best" on page 79.

MONKFISH WITH CITRUS AND GINGER

Healing Foods

Fish
Oranges
Peas

1¼ pounds monkfish fillets	2 scallions, sliced
2 tablespoons olive oil	1 tablespoon peeled minced gingerroot
2 cloves garlic, minced	1 tablespoon grated orange rind
3 cups sugar snap peas	2 cups orange sections

Trim the membrane and any discolored areas from the fish. Cut the fish diagonally into 2-inch by ¹/₂-inch strips.

In a large nonstick frying pan over medium-high heat, heat 1 tablespoon of oil. Add half of the fish and the garlic. Sauté until the fish turns white. Remove the fish with a slotted spoon.

Add the remaining fish to the pan and sauté until white. Remove from the pan. Drain off the liquid.

In the same pan, heat the remaining 1 table-spoon of oil. Add the peas, scallions, ginger, and orange rind. Cook, stirring frequently, until the peas are tender-crisp, about 6 to 8 minutes. Add the oranges and heat 1 minute.

Return the fish to the pan and heat through.

Serves 4

THYME-FLAVORED TUNA STEAKS

Healing Foods

Fish
Oil
Peppers (sweet)

2 tablespoons olive oil
1 teaspoon
  dried thyme
2 sweet red peppers,
  thinly sliced

$1/4$ teaspoon black
  pepper
1 pound tuna steaks

In a small bowl, combine the oil, thyme, and black pepper. Rub on both sides of each piece of fish.

Place the tuna in a single layer in a glass baking dish. Cover with the red peppers. Drizzle with any remaining oil mixture.

Bake at 350°F for 30 to 45 minutes, or until the fish flakes easily with a fork.

Serves 4

CHINESE BRAISED MACKEREL

Healing Foods

Carrots
Fish
Garlic

1/4 cup rice-wine vinegar
1/2 teaspoon low-sodium soy sauce
3 thin slices peeled gingerroot, julienned
5 scallions, julienned

3 cloves garlic, minced
1 pound mackerel fillets
1 cup chicken stock
3 white icicle radishes, julienned
1 large carrot, julienned

In a glass baking dish, combine the vinegar, soy sauce, ginger, and garlic. Add the mackerel, skin-side up, in a single layer. Marinate for at least 10 minutes.

In a large nonstick flying pan, bring the stock to a boil. Reduce the heat to a simmer. Add the mackerel, skin-side up, and the marinade. Cover and simmer 5 minutes.

Add the radishes and carrots. Simmer 2 to 3 minutes. With a slotted spoon, transfer the mackerel and vegetables to a serving platter.

Boil the liquid until reduced by half. Pour over the fish. Sprinkle with the scallions.

Serves 4

435

GREAT GRILLING: FISH

Want a low-fat, brimming-with-nutrients alternative to hot dogs, burgers, and barbecued chicken? Fish is made to order. For the best results:

- Use firm-fleshed fish, such as catfish, grouper, halibut, marlin, monkfish, red snapper, rockfish, sablefish, salmon, shark, swordfish, tilefish, or tuna.
- Make sure fillets and steaks are at least 1-inch thick so they're less likely to fall apart on the grill.
- Marinate the fish before grilling. Try a mixture of 2 tablespoons lime juice and 1 tablespoon canola oil. Add herbs to taste. Cover and let stand in the refrigerator for about 30 minutes.
- Coat the grilling rack with nonstick spray. Heat it until very hot.
- Place the fish on a the hot rack and cover with a lid. Cook 3 to 4 minutes. Use a spatula to reposition the fish at a 45-degree angle to its original placement (don't flip it or it may fall apart). Cover and cook 3 to 4 minutes. Don't overcook.
- For a no-cleanup fish dish, try the following succulent combination:

Fish in Foil

4 ounces firm fish	1 parsley sprig
1 thin onion slice, separated into rings	Pinch of paprika
	Pinch of ground
2 thin green pepper rings	white pepper
	2 teaspoons lemon
2 thin lemon slices	juice

Place the fish on a 12 x 14-inch piece of foil. Top with the onions, green peppers, lemons, parsley, paprika, and white pepper. Sprinkle with the lemon juice.

Fold the foil into an envelope around the fish to seal in the juice. Cook on on outdoor grill with the lid closed (or in a 450°F oven) for 15 to 20 minutes, or until the fish flakes easily with a fork.

Serves 1

Healing Foods

- Fish   • Onions   • Peppers (sweet)

FISH AND CHIPS

Healing Foods

Fish
Lemons and limes
Oil
Potatoes

437

12 small red
  potatoes
3 tablespoons olive oil
1 pound
  flounder fillets
$1/2$ teaspoon paprika
$1/4$ cup whole
  wheat flour
$1/8$ teaspoon red
  pepper
$1/4$ cup lemon juice

Scrub the potatoes, then dry thoroughly. Leaving the skins on, cut them into strips roughly 2 inches long and $1/2$ inch thick and wide. Pat dry again.

Coat a jelly-roll pan with nonstick spray. Add the potatoes. Drizzle with 2 teaspoons of the oil. Toss to coat well.

Bake at 450°F for 30 minutes, turning the potatoes frequently.

Meanwhile, pat the fish dry. Place the flour and red pepper in a plastic bag. Add the fish, a piece at a time, and shake well to coat lightly with flour. Fold each fillet in half or roll lengthwise so all the fish can later fit in a single layer in a large frying pan.

After the potatoes have been in the oven for 30 minutes, heat a large cast-iron flying pan or other heavy, ovenproof pan over medium-high heat until quite hot. Add the remaining oil. Add the fish to the pan in a single layer. Immediately tilt the pan so you can spoon some of the oil over the fish.

Transfer the pan to the oven with the potatoes. Bake both for 10 to 15 minutes (depending upon the thickness of the fillets), until the fish is cooked through and the potatoes are crisp.

Remove the fish and potatoes from the oven.

Transfer to a serving platter. Add the lemon juice to the fish pan. Stir to loosen any browned bits from the bottom. Pour over the fish. Sprinkle with the paprika.

Serves 4

GRILLED FLORIDA SNAPPER

Healing Foods

Fish
Onions
Oranges
Papayas

1 large onion, thinly sliced	1 tablespoon coarse mustard
1 tablespoon olive oil	2 cups chopped orange sections
1 pound red snapper fillets	1 cup chopped papayas
$^1/_3$ cup lime juice	
2 tablespoons honey	

In a large nonstick frying pan over medium-high heat, sauté the onion in the oil until soft and light brown, about 8 to 10 minutes. Set aside.

While the onions are cooking, rub the snapper on both sides with the mustard. Grill or broil about $5^1/_2$ inches from the heat until cooked through, about $4^1/_2$ minutes on each side. Transfer to a heated serving platter. Top with the onions, oranges, and papayas. Keep warm.

Add the lime juice and honey to the frying

439

pan. Bring to a boil over high heat and cook, stirring frequently, until reduced by half, about 3 minutes. Drizzle over the fish.

Serves 4

LOBSTER WITH MINT VINAIGRETTE

Healing Foods

Carrots
Crustaceans
Oil
Papayas
Spinach

1/4 cup lime juice
2 tablespoons olive oil
1 cup diced carrots
1 cup diced celery
2 papayas, chopped
2 cups shredded
  spinach

1/4 cup minced
  shallots
1/2 teaspoon
  dried mint
1 1/2 cups chopped
  cooked lobster

In a large bowl, combine the lime juice, oil, carrots, celery, shallots, and mint. Add the lobster and papayas. Mix well. Chill.

Serve the salad on the spinach.

Serves 4

BAY SCALLOPS WITH SAFFRON

Healing Foods

Garlic
Mollusks
Salad greens

1/4 cup orange juice
1/2 teaspoon saffron
2 cloves garlic, minced
1 pound bay scallops
1 small head
  red lettuce

1/2 cup sliced scallions
1 1/2 cups shredded
  chicory
2 tablespoons light
  mayonnaise

In a large nonstick frying pan over medium heat, heat the orange juice, saffron, and garlic to a simmer. Add the scallops and scallions. Sauté until the scallops are opaque, about 3 minutes.

Transfer the mixture to a large bowl. Add the chicory and mayonnaise. Toss well to combine.

Line a platter with red lettuce. Spoon the scallop mixture onto the platter. Serve warm or chilled.

Serves 4

SOFT-SHELL SAUTÉ

Healing Foods

Crustaceans
Oil

1/3 cup cornmeal
8 soft-shell crabs, cleaned
2 tablespoons olive oil
1/4 cup apple juice
1/4 teaspoon dried thyme
1/4 cup white grape juice
2 tablespoons raspberry vinegar
1/4 teaspoon dry mustard

Spread the cornmeal on a sheet of waxed paper. Lightly dredge the crabs in it to coat both sides.

In a large nonstick frying pan over medium heat, heat 1 tablespoon of the oil. Add four crabs. Sauté for about 3 minutes on each side, until the crabs turn a reddish color. Remove to a plate and keep warm.

Repeat with the remaining oil and crabs.

In a small saucepan, combine the apple juice, grape juice, vinegar, mustard, and thyme. Bring to a boil and cook until reduced by half. Pour over the crabs and serve immediately.

Serves 4

MACKEREL SALAD

Healing Foods

Fish
Oil
Salad greens
Watercress

2 tablespoons white-
wine vinegar
1 teaspoon Dijon
mustard
1 clove garlic,
minced
1 tablespoon minced
fresh parsley
2 tablespoons
canola oil
1 head Boston
lettuce

1 tablespoon
snipped chives
$1/4$ teaspoon
dried tarragon
1 can (15 ounces)
mackerel, drained
and flaked
1 cup thinly
sliced radishes
1 cup firmly packed
watercress leaves

In a large bowl, whisk together the vinegar, mustard, and garlic. Slowly whisk in the oil. Stir in the parsley, chives, and tarragon. Add the mackerel and toss gently. Cover and refrigerate for 1 to 2 hours.

Add the radishes. Toss gently.

Tear the lettuce into bite-size pieces. Line a platter with the lettuce and watercress. Place the mackerel salad on the greens.

Serves 4

SHARK AND STARS

Healing Foods

Fish
Tropical fruit

4 starfruit
2 tablespoons
  lime juice
2 cloves garlic,
  minced

1 teaspoon hot-
  pepper flakes
1 teaspoon canola oil
1$^1/_4$ pounds shark
  steaks

Juice three of the starfruit by running them through a food mill or using a citrus juicer. Pour the juice into a glass baking dish. Add the lime juice, garlic, pepper, and oil.

Add the shark and refrigerate for 1 hour, flipping the pieces periodically. Remove from the marinade, reserving the liquid.

Broil the shark about 5 inches from the heat for 5 to 7 minutes per side, basting occasionally with reserved marinade.

Thinly slice the remaining starfruit. Serve the fish topped with the fruit.

Serves 4

SPANISH HALIBUT

Healing Foods

Fish
Garlic
Onions
Peppers (sweet)

6 tablespoons vinegar
$^1/_4$ teaspoon
  crushed saffron
1 pound halibut fillets
1 sweet red pepper,
  thinly sliced

2 leeks, minced
2 cloves garlic, minced
1 tablespoon olive oil
1 teaspoon
  dried thyme

444

In large frying pan over medium heat, bring about 1 inch of water to a simmer. Stir in 4 tablespoons of the vinegar and the saffron. Add the halibut and red peppers. Simmer for 15 minutes, or until the fish flakes easily with a fork.

Use a spatula or slotted spoon to remove the fish and peppers from the liquid. Place in a 9 x 13-inch glass baking dish.

In a medium bowl, combine the remaining 2 tablespoons of vinegar with the leeks, garlic, oil, and thyme. Pour over the fish, cover, and refrigerate for at least 1 hour.

Serves 4

PERCH
WITH MUSTARD AND THYME

Healing Foods

Bran
Fish

1/2 cup oat bran	1/2 cup chicken stock
1 pound perch fillets	1 teaspoon Dijon
1 tablespoon olive oil	mustard
1/2 teaspoon	
dried thyme	

Place the oat bran on a large sheet of waxed paper. Dredge both sides of each fillet in the oat bran to coat.

Heat the oil in a nonstick frying pan. Add the

445

fillets and sauté until cooked through, about 3$^1/_2$ minutes on each side.

Carefully remove the fish to a heated platter. Pour the stock into the frying pan. Whisk in the mustard and thyme. Bring to a boil and cook until reduced by half. Pour over the fish.

Serves 4

MADRID TROUT

Healing Foods

Fish
Peas
Rice
Tomatoes

1 tablespoon olive oil
1 cup medium-grain brown rice
$^1/_2$ cup minced celery
$^1/_2$ cup minced onions
$^1/_2$ cup minced watercress
1 cup peeled, seeded, and chopped Italian tomatoes
3 cloves garlic, minced
$^1/_4$ teaspoon paprika
$^1/_4$ teaspoon dried thyme
2 cups chicken stock
1 pound trout fillets
1 cup peas

In a large nonstick frying pan, heat the oil. Add the rice, celery, onions, watercress, garlic, paprika, and thyme. Stirring constantly, sauté for 3 to 4 minutes, until the mixture is fragrant.

Add the stock and bring to a boil. Reduce the

heat, cover, and simmer for 35 minutes, or until the rice is almost tender.

Add the fish, cover, and simmer 8 minutes. Add the tomatoes and peas. Cover and simmer for 4 minutes, or just until the peas are tender.

Serves 4

HADDOCK BLACK RAVEN

Healing Foods

Fish
Garlic
Oil
Tomatoes

2 tablespoons olive oil
2 onions, thinly sliced
4 cloves garlic, minced
1/8 teaspoon red
   pepper
1 pound haddock
   fillets

2 cups chopped
   tomatoes
1 teaspoon
   basil vinegar
1 teaspoon
   dried basil

In a large nonstick frying pan over medium-low heat, heat the oil. Add the onions and garlic. Cook, stirring frequently, until soft, about 5 to 10 minutes.

Add the tomatoes, vinegar, basil, and red pepper to the pan. Cook for 10 minutes, or until most of the liquid from the tomatoes has evaporated.

Add the haddock. Cover the pan and cook until the fish is opaque and flakes easily, about 10 minutes.

Serves 4

BOUILLABAISSE

Healing Foods

Carrots
Crustaceans
Fish
Mollusks
Tomatoes

1 cup sliced carrots
1 cup sliced celery
1 cup sliced
  red onions
1 cup sliced
  fresh fennel
1 tablespoon olive oil
2 cups peeled,
  seeded, and
  chopped tomatoes
24 shrimp, peeled,
  and deveined

1 clove garlic, minced
$1/4$ teaspoon saffron
2 quarts stock
2 bay leaves
$1/2$ teaspoon
  fennel seed
$1/2$ teaspoon
  dried oregano
1 pound red snapper,
  cut into 1-inch
  chunks
1 pound scallops

In a 4-quart pot over medium-high heat, sauté the carrots, celery, onions, and fennel in the oil for 5 minutes. Add the tomatoes, garlic, and saffron. Sauté for 5 minutes.

Add the stock, bay leaves, fennel seed, and oregano. Bring to a boil. Reduce the heat, cover, and simmer for 30 minutes.

Add the snapper, scallops, and shrimp. Cover and simmer for 5 to 7 minutes, or until the seafood is tender. Discard the bay leaves.

Serves 6

SIZZLED SALMON WITH MINT

Healing Foods

Fish
Oranges
Tomatoes

1 pound salmon fillet
1/4 cup orange juice
2 cups chopped
  tomatoes

2 cups orange sections
2 tablespoons minced
  fresh mint
1 tablespoon olive oil

Place the salmon in a baking dish. Pour the orange juice over it. Allow to marinate for about 10 minutes.

In a small bowl, combine tomatoes, oranges, and mint. Set aside.

In a large nonstick frying pan over medium-high heat, sauté the fish in the oil for about 4 minutes per side, until brown on the outside and cooked through.

Serve topped with the tomato mixture.

Serves 4

SALMON WITH SCALLIONS

Healing Foods

Fish
Lemons and limes
Onions
Tomatoes

449

1 pound salmon fillet
1 tablespoon olive oil
1/4 cup lime juice
1/4 cup lemon juice
1/2 cup minced
  scallions

3 cloves garlic, minced
2 tablespoons minced
  fresh parsley
1/4 teaspoon hot-
  pepper sauce
2 large tomatoes,
  thinly sliced

In a large nonstick frying pan over medium-high heat, sauté the salmon in the oil for 4 to 5 minutes on each side. Handle the fish gently to keep the pieces whole.

Add the lime juice, lemon juice, garlic, parsley, and hot-pepper sauce to the pan. Cook for about 3 minutes.

Transfer the salmon to a large platter. Pour the pan juices over the fish. Cover and refrigerate until chilled.

Serve sprinkled with the scallions and topped with the tomatoes.

Serves 4

BROILED SALMON WITH CUCUMBERS

Healing Foods

Cucumbers
Fish
Garlic
Onions
Rice

1 cup diced onions
1/2 cup vinegar
4 cloves garlic,
  minced
2 teaspoons peeled
  minced gingerroot
1 tablespoon olive oil

1 teaspoon low-
  sodium soy sauce
2 cucumbers,
  thinly sliced
1 1/2 pounds
  salmon fillets
2 cups hot cooked rice

In a large nonstick frying pan over medium-high heat, combine the onions, vinegar, garlic, ginger, and soy sauce. Bring to a boil, stir, and cook for 3 minutes. Remove from the heat.

Add the cucumbers. Set aside to cool.

Rub the salmon on both sides with the oil. Broil about 6 inches from the heat for 4 to 5 minutes per side, or until cooked through.

Serve on a bed of rice topped with the cucumbers.

Serves 4

BLUEFISH IN A SEA OF GREEN

Healing Foods

Fish
Peas

1/4 cup fresh
  bread crumbs
1/4 cup thinly
  sliced scallions
3 cups snow peas
1 teaspoon sesame oil

2 tablespoons Dijon
  mustard
1 tablespoon olive oil
1 1/2 pounds bluefish
  fillets

In a small bowl, combine the bread crumbs, scallions, mustard, and oil.

Coat a piece of foil large enough to hold the fish in a single layer with nonstick spray. Place on a broiling pan, sprayed side up.

Place the fish, skin-side down, on the foil. Spread with the bread crumb mixture.

Broil 8 inches from the heat for 8 to 10 minutes, or until cooked through.

In a large nonstick frying pan, stir-fry the snow peas in the sesame oil for 3 or 4 minutes, or until crisp-tender.

Arrange the peas on a platter. Top with the fish.

Serves 4

TUNA WITH ORANGE AND GINGER SAUCE

Healing Foods

Fish
Onions
Oranges

1/4 cup orange juice
1 tablespoon all-fruit orange marmalade
1 tablespoon peeled minced gingerroot

1 tablespoon canola oil
1 pound tuna steaks
1 cup orange sections
1/2 cup chopped scallions

In a small bowl, combine the orange juice, marmalade, ginger, and oil.

Place the tuna in a single layer in a glass baking dish. Pour the juice mixture over them. Cover and allow to marinate for about 30 minutes.

Coat a broiler rack with nonstick spray. Use a fork to transfer the tuna from the dish to the rack. Reserve the marinade.

Broil the fish about 6 inches from the heat until cooked through, about 5 minutes per side.

Transfer the reserved marinade to a 1-quart saucepan. Add the oranges and scallions. Bring to a boil and cook for 1 minute. Serve the fish topped with the orange sauce.

Serves 4

DILLED SALMON TART

Healing Foods

Fish
Wheat germ
Yogurt (low-fat)

1 can (15 ounces) salmon, drained and flaked
2 cups egg substitute
1/2 teaspoon ground allspice

1 cup nonfat yogurt
1 tablespoon dillweed
1 teaspoon Dijon mustard
1/2 cup wheat germ

In a large bowl, combine the salmon, egg substitute, yogurt, dill, mustard, and allspice.

Coat four 5-inch pie pans with nonstick spray. Coat with the wheat germ, reserving any excess.

453

Divide the salmon mixture among the pans. Sprinkle with any remaining wheat germ. Bake at 400°F for 20 to 25 minutes, or until set.

Serves 4

Accent on Health: Seafood—Making It Right

Fish is only as healthy as the intentions of the cook making it. Keeping your fish cookery on the healthful—as well as tasteful—side means wise decisions when it comes to buying and preparing fish. The cardinal rules: Buy the best. Keep it light. And never overcook. Here's how:

Buying
- *Whole fish.* Look for clear eyes, ruby red gills, moist scales, firm flesh.
- *Fillets.* Clean, fresh odor; never "fishy."
- Buy fish last on your shopping trips. Rush it home and refrigerate or cook it promptly.
- *If you must store fish for a day.* Wash with cold water, wrap in plastic, and place on a container of ice in the fridge.

Steaming
This method is suitable for cod, flounder, grouper, haddock, halibut, mahimahi, pollack, red snapper, rockfish, salmon, scrod, sea bass, sole, walleye.
1. Bring 1 cup of liquid to a boil in a wok or large pot with a tight-fitting lid.
2. Place the fish on a steam rack that you've coated with nonstick spray. Add to the pot.

3. Cover with a lid and steam for 10 minutes. Do not remove the lid until the time is up.
4. Suggested steaming liquids: lemongrass tea; lemon verbena tea; water with 1 tablespoon Dijon mustard, 1 tablespoon lemon juice, and 1 teaspoon thyme.

Poaching

This method is suitable for catfish, cod, flounder, haddock, halibut, mahimahi, monkfish, orange roughy, pollack, pout, red snapper, salmon, scrod, sole, trout (whole), walleye.
1. Bring 6 cups of water or stock and herbs/spices to a boil over medium-high heat; boil for 5 minutes.
2. Add the fish and additional water to cover, if needed. Reduce the heat to a simmer. Cook 10 minutes.
3. Suggested poaching liquid: 6 cups water, 3 tablespoons wine vinegar, 12 peppercorns, 5 parsley sprigs, 3 bay leaves.
4. If desired, boil down the liquid, strain, and use as a brothy sauce.

Baking

This method is suitable for bluefish, catfish, cod, flounder, grouper, haddock, halibut, mackerel, mahimahi, orange roughy, pollack, red snapper, rockfish, salmon, scrod, sea trout, sole, trout (whole).
1. Brush the fish with juice. Sprinkle with bread crumbs.
2. Place on a baking sheet. Bake at 400°F for 6 minutes.

3. Baste with juice. Bake 6 minutes.
4. Suggested juice: equal parts orange juice, lemon juice, and lime juice.

Serving Suggestions
- Spoon on a vinaigrette made of chopped tomatoes, minced roasted garlic, olive oil, and vinegar.
- Accompany with a vegetable or fruit relish made of chopped sweet peppers, tomatoes, or mangoes. Toss with hot vinegar, honey, and scallions. Let stand 1 hour before using.
- Splash on flavored vinegars, such as raspberry, cabernet-wine, or rice-wine.
- Sprinkle with piquant seasonings. Try roasted garlic, roasted shallots, curry paste, or chili paste.

SWORDFISH AND PINEAPPLE BROCHETTES

Healing Foods

Fish
Pineapple

1 small pineapple	1 pound swordfish
1/3 cup orange juice	steaks, 1 inch thick
1/4 cup peeled	3 tablespoons light
chopped gingerroot	mayonnaise

Peel and core the pineapple. Cut part of the flesh into 12 (1-inch) cubes and reserve.

Coarsely chop the rest of the pineapple and place in a blender. Add the orange juice and ginger. Puree. Pour into a bowl or shallow baking dish.

Cut the swordfish into 16 cubes. Add to the pineapple mixture, toss to coat, cover, and allow to marinate in the refrigerator for 1 hour.

For each serving, alternate four swordfish cubes and three pineapple cubes on an 8-inch skewer. Reserve the marinade.

Place the skewers on a lightly oiled broiler pan. Broil about 4 inches from the heat for 4 to 5 minutes, turning three times to evenly broil all sides.

Place the reserved marinade in a 1-quart saucepan. Bring to a boil. Pour into a bowl. Whisk in the mayonnaise until smooth. Serve with the brochettes.

Serves 4

Accent on Health: Making Better Batter

Are you guilty of battering your fish? That's no way to treat such a healthy food! Yet batter-fried fish is extremely popular. In fact, it's one item weight watchers and health seekers miss most when they shape up their diets. Well, rejoice. Because the following no-fry batter is so close in taste and texture to the "real thing" that even long-time fans of batter-fried fish declare it *superb.*

The secret? Egg whites, skim milk, and a very light spritzing of olive oil combine to produce old-fashioned crunch without a lot of fat and calories. And this method works as well on chicken as it does on fillets such as flounder, haddock, and cod.

Batter-Dipped Fish

$1/2$ cup skim milk
4 flounder fillets
   (about 12 ounces)
$1/2$ cup whole wheat
   flour
3 egg whites,
   lightly beaten

$1/8$ teaspoon paprika
$1/8$ teaspoon ground
   white pepper
1 lemon, cut into
   wedges
$1/2$ cup bread crumbs

Place the milk in a shallow dish, such as a pie plate. Add the flounder and soak for 5 minutes.

Dredge the fish in the flour to coat. Then dip in the egg whites. Dredge in the bread crumbs.

Dip the fish in the egg whites again and then into the bread crumbs again.

Coat a slotted broiler pan with nonstick spray. Place the fish on the pan. Sprinkle lightly with the paprika and pepper. Spray the fish lightly with nonstick spray (preferably one flavored with olive oil).

Bake at 400°F for 12 minutes.

Serves 4

Healing Foods

• Fish   • Milk (low-fat)   • Whole wheat flour

MONKFISH IN GINGER SAUGE

Healing Foods

Fish
Garlic
Herbs and spices
Yogurt (low-fat)

1 pound
  monkfish fillets
1 cup nonfat yogurt
1 tablespoon olive oil
1 tablespoon
  mustard seeds
1 onion, finely
  chopped
$^1/_4$ teaspoon
  ground cloves

2 cloves garlic, minced
2 tablespoons peeled
  grated gingerroot
2 teaspoons
  ground turmeric
2 teaspoons
  ground fennel
1 teaspoon ground
  cinnamon
$^1/_4$ teaspoon ground
  black pepper

Cut the fish into individual portions. Place in a single layer in a large dish and cover with the yogurt. Cover the dish and refrigerate several hours or overnight.

Heat the oil in a large nonstick frying pan. Add the mustard seeds. Heat until the seeds start to pop. Immediately cover the pan and shake it gently, as though making popcorn, until the popping stops. Do not let the seeds burn.

Add the onions, garlic, ginger, turmeric, fennel, cinnamon, cloves, and pepper to the pan. Cook over low heat until the onion is softened, about 5 minutes. Remove from the heat and allow the mixture to cool.

Spread half of the spice mixture in the bottom of a 9 x 13-inch baking dish. Add the fish and yogurt. Cover with the remaining spice mixture. Cover the dish with foil.

Bake at 400°F for 10 to 15 minutes, or until the fish feels firm to the touch and is cooked through.

Serves 4

HERB-STEAMED MUSSELS WITH RICE PILAF

Healing Foods

Carrots
Garlic
Mollusks
Oil
Peas
Rice

1 tablespoon olive oil	1 teaspoon
1 cup chopped	dried oregano
onions	2 cups chicken stock
3 cloves garlic,	24 mussels, scrubbed
minced	and debearded
1 cup long-grain white	1 large carrot, julienned
or Basmati rice	1 cup snow peas

In a 14-inch paella pan (or other sloping-sided pan), heat the oil. Add the onions and garlic, sauté for 5 minutes. Add the rice and oregano; sauté for 3 minutes. Add the stock and bring to a boil. Reduce the heat and simmer for 20 minutes.

Add the mussels and carrots. Loosely cover the pan with foil. When the mussels begin to open, add the snow peas. Cover and simmer until the mussels are fully open. (The opening process should take about 6 minutes.) Discard any mussels that don't open.

Serves 4

SNAPPER WITH RED-PEPPER SALSA

Healing Foods

Fish
Peppers (sweet)

3 sweet red peppers
1/4 cup minced
   fresh parsley
2 tablespoons minced
   fresh coriander
1/2 teaspoon hot-
   pepper sauce

3 scallions, minced
2 tablespoons
   lemon juice
1 tablespoon
   canola oil
1 1/2 pounds red
   snapper fillets

Broil the red peppers about 4 inches from the heat until blackened on all sides. Set aside until cool enough to handle. Discard the cores and seeds; dice the flesh. Transfer to a medium bowl.

Add the parsley, coriander, scallions, lemon juice, oil, and hot-pepper sauce. Set aside.

461

Place the fish in a steamer basket. Steam over boiling water for 7 to 8 minutes, or until the fish flakes easily with a fork. Serve topped with the salsa.

Serves 4

MICRO METHOD: Fish in a Flash

Credit the microwave with being one of the fastest—and healthiest—ways to cook fish. Because the microwave speeds cooking, there's little moisture loss. That means you'll be eating tender, moist, and succulent fish that doesn't need a fatty sauce to taste good.

One pound of fish cooks in roughly 4 to 5 minutes. That's enough fish for 4 servings—at about a minute per serving. You won't find anything more convenient than that! Here are some tips for getting the best results.

- Small items, such as shrimp and bay scallops, cook more quickly than whole fish and thick steaks.
- Always peel shrimp before microwaving. Microwaving can make the shells difficult to remove.
- To prevent overcooking, choose fish fillets of uniform thickness. If the fillets are irregular, overlap thinner pieces to build them up. Or fold the thinner parts under.
- Cook fish directly on a plate or in a casserole dish. Do not use paper towels, as the fish may stick.

- Rotate the dish or rearrange the fish after half the cooking time.
- Cover the dish to facilitate cooking. Pour off any excess liquid that accumulates before serving.
- Remove fish from the oven when it's barely cooked. Let stand, covered, for a few minutes, then test for doneness. The flesh should be opaque and easy to flake with a fork.
- If your recipe contains longer-cooking ingredients, such as carrots or potatoes, partially cook them first. Add the seafood toward the end.
- Remember that fish will begin cooking as soon as it is combined with hot foods or sauces. To avoid overcooking, you may want to reduce power to medium (50 percent).
- If using full power, stir casseroles often and check fillets and steaks frequently to avoid overcooking. Remove shellfish cooked on high power from the oven while still translucent and allow them to stand for a few minutes to finish cooking.
- For best results, defrost frozen fish in the refrigerator. Just place it on a plate in the fridge in the morning if you intend serving it for dinner. If you defrost the fish in the microwave and then cook it there too, you may find the flavor and texture unpleasantly changed. Also since fish cooks so rapidly, it's difficult to defrost it without actually cooking the flesh.
- For nice flavor, you may want to add a small amount of herbs (fresh if possible), spices, flavored vinegar, lemon juice, or lime juice

before cooking. Or cook the fish on a bed of shredded vegetables.

- To cook several fillets, you might want to use this pinwheel method: Fold under the *thick* end of the fillets and arrange them facing toward the outside of a shallow dish. Position the thinner ends pointing toward the center of the dish. Microwaves tend to cook foods from the circumference of the dish toward the center, so this arrangement ensures even cooking.

- Similarly, arrange fish steaks pinwheel-fashion, with the wide ends toward the outside of the dish.

- When cooking whole fish, you have the option of removing the head and tail or leaving them on. For added flavor, place some chopped vegetables or herbs inside the cavity.

- When cooking fillets in sauce, reduce the amount of liquid in the sauce, since there will be no evaporation during the short cooking time. Because sauce will shield delicate fish, there is no need to cover the dish. Besides, excess steam produced by covering might make the sauce watery.

OYSTER FRITTERS WITH TARRAGON-MUSTARD SAUCE

Healing Foods

Bulgur
Garlic
Mollusks
Parsley
Yogurt (low-fat)

FRITTERS
1 cup boiling water
1/2 cup bulgur
1 onion, finely
  chopped
1 teaspoon oil
2 cups chopped
  oysters
1/2 cup minced
  fresh parsley
1 teaspoon
  dried tarragon
2 cloves garlic, minced
1/2 cup egg substitute
4 egg whites

SAUCE
1 cup nonfat yogurt
1 tablespoon
  Dijon mustard
1 teaspoon
  dried tarragon

To make the fritters: In a small bowl, combine the water and bulgur. Cover tightly with plastic wrap or foil. Let stand for 1 hour. Drain any excess water.

In a large nonstick frying pan, sauté the onions in the oil until rich brown in color. Add the bulgur, oysters, parsley, tarragon, and garlic. Cook, stirring, for 3 to 5 minutes, or until heated through. Remove from the heat and stir in the egg substitute.

In a large clean bowl with clean beaters, beat the egg whites until soft peaks form. Fold into the oyster mixture.

Coat a baking sheet with nonstick spray. Spoon 1/4-cup mounds of the oyster mixture onto the sheet. Bake at 375°F for 10 to 15 minutes.

To make the sauce: In a small bowl, combine the yogurt, mustard, and tarragon. Serve with the fritters.

Serves 4

SHRIMP AND ROASTED PEPPERS

Healing Foods

Crustaceans
Kale
Peppers (sweet)

1 pound large shrimp
3 sweet red peppers
1 tablespoon
 snipped chives

1 tablespoon
 balsamic vinegar
1 tablespoon olive oil
2 cups shredded kale

Steam the shrimp in their shells for 3 minutes, or until they turn bright orange. When cool enough to handle, remove the shells. Slice each shrimp in half lengthwise, removing the vein as you go.

Roast the peppers under a broiler until charred on all sides. Set aside until cool enough to handle. Remove the charred skins, seeds, and inner membranes. Slice the peppers into strips.

In a large bowl, combine the shrimp, peppers, chives, vinegar, and oil.

Arrange the kale on a serving platter. Place the shrimp mixture on top. Serve chilled.

Serves 4

FLOUNDER WITH PEPPER PUREE

Healing Foods

Fish
Garlic
Peppers (sweet)

4 sweet red peppers, sliced	1 tablespoon olive oil
1 cup water	$1/2$ teaspoon dried basil
4 cloves garlic, minced	$1/3$ cup white-wine vinegar
2 green peppers, diced	1 pound flounder fillets

In a large nonstick frying pan, combine the red peppers, water, garlic, oil, and basil. Cover and cook over medium heat until tender, about 15 minutes.

Transfer to a blender. Add the vinegar. Puree until smooth. Stir in the green peppers.

Coat a 9 x 13-inch baking dish with nonstick spray. Add the flounder in a single layer. Top with the peppers.

Bake at 450°F for 12 to 15 minutes, or until the fish flakes easily with a fork.

Serves 4

TUNA AND PEPPER BAKE

Healing Foods

Fish
Garlic
Onions
Peppers (sweet)

1 pound tuna steaks
2 teaspoons olive oil
3 tablespoons
  lime juice
1 onion, thinly sliced
1/4 cup minced
  fresh parsley

1 sweet red pepper,
  finely chopped
1 yellow pepper,
  finely chopped
2 cloves garlic,
  thinly sliced

Coat a glass baking dish with nonstick spray. Rub the tuna on both sides with the oil. Place in a single layer in the dish. Sprinkle with the lime juice.

Top with the onions, red peppers, yellow peppers, and garlic. Cover tightly with foil and bake at 375°F until the fish is just cooked through. Sprinkle with the parsley.

Serves 4

DILLED SHRIMP AND RICE SALAD

Healing Foods

Crustaceans
Oil
Peppers (sweet)
Rice
Salad greens

3 tablespoons lemon juice
3 tablespoons olive oil
1 tablespoon red-wine vinegar
1 tablespoon minced fresh dill
1 tablespoon minced fresh parsley
1 green pepper, finely chopped

2 cloves garlic, minced
1 pound medium shrimp, peeled, deveined, and cooked
$1/3$ cup minced red onions
4 cups cold cooked rice
$1/4$ cup currants
2 cups shredded arugula

In a large bowl, whisk together the lemon juice, oil, vinegar, dill, parsley, and garlic.

Add the shrimp and onions. Stir well to combine. Chill for 1 hour.

Gently fold in the rice, peppers, and currants. Serve on a bed of arugula.

Serves 4

SABLEFISH WITH BASIL AIOLI

Healing Foods

Fish
Lemons and limes
Oil

1 pound sablefish
  steaks
1/4 cup olive oil

1/2 cup chopped
  fresh basil
1/4 cup lemon juice

Rub the steaks on both sides with about 1 teaspoon of the oil. Broil or grill until cooked through, about 5 minutes on each side.

Place the basil in the bowl of a food processor. With the motor running, pour in the remaining oil and lemon juice. Process into a smooth paste, stopping to scrape down the sides of the container as needed.

Spoon the basil sauce over the fish.

Serves 4

COD WITH HERBED POTATOES

Healing Foods

Fish
Garlic
Onions
Potatoes
Tomatoes

12 small red potatoes
1 pound cod fillets
2 large tomatoes
1 large onion,
  thinly sliced
1/4 cup minced
  fresh parsley

2 tablespoons
  lemon juice
2 tablespoons water
3 cloves garlic, minced
2 teaspoons olive oil
1/4 teaspoon saffron
1 bay leaf

Steam the potatoes until tender, about 10 to 15 minutes. Let stand until cool enough to handle. Cut into quarters or eighths, depending on the size.

Coat a 9 x 13-inch baking dish with nonstick spray. Place the cod in the center of the dish. Surround with the potatoes.

Cut the tomatoes into eight wedges each. Arrange on top of the potatoes.

In a large nonstick frying pan, combine the onions, lemon juice, water, garlic, oil, bay leaf, and saffron. Cook over medium heat until the onions are soft, about 7 minutes.

Spoon the onions and any liquid over the fish.

Cover the dish with foil. Bake at 350°F for 15 to 20 minutes, or until the fish flakes easily with a fork. Discard the bay leaf.

Sprinkle with the parsley.

Serves 4

SEAFOOD-BROCCOLI TERRINE

Healing Foods

Broccoli
Fish
Milk (low-fat)
Mollusks
Peppers (sweet)

SCALLOP LAYER
$^3/_4$ cup skim milk
$^1/_2$ cup egg substitute
$^1/_2$ cup whole wheat
  bread crumbs
$^1/_2$ teaspoon
  grated nutmeg
$^1/_8$ teaspoon red
  pepper
4 ounces scallops

BROCCOLI LAYER
$^1/_4$ cup whole
  wheat flour
$1^1/_3$ cups skim milk
$^1/_4$ cup lemon juice
$^1/_2$ cup egg substitute
1 tablespoon dillweed
2 cups steamed
  chopped broccoli

ASSEMBLY
8 ounces sole fillets
1 cup steamed diced
  sweet red pepper

To make the scallop layer: In a large bowl, combine the milk, egg substitute, bread crumbs, nutmeg, and red pepper. If using sea scallops, cut them into quarters; if using bay scallops, leave them whole. Fold the scallops into egg mixture. Set aside.

To make the broccoli layer: Mix the flour with about $^1/_3$ cup milk in a 2-quart saucepan to make a paste. Gradually whisk in the remaining milk. Whisk over medium heat until the mixture thickens. Remove from the heat. Whisk in the lemon juice, egg substitute, and dill. Fold in the broccoli. Set aside.

To assemble the terrine: Coat an $8^1/_2$ x $4^1/_2$-inch loaf pan with nonstick spray. Cover the bottom of the pan with the fish fillets. Sprinkle with half of the peppers. Top with half of the broccoli mixture.

Sprinkle with the remaining peppers, then top with all of the scallop mixture. Cover with the remaining broccoli mixture.

Cover the pan tightly with foil. Place the pan on a wire rack inside a larger baking dish. Pour in enough hot water to come two-thirds of the way up the sides of the loaf pan.

Bake at 350°F for 1 hour. Uncover the pan and bake for 30 to 45 minutes, or until firm. Unmold and cut into slices.

Serves 6 to 8

OYSTER STEW

Healing Foods

Milk (low-fat)
Mollusks
Mushrooms
Onions
Potatoes

1 pint oysters with liquid (about 2 dozen)

3 tablespoons water

1 cup minced onions

1 cup minced mushrooms

$1/2$ cup minced celery

$1^1/2$ cups skim milk

1 tablespoon lemon juice

2 cups fish or chicken stock

$1^1/2$ cups diced potatoes

$1/4$ cup minced fresh parsley

1 bay leaf

$1/2$ teaspoon dried thyme

$1/4$ teaspoon paprika

$1/4$ cup julienned scallions

Remove the oysters from their liquid. Strain the liquid through a cheesecloth-lined sieve and reserve.

Rinse the oysters, rubbing lightly to loosen grit and sand. Place in a strainer to drain.

In a 4-quart pot, bring the water to a boil. Add the onions, mushrooms, and celery. Cover the pan and steam the vegetables over low heat for 5 minutes, stirring occasionally.

Add the stock, potatoes, parsley, bay leaf, and thyme. Bring to a boil. Reduce the heat, cover and simmer for 10 minutes, or until the potatoes are tender.

Add the oysters, reserved liquid, milk, lemon juice, and paprika. Heat gently for about 5 minutes (do not let boil). Discard the bay leaf. Sprinkle with the scallions.

Serves 4

CHAPTER ELEVEN

Perfect Poultry and Game

Poultry is probably the most versatile meat in the world. It takes nicely to the flavors of other ingredients and lends itself to all manner of low-fat cooking methods. And game is now being recognized for the lean meat it is. Together they're an indispensable part of the healing kitchen.

Skinless turkey breast is the undisputed king of the roost. It's about as low in fat as a meat can get, and you don't need to roast a whole bird to enjoy its benefits. Boneless, skinless cutlets are readily available and tailor-made for healthy cooking. That's why we're featuring so many delicious ways to enjoy this cut. Take your choice of Honey-Basil Turkey, Moroccan Turkey, Turkey Cacciatore, Turkey Cutlets with Pear-Pecan Stuffing, and more.

For variety, turn to boneless chicken breast. It's just marginally higher in fat than turkey but every bit as desirable from a health, taste, and convenience standpoint. It's superb for all types of international dishes.

Besides being low in fat, turkey and chicken are high in B vitamins, plus important minerals like iron, potassium, and zinc. Many of our recipes, such as Sautéed Turkey with Strawberry

Puree and Chicken with Tropical Fruit, are just what the doctor ordered for people with high blood pressure. They combine poultry with other high-potassium foods like strawberries, bananas, peaches, or tropical fruits.

If you crave a different taste sensation or just want a change of pace, give game a try. It's low in fat and increasingly available in local markets.

APRICOT-STUFFED HENS

Healing Foods

Apricots
Chicken
Herbs and spices
Rice

1 cup apple juice
1 cup apricot nectar
2 teaspoons low-sodium soy sauce
1/2 teaspoon crushed cardamom
1 bay leaf
1 cup minced onions
2 tablespoons pine nuts
1/2 teaspoon ground ginger
1/4 teaspoon black pepper
4 Cornish hens
1 1/2 cups stock
1/2 cup wild rice
1 cup chopped dried apricots

In a 9 x 13-inch baking dish, combine the apple juice, apricot nectar, soy sauce, cardamom, ginger, and pepper. Add the hens and turn to coat. Allow to marinate for 30 to 60 minutes.

In a 1-quart saucepan, combine the stock, wild rice, and bay leaf. Bring to a boil. Cover, reduce the heat, and simmer for 40 minutes, or until the rice is tender and the liquid has been absorbed. Discard the bay leaf.

Remove the hens from the marinade (reserve the marinade).

In a 2-quart saucepan, cook the onions in 2 tablespoons of the marinade until wilted, about 5 minutes. Add the apricots, pine nuts, and rice. Heat through, adding more marinade if the mixture is too dry.

Distribute the stuffing among the hens, filling the cavities. (Place any remaining stuffing in a small casserole dish that you've coated with non-stick spray.)

Coat a roasting pan with nonstick spray. Add the hens. Bake at 350°F for 45 minutes, basting occasionally with the marinade. Add the casserole dish to the oven and bake for 15 minutes more, or until the hens are tender when pierced with a fork. If the hens appear to be getting too brown, cover with foil.

Transfer the remaining marinade to a 1-quart saucepan. Boil until reduced by half. Serve as a sauce with the hens. Remove the skin before eating.

Serves 4

CHICKEN
WITH KASHMIRI RICE

Healing Foods

Chicken
Garlic
Onions
Raisins
Rice

1 large onion, minced
3 cloves garlic, minced
2 teaspoons olive oil
1 cup long-grain
  brown rice
2$^1/_4$ cups chicken
  stock
$^1/_4$ teaspoon
  ground cinnamon
1 bay leaf

$^1/_4$ cup raisins
1 teaspoon grated
  lemon rind
$^1/_2$ teaspoon peeled
  minced gingerroot
$^1/_4$ teaspoon ground
  cardamom
1 roasting chicken
  (3$^1/_2$–4 pounds)

In a 3-quart saucepan, sauté the onions and garlic in the oil until soft, about 5 minutes. Add the rice and stir for 3 minutes. Add the stock. Bring to a boil.

Add the raisins, lemon rind, ginger, cardamom, cinnamon, and bay leaf. Cover, reduce the heat and simmer for 30 minutes, or until the rice is almost tender but has not absorbed all the liquid. Discard the bay leaf. Cover the pan and set it aside.

Remove all visible fat from the chicken, especially in the cavity area. Pat the chicken dry. Place in a small roasting pan. Loosely stuff the cavity with the rice mixture. (Place the remaining rice in a small baking dish that you've coated with nonstick spray. Cover the dish with foil and refrigerate until needed.)

Loosely cover the chicken with foil. Bake at 350°F for 1 hour, basting often with pan juices. Add the extra rice to the oven at this point. Bake the chicken for 15 minutes more, then remove the foil and bake another 15 minutes, or until the chicken is tender and the juices run clear when you pierce a thigh with a fork. Remove the skin before eating.

Serves 4

ROAST CHICKEN WITH FENNEL AND MUSTARD

Healing Foods

Chicken
Garlic
Lemons and limes
Potatoes

1/4 cup minced fresh parsley
1 tablespoon Dijon mustard
2 cloves garlic, minced
1 teaspoon red-pepper flakes

1 teaspoon crushed fennel seeds
1/2 cup lemon juice
1 roasting chicken (3 1/2–4 pounds)
4 large baking potatoes

In a small bowl, combine the parsley, mustard, garlic, pepper flakes, and fennel. Stir in the lemon juice to make a paste.

Rub the chicken with two-thirds of the marinade. Let stand, refrigerated, for 1 hour.

Place the chicken on a roasting rack in a large baking dish. Rub the potatoes with the remaining marinade and place them on the rack.

Bake at 350°F for about $1\frac{1}{2}$ hours, or until the juices run clear when you pierce the thickest part of a thigh with a fork and the potatoes are tender. Remove the skin from the chicken before eating.

Serves 4

POACHED TURKEY PAPRIKA

Healing Foods

Oil
Turkey
Yogurt (low-fat)

1 pound turkey cutlets
3 tablespoons olive oil
1 teaspoon paprika
1 teaspoon dillweed
$\frac{1}{4}$ teaspoon black pepper
3 tablespoons lemon juice
1 cup nonfat yogurt

Place the cutlets between sheets of waxed paper or plastic wrap and pound to an even thickness (about $\frac{1}{3}$ to $\frac{1}{2}$ inch) with a mallet.

In a pie plate, combine the oil, paprika, and

pepper. Dip the turkey in the mixture to coat both sides of each cutlet.

Place in a nonstick frying pan in a single layer. Sprinkle with the lemon juice. Cover and cook over medium-high heat for 8 to 10 minutes, or until turkey is opaque. Do not overcook.

In a small bowl, mix the yogurt and dill. Serve as a sauce for the turkey.

Serves 4

JASMINE CHICKEN WITH STRAWBERRY COULIS

Healing Foods

Chicken
Strawberries

2 cups water
1 cup chicken stock
3 jasmine-flower
 tea bags
2 tablespoons
 evaporated skim milk

1 pound boneless,
 skinless chicken
 breasts
2 cups strawberries

In a 2-quart saucepan, bring the water and stock to a boil. Add the tea bags. Cover, remove from the heat and let steep for 15 minutes. Remove the tea bags.

Cut the chicken into 1-inch strips. Add to the pan and simmer for 10 minutes. Remove the saucepan from the heat and let the chicken cool in the tea. Remove with a slotted spoon to a serving platter.

In a food processor or blender, puree the strawberries. Stir in the milk. Serve as a sauce with the
chicken.

Serves 4

TURKEY CUTLETS
WITH PEAR-PECAN STUFFING

Healing Foods

Nuts
Pears
Turkey

$^1/_2$ cup minced celery
$^1/_4$ cup minced
  shallots
1 tablespoon olive oil
$^1/_4$ cup chopped
  pecans
1 cup diced pears
1 pound turkey
  cutlets
2 tablespoons minced
  fresh parsley

$^1/_2$ cup whole wheat
  bread crumbs
$^3/_4$ teaspoon
  dried thyme
$^1/_8$ teaspoon
  ground allspice
$^1/_4$ cup chicken stock
$^1/_4$ cup pear juice
2 tablespoons
  snipped chives

In a large nonstick frying pan, sauté the celery
and shallots in the oil until soft, about 4 minutes.
Stir in the pecans and toast for 1 minute. Remove
from the heat.

Add the pears, bread crumbs, thyme, allspice,
and 1 tablespoon of stock.

Place the cutlets between sheets of waxed paper

or plastic wrap and pound to an even thickness (about $^1/_3$ to $^1/_2$ inch) with a mallet.

Divide the stuffing among the cutlets, mounding it in the center of each. Carefully roll up each cutlet to enclose stuffing (if necessary tie with string or use skewers).

Coat a 9 x 9-inch baking dish with nonstick spray. Add the cutlets. Lightly mist the top of each with nonstick spray.

In a cup, combine the remaining 3 tablespoons stock and the pear juice. Spoon over the cutlets. Cover the dish tightly with foil.

Bake at 350°F for 20 minutes. Remove the foil. Bake, basting occasionally, for 10 to 15 minutes, or until lightly browned.

Sprinkle with the chives and parsley.

Serves 4

MICRO METHOD: Bird Talk

There are several reasons to reach for the microwave when cooking poultry. One is the expected savings of time. Most poultry microwaved on full power is table-ready in one-third to one-half the time that conventional methods require. (Stewing hens are an exception. Because they are large and best microwaved at 50 percent power, they take nearly as long as conventional cooking. Further, the skin will not become tender. You're better off using another method.)

Another advantage to microwaving most birds is that dark meat is less likely to discolor next to the bone. Also white meat remains nice and moist. But the most important health advantage is that microwaving does a good job of liquefying fat so it drains off. For best drainage, cook poultry on a microwave drainer or ridged microwave rack. If you'd like to brown the meat, microwave it until almost done, then grill or broil as desired.

Because microwaves cook food from the circumference of a dish toward the center, always position the parts of chicken that take longest to cook—the dark meat and thick sections of white meat—toward the outside of your dish. When cooking a split chicken breast, arrange it so that the thick breastbone sections face outward. If doing several split breasts, arrange them pinwheel fashion, with the thin pointed ends toward the center and the meatier sections toward the outside.

Cooking a small amount of chicken for salad is simple in the microwave. Allow one-half boneless, skinless breast per person and cook it on full power just until opaque. Four breast halves cook in as little as 5 minutes in a full-size microwave; smaller quantities take less time.

When using poultry in a casserole, reduce the liquid by one-third to one-half (unless the liquid is needed to rehydrate dry pasta or rice). Because brown rice requires longer cooking than most poultry, cook the rice by itself until almost tender, then add the chicken.

ORANGE-SCENTED ROAST GOOSE

Healing Food

Waterfowl

1 goose (8 pounds)
1 orange, thinly
sliced crosswise

1 tablespoon
dried rosemary

Rinse the goose with cold water. Pat dry with paper towels. Remove all visible fat from the neck and cavity areas. Prick the goose all over with a fork.

Bring a very large pot of water to a boil. Add the goose and cook for about 30 minutes. Drain.

Loosen the skin over the breast and back portions. Slide orange slices under the skin. Also distribute the rosemary under the skin. Both will help flavor the meat as it roasts.

Put the goose on a rack in a roasting pan. Roast the goose at 350°F for about 2 hours. Remove the skin before eating.

Serves 8

POACHED CHICKEN
WITH CHINESE VINAIGRETTE

Healing Foods

Chicken
Garlic
Peppers (sweet)
Salad greens

1 pound boneless, skinless chicken breasts

2 cloves garlic, crushed

1 teaspoon peeled minced gingerroot

1 green pepper, julienned

4 scallions, julienned

2 tablespoons vinegar

1 teaspoon sesame oil

1 head green lettuce

In a large frying pan over medium heat, combine the chicken, garlic, and ginger. Add cold water to cover. Bring to a simmer, cover and cook until the chicken is tender, about 10 to 15 minutes. Drain the chicken and place in the refrigerator to chill.

Shred the chicken and place in a large bowl. Add the peppers and scallions.

In a small bowl, whisk together the vinegar and oil. Pour over the chicken and toss well to combine.

To serve, mound the chicken on a serving platter. Divide the head of lettuce into individual leaves. Place a little chicken on each lettuce leaf, roll, and eat.

Serves 4

MARINADE MAGIC FOR POULTRY

Tasty, low-fat marinades impart great flavor to poultry. And they're excellent for basting the meat as it cooks to help keep it juicy. For best results, simply skin the poultry and place it in a large bowl or shallow baking dish with the marinade. Flip the pieces often to ensure even coverage. Cover the meat and let stand at room temperature for no longer than 1 hour. Then cook immediately. For longer marinating, place the poultry in the refrigerator.

Here are five tasty marinades suitable for any type of poultry. Vary the proportions to suit your taste.

- Chicken stock, minced garlic, minced fresh ginger, low-sodium soy sauce, and grated orange rind
- Tomato juice, minced garlic, minced fresh oregano, ground cumin, and ground coriander
- Buttermilk, curry powder, and minced fresh coriander or parsley
- Chicken stock, minced fresh thyme, ground black pepper, dried mustard, and ground red pepper
- Chicken stock, lemon juice, minced onions, minced garlic, minced fresh oregano, and crushed celery seeds

CURRIED CHICKEN BREASTS

Healing Foods

Chicken
Garlic
Herbs and spices
Yogurt (low-fat)

$1/4$ cup chicken stock
3 cloves garlic, minced
2 teaspoons
  curry powder
2 teaspoons honey
1 teaspoon
  dried marjoram
1 teaspoon
  ground fennel
$1/8$ teaspoon
  black pepper

1 teaspoon
  ground cumin
1 teaspoon ground
  coriander
$1/2$ teaspoon
  ground fenugreek
$1/2$ teaspoon red-
  pepper flakes
$1/2$ teaspoon saffron
$1/2$ cup nonfat yogurt
1 pound boneless,
  skinless chicken
  breasts

In a large nonstick frying pan over medium-high heat, combine the stock, garlic, curry powder, honey, marjoram, fennel, cumin, coriander, fenugreek, red pepper, saffron, and black pepper. Simmer, stirring constantly, until the spices are fragrant, about 3 minutes. Remove from the heat and let cool for 5 minutes. Whisk in the yogurt.

Place the chicken breasts between sheets of waxed paper or plastic wrap and pound to an even thickness (about $1/3$ to $1/2$ inch) with a mallet.

Place the chicken in the spice mixture and turn to coat. Marinate for about 30 minutes, flipping the pieces occasionally.

Coat a 9 x 13-inch baking dish with nonstick spray. Add the chicken. Bake at 350°F until cooked through, about 20 minutes.

Serves 4

DIAMOND HEAD TURKEY WITH PINEAPPLE

Healing Foods

Garlic
Peppers (sweet)
Pineapple
Turkey

12 ounces turkey cutlets
1/2 cup pineapple juice
1/2 cup minced onions
3 tablespoons apple-cider vinegar
2 tablespoons low-sodium soy sauce
1 tablespoon peeled minced gingerroot
3 cloves garlic, minced
1 ripe pineapple
1 tablespoon cornstarch
1 green pepper, cut into thin strips
1 sweet red pepper, cut into thin strips

Cut the turkey into bite-size pieces.

In a large bowl, combine the pineapple juice, onions, vinegar, soy sauce, ginger, and garlic. Add the turkey. Cover and refrigerate for 4 hours.

Peel, core, and slice the pineapple into $1/2$-inch cubes.

Drain the turkey and onions, reserving the marinade.

Heat a large nonstick frying pan over medium-high heat. Add 3 tablespoons of the marinade and heat for 1 minute. Add the turkey and onions. Stir-fry just until brown. Remove from the pan and keep warm.

Dissolve the cornstarch in the remaining marinade. Add to the pan. Cook, stirring constantly, until thick.

Add the green peppers, red peppers, pineapple, and turkey. Toss to coat with sauce and reheat the turkey.

Serves 4

STEAMED WONTONS

Healing Food

Chicken

WONTONS
8 ounces boneless, skinless chicken breasts
$1/4$ cup minced scallions
1 teaspoon low-sodium soy sauce
1 teaspoon peeled grated gingerroot

SAUCE
3 tablespoons low-sodium soy sauce
3 tablespoons stock
$1/2$ teaspoon sesame oil

490

(WONTONS, cont'd)
$^1/_4$ teaspoon honey
1 clove garlic, minced
24 round wonton skins

To make the wontons: Cut the chicken into 1-inch pieces. In a food processor, combine the chicken, scallions, soy sauce, ginger, honey, and garlic with on/off turns until finely chopped.

Place 1 teaspoon of filling in the center of each wonton skin. Lightly moisten the circumference with water so edges will stick together. Pleat the edges around the filling so the wontons resemble flowers.

Steam over boiling water in batches for 8 to 10 minutes.

To make the sauce: In a small bowl, combine the soy sauce, stock, and oil. Use as a dipping sauce for the wontons.

Serves 6

POLLO SEVILLA

Healing Foods

Chicken
Garlic
Oranges
Peppers (sweet)
Rice
Tomatoes

491

1 pound boneless, skinless chicken breasts
1 tablespoon olive oil
1/4 teaspoon black pepper
1 large green pepper, chopped
1 large tomato, chopped
3 cloves garlic, minced
2 cups orange segments
2 cups hot cooked rice

Cut the chicken into 1-inch chunks.

In a large nonstick frying pan over medium-high heat, sauté the chicken in the oil for 3 to 5 minutes.

Add the green peppers, tomatoes, garlic, and black pepper. Cover and cook over low heat for 10 minutes.

Add the oranges, cover and cook for 5 minutes.

Serve over the rice.

Serves 4

POULTRY PÂTÉ

Healing Foods

Carrots
Chicken
Garlic
Rice
Turkey

8 ounces skinless, boneless chicken breasts
8 ounces skinless, boneless turkey breasts
1 cup cooked rice
1/2 cup shredded carrots
1/4 cup egg substitute
1 leek, coarsely chopped
2 tablespoons skim milk

2 cloves garlic,   1 teaspoon Dijon
   minced   mustard
1 teaspoon dried sage $1/2$ teaspoon dried
                                      thyme

Cut the chicken and turkey into 1-inch cubes. Place in the bowl of a food processor and chop coarsely with on/off turns. Add the rice, carrots, egg substitute, leeks, milk, garlic, mustard, sage, and thyme. Process until finely chopped.

Coat an $8^1/_2$ x $4^1/_2$-inch loaf pan with non-stick spray. Add the pâté mixture, smoothing the top with a spatula. Cover the pan with foil. Set in a larger pan; add 2 inches of water to the larger pan.

Bake at 350°F for 1 hour.

Remove the smaller pan from the water and refrigerate overnight.

Unmold the pâté from the pan and cut into slices to serve.

Serves 4

TURKEY AND SHRIMP KABOBS WITH TOMATOES

Healing Foods

Crustaceans
Garlic
Peppers (chili)
Rice
Tomatoes
Turkey

8 ounces skinless, boneless turkey breast

8 ounces shrimp, peeled and deveined

2 tablespoons lemon juice

1/4 cup minced fresh parsley

4 cloves garlic, minced

2 cups hot cooked rice

1 jalapeño pepper, minced

2 tablespoons minced shallots

1 tablespoon olive oil

1 teaspoon red-pepper flakes

1 teaspoon dried basil

1 1/2 pounds tomatoes, peeled, seeded, and chopped

Cut the turkey into 1-inch cubes. Combine in a large bowl with the shrimp and lemon juice. Cover and let stand about 30 minutes.

In a large frying pan, combine the parsley, garlic, peppers, shallots, oil, pepper flakes, and basil. Sauté over medium heat for 5 minutes. Add the tomatoes, cover the pan, and cook for 10 minutes.

Thread the turkey and shrimp onto skewers. Broil about 4 inches from the heat until cooked through, about 3 minutes per side.

Serve with the rice and cooked tomatoes.

Serves 4

CHICKEN WITH THAI FLAVORS

Healing Foods

Chicken
Garlic
Lemons and limes

1/4 cup minced
  fresh parsley
1/4 cup lime juice
1/4 cup lemon
  juice
2 teaspoons low-
  sodium soy sauce
1 teaspoon red-
  pepper flakes

1/2 teaspoon peeled
  grated gingerroot
3 cloves garlic,
  minced
1 pound boneless,
  skinless chicken
  breasts
1 teaspoon canola oil
2 scallions, minced

In a shallow glass dish, combine the parsley, lime juice, lemon juice, soy sauce, pepper, ginger, and garlic.

Place the chicken breasts between sheets of waxed paper or plastic wrap and pound to an even thickness (about 1/3 to 1/2 inch) with a mallet.

Add the chicken to the dish, turning to coat the pieces with marinade. Cover and allow to marinate for 30 minutes, flipping the pieces midway.

In a large nonstick frying pan over medium-high heat, warm the oil. Add the chicken (reserve the marinade). Sizzle about 5 minutes per side, or until cooked through. Transfer to a platter.

Add the marinade to the pan. Boil for about 30 seconds. Drizzle over the chicken. Sprinkle with the scallions.

Serves 4

GARLIC-ROASTED TURKEY BREAST

Healing Foods

Carrots
Garlic
Mushrooms
Turkey

1 skinless turkey
  breast (5 pounds)
12 cloves garlic
1 teaspoon
  dried thyme
1 tablespoon flour
1 bay leaf

8 ounces mushrooms
4 carrots, cut into
  3-inch sticks
1 cup stock
1 teaspoon
  dried rosemary

With a sharp knife, make 12 slits in the turkey breast. Fully insert a whole garlic clove into each slit. Rub the breast with the thyme.

Place the flour in a large oven-cooking bag. Shake to coat the inside of the bag with the flour. Place the turkey in the bag. Arrange the mushrooms and carrots around the breast. Add the stock, rosemary, and bay leaf.

Follow the manufacturer's directions for tying the bag and making slits for steam to escape. Place the bag in a roasting pan.

Bake at 350°F for about 1$^1\!/_4$ hours, or to an internal temperature of 175°F. Discard the bay leaf. Serve the turkey with the vegetables.

Serves 10

PESTO TURKEY

Healing Foods

Garlic
Oil
Turkey

1 1/2 cups basil leaves
4 cloves garlic,
  minced
1/3 cup olive oil
1 pound turkey
  cutlets
12 mushrooms, sliced

4 small tomatoes,
  sliced
2 tablespoons grated
  Sapsago or
  Parmesan cheese
2 tablespoons chopped
  pine nuts

In a blender or food processor, process the basil and garlic until well chopped. With the machine running, add the oil in a stream. Process until a smooth paste forms.

Cut four large squares of foil. Coat one side with nonstick spray.

Divide the cutlets among the foil. Spread each with 1 tablespoon of the basil pesto.

Top with the mushrooms and tomatoes. Cover with the remaining pesto. Sprinkle with the cheese and pine nuts.

Fold the foil to enclose the filling and seal tightly. Place the packets on a baking sheet. Bake at 375°F for 20 minutes.

Serves 4

FOWL TIPS

Poultry seems tailor-made for light, low-fat eating. It tends to be lower in calories and fat than red meat. And it's so versatile you can serve it often without repeating yourself or tiring of your creations. To keep poultry at its healthy best:

- Remove all visible fat before cooking. Be especially mindful of large fat deposits in the cavity and neck areas of whole birds.
- Discard the skin before eating. Although the skin itself contains a good deal of fat, you may choose to leave it on during cooking to keep the meat from drying out (especially for baking, grilling, and roasting). That's fine. Just don't eat it.
- Use as little added fat during cooking as possible. That means poaching or sautéing in a little liquid instead of frying. And not rubbing butter, margarine, or other fat onto poultry skin before cooking.
- Baste meat as it cooks with orange juice, stock, or other liquid. That imparts nice flavor to the meat so you don't need a fatty sauce.
- When roasting a whole bird, first prick the skin all over with a sharp skewer or fork so that fat just under the skin can drain easily.
- Additionally, when roasting, use a roasting rack. Both vertical and horizontal versions are available. Both keep the meat from standing in fat drippings as it cooks. You can also buy little roasting prongs that accomplish the same task by holding the meat above its pan.

To prevent the hot fat from smoking as it hits the pan, place about $1/2$ inch of water in the drip pan.

VENISON BROCHETTES

Healing Foods

Game
Garlic
Herbs and spices
Rice

4 cloves garlic,
  minced
2 teaspoons
  orange juice
$1/2$ teaspoon grated
  orange rind
$1/2$ teaspoon
  ground mace
2 cups hot
  cooked rice

$1/2$ teaspoon
  ground cumin
$1/8$ teaspoon
  ground cinnamon
$1/8$ teaspoon
  ground ginger
$1/2$ cup nonfat yogurt
1 pound venison
  saddle or loin

In a large bowl, combine the garlic, orange juice, orange rind, mace, cumin, cinnamon, and ginger. Whisk in the yogurt.

Cut the venison into $1^1/2$-inch cubes. Add to the yogurt mixture and stir to combine well. Cover and refrigerate overnight. Stir occasionally.

Thread the venison onto skewers, taking care not to crowd the pieces. Reserve the yogurt. Broil about 5 inches from the heat, turning frequently and basting with leftover yogurt mixture, until cooked through, about 10 to 12 minutes.

Serve over the rice.

Serves 4

MOROCCAN TURKEY

Healing Foods

Herbs and spices
Nuts
Oil
Turkey

1 pound turkey cutlets
2 tablespoons olive oil
$1/2$ teaspoon
   ground ginger
$1/2$ teaspoon ground
   cinnamon
1 tablespoon honey

$1/4$ teaspoon
   ground cumin
$1/8$ teaspoon ground
   red pepper
$1/8$ teaspoon turmeric
2 tablespoons
   ground almonds

Place the cutlets between sheets of waxed paper or plastic wrap and pound to an even thickness (about $1/3$ to $1/2$ inch) with a mallet.

In a pie plate, combine the oil, ginger, cinnamon, cumin, red pepper, and turmeric. Dip the turkey in the mixture to coat both sides of each cutlet.

Place in a large nonstick frying pan in a single layer. Sprinkle with the almonds and drizzle with the honey.

Cover the pan and cook over medium-high heat for 8 to 10 minutes, or until the turkey is opaque. Do not overcook.

Serves 4

CHINESE-STYLE RABBIT

Healing Foods

Game
Garlic
Rice

1 tablespoon canola oil
2 pounds rabbit pieces
1 1/2 cups chicken stock
2 tablespoons tomato paste
1 tablespoon low-sodium soy sauce
1 tablespoon honey
1 teaspoon peeled minced gingerroot
4 cloves garlic, minced
1 teaspoon hot-pepper sauce
2 cups hot cooked rice

In a large nonstick frying pan over medium heat, heat the oil. Add rabbit and sauté until it begins to brown, about 5 minutes.

In a medium bowl, combine the stock, tomato paste, soy sauce, honey, ginger, garlic, and hot-pepper sauce. Pour over the rabbit.

Reduce the heat to medium low, partially cover the pan, and simmer the rabbit until cooked through, about 20 to 25 minutes.

Serve with the rice.

Serves 4

ROAST DUCK WITH FRESH ROSEMARY

Healing Foods

Garlic
Potatoes
Waterfowl

1 Muscovy duck
(6 pounds)
$1/3$ cup orange juice
2 tablespoons minced
fresh rosemary
3 cloves garlic,
minced
1 pound new potatoes

2 teaspoons Dijon
mustard
$1/2$ teaspoon grated
orange rind
1 onion, quartered
1 orange, quartered
3 sprigs fresh
rosemary

Use poultry shears to remove the wing tips from the duck. Discard, along with any visible fat from the neck and tail areas. Also remove and discard the neck if it's still attached.

In a small bowl, combine the orange juice, minced rosemary, garlic, mustard, and orange rind.

Set the duck in a 9 x 13-inch baking dish. Loosen the skin over most of the duck with your fingers. Rub the rosemary mixture under the skin and over the flesh. Cover, refrigerate, and allow to marinate at least 4 hours.

Place the duck on a raised rack in a roasting pan. Pour about 1 inch of water into the pan to keep any dripping fat from smoking during roasting.

Place the onions, oranges, and rosemary sprigs in the cavity.

Roast at 400°F for 2 hours, or until the duck is tender and cooked through. (Check occasionally: If the temperature seems too hot, lower it to 350°F. If the duck begins to darken too quickly, cover with foil. Remove the tent for the last 30 minutes.)

Remove from the oven and let stand 20 minutes before carving. Remove and discard the skin, onions, oranges, and rosemary sprigs.

While waiting to carve the duck, steam the potatoes until tender, about 15 minutes. Serve with the duck.

Serves 4

CHICKEN BREASTS WITH HARVEST VEGETABLES

Healing Foods

Chicken
Corn
Mushrooms
Peppers (sweet)

1/2 cup chicken stock

2 teaspoons white-wine vinegar

1 teaspoon Dijon mustard

1 clove garlic, minced

1 pound boneless, skinless chicken breasts

1/2 teaspoon cornstarch

1 tablespoon water

1 cup diced sweet red peppers

1/2 cup sliced scallions

1 tablespoon olive oil

1 1/4 cups sliced mushrooms

1/2 teaspoon	1 cup corn
dried basil	2 tablespoons chopped
1/4 teaspoon	fresh parsley
black pepper	

In a large bowl, whisk together the stock, vinegar, mustard, and garlic. Add the chicken and turn to coat. Cover, refrigerate, and allow to marinate at least 4 hours.

Coat a broiler rack with nonstick spray. Remove the chicken from the marinade (reserve the marinade) and set on the rack. Broil about 5 inches from the heat for about 5 minutes per side, or until cooked through.

While the chicken is cooking, transfer the marinade to a 1-quart saucepan. In a cup, dissolve the cornstarch in the water. Whisk into the marinade. Bring to a boil, stirring constantly. Simmer for 2 to 3 minutes. Keep warm.

In a large nonstick frying pan over medium heat, sauté the red peppers and scallions in the oil for 2 to 3 minutes. Add the mushrooms, corn, basil, parsley, and black pepper. Sauté for 5 minutes.

Place the vegetables on a serving platter. Top with the chicken and spoon on the sauce.

Serves 4

GRILLED CHICKEN AND ARTICHOKES WITH MIXED GREENS

Healing Foods

Artichokes
Chicken
Oil
Peppers (sweet)
Salad greens
Sprouts
Tomatoes

2 bunches arugula
1 head radicchio
3 ounces alfalfa
sprouts
12 artichoke hearts,
halved
8 sun-dried tomatoes,
sliced, or cherry
tomatoes, halved
1/4 teaspoon ground
black pepper

1 sweet yellow pepper,
thinly sliced
1 pound boneless,
skinless chicken
breasts
1/3 cup balsamic
vinegar
2 tablespoons olive oil
1 tablespoon minced
fresh basil or thyme

Divide the arugula, radicchio, sprouts, arti-chokes, tomatoes, and peppers among serving plates. Set aside.

Grill or broil the chicken for about 5 minutes per side, or until cooked through. Slice as desired and place on the greens.

In a small bowl, whisk together the vinegar, oil, basil or thyme, and pepper. Spoon over the salad.

Serves 4

RABBIT SAUTÉ WITH MUSHROOMS

Healing Foods

Game
Garlic
Mushrooms
Oil
Pasta

2 pounds rabbit pieces
2 tablespoons flour
2 tablespoons olive oil
2 cups chicken stock
2 cups sliced shiitake
  mushrooms
1/2 teaspoon dried
  thyme
8 ounces broad noodles

1 large onion, sliced
  crosswise into rings
2 tablespoons vinegar
2 cloves garlic, minced
1 teaspoon Dijon
  mustard
1 bay leaf
1/2 cup minced
  fresh parsley

Dredge the rabbit in the flour.

In a large nonstick frying pan over medium heat, sauté the rabbit in the oil until golden, about 5 minutes on each side.

Add the stock, mushrooms, onions, vinegar, garlic, mustard, thyme, and bay leaf. Stir to combine. Bring to a boil. Lower the heat and cover loosely. Simmer until tender, about 40 minutes, stirring occasionally.

Cook the noodles in a large pot of boiling water until tender. Drain and transfer to a serving platter. Add the rabbit and sauce. Sprinkle with the parsley.

Serves 4

POACHED CHICKEN WITH PEAR AND KIWIFRUIT

Healing Foods

Carrots
Chicken
Kiwifruit
Pears

4 pears
2 cups pear juice
1/4 teaspoon
  ground cinnamon
1 cup stock
1 pound boneless,
  skinless chicken
  breasts

1 stalk celery,
  coarsely chopped
1 onion, coarsely
  chopped
1 bay leaf
8 ounces carrots,
  julienned
4 kiwifruit, thinly
  sliced

Quarter the pears and remove the cores. Place in a large frying pan. Add the pear juice and cinnamon. Bring to a boil, then reduce the heat and simmer until the pears are just tender, about 10 to 20 minutes. Remove the pears from the liquid and keep warm. Reserve the juice for another use.

In the same frying pan, combine the stock, chicken, celery, onions, and bay leaf. Cover and simmer over medium heat for 12 minutes, or until the chicken is cooked through. Remove the chicken from the liquid. Keep warm.

Strain the liquid and return it to the frying pan. Add the carrots. Cover and cook over medium heat until tender, about 8 to 10 minutes. Drain.

Serve the chicken with the pears, carrots, and kiwis.

Serves 4

GINGER TURKEY WITH SPICY TOMATO SAUCE

Healing Foods

Herbs and spices
Peppers (sweet)
Turkey
Yogurt (low-fat)

12 ounces turkey
    cutlets
1 1/4 cups nonfat
    yogurt
1/4 cup tomato puree
1 tablespoon paprika
2 teaspoons turmeric
2 cloves garlic, minced
1 tablespoon peeled
    grated gingerroot

1 teaspoon
    ground cinnamon
1 teaspoon
    ground cardamom
1/4 teaspoon
    ground cloves
1/4 teaspoon red
    pepper
2 teaspoons canola oil
1 sweet red pepper,
    cut into 1/4-inch
    strips

Cut the turkey into 1-inch strips. Place in a large bowl and add 1/2 cup yogurt. Combine well, cover, and marinate in the refrigerator for 2 to 3 hours.

In a small bowl, whisk together the remaining

yogurt, tomato puree, paprika, and turmeric. Set aside.

In another small bowl, combine the garlic, ginger, cinnamon, cardamom, cloves, and red pepper. Set aside.

Drain the turkey of excess marinade and pat dry with paper towels.

In a large nonstick frying pan over medium-high heat, heat the oil. Add the turkey and brown on all sides. Remove from the pan.

Add the spice mixture to the pan and cook over low heat, stirring constantly, until fragrant, about 1 minute. Then immediately add the yogurt mixture to the pan. Bring to a boil.

Return the turkey to the pan. Add the red peppers. Simmer for 10 minutes, or until the sauce thickens and coats the turkey.

Serves 4

JAMAICAN CHICKEN

Healing Foods

Celery
Chicken
Garlic
Mushrooms
Peppers (sweet)

1/3 cup chicken stock
1 tablespoon low-sodium soy sauce
1 teaspoon peeled minced gingerroot

1/4 teaspoon ground allspice
12 ounces boneless, skinless chicken breasts

1 bay leaf
1 clove garlic, minced
1/2 cup thinly sliced
  yellow peppers
1 teaspoon honey

1/2 cup sliced
  mushrooms
1/2 cup sliced celery
1 teaspoon cornstarch

In a large bowl, combine the stock, soy sauce, ginger, bay leaf, garlic, allspice.

Cut the chicken into 1/4-inch strips. Add to the bowl and stir well. Cover, refrigerate, and marinate for at least 4 hours, stirring occasionally. Remove the chicken from the bowl and reserve the marinade. Discard the bay leaf.

Coat a large nonstick frying pan with nonstick spray. Stir-fry the chicken over medium-high heat for 3 to 5 minutes, adding a bit of marinade if necessary to prevent scorching. Remove the chicken and drain on paper towels. Transfer to a bowl. Wipe the pan clean.

In the same pan over medium-high heat, sauté the mushrooms, peppers, and celery with 1 tablespoon of the marinade for 1 minute. Add the vegetables to the chicken.

In a small bowl, combine the remaining marinade with the cornstarch and honey.

Pour into the frying pan and heat, stirring constantly, until thick and shiny. Add the chicken and vegetables. Toss to coat with sauce.

Serves 4

CHICKEN WITH TROPICAL FRUIT

Healing Foods

Bananas
Chicken
Papayas
Tropical fruit
Yogurt (low-fat)

1 papaya, thinly sliced
1 starfruit, sliced
1 banana, sliced
1 tablespoon
  lime juice
1 pound boneless,
  skinless chicken breasts

1 tablespoon olive oil
$1/4$ cup chicken stock
2 teaspoons
  curry powder
1 cup nonfat yogurt

In a large bowl, combine the papayas, starfruit, bananas, and lime juice.

Place the chicken breasts between sheets of waxed paper or plastic wrap and pound to an even thickness (about $1/3$ to $1/2$ inch) with a mallet.

Heat a large, heavy cast-iron frying pan on high for 3 minutes. Add half of the oil and half of the chicken. Sauté for 5 minutes per side. Transfer to the bowl with the fruit and toss to combine.

Repeat with the remaining oil and chicken.

Using the same frying pan, heat the stock until just boiling. Scrape the bottom with a wooden spoon to incorporate any browned bits. Add the curry powder and stir to form a paste. Transfer to a small bowl. Stir in the yogurt.

Arrange the chicken and fruit on a serving platter. Drizzle with the yogurt.

Serves 4

HONEY-BASIL TURKEY

Healing Foods

Garlic Turkey

1/2 cup apple-cider vinegar
1/4 cup minced fresh basil
2 tablespoons Dijon mustard
2 tablespoons honey

1 tablespoon low-sodium soy sauce
3 cloves garlic, minced
1/2 teaspoon dried thyme
1 pound turkey cutlets

In a shallow baking dish, combine the vinegar, basil, mustard, honey, soy sauce, garlic, and thyme.

Add the turkey and turn to coat. Cover and marinate for 15 minutes.

Remove the turkey from the marinade. Transfer the marinade to a large frying pan. Place the turkey on a broiler rack. Broil about 6 inches from the heat until cooked through, about 5 minutes per side.

Bring the marinade to a boil and cook until reduced by half, about 5 minutes. Add the turkey and reheat briefly.

Serves 4

SUMMER CHICKEN SALAD SANDWICHES

Healing Foods

Chicken
Grapes
Nectarines
Nuts

3 cups cubed cooked chicken breast
1/2 cup halved grapes
1/4 cup minced scallions
1/4 cup minced fresh parsley
12 slices pumpernickel bread
2 tablespoons chopped pecans
1/2 cup nonfat yogurt
2 tablespoons light mayonnaise
1 1/2 teaspoons curry powder
2 nectarines, thinly sliced

In a large bowl, combine the chicken, grapes, scallions, parsley, and pecans.

In a cup, combine the yogurt, mayonnaise, and curry powder. Mix the dressing with the chicken.

Divide the chicken among six slices of the bread. Top with the nectarines and the remaining bread.

Serves 6

SAUTÉED TURKEY WITH STRAWBERRY PUREE

Healing Foods

Oil
Strawberries
Turkey

1 pound turkey cutlets	1 tablespoon canola oil
1/4 cup whole wheat flour	1 1/2 cups sliced strawberries
	1 teaspoon honey

Place the cutlets between sheets of waxed paper or plastic wrap and pound to an even thickness (about 1/3 to 1/2 inch) with a mallet. Lightly dredge the cutlets in the flour; shake off the excess.

In a large nonstick frying pan over medium-high heat, sauté the turkey in the oil for 3 minutes per side, or until cooked through. Remove to a platter and keep warm.

In a blender or food processor, puree half of the strawberries. Add to the frying pan with the honey and stir until heated. Add the remaining strawberries and fold in gently.

Spoon the sauce over the turkey.

Serves 4

BUFFALO CHILI

Healing Foods

Game
Garlic
Herbs and spices

1 pound buffalo
top round
2 tablespoons whole
wheat flour
1/2 teaspoon
dried oregano
1/2 teaspoon
ground coriander
3 cloves garlic, minced
8 corn tortillas,
warmed

1/2 teaspoon
ground cumin
1/8 teaspoon
ground allspice
1 tablespoon olive oil
1 2/3 cups beef stock
2 tablespoons chili
powder
1/2 teaspoon hot-
pepper sauce
1 bay leaf

Cut the buffalo into 1-inch cubes.

In a pie plate, combine the flour, oregano, coriander, cumin, and allspice. Add the meat and toss well to coat.

In a large nonstick frying pan, sauté the meat in the oil until the pieces are almost all brown.

Add the stock, chili powder, garlic, hot-pepper sauce, and bay leaf. Bring to a boil. Reduce the heat and simmer for 30 minutes, or until the meat is tender. If necessary, add more stock to prevent sticking. Discard the bay leaf.

Divide the mixture among the tortillas and roll up.

Serves 4

MANDARIN CHICKEN WITH BEAN SPROUTS

Healing Foods

Chicken
Oil
Peas
Peppers (sweet)
Rice
Sprouts

12 ounces boneless, skinless chicken breasts
1 egg white
2 tablespoons canola oil
1/4 cup julienned scallions
1 tablespoon honey
2 cups hot cooked rice

1 tablespoon stock
1 1/2 cups bean sprouts
1/2 cup julienned snow peas
1/2 cup julienned sweet red or green peppers
1 tablespoon vinegar
1/8 teaspoon black pepper

Slice the chicken into thin pieces.

In a medium bowl, whisk the egg white with a fork until frothy. Add the chicken and toss to coat.

In a wok or large frying pan over medium-high heat, heat 1 tablespoon of the oil. Add the chicken and stir-fry for 2 to 3 minutes, or until the pieces turn white. Remove the chicken to a plate.

Heat the remaining oil. Add the scallions. Stir-fry until slightly browned, about 1 minute.

Add the stock and heat for 30 seconds. Add the sprouts, snow peas, and peppers. Stir-fry for 2 minutes.

Add the chicken, vinegar, honey, and black pepper. Stir-fry for 2 minutes to reheat the chicken. Serve over the rice.

Serves 4

ORANGE-SCENTED CHICKEN BREASTS

Healing Foods

Chicken
Garlic

2 tablespoons paprika
1 teaspoon
  dried oregano
$1/2$ teaspoon
  ground cumin
3 garlic cloves,
  minced

$1/3$ cup orange juice
3 tablespoons
  lime juice
2 tablespoons red-
  wine vinegar
1 tablespoon olive oil
1 pound boneless,
  skinless chicken
  breasts

In a 9 x 13-inch baking dish, combine the paprika, oregano, cumin, and garlic. Whisk in the orange juice, lime juice, vinegar, and oil.

Place the chicken breasts between sheets of waxed paper or plastic wrap and pound to an even thickness (about $1/3$ to $1/2$ inch) with a mallet.

Add the chicken to the dish and turn to coat well. Arrange in a single layer.

517

Bake at 400°F, basting occasionally, for 20 minutes, or until cooked through.

Serves 4

TURKEY MEDALLIONS WITH PEACHES

Healing Foods

Nuts
Oil
Peaches
Turkey

1 pound turkey
  cutlets
$^1/_4$ cup whole
  wheat flour
$^1/_4$ cup almonds

2 cups sliced peaches
2 tablespoons olive oil
$^3/_4$ cup water
2 teaspoons ground
  dried rosemary

Place the cutlets between sheets of waxed paper or plastic wrap and pound to an even thickness (about $^1/_3$ to $^1/_2$ inch) with a mallet.

Combine the flour and rosemary in a pie plate. Lightly dredge the turkey in the flour; shake off the excess.

In a large nonstick frying pan over medium-high heat, sauté the peaches in 1 tablespoon of the oil for about 3 minutes. Remove from the pan and reserve.

Sauté the cutlets in the remaining 1 tablespoon oil over medium-high heat for 1 minute on each side. Remove the pan from the heat.

518

In a blender, combine the water and almonds. Process on low speed until finely chopped. Pour the mixture into the pan with the turkey. Add the peaches. Return the pan to the heat and cook over low heat for 10 minutes.

Serves 4

IS IT DONE?

For maximum flavor, as well as safety, always cook poultry until well done. Here are some fail-safe ways to test a bird.

- Press the thick muscle of the drumstick. If the meat feels soft, the poultry is done.
- If cooking a whole or half bird, the leg should move up and down easily (the hip joint may even break).
- Insert a fork into the breast or a thick part of the thigh. When the meat is done, the fork slides in easily.
- Use a meat thermometer. Insert the thermometer into the fleshy inner thigh or through the carcass into the center of the stuffing. It should never touch bone. In the thigh, the thermometer should register from 180°F to 185°F when the meat is done; in the stuffing, it should read 165°F.
- Pierce the thickest part of the thigh with a skewer, fork, or the tip of a sharp knife. The escaping juices will be clear if the meat is done.

CORNISH HENS STUFFED WITH APPLES, ALMONDS, AND RAISINS

Healing Foods

Apples
Bulgur
Chicken
Lemons and limes
Nuts
Oil

2 large onions, minced
3/4 cup lemon juice
4 Cornish hens
1 cup chopped apples
2 1/4 cups chicken stock
1 teaspoon dried mint
1/2 cup chopped almonds
2 tablespoons raisins
2 tablespoons olive oil
2 cups bulgur
1/2 cup minced fresh parsley

In a large bowl, combine the onions and lemon juice. Add the hens and allow to marinate for at least 20 minutes, turning occasionally.

Transfer the hens to a roasting pan. Strain the marinade, reserving both the onions and the lemon juice.

In a large nonstick frying pan, sauté the reserved onions, apples, almonds, and raisins in the oil for 5 minutes. Add the bulgur and cook for 3 minutes, or until the bulgur is lightly toasted.

In a 1-quart saucepan, bring the stock and 1/2 cup of the reserved lemon juice to a boil. Add

$1^3/_4$, cups of stock to the bulgur mixture and simmer for 5 minutes, or until the stock has been absorbed. Fluff with a fork and stir in the parsley and mint.

Loosely stuff each hen with part of the bulgur mixture.

Combine the remaining 1 cup stock and the remaining stuffing. Coat a small casserole dish with nonstick spray and add the stuffing. Cover with foil and set aside.

Bake the hens at 350°F for 45 minutes, basting often with the remaining lemon juice. Add the casserole dish to the oven. Bake the hens another 30 minutes, or until tender. Remove the skin before eating.

Serves 4

TURKEY CACCIATORE

Healing Foods

Garlic
Mushrooms
Oil
Peppers (sweet)
Tomatoes
Turkey

8 ounces turkey cutlets	1 green pepper, thinly sliced
1 tablespoon whole wheat flour	3 cloves garlic, minced
2 tablespoons olive oil	$3^1/_2$ cups sliced tomatoes

1/2 cup chicken stock
1 large onion,
  thinly sliced
1/4 cup minced
  fresh parsley
1 bay leaf

3/4 cup thinly
  sliced mushrooms
1 teaspoon
  dried rosemary
1/2 teaspoon
  dried marjoram

Cut the turkey into 1/2-inch strips. Toss with the flour.

In a large nonstick frying pan over medium-high heat, sauté the turkey in the oil until opaque. Remove with a slotted spoon.

Add the stock to the pan and boil rapidly, scraping the bottom of the pan, until the stock is reduced by half. Reduce the heat to low and add the onions, peppers, and garlic. Cook until the vegetables are tender, about 5 minutes.

Add the tomatoes, mushrooms, parsley, rosemary, marjoram, and bay leaf. Cover and simmer 8 to 10 minutes, stirring occasionally.

Add the turkey and heat through. Discard the bay leaf.

Serves 4

CHAPTER TWELVE

Lean Meats

Of course you can eat meat on a healing diet! Just choose your cuts carefully and be extra resourceful about how you prepare them. If you're unsure how to do that, let the recipes in this chapter be your guide to maximizing the health potential of red meat.

As always, start with naturally lean cuts like flank steak, pork tenderloin, and lamb leg. And make sure to trim off every speck of visible fat. That way you get all the advantages of meat, like lots of protein, iron, and zinc, without any of its fatty drawbacks.

That done, you can concentrate on ways to use just a little meat with a lot of other healthy ingredients. Keep portions modest (3 or 4 ounces is plenty) and combine the meat with high-fiber, nutrient-dense foods like potatoes, pasta, beans, vegetables grains, or even fruit. Beef recipes that follow this guideline include Spicy Beef with Orange Vinaigrette, Orchard Meat Loaf, and Pan-Fried Noodles with Beans and Beef. If lamb or veal is more your style, you'll like Fruited Lamb Curry or Veal Loin with Mango Sauce.

Pork, too, marries well with fruit, like pears and peaches. Pear and Pork Stir-Fry, for example, incorporates fiber-rich pears and spinach. Likewise, Peaches and Pork contains fiber plus beta-carotene to help protect against certain kinds of cancer.

For last-minute entertaining, take a hint from the Chinese. Let a small amount of meat share the plate with an extra-large helping of delicious, health-building vegetables. Mix-and-Match Stir-Fries are guaranteed to both please your guests and appease your good conscience. And that's one challenge worth meating!

LONDON BROIL WITH GARLIC MARINADE

Healing Foods

Beef (lean)
Garlic

12 ounces lean top round, $^3/_4$ inch thick

2 teaspoons olive oil

3 cloves garlic, minced

3 bay leaves

$^1/_3$ cup red-wine vinegar

Trim all visible fat from the meat, then pierce it with a fork in about a dozen places. Place the meat in shallow baking dish or ovenproof casserole.

In a cup, combine the vinegar, garlic, bay leaves, and oil. Pour over the meat, cover, and refrigerate overnight. Discard the bay leaves.

Transfer the meat to a rack and broil about 5 inches from the heat until cooked through, about 5 minutes on each side for medium rare.

Serves 4

LAMB MEATBALLS WITH PEAR-TURNIP PUREE

Healing Foods

Lamb (lean)
Pears
Turnips
Wheat germ

1 pound turnips, thinly sliced

2 large pears chopped

1/2 cup chopped scallions

1/4 cup crumbled blue cheese

1/4 cup minced fresh parsley

1 teaspoon grated nutmeg

1 1/2 pounds extra-lean ground lamb

1 cup wheat germ

1 onion, minced

1/4 cup egg substitute

1 tablespoon canola oil

2 teaspoons dried thyme

Steam the turnips until tender, about 30 minutes. Add the pears and steam 5 minutes more.

In a small pan, sauté the scallions in the oil until tender. Transfer to a blender or food processor. Add the turnips, pears, 2 tablespoons of the cheese, and nutmeg. Process until well blended. Pour into a 2-quart saucepan and keep warm.

In a large bowl, combine the lamb, wheat germ, remaining cheese, onions, egg substitute, parsley, and thyme. Mix well. Shape into small meatballs.

In a large nonstick frying pan over medium

heat, sauté the meatballs until cooked through, about 5 to 10 minutes. Blot on paper towels to remove any excess fat.

Serve the meatballs with the puree.

Serves 6 to 8

ORCHARD MEAT LOAF

Healing Foods

Apples
Beef (lean)
Oats
Onions

1 1/4 pounds extra-
  lean ground beef
1 cup rolled oats
1 large onion, diced
1 cup shredded apples
1/2 teaspoon
  dried oregano

1/2 cup minced
  fresh parsley
1/4 cup egg substitute
1 1/2 teaspoons
  Worcestershire sauce
1/2 teaspoon
  dried basil
1/4 teaspoon
  hot-pepper sauce

In a large bowl, combine the beef, oats, onions, apples, parsley, egg substitute, Worcestershire, basil, oregano, and hot-pepper sauce.

Coat a 9 x 5-inch loaf pan with nonstick spray. Add the meat mixture. Bake at 350°F for 1 hour.

Serves 6

STUFFED BAKED POTATOES

Healing Foods

Beef (lean)
Onions
Peppers (sweet)
Potatoes

4 large potatoes
8 ounces extra-lean
    ground beef
1 onion, minced
1 sweet red pepper,
    minced
1/4 teaspoon
    dried thyme

1/4 cup minced
    fresh parsley
1 teaspoon Dijon
    mustard
1/4 teaspoon
    dried basil
1/8 teaspoon red
    pepper

Bake the potatoes at 375°F for 1 hour, or until easily pierced with a fork.

In a large nonstick frying pan over high heat, brown the beef for 5 minutes. Add the onions, peppers, parsley, mustard, basil, thyme, and red pepper. Cook for 3 minutes. Reserve 1/2 cup.

Cut a thin slice off the top of each potato. With a spoon, scoop out the insides, leaving a 1/4-inch-thick shell. Mash the scooped-out potatoes and add to the beef mixture in the pan.

Spoon the mixture into the shells, mounding it. Sprinkle with the reserved mixture. Reheat in the oven for 5 minutes.

Serves 4

TOMATOES STUFFED WITH LAMB HASH

Healing Foods

Lamb (lean)
Potatoes
Tomatoes
Yogurt (low-fat)

1^1/$_2$ cups diced
  cooked lean lamb
1^1/$_2$ cups diced
  cooked potatoes
^{1}/$_4$ cup snipped
  chives
4 extra-large tomatoes

1 cup nonfat yogurt
^{1}/$_4$ cup light
  mayonnaise
1 tablespoon vinegar
1 teaspoon dillweed
^{1}/$_4$ cup chopped
  fresh parsley

In a large bowl, combine the lamb, potatoes, and chives.

In a small bowl, whisk together the yogurt, mayonnaise, vinegar, and dill. Pour over the lamb and mix well.

Cut off the tops of the tomatoes. Scoop out the pulp, being careful not to pierce the skins. Mince 1 cup of the tomato pulp and add it to the lamb mixture.

Stuff the tomato shells with the hash. Sprinkle with the parsley.

Serves 4

MARINADE MAGIC FOR MEAT

Low-fat meats are tougher than marbleized cuts, but they can be tenderized by a good marinade. Marinades also offer added flavor as the meat absorbs the liquids and spices used in the recipe.

Marinades work best on small pieces of meat. For maximum effect, marinate the meat overnight and turn the pieces frequently to expose as much surface as possible to the marinade's flavorful ingredients. After marinating, broil, bake, grill, or stir-fry the meat.

Since most marinades are acid-based, always use a nonreactive container, such as glass, ceramic, or stainless steel. Don't use aluminum or plastic. And remember that although acidic ingredients help protect the food from bacterial growth, refrigerating the meat during marination is the safest course.

Here are some savory citrus marinades suitable for any type of meat. Vary the proportions to suit your own taste.

- Lemon juice and pulp, dried tarragon, and minced shallots
- Lime juice and pulp, nonfat yogurt, and curry powder
- Lemon juice and pulp and cranberry sauce
- Lemon juice and pulp, crushed fennel seeds, and minced garlic
- Orange juice and pulp, low-sodium soy sauce, minced ginger and sesame oil

529

- Lime juice and pulp, peanut oil, and hot-pepper sauce
- Lime juice and pulp and minced fresh ginger
- Lemon juice and pulp, tomato puree, dried oregano, and dried basil
- Lime juice and pulp, grated nutmeg, and ground allspice
- Lemon juice and pulp, coarse mustard, and dried sage

SIZZLING FAJITAS

Healing Foods

Avocados
Beef (lean)
Lemons and limes
Peppers (chili)
Tomatoes

1 pound skirt steak, trimmed of all visible fat

1/2 cup lime juice

2 tablespoons minced fresh coriander

1 teaspoon olive oil

3 chili peppers, cut into thin strips

1 cup diced tomatoes

1 ripe avocado, peeled and chopped

1 clove garlic, minced

3/4 teaspoon ground cumin

1/4 teaspoon dried oregano

1/4 teaspoon black pepper

1 cup thinly sliced onions

6 flour tortillas, warmed

Freeze the beef until firm enough to slice easily, about 30 minutes. Cut across the grain and slightly on the bias into $1/4$-inch slices.

In a large bowl, combine $1/4$ cup lime juice, coriander, oil, garlic, cumin, oregano, and black pepper. Add the steak. Cover, refrigerate, and allow to marinate 2 hours, stirring occasionally.

Coat a broiler rack with nonstick spray. With tongs, remove the steak from the marinade (reserve the marinade) and arrange in a single layer on the rack. Broil about 5 inches from the heat for 4 minutes. Turn and broil another 4 minutes, or until lightly browned.

In a large nonstick frying pan over medium-high heat, combine the reserved marinade and the onions and chili peppers. Cook for 3 to 4 minutes, or until crisp-tender.

Add the tomatoes and remaining $1/4$ cup lime juice. Cook, stirring occasionally, for 3 minutes, or until just heated. Add the meat and toss to combine.

Divide the mixture among the tortillas. Sprinkle with avocados. Roll to enclose the filling.

Serves 6

PEACHES AND PORK

Healing Foods

Garlic
Nuts
Peaches
Pork (lean)

12 ounces pork
  tenderloin,
  trimmed of all fat
2 teaspoons cornstarch
$1/4$ cup stock
1 tablespoon peeled
  minced gingerroot
1 tablespoon canola oil
2 cups julienned
  peaches
3 scallions, minced

1 egg white, lightly
  beaten
3 cloves garlic,
  minced
1 teaspoon low-
  sodium soy sauce
$1/2$ teaspoon Chinese
  5-spice powder
2 tablespoons
  toasted pine nuts

Freeze the pork until firm enough to slice easily, about 30 minutes. Cut against the grain into thin slices. Sprinkle with the cornstarch.

In a large bowl, combine the stock, ginger, egg white, garlic, soy sauce, and 5-spice powder. Add the pork, toss to combine, and allow to marinate for 30 minutes.

In a large nonstick frying pan over medium-high heat, heat 2 teaspoons oil for 1 minute. Add the pork and marinade. Stir-fry for 3 minutes, or until cooked through. Remove the pork from the pan.

Add the remaining 1 teaspoon oil to the pan. Add the peaches and stir-fry for about 30 seconds. Add the pine nuts, scallions, and pork. Stir-fry until heated through.

Serves 4

Accent on Health:
Sweet and Savory Chutneys

Chutneys are flavorful condiments of Indian origin that are a *must* for the health-conscious kitchen. They add needed pizzazz to no-salt, low-fat cookery. And they're especially good with very lean meats that must be braised a long time to be tender. (They're also delicious with plain poached chicken breasts or steamed fish fillets—foods that need a little extra culinary oomph.)

Fresh Pineapple Chutney

1 pineapple, peeled, cored, and diced
1/4 cup minced fresh coriander
1/4 cup minced fresh mint
1 green chili pepper, seeded and finely chopped
2 tablespoons lime juice
1 tablespoon peeled grated gingerroot

In a large bowl, mix the pineapple, coriander, mint, peppers, lime juice, and ginger. Cover and let stand for 30 minutes.

Makes about 3 cups

Healing Foods

• Peppers (chili) • Pineapple

Peach Chutney

1/4 cup honey
1/4 cup white-wine
    vinegar
1/4 cup minced
    onions
1 pound peaches

1 tablespoon peeled
    minced gingerroot
1/4 teaspoon
    ground cumin
3 tablespoons
    raisins, chopped

In a 2-quart saucepan, combine the honey, vinegar, onions, raisins, ginger, and cumin. Simmer for 10 minutes.

Pit and coarsely chop the peaches. Add to the pan and simmer, stirring occasionally, for 30 minutes, or until thick.

Transfer to a medium bowl. Serve warm or cold. Store tightly covered in the refrigerator.

Makes about 2 1/4 cups

Healing Foods

• Peaches   • Raisins

Apple-Tomato Chutney

2 pounds tomatoes,
    peeled, seeded,
    and chopped
1/2 cup minced
    red onions
1/2 cup chopped
    celery
1 tablespoon
    apple juice

2 large apples,
    coarsely chopped
1/4 cup apple-cider
    vinegar
4 allspice berries,
    crushed
1/2 teaspoon
    ground cinnamon
1 bay leaf

In a medium saucepan, combine the tomatoes, onions, celery, bay leaf, and apple juice. Simmer for 5 minutes.

Add the apples, vinegar, allspice, and cinnamon. Partially cover and simmer, stirring frequently, for 40 minutes, or until thick. Discard the bay leaf.

Transfer to a medium bowl. Serve warm or cold. Store tightly covered in the refrigerator.

Makes about 3 cups

Healing Foods

• Apples   • Tomatoes

SPICY BEEF WITH ORANGE VINAIGRETTE

Healing Foods

Beef (lean)
Oranges
Peppers (sweet)
Potatoes
Salad greens

BEEF
1 teaspoon paprika
$1/2$ teaspoon
   dried oregano
$1/2$ teaspoon
   dried thyme
$1/2$ teaspoon ground
   red pepper

VINAIGRETTE
$1/3$ cup orange juice
1 tablespoon apple-
   cider vinegar
1 tablespoon olive oil
1 tablespoon
   snipped chives

BEEF (cont'd)
12 ounces beef
  tenderloin, trimmed
  of all visible fat
20 new potatoes,
  halved
1 cup orange sections
1 sweet red pepper,
  julienned
1 head red lettuce

VINAIGRETTE
(cont'd)
1 teaspoon Dijon
  mustard
1 teaspoon peeled
  minced gingerroot

To make the beef: In a cup, combine the paprika, oregano, thyme, and ground pepper. Rub the mixture into the beef on all sides.

Heat a large ovenproof frying pan over medium-high heat. Add the beef and sear on all sides. Add the potatoes to the pan. Transfer to the oven and roast at 400°F for 20 minutes, or until a meat thermometer registers 130°F (for rare) and the potatoes are tender. Remove the pan from the oven. Slice the meat thinly across the grain and keep warm.

Transfer the potatoes to a large bowl. Add the oranges and red peppers to the potatoes.

Divide the lettuce among serving plates.

To make the vinaigrette: In a cup, whisk together the orange juice, vinegar, oil, chives, mustard, and ginger. Pour over the vegetables and toss lightly.

Divide the meat and vegetables among the plates.

Serves 4

ORANGE BEEF WITH RICE

Healing Foods

Beef (lean)
Carrots
Peppers (chili)
Rice
Salad greens

1 pound flank steak, trimmed of all visible fat
1 orange
3 tablespoons lemon juice
3 cloves garlic, minced
1 tablespoon olive oil
2 small hot green chili peppers, minced

3 cups stock
1$^1/_4$ cups brown rice
2 carrots, shredded
1 teaspoon ground cumin
$^1/_2$ teaspoon ground cinnamon
4 scallions, thinly sliced
3 cups shredded escarole

Freeze the beef until firm enough to slice easily, about 30 minutes. Cut across the grain into paper-thin strips about 2 inches long.

Grate about 1 tablespoon of orange rind into a large shallow bowl. Squeeze the juice from the orange into the bowl. Add the lemon juice, garlic, chili peppers, and beef. Combine well. Cover, refrigerate, and allow to marinate for 2 hours (or overnight).

About 1 hour before serving, bring the stock to a boil in a 2-quart saucepan. Add the rice, carrots, cumin, and cinnamon. Cover, reduce the heat and simmer for 40 minutes, or until the rice is tender and the water has been absorbed. Fluff with a fork and fold in the scallions.

In a large nonstick frying pan over medium-high heat, heat the oil. Transfer the beef to the pan with a slotted spoon (save the marinade). Cook rapidly, stirring constantly, for 2 minutes, or until just cooked. Add the escarole, toss, and cook until just wilted.

Remove the meat mixture from the pan and keep warm. Add the marinade to the pan. Cook over high heat, stirring constantly to scrape up browned bits from the pan, for about 1 minute.

Mound the rice on a large serving platter. Spoon the meat mixture on top. Pour the marinade over the meat.

Serves 4 to 5

BARBECUED BEEF SATAY

Healing Foods

Beef (lean)
Garlic
Herbs and spices
Onions
Rice

1 pound top round, trimmed of all visible fat
1 large onion, minced

2 teaspoons low-sodium soy sauce
1 teaspoon caraway seeds

1/4 cup stock	1 teaspoon
1/4 cup lemon	ground coriander
juice	1/2 teaspoon turmeric
1 tablespoon peeled	1/2 ground red pepper
grated gingerroot	3–4 cups hot
3 cloves garlic, minced	cooked rice

Cut the beef into 1-inch cubes. In a large bowl, combine the beef, onions, stock, lemon juice, ginger, soy sauce, caraway, coriander, turmeric, red pepper, and garlic. Cover and allow to marinate for 2 hours.

Thread the meat onto small skewers. Reserve the marinade and transfer to a 1-quart saucepan.

Broil the meat 4 inches from the heat for 6 minutes, turning once and brushing with marinade.

Boil the marinade for 1 minute.

Serve the meat atop the rice. Spoon on the marinade.

Serves 4 to 5

MICRO METHOD: Moist Meats

When time's at a premium, remember that you can cook most meats in the microwave. Here's how to get the best results.

- Remember that because microwaving is a moist medium, meats don't stick as they might in a frying pan. Therefore you don't need added fat to prevent sticking.

539

- Ground meat (choose lean ground top round) cooks wonderfully in the microwave. Although it will not brown, it will render a lot of fat—more fat than broiling, charbroiling, roasting, convection heating, or frying will release. Pour off the fat before adding the meat to a casserole or other dish.
- Lean, thin strips of meat cook more quickly and evenly than thick chunks. For best results, slice the meat against its grain.
- If you're cooking meat without a sauce, don't cover it. That way you won't steam the meat and toughen the protein.
- Microwave pork to an internal temperature of 170°F. Check it with a meat thermometer when you remove the meat from the oven.
- When converting a conventional recipe that calls for a good deal of liquid or a long baking time, reduce the liquid by one-third. Liquid doesn't evaporate during microwaving the way it does on the stove or in the oven. Check the dish as it cooks and add more liquid if necessary to achieve the desired consistency. But be aware that dry foods, such as uncooked rice or pasta, will absorb moisture as they cook; so don't reduce the liquid in those recipes.
- Because microwaving can intensify the flavors of certain seasonings, cut back on herbs and spices before cooking. Taste the dish after microwaving and season it then.
- If you're increasing or decreasing a casserole recipe, try to choose a baking dish that will maintain the ingredients at the same depth as

they were in the original recipe. In other words, if you're halving a recipe, choose a proportionately smaller dish. But make sure it's deep enough to prevent boilovers.

SPICY PORK AND CHICKEN WITH PINEAPPLE

Healing Foods

Bananas
Chicken
Garlic
Lemons and limes
Peppers (chili)
Pineapple
Pork (lean)
Seeds

1 pound lean pork, trimmed of all visible fat
2 tablespoons canola oil
1 onion, coarsely chopped
4 cloves garlic, halved
1/2 cup toasted pumpkin seeds
2 1/2 cups stock
1/4 cup minced fresh coriander
3 jalapeño peppers, seeded and chopped
2 tablespoons cornmeal
1 teaspoon hot-pepper flakes
1 pound boneless, skinless chicken breast
4 bananas
1 pineapple, peeled, cored, and cut into chunks
4 limes, quartered

Cut the pork into 2-inch cubes.

In a 6-quart pot over medium heat, brown the pork in 1 tablespoon oil. Remove from the pan and set aside.

Add the onions and garlic to the pan. Cook for 3 to 4 minutes. Add the stock, coriander, peppers, cornmeal, and pepper flakes. Bring to a boil, cover the pan, reduce the heat and simmer for 15 minutes. Transfer to a blender or food processor and puree until smooth.

Return the mixture to the pan. Add the pork, cover, and simmer over low heat for 1 hour, or until the pork is very tender.

Cut the chicken into 1-inch pieces. Add to the pan. Simmer for 20 minutes.

Cut the bananas in half lengthwise, then in half crosswise.

In a large nonstick frying pan, heat the remaining 1 tablespoon oil. Add the bananas and cook until lightly browned on each side.

To serve, spoon the meat mixture onto a large platter. Sprinkle with the pumpkin seeds. Surround with bananas, pineapples, and limes. To eat, squeeze lime juice over the food as you go.

Serves 6

PAN-FRIED NOODLES WITH BEANS AND BEEF

Healing Foods

Beans (snap)
Beef (lean)
Pasta
Peppers (sweet)

8 ounces top round, trimmed of all visible fat
2 teaspoons water
1 teaspoon low-sodium soy sauce
1 teaspoon honey
1 tablespoon cornstarch
2 cups cooked spaghetti, snipped into short pieces

2 tablespoons oyster sauce
2 tablespoons apple juice
1 teaspoon canola oil
1 pound green beans, trimmed and halved
1 sweet red pepper, julienned

Freeze the beef until firm enough to slice easily, about 30 minutes. Slice against the grain into very thin slices.

In a large bowl, whisk together the water, soy sauce, honey, and 1 teaspoon of the cornstarch. Add the beef and toss to combine. Cover and allow to marinate for 30 minutes.

In a small bowl, combine the remaining 2 teaspoons cornstarch with the oyster sauce and apple juice. Set aside.

In a large nonstick frying pan, heat the oil for

about 30 seconds. Add the meat and stir-fry for several minutes, or until cooked through.

Remove the meat with a slotted spoon and set aside. Add the beans, peppers, and spaghetti to the pan. Stir-fry for 2 minutes. Add the beef and push everything to the sides of the pan, leaving an empty space in the middle.

Give the oyster sauce mixture a stir and add it to the pan. Stir constantly until the sauce is thick and shiny. Toss the sauce with the noodle mixture until all the pieces are coated.

Serves 4

SCALLOPS OF VEAL WITH FENNEL AND GRAPES

Healing Foods

Grapes
Onions
Veal (lean)

1 pound veal scallops
1 tablespoon
 canola oil
1 tablespoon minced
 fresh parsley
$1/2$ teaspoon
 dried savory
$1/2$ teaspoon
 dried rosemary

$1/2$ cup chicken stock
1 fennel bulb, halved
 lengthwise and
 thinly sliced
$1/2$ cup minced
 shallots
2 cups small red
 grapes

Pat the veal dry with paper towels. Place between

sheets of waxed paper and flatten with a mallet until about $1/8$ inch thick.

In a cup, combine the oil, parsley, savory, and rosemary. Brush over the veal. Cover with plastic and refrigerate for 3 to 4 hours.

Coat a large nonstick frying pan with nonstick spray. Over medium-high heat, sauté the veal in batches for 2 minutes per side, or until slightly browned. Remove to a serving dish and keep warm.

In the same pan, combine the stock, fennel, and shallots. Cook over medium-high heat until the stock is reduced by half and the fennel is tender, about 10 minutes. Add the grapes and heat for 30 seconds.

Serve over the veal.

Serves 4

VEAL IN APPLE-LEMON SAUCE

Healing Foods

Apples
Lemons and limes
Mushrooms
Oil
Veal (lean)

$1^1/2$ pounds veal scallops
$1/2$ cup whole wheat flour
4 large apples, cut into $1/2$-inch slices
$1/2$ cup lemon juice

2 tablespoons olive oil
1 cup thinly sliced mushrooms
$1^1/2$ cups chicken stock

545

Pat the veal dry with paper towels. Place between sheets of waxed paper and flatten with a mallet until about $1/8$ inch thick. Dredge in the flour. Shake off the excess.

In a 2-quart saucepan, cook the apples in the lemon juice until tender, about 5 to 7 minutes. Puree half of the apples in a blender. Reserve the remaining slices separately.

In a large nonstick frying pan, heat 1 tablespoon oil. Add the mushrooms and sauté until tender, about 5 minutes. Remove with a slotted spoon and set aside.

Add the remaining 1 tablespoon oil to the pan. Sauté the veal about $1^1/2$ minutes on each side. Remove the veal to a platter and keep warm.

Add the stock to the pan and bring to a boil, scraping the bottom of the pan to loosen browned bits. Lower the heat, add the apple puree, and cook 2 to 3 minutes.

Add the veal, mushrooms, and apple slices. Cook 5 minutes.

Serves 6

MIX-AND-MATCH STIR-FRIES

Oriental cuisine has a healthy reputation because its foremost practitioners, the Chinese and Japanese, are relatively free of the heart disease that plagues Westerners. Nutrition researchers believe the Orientals' low-fat, high-fiber diet is largely responsible for this.

Of all the dishes we associate with Oriental cuisine, stir-fry dishes seem most typical. They permit versatility in the diet and combine a generous amount of vegetables with just a small portion of meat. That gives you a very healthy balance of nutrients.

You can take advantage of the speed, nutritiousness, and versatility of stir-fry cooking without having to rely on complicated recipes. Use the chart on the next few pages to assemble your meal by choosing one ingredient from each section. (The amounts given serve 4.) Then follow these easy directions:

1. *Prepare a basic stir-fry sauce:* In a 1-quart saucepan, combine $1/4$ cup water, 2 tablespoons low-sodium soy sauce, 2 tablespoons mirin or other vinegar, 2 teaspoons honey, 1 teaspoon minced garlic, 1 teaspoon sesame oil, and 1 teaspoon minced fresh ginger. Bring to a boil, stirring constantly. Stir in 2 teaspoons cornstarch that you've dissolved in 2 tablespoons water. Cook, stirring, until the sauce is shiny and thick. Remove from the heat and set aside.

2. Cut all ingredients into uniform, bite-size pieces. Arrange each category on a separate plate near the stove.

3. Heat a wok or large frying pan on medium-high heat for 1 minute. Add 1 teaspoon of oil, swirl to distribute, and let heat for 1 minute.

4. Add the Basic Ingredient. Stir-fry until the food is lightly browned on the outside, from 1 to 5 minutes. Remove with a slotted spoon and set aside.

5. Add 1 teaspoon oil to the pan. Add your choice of Hearty Vegetables. Stir-fry for 3 minutes, or until slightly tender.
6. Immediately return the first ingredient to the pan along with your Tender Vegetables. Stir-fry for 1 minute. Add the reserved sauce and Toppings. Toss all ingredients quickly to coat them with the sauce. Serve immediately.

Basic Ingredient (choose 8 ounces)

Bay scallops
Beef, slivered
Chicken, cubed
  or slivered
Clams, shucked
Duck, slivered
Firm fish, cubed
Lamb, slivered

Oysters, shucked
Pork, slivered
Sea scallops, halved
Shrimp, peeled
  and deveined
Tofu, cubed
Turkey, cubed
  or slivered

Hearty Vegetables (choose 2–3 cups)

Asparagus, sliced
  diagonally
Bamboo shoots,
  julienned
Bok choy ribs,
  sliced diagonally
Broccoli florets or
  stalks, julienned
Carrots, lightly
  steamed and
  julienned
Cauliflower florets

Celery, sliced
  diagonally
Daikon radish,
  julienned
Green beans, whole
  or sliced
Mushrooms, sliced
Onions, slivered
Peas
Peppers, cubed
  or sliced
Snow peas

Water chestnuts,
sliced into coins
or quartered

Yellow squash,
julienned or cubed
Zucchini, julienned
or cubed

Tender Vegetables (choose 1–2 cups)

Bean sprouts
Bok choy leaves,
shredded
Lettuce, shredded
Napa cabbage,
shredded

Scallions, cut
into matchsticks
Spinach or kale,
shredded
Watercress, shredded

Toppings (choose 2 tablespoons)

Almonds, roasted
and slivered
Peanuts, chopped

Pine nuts
Scallions, chopped
Sesame seeds

MEXICAN PICADILLO

Healing Foods

Apples
Beef (lean)
Garlic
Onions
Peppers (sweet)
Raisins
Salad greens

1½ pounds extra-lean ground beef
2 onions, minced
1 green pepper, minced
3 cloves garlic, minced
1 cup tomato sauce
2 apples, finely chopped
⅓ cup raisins
2 teaspoons dried oregano
2 teaspoons ground cumin
1 head romaine lettuce
1 lime, cut into wedges

In a large nonstick frying pan over medium heat, brown the beef, breaking it up with a wooden spoon. As soon as the meat begins to lose its pink color, add the onions, peppers, and garlic. Cook, stirring often, until beef has browned and the onions are translucent. Drain any accumulated fat.

Add the tomato sauce, apples, raisins, oregano, and cumin. Cover and simmer for 30 minutes.

Transfer to a large platter. Surround with romaine leaves.

To eat, spoon some meat onto a lettuce leaf, squeeze on some lime juice, then roll up the leaf like a tortilla.

Serves 6 to 8

PEAR AND PORK STIR-FRY

Healing Foods

Oil
Pears
Pork (lean)
Spinach

12 ounces pork shoulder, trimmed of all visible fat
2 tablespoons chicken stock
2 teaspoons low-sodium soy sauce
1 teaspoon vinegar
1 teaspoon cornstarch

1/8 teaspoon ground cinnamon
2 tablespoons canola oil
2 scallions, shredded
2 tablespoons peeled minced gingerroot
1 clove garlic, minced
2 large pears, sliced 1/4 inch thick
1 cup shredded spinach

Freeze the pork until firm enough to slice easily, about 30 minutes. Slice across the grain into thin slices. Cut into 1- by 2-inch pieces.

In a large bowl, combine the stock, soy sauce, vinegar, cornstarch, and cinnamon. Add the pork and toss gently. Cover and let stand 20 minutes.

In a large nonstick frying pan over medium-high heat, heat the oil for 2 minutes. Add the scallions, ginger, and garlic. Stir-fry for 10 seconds, or until the scallions are translucent.

Add the pork and marinade. Stir-fry until the pork begins to brown, 2 to 3 minutes.

Add the pears and stir-fry 1 minute. Add the spinach. Cook until the spinach begins to wilt, about 1 minute.

Serves 4

FRUITED LAMB CURRY

Healing Foods

Apples
Bananas
Garlic
Lamb (lean)
Oil
Potatoes
Raisins

1/2 cup raisins
1/2 cup hot water
2 potatoes, cubed
2 tablespoons
  canola oil
1 large onion,
  chopped
1 pound lamb loin,
  trimmed of all
  visible fat

1 banana, diced
2 cloves garlic, minced
1 tablespoon
  curry powder
6 ounces tomato
  paste
1 cup chicken stock
1 bay leaf
2 tart apples, diced

In a cup, soak the raisins in the water for 15 to 30 minutes, until plump.

Steam the potatoes until just tender.

In a 3-quart saucepan over medium heat, heat 1 tablespoon oil. Add the onions. Sauté until transparent, about 5 minutes.

Add the apples, bananas, garlic, and curry powder. Cook, stirring often, until the apple is soft, about 3 minutes. Transfer to a blender or food processor. Add the tomato paste and stock. Blend well.

Return the mixture to the saucepan. Add the potatoes, bay leaf, and raisins (including the soaking water).

Simmer over low heat, stirring, for 10 minutes.

Cut the lamb into $1/2$-inch cubes.

In a large nonstick frying pan over high heat, heat the remaining 1 tablespoon oil. Add the lamb and brown it quickly over high heat until cooked through. Add the lamb to the sauce. Discard the bay leaf.

Serves 4 to 6

VEAL LOIN WITH MANGO SAUCE

Healing Foods

Mangoes
Rice
Veal (lean)

1 mango
1 teaspoon cornstarch
1 tablespoon water
$1/4$ cup stock
$1/4$ cup skim milk

2 tablespoons snipped chives
1 tablespoon peeled grated gingerroot
1 teaspoon minced garlic

1 tablespoon canola   4 veal tenderloin
  oil   medallions
2 cups hot cooked rice

Peel and seed the mango. In a blender or food processor, puree the flesh.

In a small bowl, dissolve the cornstarch in the water. Whisk in the stock, milk, and mango puree. Set aside.

In a 1-quart saucepan over medium heat, sauté the chives, ginger, and garlic in the oil for 2 minutes. Whisk in the mango mixture. Cook over medium heat until slightly thickened, about 5 minutes.

Broil the veal about 5 inches from the heat until cooked through, about 5 minutes on each side.

Serve with the rice and top with the sauce.

Serves 4

CHAPTER THIRTEEN

Vegetable Side Dishes

From asparagus to zucchini, vegetables add a hefty dose of healing oomph to any meal. And while family members may square off over their favorites, all are bound to find something they like.

You might say green and gold are the official colors of the vegetable class. Dark green and yellow vegetables like spinach, Swiss chard, squash, and sweet potatoes get their vibrant hues from carotenoids, plant forms of cancer-fighting vitamin A. Pumpkin, for example, is so high in healing potential that it's a shame to use it for decoration only. And it's not just for dessert either. Onions and Apples in a Pumpkin are a creative way to reap its significant healing benefits.

All the recipes in this chapter aim to help you see your old favorite vegetables in a new light. Instead of serving plain peas or carrots, for example, try Sesame Snow Peas or Carrot Fritters. Instead of buttered green beans (who needs all that saturated fat?), try Chinese Beans with Sesame Seeds. And as a change of pace from Eggplant Parmesan, help yourself to Hunan Eggplant, yet another Oriental dream.

Cruciferous vegetables like brussels sprouts

really shine when dressed up in Mushroom Glaze or Three-Root Sauce. And Marinated Cauliflower is a new way to savor another cancer-fighting crucifer.

And what about those root vegetables—like parsnips, rutabagas, and turnips—that you may have passed by until now because you just couldn't figure out what to do with them? We've got tantalizing recipes for them too, such as Parsnip-Corn Cakes, Far Eastern Rutabagas, and Creamed Turnips.

GARDEN-PUFF POTATOES

Healing Foods

Broccoli
Carrots
Peppers (sweet)
Potatoes

4 large baking
  potatoes
1 1/2 cups bite-size
  broccoli florets
1/2 cup diced
  green peppers

1/4 cup diced onions
1 cup shredded
  carrots
1/3 cup buttermilk
2 teaspoons dillweed
1 tablespoon
  snipped chives

Bake the potatoes at 375°F for 1 hour, or until easily pierced with a fork.

Steam the broccoli for 3 minutes. Add the peppers and onions. Steam for 2 minutes.

Cut a thin slice off the top of each potato. Scoop out the pulp, leaving a $^1/_4$-inch shell. Reserve the shells and transfer the pulp to a blender.

Add the carrots, buttermilk, and dill. Whip on high speed for 5 minutes, or until light and fluffy. Add more buttermilk, if needed.

Transfer to a medium bowl. Fold in the steamed vegetables.

Spoon the potato mixture into the reserved shells. Broil about 4 inches from the heat for 5 minutes, or until lightly browned. Sprinkle with the chives.

Serves 4

FAR EASTERN RUTABAGAS

Healing Foods

Garlic
Rutabagas

2 pounds rutabagas
1 tablespoon low-
 sodium soy sauce
1 tablespoon
 canola oil
$^1/_4$ cup thinly
 sliced scallions

$^1/_2$ teaspoon
 sesame oil
2 cloves garlic,
 minced
$^1/_4$ teaspoon red
 pepper

Peel the rutabagas and cut into $^1/_2$-inch chunks. Place in a 3-quart saucepan, cover with cold water, and cook over medium heat until tender,

557

about 20 to 25 minutes. Drain. Return to the pan and stir over medium heat until all the excess moisture evaporates, about 2 minutes.

In a large frying pan, combine the soy sauce, canola oil, sesame oil, garlic, and pepper. Heat for 4 minutes. Add the rutabagas and toss to combine. Heat for 2 minutes. Sprinkle with the scallions.

Serves 4

GREEN BEANS AND PEPPERS

Healing Foods

Artichokes
Beans (snap)
Oil
Peppers (sweet)
Potatoes

12 ounces small red potatoes	1/3 cap tarragon vinegar
8 ounces green beans	3 tablespoons olive oil
2 sweet red peppers	1 teaspoon Dijon mustard
8 cooked artichoke hearts, halved	1/4 teaspoon black pepper
1/2 teaspoon dried marioram	1/4 teaspoon Worcestershire sauce
1 clove garlic, minced	

Steam the potatoes until tender, about 15 minutes. Cool to warm and slice thinly. Place in a large bowl.

Blanch the beans in boiling water for 5 minutes. Drain and add to the bowl.

Broil the peppers until charred on all sides. Let cool slightly, then peel, seed, and dice. Add to the bowl.

Add the artichokes and toss to combine.

In a small bowl, whisk together the vinegar, oil, mustard, garlic, marjoram, black pepper, and Worcestershire.

Pour over the vegetables and toss to combine.

Serves 4

FRESH TALK ABOUT VEGETABLES

Safeguard the nutrients in your produce by choosing and storing your selections properly.

Vegetable	Look For	Storage
Asparagus	Firm, smooth, round spears; closed, compact tips; rich green color	Wrap stems in moist toweling; refrigerate in plastic bags; will keep 2–3 days
Broccoli	Small, closed buds with no trace of yellow; moderate size; firm yet tender stems and branches	Refrigerate in plastic bags; will keep 3–5 days

Vegetable	Look For	Storage
Corn	Moist, green husks; bright, plump kernels	Refrigerate in husks; will keep 1–2 days
Eggplant	Firm, heavy body; small blossom-end scar; rich purple color; shiny, tight, smooth skin	Store in cool place or in refrigerator; put in plastic bag to retain moisture; will keep 2–4 days
Lima beans	Well-filled, clean, shiny green pods	Refrigerate in shells; will keep 2–5 days
Peas	Crisp, bright green pods filled but not bulging with peas	Refrigerate uncovered in pods; will keep 2–4 days
Snap beans	Crisp, long, slender pods; seeds less than half grown; good color	Refrigerate in plastic bags; will keep 2–5 days
Snow or sugar snap peas	Crisp, slender, bright green pods with immature peas	Refrigerate in plastic bags; will keep 1–2 days

Vegetable	Look For	Storage
Summer squash	Firm, glossy tender skin; fairly heavy for size; slender	Refrigerate in plastic bags; will keep 3–5 days
Tomatoes	Firm plump bodies with uniform color; small blossom-end scar	Ripen and store at room temperature; will keep at least 1 week

ZUCCHINI WITH CARAWAY

Healing Food

Squash (summer)

1 tablespoon olive oil
12 ounces zucchini, thinly sliced
1/4 cup chopped onions
1/4 cup sliced mushrooms
2 cloves garlic, minced
1/4 teaspoon caraway seeds, crushed
1 tablespoon minced fresh parsley

In a large nonstick frying pan over medium-high heat, heat the oil. Add the zucchini, onions, mushrooms, garlic, and caraway seeds.

Sauté until the zucchini is tender and a bit brown, about 8 minutes. Sprinkle with the parsley.

Serves 4

BROCCOLI WITH PARSLEY SAUCE

Healing Foods

Broccoli
Parsley

1 cup fresh parsley
1 small onion, minced
1 pound broccoli
  florets

2 tablespoons part-
  skim ricotta
$^1/_2$ cup buttermilk

In a food processor, finely chop the parsley with the onions and ricotta.

With the motor running, pour in the buttermilk and continue to process just until combined.

Steam the broccoli until tender, about 8 minutes.

Drizzle the sauce over the broccoli.

Serves 4

STUFFED ACORN SQUASH

Healing Foods

Cheese (low-fat)
Seeds
Squash (winter)

2 large acorn squash
$^1/_2$ cup diced onions
$^1/_2$ cup diced celery

2 tablespoons olive oil
1 cup fresh
  bread crumbs

1/2 cup sunflower
  seeds
2 cloves garlic,
  minced
1/2 cup shredded
  low-fat Cheddar
  cheese

1/4 cup raisins
2 tablespoons
  lemon juice
1/2 teaspoon dried sage
1/4 teaspoon black
  pepper
1/2 teaspoon
  dried thyme

Cut the squash in half lengthwise. Scoop out and discard the seeds.

In a large frying pan, sauté the onions, celery, sunflower seeds, and garlic in the oil until the onions are soft, about 5 minutes.

Add the bread crumbs, raisins, lemon juice, sage, thyme, and pepper. Cook, stirring, over low heat for 5 minutes.

Remove from the heat and mix in the cheese. Pack the stuffing into the squash cavities.

Coat a 9 x 13-inch baking dish with nonstick spray. Add the squash, filling side up. Bake at 350°F for 25 to 35 minutes, or until tender.

Serves 4

WINTER GREENS WITH ROASTED GARLIC

Healing Foods

Garlic
Kale

1/3 cup chicken stock
8 cloves unpeeled
   garlic
1 pound kale,
   shredded
1/2 teaspoon red
   pepper flakes

2 tablespoons
   lemon juice
2 tablespoons
   tomato juice
1 teaspoon olive oil
8 slices French bread

In an ovenproof custard cup, combine the stock and garlic. Bake at 350°F, stirring occasionally, until the garlic is soft, about 30 minutes.

Steam the kale until just tender, about 4 minutes.

In a large bowl whisk together the lemon juice, tomato juice, oil, and red pepper. Add the kale and toss to coat.

To serve, peel each clove of garlic and spread on a slice of bread. Mound the greens on the bread.

Serves 4

CUCUMBERS WITH CUMIN AND CORIANDER

Healing Foods

Cucumbers
Yogurt (low-fat)

2 cups nonfat yogurt
1 teaspoon
   ground cumin
1/8 teaspoon red pepper
1 large cucumber

1 tomato, chopped
2 tablespoons minced
   red onions
2 tablespoons minced
   fresh coriander

Line a strainer with cheesecloth or a coffee filter. Place over a bowl. Spoon in the yogurt and allow to drain for 30 minutes.

Transfer to a medium bowl. Whisk in the cumin and red pepper.

Peel and coarsely shred the cucumber. Doing a handful at a time, gently squeeze the pulp to remove excess moisture. Place the cucumbers in a large bowl. Add the tomatoes, onions, and coriander. Toss gently to combine.

Add the yogurt and mix well. Chill before serving.

Serves 4

SWEET-CORN FRITTERS

Healing Foods

Corn
Yogurt (low-fat)

1 cup nonfat yogurt	$^1/_3$ cup unbleached
$^1/_2$ cup applesauce	flour
1 cup corn	$^1/_2$ teaspoon
$^1/_2$ cup egg substitute	baking powder
$^1/_4$ cup skim milk	2 tablespoons
$^1/_4$ teaspoon	snipped chives
dried oregano	1 tablespoon canola oil

Line a strainer with cheesecloth or a coffee filter. Place over a bowl. Spoon in the yogurt and allow to drain for 30 minutes.

Transfer to a small bowl. Whisk in the applesauce. Set aside.

In a food processor, chop the corn with on/off turns until crushed but not pureed. Transfer to a medium bowl. Stir in the egg substitute and milk.

Add the flour, baking powder, chives, and oregano. If the batter is too thick, stir in additional milk.

Heat a large nonstick frying pan over medium heat. Brush lightly with oil. Drop batter by heaping teaspoonfuls into the pan. Cook the fritters until golden brown on both sides, about 4 minutes. Repeat, brushing the pan with additional oil, until all the batter is used.

Serve the fritters with the applesauce mixture.

Serves 4 to 6

BRUSSELS SPROUTS WITH THREE-ROOT SAUCE

Healing Foods

Brussels sprouts
Parsnips
Potatoes

1 large potato, diced
1 small celery root, peeled and chopped

2 parsnips, chopped
1 cup chicken stock
1 pound brussels sprouts

In a 2-quart saucepan, cook the potato in water to cover until tender, about 15 minutes. Drain and mash using a food mill or hand-held masher. Transfer to a large bowl.

In the same saucepan, cook the celery root and parsnips in water to cover until tender, about 15 minutes. Drain and puree in a food processor with the stock until smooth. Add to the potatoes and combine well. Return to the saucepan and keep warm.

Steam the brussels sprouts until tender, about 10 minutes. Serve with the sauce.

Serves 4

CREAMED TURNIPS

Healing Foods

Milk (low-fat)
Turnips

2 pounds small turnips	$1/4$ teaspoon dried thyme
1 cup thinly sliced onions	$1/4$ teaspoon grated nutmeg
$1^1/2$ tablespoons unbleached flour	$1/8$ teaspoon black pepper
1 cup skim milk	2 tablespoons shredded low-fat Swiss cheese

Peel and quarter the turnips. Steam the turnips and onions until the turnips are tender, about 10 minutes. Transfer to a large bowl.

In a 1-quart saucepan, whisk the flour with about 2 tablespoons of milk until smooth. Whisk in the remaining milk. Cook over medium heat, whisking constantly, until thickened. Add the thyme, nutmeg, and pepper.

Pour the sauce over the turnips and mix well.

Coat a $1^1/_2$-quart casserole with nonstick spray. Add the turnip mixture. Sprinkle with the cheese.

Bake at 350°F for 15 minutes.

Serves 4

INDIAN-STYLE WILTED GREENS

Healing Foods

Herbs and spices
Onions
Peppers (chili)
Salad greens

2 cups shredded endive

2 cups shredded mustard greens

2 cups shredded red chard

1 tablespoon olive oil

1 teaspoon ground cumin

1 tablespoon peeled grated gingerroot

1 onion, thinly sliced

1 bunch scallions, cut into 1-inch pieces

1 green chili pepper, seeded and chopped

$1^1/_2$ teaspoons turmeric

1 teaspoon ground coriander

$^1/_2$ teaspoon ground cinnamon

$^1/_8$ teaspoon ground cloves

$^1/_8$ teaspoon black pepper

Wash the endive, mustard greens, and chard in cold water. Drain and combine in a large bowl with just the water left clinging to the leaves. Set aside.

In a large nonstick frying pan over low heat, stir the oil and cumin until fragrant, about 1 minute. Do not allow to burn. Add the ginger, chili pepper, turmeric, coriander, cinnamon, cloves, and pepper. Sauté over low heat for 3 minutes.

Add the onions and scallions. Sauté for 3 minutes.

Add a large handful of the mixed greens. Stir until they shrink considerably. Keep adding greens until all are thoroughly wilted.

Serves 4

MICRO METHOD: Appetite Appeal

Even finicky eaters—like children—will feel more kindly toward vegetables if you make them look appealing. Cut the veggies into interesting shapes and then aim for a pleasing mix of colors, flavors, and textures. Choose two or more compatible vegetables that you can cook and serve together. Then let your microwave see to it that the vegetables will be ready to serve at the same time.

As a bonus, microwaving helps vegetables retain their individual shapes and attractive colors. And it brings out flavors so well that you won't need butter to make produce palatable.

There are three basic ways to microwave an assortment of vegetables at the same time:

- Choose vegetables with similar densities so they'll cook in the same amount of time. Rotate the dish or stir the vegetables once or twice during microwaving to ensure even cooking.
- Microwave the long cookers first, then add the more tender vegetables near the end of the microwaving time.
- Take advantage of the microwave's tendency to cook foods from the outside circumference of a dish toward the center. By arranging vegetables carefully, you can cook and serve a stunning presentation in the same dish. Take thinly sliced long-cooking vegetables, such as carrots and winter squash, and arrange them around the outer edge of the dish. Cut more tender vegetables, like cauliflower and broccoli, into slightly larger pieces and place them just inside the outer circle. Position very delicate vegetables, such as zucchini, in the center of the dish.

No matter which method you're using, if the vegetables are still damp from being rinsed, you don't need to add any water to the dish. Just cover it with microwave-safe plastic wrap and cook on high until the vegetables are crisp-tender. Total cooking time will depend on the exact amounts and types of vegetables you're using. Remember that food continues to cook after being removed from the microwave, so don't overcook your selections. If desired, spoon a low-fat dressing or sauce over the vegetables before serving.

ORIENTAL GINGERED VEGETABLES

Healing Foods

Asparagus
Beans (snap)
Broccoli
Carrots

1 cup sliced
green beans

1 cup broccoli florets

1 cup thinly sliced
carrots

1 cup sliced asparagus

1 cup thinly
sliced mushrooms

$^1/_2$ cup julienned
sweet red peppers

1 tablespoon peeled
minced gingerroot

1 clove garlic, minced

1 tablespoon
canola oil

1 tablespoon low-
sodium soy sauce

Steam the beans, broccoli, carrots, and asparagus until crisp-tender, about 5 minutes.

In a large nonstick frying pan over medium-high heat, sauté the mushrooms, peppers, ginger, and garlic in the oil until light brown, about 3 minutes.

Add the steamed vegetables and soy sauce. Stir-fry for 1 to 2 minutes.

Serves 4

TOMATO AND ZUCCHINI GRATIN

Healing Foods

Rice
Squash (summer)

1 large onion, thinly sliced	1/4 teaspoon dried thyme
1 tablespoon olive oil	1/4 teaspoon dried basil
1 pound zucchini, thinly sliced	3 cups cooked rice
1 large tomato, thinly sliced	1/4 cup grated Parmesan cheese

In a large frying pan over medium heat, sauté the onions in the oil for 2 minutes. Add the zucchini and sauté until tender, about 4 minutes. Stir in the thyme and basil. Remove from the heat.

Coat a 1 1/2-quart casserole with nonstick spray. Layer half of the rice in the dish. Top with half of the zucchini and half of the tomatoes. Sprinkle with half of the cheese. Repeat.

Bake at 375°F for 15 minutes, or until heated through and lightly browned.

Serves 4

SAVOY PUREE
IN POTATO SHELLS

Healing Foods

Cabbage
Potatoes

4 large baking
   potatoes
1 pound savoy
   cabbage, shredded
$1/2$ teaspoon
   dried chervil

2 tablespoons
   olive oil
$1/4$ cup minced
   fresh parsley
$1/4$ teaspoon ground
   black pepper

Bake the potatoes at 375°F for 1 hour, or until easily pierced with a fork.

In a large frying pan, combine the cabbage and oil. Cover and cook over low heat, stirring frequently, until caramelized and very tender, about 40 minutes.

Cut a thin slice off the top of each potato. Scoop out the pulp, leaving a $1/4$-inch shell. Reserve the shells and transfer the pulp to a large bowl. Mash well. Add the cabbage, parsley, chervil, and pepper.

Spoon into the potato shells.

Serves 4

STUFFED RED BEETS

Healing Foods

Beets

$^1/_2$ cup nonfat yogurt
$^1/_3$ cup minced
    celery
2 tablespoons finely
    chopped almonds
4 large beets, cooked

1 tablespoon olive oil
1 teaspoon
    lemon juice
1 clove garlic, minced
$^1/_4$ teaspoon
    dried thyme

Line a strainer with cheesecloth or a coffee filter. Place over a bowl. Spoon in the yogurt and allow to drain for 30 minutes.

Transfer to a medium bowl. Add the celery, almonds, oil, lemon juice, garlic, and thyme.

Using a melon scoop or small spoon, scoop out the centers from the beets, leaving a $^1/_4$-inch shell. Set the shells aside.

Dice the scooped-out part of the beets. Add to the yogurt mixture.

Spoon the mixture into the beet shells.

Serves 4

CORN AND ONION PUDDING

Healing Foods

Corn
Milk (low-fat)

1 1/2 cups skim milk
1/2 cup egg substitute
1/4 teaspoon chili
  powder

1/4 teaspoon hot-
  pepper sauce
1 cup corn
1 cup minced onions

In a large bowl, whisk together the milk, egg substitute, chili powder, hot-pepper sauce. Stir in the corn and onions.

Coat a 1 1/2-quart baking dish with nonstick spray. Add the corn mixture.

Bake at 350°F for 1 hour, or until set and light brown on top.

Serves 4

CARROT FRITTERS

Healing Foods

Carrots

1/4 cup egg substitute
1 tablespoon flour
2 cups shredded
  carrots
2 scallions, minced
1 tablespoon olive oil

2 tablespoons
  minced parsley
1/2 teaspoon
  dried tarragon
2 egg whites

In a large bowl, combine the egg substitute and flour. Stir in the carrots, scallions, parsley, and tarragon.

In a separate bowl, whip the egg whites with clean beaters until stiff. Fold into the carrot mixture.

Heat the oil on a nonstick griddle. Drop $1/4$-cup mounds of batter onto the hot griddle. Flatten a bit with the back of a spatula. Fry on both sides until golden brown.

Serves 4

CARROTS AND PARSNIPS

Healing Foods

Carrots
Parsnips
Pears

1 pound carrots, chopped
1 pound parsnips, chopped

1 ripe pear, chopped
2 tablespoons minced fresh chervil or parsley

In a 3-quart saucepan, steam the carrots and parsnips until tender, about 10 minutes. Reserve the steaming liquid.

Transfer the carrots and parsnips to a food processor. Add the pears. Puree until smooth, adding just enough cooking liquid to facilitate blending.

Reheat gently before serving. Stir in the chervil or parsley.

Serves 8

CHRISTMAS CABBAGE

Healing Foods

Apples
Cabbage
Oranges
Pears

2 pounds cabbage, chopped into $1/2$-inch pieces
1 tart apple, cubed
1 pear, cubed
1 large onion, diced
1 tablespoon red-wine vinegar

1 navel orange, sectioned and chopped
$1/4$ cup stock
1 tablespoon honey
$1^1/2$ teaspoons peeled minced gingerroot
1 tablespoon all-fruit marmalade

In a 4-quart pot, combine the cabbage, apples, pears, onions, oranges, stock, honey, and ginger. Cover and simmer, stirring occasionally, for 30 minutes. Add the vinegar and marmalade. Cook for 5 minutes.

Serves 6 to 8

FRENCH-STYLE CHARD

Healing Foods

Garlic
Swiss chard

4 cups coarsely
  shredded Swiss
  chard
2 cloves garlic,
  minced

2 tablespoons grated
  Sapsago or
  Parmesan cheese
1 tablespoon olive oil

In a large nonstick frying pan, sauté the chard
and garlic in the oil until wilted, about 5 minutes.
Sprinkle with the cheese.

Serves 4

WHAT TO DO ABOUT PESTICIDES

Many healing fruits and vegetables—like broccoli, carrots, and spinach—are routinely sprayed
with chemical pesticides, some of which are
suspected of causing cancer. You can minimize
your exposure to questionable chemical sprays
by buying produce that's been grown organ-
ically. If that's not possible, try to find locally
grown produce, including fruits and vegetables
from farmer's markets and roadside stands.
Often these small producers use fewer pesticides
than large growers. And since you'll be dealing
with the actual growers, you can quiz them about
their pesticide use.

Whenever possible, let your supermarket produce manager know that you are interested in
buying nonsprayed groceries. Create a demand
for pesticide-free fruits and vegetables.

In addition, buy seasonal fruits and vegetables.
Out-of-season varieties are often imported and
may not be as carefully checked for pesticide
residue.

If you can't find nonsprayed produce, peeling fruits and vegetables such as apples, carrots, and cucumbers can help cut exposure. Be aware that you will lose some fiber and also that some vitamins are concentrated just under the skin.

When peeling isn't practical or desirable, give your produce a nice hot bath to clean away traces of pesticides that cling to the surface.

"Wash, scrub, and rinse carefully" is the advice from Shannon Sullivan, former assistant project coordinator at the Natural Resources Defense Council, based in Washington, D.C. Add a cup of vinegar or the juice of a fresh lemon to a bowl of water. Let the produce soak for 3 minutes, then rinse very, very thoroughly. This is practical with hard or thick-skinned produce, such as apples, pears, peppers, or squash. It's not really suitable for berries or other very delicate items.

"Many pesticides are oil-based, and introducing an agent (like an acid) that breaks the bonds between the pesticides and the vegetables can help remove some of the chemicals from the surface," says Sullivan.

To learn more about pesticides in foods or pesticide use in home gardens, contact the Environmental Protection Agency's toll-free hotline: 800-858-PEST.

MOROCCAN CARROT SALAD

Healing Foods

Carrots
Garlic
Herbs and spices

1 pound carrots,
  julienned
2 cloves garlic,
  minced
1 scallion, minced
2 tablespoons minced
  fresh parsley
1/8 teaspoon
  ground cinnamon

2 teaspoons dillweed
2 tablespoons
  lemon juice
1 tablespoon olive oil
1/2 teaspoon
  ground cumin
1/4 teaspoon paprika
1/8 teaspoon red
  pepper

Steam the carrots and garlic for 5 minutes, until crisp-tender. Transfer to a large bowl. Add the scallions, parsley, and dill.

In a small bowl, whisk together the lemon juice, oil, cumin, paprika, cinnamon, and red pepper. Pour over the carrots and mix well. Refrigerate until cold.

Serves 4

CHINESE BEANS WITH SESAME SEEDS

Healing Foods

Beans (snap)
Peppers (sweet)
Seeds

12 ounces green beans
3 tablespoons rice-wine vinegar
1 tablespoon canola oil
2 teaspoons low-sodium soy sauce
1 teaspoon honey
1 sweet red or yellow pepper, cut into strips
1 tablespoon peeled minced gingerroot
1 tablespoon snipped chives
1 clove garlic, minced
$1/8$ teaspoon red pepper
4 scallions, sliced diagonally
3 tablespoons toasted sesame seeds

If the beans are young and small, leave them whole. Otherwise, snap in half or slice lengthwise. Blanch in boiling water for 2 to 3 minutes. Drain and rinse under cold water.

In a small bowl, whisk together the vinegar, oil, soy sauce, and honey. Stir in the ginger, chives, garlic, and red pepper.

In a large nonstick frying pan over medium-high heat, heat 1 tablespoon of the dressing. Add the beans and toss to coat. Cover and cook for 3 to 4 minutes, or until crisp-tender.

Transfer to a serving platter. Top with the scallions and sliced peppers. Lightly drizzle with the dressing and sprinkle with the sesame seeds.

Serves 4

STIR-FRY WITH SNOW PEAS, CELERY, AND PISTACHIOS

Healing Foods

Celery
Nuts
Peas

1 cup sliced celery
1/4 cup minced
  scallions
1 tablespoon
  canola oil
1/4 cup chopped
  pistachios

1 cup snow peas
1 teaspoon
  dried thyme
1/4 teaspoon
  black pepper
1/4 cup minced
  fresh parsley

In a 1-quart saucepan, cook the celery in water to cover until crisp-tender, about 3 to 5 minutes. Drain.

In a large nonstick frying pan over medium heat, sauté the scallions in the oil until light brown, about 5 minutes. Add the celery, snow peas, thyme, and pepper. Sauté for several minutes. Remove from the heat and add the pistachios and parsley.

Serves 4

ROSEMARY ASPARAGUS

Healing Food

Asparagus

582

1 cup chicken stock
1 clove garlic, halved
1 teaspoon
   dried rosemary
1 tablespoon minced
   fresh parsley

1 bay leaf
1 pound thin
   asparagus spears
$1/2$ cup chopped
   onions

Pour the stock into a large frying pan. Add the garlic, rosemary, and bay leaf. Bring to a simmer.

Prepare the asparagus by holding each spear at its ends and bending until it snaps. Discard the tough bottom part. Set the spears in the frying pan and cover with the onions. Partially cover the pan. Simmer for 4 minutes.

Remove the spears from the stock and place on a serving platter. Discard the bay leaf. Strain the stock into a small bowl, reserving the onions and garlic.

Place the onions, garlic, and parsley in a blender or food processor. Add $1/3$ cup of the reserved stock. Process until smooth. Drizzle the sauce over the warm asparagus.

Serves 4

BEETS WITH PECANS AND DILL

Healing Foods

Beets
Nuts
Onions

2 pounds beets
1 pound onions,
  thinly sliced
$1/3$ cup chicken stock
$1/2$ cup minced
  shallots
$1/4$ teaspoon dillweed

$1/4$ cup minced
  fresh parsley
2 tablespoons
  chopped pecans
2 tablespoons olive oil
$1/2$ teaspoon
  black pepper

In a 3-quart saucepan, cook the beets in water to cover until easily pierced with a skewer, about 50 minutes. Drain and plunge into cold water. Trim off the tops and slip off the skins. Thinly slice the beets crosswise.

In a large frying pan, combine the onions and stock. Cover and cook over medium heat until very soft, about 20 minutes. Add the shallots and cook for 5 minutes.

In a cup, combine the parsley, pecans, oil, pepper, and dill.

Coat a 9 x 9-inch baking dish with nonstick spray. Add one-fourth of the beets in a single layer. Top with one-third of the onions. Sprinkle with one-third of the parsley mixture.

Repeat two times. End with a layer of beets.

Cover the dish with foil. Bake at 325°F for 35 to 45 minutes.

Serves 4

HUNAN EGGPLANT

Healing Foods

Eggplant
Garlic

1^1/$_2$ pounds eggplant
1 tablespoon
  canola oil
1 teaspoon peeled
  minced gingerroot
1 teaspoon honey

2 cloves garlic, minced
1 tablespoon
  lemon juice
1 teaspoon low-
  sodium soy sauce
1 teaspoon sesame oil

Slice the eggplant into 1-inch chunks. Steam until tender, about 12 minutes.

In a large nonstick frying pan over medium heat, heat the canola oil. Add the ginger and garlic. Sauté until fragrant, about 3 minutes. Stir in the lemon juice, soy sauce, honey, and sesame oil.

Add the eggplant and toss to coat.

Serves 4

CHIC SHALLOTS AND THE REST OF THE ONION FAMILY

The culinary contributions of the heart-healthy onion clan have been recognized and valued for centuries. Here are some tips, tricks, and techniques for getting the best from these aromatic vegetables, collectively known as the allium family.

Onions

- The easiest way to peel tiny pearl onions is to place them in boiling water for 1 minute. Drain, cut a thin slice off each end, and slip off the peel.
- Impart a golden brown hue to pale stocks and soups by adding onion skins during cooking. Add them loose to stock (you'll be straining it later). For soup, tie them in a piece of cheesecloth for easy removal.
- For extra flavor in soups and stews, peel an onion and press about a dozen cloves into it. Add it to the pot and remove just before serving. If desired, discard the cloves and eat the onion.
- Make stuffed onions by boiling medium to large peeled onions for 5 minutes. Drain and set aside until cool enough to handle. Remove the middles with a melon scoop, leaving a sturdy shell. Chop the centers and add to cooked rice, mashed sweet potatoes, or cooked diced summer squash. Season with herbs, bread crumbs, and a little shredded low-fat cheese. Fill the onions with the stuffing and bake at 350°F for 1 hour, or until brown, sweet, and tender.
- Wrap large unpeeled onions in foil and bake them at 350°F for about 1 hour. Or bury them in hot coals for the same amount of time when grilling. Remove the foil, peel, and serve as an accompaniment to fish, meat, or poultry.

Garlic

- Peel garlic by laying cloves flat on a counter or cutting board. Cover with an unslotted spatula or the broad side of a chef's knife. Press down on the spatula or knife with the heel of your hand to crush the clove. The peel will then slip right off.
- For best flavor, don't refrigerate garlic. Store it in a cool, well-ventilated place.
- When sautéing garlic, take care not to let it burn or it will turn bitter.
- To get a sweet, nutty flavor from garlic, roast it. Toss unpeeled cloves into a baking dish and bake at 350°F for 15 to 30 minutes. Stir occasionally to prevent scorching. Slip off the peels, mash, and add to sauces, marinades, and purees. Or serve on bread or pasta.
- Become acquainted with elephant garlic. Its cloves are five to ten times larger than regular garlic (sometimes a bulb is as big as an apple). But its flavor is more subtle. It's so mild that you can serve it thinly sliced in sandwiches and salads, like Bermuda onions.

Shallots

- Shallots have a milder, more refined flavor than onions. Peel the garlic-like cloves, mince, and add to sauces, sautes, and salads.
- If you grow your own, use the leaves like chives.
- Store in a cool, well-ventilated place. But for best results, don't refrigerate.
- Bake shallots as an elegant accompaniment

to roast pork, poultry or veal. Peel the cloves, place in a small baking dish and cover with stock. Bake at 350°F for 45 minutes. Remove from the stock and serve.

Chives

- Mince the slender green spears and use to top cottage cheese, baked potatoes, or cooked vegetables.
- If you grow your own, use the spicy purple flowers as edible garnishes or additions to green salads. But don't eat the flower stalks; they tend to be woody.
- Look for garlic chives (also called Chinese chives) in the market. They're larger, flatter, and more silvery in color than regular chives. They have a more pronounced flavor.

Leeks

- Buy leeks with firm white stalks and fresh green tops. The root end should show several inches of blanched, white skin. Avoid bulbs with splits, which may be tough and stringy.
- Store leeks in the refrigerator (wrap in plastic) and use within a few days.
- To use, cut off the root end and tough upper leaves (reserve those leaves for stock). To remove grit that may be lodged between the layers, cut leeks in half lengthwise and wash well under cold running water. Fan out the layers for maximum effect.
- Braise in stock to cover until tender and serve as a vegetable. Figure on two leeks per serving.

PARSNIP-CORN CAKES

Healing Foods

Corn
Parsnips
Potatoes

2 potatoes, shredded
4 parsnips, shredded
$1^1/2$ cups corn
2 tablespoons
  snipped chives
2 teaspoons flour
1 tablespoon
  canola oil

$1/2$ teaspoon
  grated nutmeg
$1/2$ teaspoon
  black pepper
$1/2$ cup egg substitute
3 egg whites
$1/4$ cup maple
  syrup (optional)

Working a handful at a time, squeeze the potatoes to extract all excess moisture. Place the potatoes in a large bowl.

Add the parsnips, corn, chives, nutmeg, and pepper. Stir in the egg substitute and flour.

In a separate bowl with clean beaters, beat the egg whites until stiff. Fold into the vegetable mixture.

Brush a large nonstick frying pan with oil. Heat over medium heat. Drop spoonfuls of the batter into the pan, shape into rounds and fry until golden on both sides. Repeat, brushing the pan with additional oil, until all the batter is used.

If desired, serve with maple syrup.

Serves 4

POTATOES WITH CREAMY MUSTARD TOPPING

Healing Foods

Cottage cheese (low-fat)
Potatoes

4 large baking
  potatoes
1 cup low-fat
  cottage cheese
1 tablespoon Dijon
  mustard

1 tablespoon chopped
  scallions
1 tablespoon
  snipped chives

Bake the potatoes at 375°F for 1 hour, or until easily pierced with a fork.

Cut a thin slice off the top of each potato. Scoop out the pulp, leaving a 1/4-inch shell. Reserve the shells and transfer the pulp to a large bowl. Mash well.

In a food processor, puree the cottage cheese, mustard, and scallions until smooth. Fold into the mashed potatoes. Spoon the mixture into the reserved shells. Sprinkle with the chives.

Serves 4

ROSEMARY ROASTED PEPPERS

Healing Foods

Garlic
Peppers (sweet)

5 sweet red peppers ¹/₂ teaspoon dried
1 tablespoon olive oil   rosemary, crushed
3 cloves garlic, minced 1 teaspoon capers,
2 tablespoons vinegar   rinsed and mashed

Broil the peppers about 5 inches from the heat until charred on all sides. Transfer to a paper bag and allow to stand until cool enough to handle, about 10 minutes. Remove the skin, seeds, and stems. Cut the peppers into strips. Place in a large bowl.

In a 1-quart saucepan, heat the oil, garlic, capers, and rosemary for 2 to 3 minutes, or until fragrant. Do not allow the garlic to brown. Stir in the vinegar and pour over the peppers. Toss well to combine. Serve warm or cold.

Serves 4

SPINACH WITH PISTACHIOS

Healing Foods

Nuts
Onions
Spinach

3 tablespoons   ¹/₂ teaspoon
  pistachios   grated nutmeg
¹/₄ cup chicken stock 1 pound spinach
2 large red onions,   1 tablespoon grated
  thinly sliced   Parmesan cheese

In a large nonstick frying pan over medium-high

591

heat, stir the pistachios until fragrant and lightly toasted, about 2 minutes. Set aside.

Wash the spinach in plenty of cold water to remove any grit. Discard tough stems. Shake off excess water.

In the frying pan, heat the stock and add the onions. Sauté until tender, about 3 to 5 minutes. Add the spinach and nutmeg. Sauté until the spinach wilts, about 2 minutes.

Add the pistachios. Toss lightly. Sprinkle with the cheese.

Serves 4

HOT-TOPPED POTATOES

Spuds are a health-watcher's dream: high in nutrients and low in fat. Just don't cancel out their healthy qualities with a blanket of butter, sour cream, or bacon bits. Instead try these tasty low-fat toppings:

- Chopped tomatoes, mashed pinto beans, minced jalapeño peppers, and melted low-fat Monterey Jack cheese
- Stir-fried sweet red peppers, sliced mushrooms, and snow peas flavored with minced ginger and garlic
- Chopped steamed asparagus, toasted pine nuts, and blenderized low-fat cottage cheese
- Sliced wild mushrooms, shredded spinach, and minced garlic sautéed in olive oil and sprinkled with grated Sapsago or Parmesan cheese

- Toasted walnuts, chopped red onions, chopped black olives, and a sprinkling of crumbled feta cheese

SESAME SNOW PEAS

Healing Foods

Carrots
Peas

12 ounces snow peas
1 carrot, julienned
1 tablespoon toasted
sesame seeds

1 teaspoon sesame oil
1/2 teaspoon grated
orange rind

Steam the snow peas and carrots until tender, about 4 minutes.

Transfer to a medium bowl. Add the sesame seeds, oil, and orange rind. Toss to combine.

Serves 4

VEGETABLE EGG ROLL-UPS

Healing Foods

Carrots
Onions
Salad greens
Sprouts

1 tablespoon olive oil
1 cup shredded
  carrots
1 cup thinly
  sliced onions
4 egg whites
1 cup mung bean
  sprouts
1 cup sliced
  mushrooms
1 small head
  Boston lettuce

In a large nonstick frying pan over medium-high heat, heat the oil. Add the carrots and onions. Stir-fry for 3 minutes.

Add the sprouts and mushrooms. Stir-fry for 3 minutes.

In a cup, whisk the egg whites with a fork until frothy. Add to the vegetables. Stir slowly with a fork until the whites are cooked, about 1 minute.

Separate the lettuce into individual leaves. Divide the vegetable mixture evenly among the lettuce. Loosely roll up the leaves and eat with your hands.

Serves 4

BRUSSELS SPROUTS WITH MUSHROOM GLAZE

Healing Foods

**Brussels sprouts
Mushrooms**

1 pound brussels
  sprouts
1 cup beef stock
2 teaspoons Dijon
  mustard
1 teaspoon dried
  thyme

| 2 teaspoons | 1 cup thinly sliced |
| lemon juice | mushrooms |

Trim the brussels sprouts and halve lengthwise. Steam until tender, about 10 minutes. Set aside.

In a large nonstick frying pan over medium-high heat, bring the stock to a boil. Whisk in the lemon juice, mustard, and thyme. Add the mushrooms. Boil until the stock is reduced by half, about 5 minutes. Add the brussels sprouts. Toss well to coat with the glaze.

Serves 4

SPICY ROASTED POTATOES

Healing Food

Potatoes

1 tablespoon	1 teaspoon
coarse mustard	dried tarragon
1 tablespoon olive oil	$1/4$ teaspoon paprika
1 clove garlic, minced	$1/8$ teaspoon red
2 large baking potatoes	pepper

In a medium bowl, mix the mustard, oil, garlic, tarragon, paprika, and red pepper into a smooth paste.

Cut the potatoes into 1-inch pieces. Pat dry with paper towels. Add to the bowl and toss to coat.

Coat a baking sheet with nonstick spray. Add

the potatoes in a single layer. Bake at 425°F for 30 to 35 minutes, or until tender.

Serves 4

MAPLE SWEET POTATOES

Healing Food

Sweet potatoes

4 large sweet potatoes
3 tablespoons orange juice

3 tablespoons maple syrup
$1/4$ cup nonfat yogurt

Bake the potatoes at 375°F for $1^1/4$ hours, or until easily pierced with a fork. Slice in half lengthwise. Scoop out the pulp, leaving a $1/4$-inch shell. Reserve the shells and transfer the pulp to a large bowl.

Mash the pulp and stir in the yogurt, maple syrup, and orange juice. Spoon the filling into the reserved shells.

Return to the oven and bake for 5 minutes to heat through.

Serves 4

GREEN BEANS WITH WALNUTS

Healing Food

Beans (snap)

12 ounces green
  beans, split
  lengthwise
2 tablespoons
  chicken stock
2 tablespoons
  chopped walnuts

2 tablespoons
  snipped chives
1 tablespoon minced
  shallots
2 cloves garlic, minced
$1^1/_2$ teaspoons
  olive oil

Steam the beans until tender, about 5 minutes.

In a large nonstick frying pan over medium heat, combine the stock, walnuts, chives, shallots, garlic, and oil. Sauté for 5 minutes, or until the shallots are tender and the liquid has evaporated.

Add the beans and warm through.

Serves 4

CIDERED PARSNIPS

Healing Food

Parsnips

$1^1/_2$ pounds parsnips,
  thinly sliced

1 cup cider

Steam the parsnips until tender, about 10 minutes.

In a large frying pan over medium-high heat, boil the cider until reduced to $1/_3$ cup. Add the parsnips and toss to coat.

Serves 4

ONIONS AND APPLES IN A PUMPKIN

Healing Foods

Apples
Cheese (low-fat)
Onions
Pumpkin

1 small pumpkin (about 2¹/₂ pounds)	¹/₂ teaspoon dillweed
2 large onions, minced	¹/₄ cup grated Sapsago or
1 large apple, minced	Parmesan cheese

Cut the top off the pumpkin and set it aside. Use a large spoon to remove the seeds.

In a medium bowl, mix the onions, apples, dill, and 2 tablespoons of the cheese. Spoon the mixture into the pumpkin. Cover with the top. If the top has a stem, cover it with foil so it won't burn.

Set the pumpkin in a baking dish for easy handling. Bake at 350°F until the pumpkin is tender, about 2 hours.

Open the pumpkin and sprinkle with the remaining cheese. To serve, scoop out cooked pumpkin along with the filling.

Serves 4

MARINATED CAULIFLOWER

Healing Foods

Cauliflower
Garlic
Onions

1 head cauliflower
2 red onions,
   thinly sliced
1 tablespoon olive oil
1 tablespoon white-
   wine vinegar
1/2 teaspoon dillweed

1 tablespoon
   lemon juice
3 tablespoons minced
   fresh parsley
2 cloves garlic, minced
1/4 teaspoon
   dried thyme

Break the cauliflower into florets. Steam the cauliflower and onions until tender, about 5 minutes.

In a large bowl, whisk together the oil, vinegar, and lemon juice. Stir in the parsley, garlic, dill, and thyme.

Refrigerate for several hours, turning the vegetables in the marinade occasionally.

Serves 4

CHAPTER FOURTEEN

Grand Finales

The perfect "grand finale" finishes off a healthy meal with its own positive contributions. It never sabotages a good diet with an overload of sugar, fat, or calories. That's why the accent is on sweet, succulent fruits and other healthy ingredients in this dessert chapter.

The very best desserts, of course, are juicy, sun-ripened fruits savored all by themselves. But when you hanker for a special indulgence, appease your sweet tooth the *right* way—with nutrient-dense desserts.

When you want a traditional cake, for example, try our Classic Carrot Cake. It's high in fiber and low in saturated fat and offers lots of beta-carotene—rich carrots, no-cholesterol egg substitute, and monounsaturated canola oil for extra healing potential. The icing is made with reduced-fat "cream cheese" and just a little honey. It's still not everyday fare, but it's a wise choice for special occasions.

For more frequent enjoyment, reach for a fruit-based sweet, such as Spiced Apples, Cranberry Pears, Tropical Compote, or Peach Soufflé. They're easy as pie and delightfully lean.

Speaking of pie, choosing a single-crust tart cuts fat and calories. For extra measure, replace the saturated butter, lard, or hydrogenated short-ening in standard recipes with healthy canola oil. Then pile the shell high with pectin-rich berries or tree fruit, as in Peach-Blackberry Pie, Apple Tart, or Pear-Cheese Pie. Or have your pie without a crust as in Lemon Pumpkin Pie. For variety, make an all-American cobbler, crisp, or crunch—no crust needed, just a streusel-like topping of fiber-filled rolled oats and maybe a sprinkling of healthy nuts.

LEMON PUMPKIN PIE

Healing Foods

Milk (low-fat)
Pumpkin
Yogurt (low-fat)

$1^1/_2$ cups pumpkin
  puree
$3/_4$ cup egg substitute
$3/_4$ cup evaporated
  skim milk
$1/_3$ cup maple syrup
1 cup nonfat
  vanilla yogurt
2 teaspoons grated
  lemon rind

$1/_2$ teaspoon
  ground cinnamon
$1/_2$ teaspoon
  ground ginger
$1/_4$ teaspoon
  grated nutmeg
1 tablespoon lemon
  juice

Coat a 9-inch pie plate with nonstick spray.

In a large bowl, beat together the pumpkin, egg substitute, milk, maple syrup, cinnamon, ginger, and nutmeg.

Pour into the pie plate and bake at 350°F for 55 minutes, or until a knife inserted near the center comes out clean. Cool on a wire rack.

In a small bowl, whisk together the yogurt, lemon juice, and lemon rind. Spread on top of the pie. Chill.

Serves 8

CHEESECAKE TART

Healing Foods

Cottage cheese (low-fat)
Kiwifruit
Tangerines
Wheat germ

CRUST
1 cup wheat germ
2 tablespoons
    canola oil
2 tablespoons
    maple syrup

CHEESECAKE
2 cups low-fat
    cottage cheese
$1/2$ cup egg substitute
$1/4$ cup maple syrup
1 teaspoon
    vanilla extract
$1/4$ teaspoon
    almond extract
2 tangerines, sectioned
2 kiwifruit, sliced

To make the crust: Lightly oil a 9-inch tart pan with removable bottom.

In a small bowl, combine the wheat germ,

oil, and maple syrup. Press the mixture in the bottom and up the sides of the tart pan.

To make the cheesecake: In a food processor, combine the cottage cheese, egg substitute, maple syrup, vanilla, and almond extract until smooth.

Spoon the filling into the pan. Bake at 325°F for 30 minutes, or until firm.

Let cool on a wire rack. Then chill for at least 3 hours. Top with the tangerines and kiwis before serving.

Serves 8

STRAWBERRIES WITH TWO MELONS

Healing Foods

**Lemons and limes
Melons
Strawberries
Yogurt (low-fat)**

1 1/2 cups cantaloupe chunks

1 1/2 cups honeydew chunks

2 cups halved strawberries

1 lime, thinly sliced

1 cup nonfat vanilla yogurt

1 tablespoon lime juice

1/4 teaspoon ground cardamom

In a large bowl, combine the cantaloupe, honeydew, strawberries, and lime.

In a small bowl, combine the yogurt, lime juice, and cardamom. Pour over the fruit and toss to combine.

Serves 4

MICRO METHOD: Bring Out the Best

Recapture the just-picked sweetness of sun-ripened fruit by microwaving it briefly. Some suggestions:

- Accentuate the flavor of strawberries, raspberries, pineapple, apricots, figs, peaches, nectarines, and other summer fruit by microwaving until just barely warm. Exact time will depend on the quantity, size, and temperature of the fruit. For instance, 10 large room temperature strawberries (arrange in a circle with tips pointing in) will take about 10 to 20 seconds.
- Get more juice from citrus fruit. Before cutting and squeezing (or eating out of hand), microwave a whole lemon, lime, orange, or tangerine on full power for 15 to 35 seconds, until just slightly warm to the touch. If using the fruit for juice, roll it on the kitchen counter for a few seconds, exerting pressure with your palm, to help break the cell walls for easier juice extraction.
- Warm grapefruit for an extra-sweet breakfast treat. Halve and section a grapefruit as usual. Heat each half for 45 to 60 seconds.
- Soften an underripe avocado (yes, avocados are fruit). Prick the skin and microwave for about 1 minute. Let cool before slicing.

CRAN-APPLE SAUCE

Healing Foods

Apples
Cranberries

2 cups cranberries
2 apples, chopped
1/2 teaspoon
   ground cinnamon

3 tablespoons
   maple syrup
2 tablespoons raisins

In a 2-quart saucepan, combine the cranberries, apples, maple syrup, raisins. Simmer over medium heat, stirring frequently, until the berries and apples begin to soften, about 5 minutes. Use a potato masher to slightly crush the fruit.

   Add the cinnamon and reduce the heat to low. Cook until the sauce is thick and bubbly, about 15 minutes.

Serves 4

EMERALD ISLE RICE PUDDING

Healing Foods

Milk (low-fat)
Raisins
Rice
Squash (summer)

5 cups skim milk
3/4 cup short-
   grain brown rice
1/4 teaspoon
   grated nutmeg

1/4 cup honey
1/4 cup raisins
1 teaspoon
   vanilla extract
2 cups grated zucchini

In the top of a double boiler over boiling water, bring the milk just to a boil. Add the rice slowly and return to a boil. Reduce the heat to medium and cover the pan.

Cook the rice for 2 hours, or until tender and creamy. Stir occasionally. (Check to make sure water does not boil away.)

Stir in the honey, raisins, vanilla, and nutmeg.

Squeeze all excess liquid from the zucchini. Add to the rice. Simmer the mixture for 10 minutes. Serve warm or cold.

Serves 6 to 8

BLACK-RASPBERRY PIE

Healing Food

Raspberries

1 envelope
   unflavored gelatin
1/3 cup white
   grape juice
4 cups black
   raspberries

1/3 cup honey
1 9-inch Whole Wheat
   Pie Shell, baked
   (page 272)

In a cup, sprinkle the gelatin over the grape juice. Set aside to soften 5 minutes.

606

In a 2-quart saucepan, lightly crush the raspberries with a potato masher. Add the gelatin and honey.

Over medium-high heat, bring the mixture to a boil, stirring constantly. Remove from the heat and cool about 5 minutes.

Spoon the filling into the pie shell. Cool completely before slicing.

Serves 8

PEACH SOUFFLÉ

Healing Food

Peaches

1 1/2 cups chopped peaches	1 tablespoon lemon juice
3 tablespoons honey	1/2 teaspoon grated nutmeg
1/8 teaspoon ground cinnamon	5 egg whites

In a food processor or a blender, puree the peaches.

In a 1-quart saucepan, combine the puree and honey. Cook over low heat, stirring often, for 20 minutes, or until thickened. Add the lemon juice and nutmeg. Cool the mixture to lukewarm.

In a large bowl, beat the whites until stiff peaks form. Gently whisk one-third of the whites into the peach mixture. Then fold the peach mixture into the remaining whites.

Spoon the mixture into an ungreased 1^1/$_2$-quart soufflé dish. Sprinkle with the cinnamon.

Place the dish in a pan of hot water. Bake at 300°F for 1 hour, or until firm to the touch and browned. Do not open the oven door until near the end of the required baking time or the soufflé may fall. Serve immediately.

Serves 6

MARINATED FIGS AND APRICOTS

Healing Foods

Apricots
Figs
Yogurt (low-fat)

8 ounces dried
  black figs
8 ounces dried
  apricots
^{1}/$_2$ cup orange juice
2 tablespoons
  lime juice
1 tablespoon grated
  lime rind

^{1}/$_4$ teaspoon
  vanilla extract
1^1/$_2$ cups nonfat
  yogurt
1 tablespoon maple
  syrup
^{1}/$_4$ teaspoon
  grated nutmeg

Remove and discard the stems from the figs.

In a 2-quart saucepan, combine the figs, apricots, orange juice, lime juice, and vanilla. Simmer gently for 7 minutes or until the fruit is just beginning to plump. Remove from the heat, cover, and refrigerate overnight.

Spoon the yogurt into a cheesecloth-lined sieve. Place over a bowl and allow to drain until thick, about 2 hours.

Transfer to a small bowl, stir in the maple syrup, nutmeg, and lime rind.

Serve the fruit with the yogurt mixture.

Serves 6

BAKED PRUNE COMPOTE

Healing Foods

Apricots
Figs
Pears
Prunes

1 cup applesauce
1 cup apple juice
3 tablespoons
    lemon juice
1 tablespoon
    vanilla extract
$^1/_2$ teaspoon
    ground cinnamon
1 pear, thinly sliced

$^1/_4$ teaspoon
    ground ginger
$^1/_4$ teaspoon
    grated nutmeg
$^1/_2$ cup dried
    apricot halves
$^1/_2$ cup pitted prunes
12 dried figs, halved

In a 2-quart casserole, combine the applesauce, apple juice, lemon juice, vanilla, cinnamon, ginger, and nutmeg.

Stir in the apricots, prunes, figs, and pears. Cover and bake at 300°F for $1^1/_2$ hours. Serve warm or cold.

Serves 4

PEACH-BLACKBERRY PIE

Healing Foods

Blackberries
Peaches

1/4 cup cornstarch
3 tablespoons quick-
cooking tapioca
1 9-inch Whole
Wheat Pie Shell,
unbaked (page 272)

3/4 cup honey
2 cups sliced peaches
2 cups blackberries
1 tablespoon
lemon juice
1/2 teaspoon
ground cinnamon

In a small bowl, combine the cornstarch, tapioca, and cinnamon. Add honey and mix well.

In a large bowl, toss the peaches and black-berries with the lemon juice. Fold in the honey mixture.

Transfer to the pie shell. Place the pie plate on a baking sheet to catch drips. Bake at 375°F for 35 minutes, or until the filling is bubbly and the crust is lightly browned. Cool before cutting.

Serves 8

APPLE AND PERSIMMON COBBLER

Healing Foods

Apples
Nuts
Oats
Persimmons

FILLING
4 Japanese
  persimmons
4 apples, thinly
  sliced
1 tablespoon honey
1 teaspoon ground
  cinnamon
1/4 teaspoon
  ground cloves

TOPPING
1/2 cup rolled oats
1/3 cup ground
  almonds
2 tablespoons
  whole wheat flour
1 teaspoon ground
  cinnamon
1/3 cup honey
3 tablespoons
  light margarine

To make the filling: Peel the persimmons and slice thinly, removing any seeds.

In a large bowl, combine the persimmons, apples, honey, cinnamon, and cloves.

Coat a 9-inch pie plate with nonstick spray. Add the filling, mounding it to fit. Bake at 350°F for 40 minutes.

To make the topping: In a medium bowl, mix the oats, almonds, flour, and cinnamon. Drizzle with the honey. Cut in the margarine with a pastry blender until well mixed.

611

Remove the pie from the oven and add the topping. Bake for 20 minutes, or until crisp.

Serves 8

TROPICAL COMPOTE

Healing Foods

Grapes
Mangoes
Oranges
Papayas
Tropical fruit

2 starfruit
1 papaya
1 mango
1 1/2 cups seedless
grapes

2 oranges, sectioned
1/4 cup lime juice
2 tablespoons apple
juice concentrate

Cut the starfruit crosswise into slices. Remove any seeds.

Peel and halve the papaya. Discard the seeds. Cut the flesh into thick slices.

Peel the mango. Use a serrated knife to cut the flesh from the large inner pit. Cut the flesh into thick slices.

Arrange the starfruit, papayas, mangoes, grapes, and oranges on a shallow heatproof platter. Sprinkle with the lime juice and apple juice concentrate.

Bake at 350°F for 15 to 20 minutes, or until all the fruit is warmed through. Serve warm.

Serves 8

FRESH-FRUIT TART

Healing Foods

Blueberries
Oats
Strawberries

CRUST
1/2 cup bud-type
  bran cereal
1/2 cup rolled oats
1/2 teaspoon ground
  cinnamon
2 egg whites
1 tablespoon canola oil

FILLING
1/2 cup low-fat
  cottage cheese
1 tablespoon orange
  juice concentrate
1 cup blueberries
1 cup sliced
  strawberries

To make the crust: In a large bowl, mix the cereal, oats, and cinnamon.

In a small bowl, whisk the egg whites until frothy. Add the oil and stir into the cereal mixture. Mix well.

Coat a 9-inch pie plate with nonstick spray. Firmly press the cereal mixture into bottom of the plate to make a crust. (Don't leave any holes in the crust and don't go up the sides of the plate.)

Bake at 350°F for 10 minutes, or until firm. Let cool for 10 minutes before removing from the pan.

To make the filling: In a blender or food processor, puree the cottage cheese and juice concentrate until smooth. Spread over the crust.

Top with the blueberries and strawberries.

Use kitchen shears or a pizza cutter to cut the tart into wedges.

Serves 4

SWEET PLUMS AND ORANGES

Healing Foods

Nuts
Oranges
Plums

4 large plums,
halved and sliced
2 oranges, sectioned
2 tablespoons
lime juice

1 tablespoon maple
syrup
2 tablespoons
chopped hazelnuts

In a medium bowl, combine the plums and oranges.

In a small bowl, whisk together the lime juice and maple syrup. Pour over the fruit. Toss well to combine.

Sprinkle with the hazelnuts.

Serves 4

THE ICE AGE: FREEZING FRUIT

Stock up on fresh fruit when it's in season and at its very best in terms of flavor and vitamin content. The ideal way to store fruit for winter enjoyment is to freeze it. Here are some pointers for maximum success.

• Choose fruit for freezing that is perfectly ripe. Avoid fruit that is cheap because it's slightly over the hill. Fruit that is already soft will not fare well in the freezer, where fruit inevitably softens anyway.

- Don't buy fruit in quantity unless you have the time to freeze it immediately. Your goal is to freeze fruit while it is very fresh.
- Sort and wash fruit gently. It's best to use cold—even iced—water, particularly for berries. Warm water may soften or even bleed juice from fruit; cold water firms fruit.
- Don't let your fruit stand in water after washing; it will lose vitamins. Drain it thoroughly and pat dry gently.
- Peel and pit the fruit. Cut into uniform pieces.
- To tray-freeze fruit for easier retrieval later, arrange the fruit in a single layer on a tray lined with waxed paper. Leave space between the pieces so they don't clump together. Cover the tray and place in the freezer until the fruit is solid. Transfer the pieces to freezer bags or containers.
- Remember not to overload your freezer in your zeal to dispatch your bounty. The rule of thumb is to freeze only 2 to 3 pounds of food at one time for each cubic foot of freezer capacity.
- Thaw fruit in the refrigerator in its sealed container and eat it while still icy or just barely thawed for best texture.
- You may also thaw fruit in the microwave on medium power for short periods of time. Check the pieces frequently to keep from over-thawing or cooking them.
- Use fruit within a year of freezing.

NECTARINES WITH SAUCE CARDINALE

Healing Foods

Nectarines
Raspberries

1 cup raspberries
2 tablespoons all-
    fruit apricot preserves
1 teaspoon cornstarch

1 tablespoon water
4 cups sliced
    nectarines

Puree the raspberries in a blender or food processor. Transfer to a 1-quart saucepan. Add the preserves.

In a cup, dissolve the cornstarch in the water. Add to the saucepan.

Cook over medium heat, stirring constantly, until the sauce is thickened. Cool.

Serve the sauce over the nectarines.

Serves 4

APPLE TART

Healing Foods

Apples
Oats
Yogurt (low-fat)

CRUST

2 cups rolled oats
1/4 cup apple juice
   concentrate
1 tablespoon ground
   cinnamon

FILLING

3 large apples,
   thickly sliced
1/2 cup apple juice
   concentrate
1/2 teaspoon
   almond extract
1/2 teaspoon ground
   cinnamon
1 envelope
   unflavored gelatin
2 tablespoons honey
2 cups nonfat yogurt
1 cup halved grapes

To make the crust: In a medium bowl, combine the oats, apple juice concentrate, and cinnamon. Press into a 9-inch pie plate. Bake at 350°F for 5 minutes.

To make the filling: In a 3-quart saucepan, combine the apples, 1/4 cup of the apple juice concentrate, almond extract, and cinnamon. Simmer just until the apples are tender, about 10 minutes. Drain and let cool.

In a 1-quart saucepan, place the remaining 1/4 cup apple juice concentrate. Sprinkle with the gelatin. Let stand 5 minutes, or until the gelatin is softened. Cook over low heat until the gelatin dissolves. Remove from the heat and stir in the honey.

In a small bowl, whisk the yogurt until smooth. Add to the gelatin mixture. Pour into the crust and refrigerate for 1 hour.

Place the apples and grapes over the filling in a decorative pattern.

Serves 8

SPICED APPLES

Healing Foods

Apples
Oil

3 large apples,
    thinly sliced
2 tablespoons
    canola oil
1/2 cup cranberry
    juice

1 tablespoon honey
1/4 teaspoon ground
    cinnamon
1/8 teaspoon
    ground allspice
1/8 teaspoon
    grated nutmeg

In a large nonstick frying pan over medium heat, sauté the apples in oil until tender but not mushy, about 10 minutes. Remove and keep warm.

Add the juice, honey, cinnamon, allspice, and nutmeg to the pan. Cook over medium-high heat until syrupy, about 5 minutes. Add the apples and heat for 1 minute, turning to glaze the apples.

Serves 4

MICRO METHOD: Fruit Pies Made Easy

Fruit takes to the microwave like a duck to water. That's because microwaving is so fast it safeguards the luscious, just-picked flavor of vine-ripe fruit in a way no other cooking method can match. Here are some tips to keep in mind when preparing fruit pies.

- To prevent boil-overs, be sure your glass or ceramic pie plate actually measures 9 inches across the top and is at least $1^1/2$ inches deep. (If your plate is smaller, reduce the amount of fruit filling or microwave the excess in custard cups.)
- Microwaved fruit pies must be made in a pre-baked shell. If the pastry is not baked first, it may absorb moisture from the filling and become soggy.
- For best results, don't use a top crust.
- A high, fluted rim on the pie shell will help contain bubbling.
- Place a sheet of waxed paper on the bottom of the oven to catch any spills.
- If the pie bubbles excessively, reduce the power to medium-high (70 percent) or medium (50 percent) and increase the time.
- Microwaving time depends on the fruits used, with apples taking longer than most other selections. Berries cook very fast; check berry pies after 10 minutes.
- When the filling is hot and has started to cook in the center, the fruit pie is done. As with all microwave recipes, the pie will continue cooking after removal from the oven.

- You can microwave fruit cobblers and crumbles the same way as fruit pie fillings. However, be aware that the toppings will not brown.

The Shell Game

When it comes to the matter of a pie shell for your microwave pies, you can use your favorite recipe. But you have two choices as far as baking the crust goes.

You may prebake your shell in a *conventional* oven according to the usual directions: Prick the dough all over with a fork, then line the crust with a sheet of foil. Add some pie weights or dried beans reserved for this purpose. Bake the crust at 400°F for 15 minutes. Remove the foil and weights. Bake for another 5 to 7 minutes, or until the shell is lightly browned and thoroughly baked.

Or you may microwave it. Just be aware that although a microwaved shell can be quite tender and flaky, it will not brown. Here's how to microwave a crust.

1. Roll out the dough as usual and line your pie plate with it. Form a high, fluted edge to help guard against boil-overs.
2. Prick the crust with a fork at $1/8$-inch intervals where bottom and sides meet and at $1/2$-inch intervals over the remaining surface. That helps prevent shrinking.
3. Microwave the crust on full power for $4^1/2$ to $6^1/2$ minutes, or until the crust is dry and the bottom is opaque. (Rotate the dish after half

the cooking time.) If you have a glass pie plate, you can also check through the bottom for doneness.

4. If your pie filling will be quite liquid, seal the prick holes by brushing the crust with a small amount of well-beaten egg yolk, egg white, or egg substitute. Microwave the crust on high for 30 seconds to set the egg.

BERRY CUSTARD

Healing Foods

Milk (low-fat)
Raspberries
Strawberries

$^1/_3$ cup cornstarch
3 cups skim milk
$^1/_3$ cup honey
$^1/_4$ cup egg substitute

2 cups sliced
  strawberries
1 cup raspberries
1 teaspoon vanilla
  extract

In a 2-quart saucepan, combine the cornstarch with $^1/_2$ cup milk until smooth. Whisk in the remaining milk and the honey. Cook over low heat, stirring constantly, until the mixture thickens to a syrupy consistency. Remove from the heat.

Place the egg substitute in a cup. Stir in several spoonfuls of the hot mixture. Whisk the mixture into the pan.

Cook over low heat, stirring constantly, until

the mixture reaches a light-custard consistency. Stir in the vanilla.

Divide the mixture among six custard cups. Chill thoroughly.

Just before serving, top each serving with the strawberries and raspberries.

Serves 6

BLUEBERRY-APPLE CRISP

Healing Foods

Apples
Blueberries
Oats

6 apples, thinly sliced
2 cups blueberries
2 tablespoons lemon juice
2 cups rolled oats
$1/3$ cup honey

$3/4$ cup whole wheat flour
$1/2$ cup raisins
2 teaspoons ground cinnamon
$1/2$ cup apple juice
2 tablespoons canola oil

Coat a 9 x 13-inch baking dish with nonstick spray. Add the apples, blueberries, and lemon juice. Toss to combine.

In a large bowl, combine the oats, flour, raisins, and cinnamon. Drizzle with the apple juice, honey, and oil. Combine well. Sprinkle over the fruit.

Bake at 350°F for 30 to 40 minutes, or until the apples are tender.

Serves 12 to 15

WINTER-JUBILEE FRUIT

Healing Foods

Figs
Papayas
Pears
Pomegranates

2 pears, sliced	$1/2$ cup chopped
2 papayas, peeled,	dried figs
seeded, and sliced	1 pomegranate
2 tablespoons	1 cup nonfat
orange juice	vanilla yogurt

In a large bowl, combine the pears, papayas, and figs.

Break open the pomegranate. Gently dislodge the seeds from the surrounding membranes. Reserve 2 tablespoons of seeds. Add the remainder to the fruit mixture.

In a small bowl, combine the yogurt and orange juice. Stir into the fruit. Sprinkle with the reserved pomegranate seeds.

Serves 4 to 6

ALMOND-TOPPED BAKED PLUMS

Healing Foods

Nuts
Oil
Plums

PLUMS

3 cups halved plums
1 tablespoon
  canola oil
1/4 cup honey
3 tablespoons
  lemon juice

TOPPING

1/2 cup sliced almonds
1/3 cup whole
  wheat flour
2 tablespoons honey
2 tablespoons canola oil
1 teaspoon vanilla
  extract

To make the plums: In a large frying pan over medium heat, sauté the plums in the oil until soft, about 5 minutes. Add the honey and lemon juice.

Spoon the plums into a 2-quart baking dish.

To make the topping: In a medium bowl, mix the almonds, flour, honey, oil, and vanilla until crumbly. Sprinke over the plums.

Bake at 350°F for 25 minutes. Serve hot or cold.

Serves 6

BLUEBERRY PUDDING

Healing Foods

Blueberries
Cottage cheese (low-fat)
Yogurt (low-fat)

2 cups low-fat
  cottage cheese
2 cups blueberries
2 tablespoons honey

1 cup nonfat yogurt
3 tablespoons
  lemon juice

In a food processor, blend the cottage cheese until smooth, about 3 minutes. Add the blueberries and blend again until smooth.

Transfer to a large bowl. Whisk in the yogurt, lemon juice, and honey. Divide the mixture among six custard cups. Chill before serving.

Serves 6

PEAR-CHEESE PIE

Healing Foods

Cottage cheese (low-fat)
Pears

3 cups thinly
  sliced pears
1 9-inch Whole Wheat
  Pie Shell, unbaked
  (page 272)
2 cups low-fat
  cottage cheese
1 cup egg substitute
1/4 cup honey
1 tablespoon
  orange juice
1 tablespoon
  lemon juice
2 cups apple juice

2 teaspoons grated
  orange rind
2 teaspoons
  unbleached flour
1/4 teaspoon
  ground cinnamon
1/8 teaspoon
  grated nutmeg
1 teaspoon
  vanilla extract
1/4 teaspoon
  almond extract
3 tablespoons all-fruit
  orange marmalade

Arrange 1 cup of the pears in the pie shell.

In a food processor, puree the cottage cheese until smooth. Add the egg substitute, honey, orange juice, orange rind, flour, cinnamon, nutmeg, vanilla, and almond extract. Mix well. Pour into the pie shell.

Bake at 350°F for 15 minutes. Reduce the temperature to 325°F and bake another 45 minutes, or until the filling is set.

In a large bowl, combine the remaining pears and the lemon juice. In a large frying pan, bring the apple juice to a boil. Add the pears and cook for 1 minute, stirring constantly. Remove with a slotted spoon and drain well on paper towels.

Arrange the pears in a circle around the edge of the crust, overlapping the slices slightly.

In a 1-quart saucepan, melt the marmalade over low heat. Brush the pears with the marmalade. Chill the pie at least 4 hours.

Serves 8

FRESH TALK ABOUT FRUIT

Here's how to choose and store the cream of the crop.

Fruit	Look For	Storage
Apricots	Plump, juicy looking; smooth skin; bright golden-orange color; yield to gentle pressure	Ripen at room temperature, refrigerate ripe apricots; will keep 3–5 days

626

Fruit	Look For	Storage
Blackberries	Plump; bright color	Refrigerate, unwashed and uncovered; will keep 1–2 days
Blueberries	Firm; dry; well-rounded shape; bright purple-blue color with slightly frosted appearance	Refrigerate, unwashed and uncovered; will keep 1–2 days
Cherries	Firm; stems attached; good color	Refrigerate, unwashed and uncovered; will keep 1–2 days
Currants (fresh)	Firm; plump; bright red, almost translucent color	Refrigerate, unwashed and uncovered; will keep 1–3 days
Melons	Heavy for size; pleasant, fruity aroma; yield to slight pressure at blossom end	Ripen at room temperature; refrigerate ripe melons; will keep 2–3 days
Nectarines	Firm; plump smooth skin; reddish yellow color; slight softening along seam edge	Ripen at room temperature; refrigerate ripe nectarines; will keep 3–5 days

Fruit	Look For	Storage
Peaches	Firm; plump; slightly fuzzy skin; white to yellow to blush color; yield to gentle pressure	Ripen at room temperature; refrigerate ripe peaches; will keep 3–5 days
Raspberries	Plump; bright color	Refrigerate, unwashed and uncovered; will keep 1–2 days
Rhubarb	Crisp, reddish-green; stalks	Refrigerate; will keep 3–5 days

FRAGRANT PEAR CHARLOTTE

Healing Foods

Pears
Raspberries
Yogurt (low-fat)

3 pounds ripe pears, chopped
1 teaspoon grated orange rind
1 teaspoon vanilla extract
$1/2$ cup all-fruit raspberry preserves

$1/4$ cup apple juice
12 slices whole-grain bread, crusts removed
2 cups nonfat vanilla yogurt
2 cups raspberries

In a large frying pan over medium-low heat,

combine the pears, orange rind, and vanilla. Simmer, stirring frequently, for about 30 minutes, or until the pears are very soft and thick. If necessary, drain any excess liquid.

In a 1-quart saucepan, combine the preserves and apple juice. Heat until melted and well combined.

Coat an $8^1/_2$-inch round glass baking dish with nonstick spray. Place a round of waxed paper in the bottom of the dish.

Cut 5 slices of bread in half diagonally. Dip 1 side of each into the preserves. Fit the slices, dipped side down, into the bottom of the dish, trimming the slices as necessary to cover the bottom.

Cut the remaining slices into 1-inch strips. Dip one side of each into the preserves. Fit the slices, dipped side out, around the sides of the pan to completely cover.

Brush the bread with the remaining preserves.

Spoon the pear mixture into the pan. Bake at 450°F for 15 minutes. Reduce the oven temperature to 350°F and bake for 30 minutes.

Let cool in the pan. Cover and refrigerate overnight.

To serve, run the blade of a knife around the edge of the pan to loosen the bread. Invert the charlotte onto a serving plate. Peel off and discard the waxed paper. Serve the charlotte with the yogurt and raspberries.

Serves 8

CLASSIC CARROT CAKE

Healing Foods

Carrots
Cheese (low-fat)
Nuts
Oil
Raisins
Whole wheat flour

CAKE

1 1/2 cups whole
wheat flour
1 1/2 cups
unbleached flour
2 teaspoons
baking powder
1/2 teaspoon
baking soda
1 1/2 teaspoons
ground cinnamon
1/4 teaspoon
ground mace
1/4 teaspoon
ground allspice
1 cup canola oil
3/4 cup egg substitute
3/4 cup honey, warmed
2 cups finely
shredded carrots
1 cup raisins
1/2 cup chopped
pecans
1 teaspoon vanilla extract

FROSTING

8 ounces Neufchâtel
cheese, softened
1/3 cup honey,
warmed
1 teaspoon
vanilla extract

To make the cake: Sift the whole wheat flour, unbleached flour, baking powder, baking soda, cinnamon, mace, and allspice into a large bowl.

In a medium bowl, beat the oil, egg substitute, and honey until blended. Stir in the carrots, raisins, pecans, and vanilla.

Stir the liquid ingredients into the flour mixture, 1 cup at a time, blending well after each addition.

Coat a 9 x 13-inch baking dish with nonstick spray. Add the batter. Bake at 350°F for 40 to 50 minutes, or until a toothpick inserted in the center comes out clean. Cool on a wire rack before frosting.

To make the frosting: In a medium bowl, cream together the Neufchâtel, honey, and vanilla until smooth, about 5 minutes.

Serves 20

STUFFED PEACHES

Healing Foods

Peaches
Raisins

4 large peaches
2 tablespoons
  lemon juice
1/4 cup chopped
  raisins
1 tablespoon honey

1 teaspoon
  vanilla extract
1 teaspoon grated
  lemon rind
1/2 teaspoon
  ground cinnamon
1/3 cup low-fat yogurt

Scald the peaches in boiling water for 1 minute to loosen skins. Drain, slip off peels, cut the peaches in half, and discard the pits. Brush the fruit with the lemon juice to prevent discoloration.

With a grapefruit spoon or melon scoop, remove about half of the pulp from each peach, leaving a sturdy shell. Brush the insides of the shells with more lemon juice. Chop the pulp and set it aside.

In a small bowl, combine the raisins, honey, vanilla, lemon rind and cinnamon. Add the reserved peach pulp. Fold in just enough yogurt to bind the stuffing together.

Divide the stuffing among the peach halves. Serve immediately.

Serves 4

PINEAPPLE FRUIT COCKTAIL

Healing Foods

Kiwifruit
Oranges
Pineapple
Tangerines

1¹/₄ cups chopped
   pineapple
2 oranges, sectioned
1 tablespoon
   toasted coconut
2 tangerines, sectioned
3 kiwifruit, sliced
2 tablespoons lime
   juice

In a large bowl, combine the pineapple, oranges,

tangerines, and kiwis. Drizzle with the lime juice. Cover and allow to marinate in the refrigerator for 1 hour.

Just before serving, sprinkle with the coconut.

Serves 6

CRANBERRY PEARS

Healing Foods

Cranberries
Pears

8 firm pears	2 tablespoons honey
1 tablespoon	$1/2$ teaspoon
lime juice	ground cinnamon
2 cups cranberries	$1/8$ teaspoon
1 cup pear juice	ground cloves

If desired, peel the pears, leaving the stems intact. Using a melon scoop, core the pears from the bottom. Brush the pears with the lime juice and arrange them upright in a shallow baking dish.

In a 2-quart saucepan, combine the cranberries and pear juice. Cook over medium heat until the cranberries pop, about 5 minutes. Stir in the honey, cinnamon, and cloves. Pour over the pears.

Bake at 350°F for 30 minutes, or until the pears can be easily pierced with a knife but still hold their shape. Serve warm.

Serves 8

CHERRY-MAPLE CRUNCH

Healing Foods

Cherries
Oats

3 cups pitted sour
  cherries
1 teaspoon corn-
  starch

$1/3$ cup maple syrup
$1/2$ cup rolled oats
2 tablespoons
  canola oil

Coat a 9-inch pie plate with nonstick spray. Add the cherries.

In a cup, dissolve the cornstarch in the maple syrup. Pour over the cherries.

In a small bowl, combine the oats and the oil. Sprinkle over the cherries.

Bake at 350°F for about 40 minutes, or until lightly browned on top.

Serves 6

APRICOT MOUSSE

Healing Foods

Apricots
Bananas
Yogurt (low-fat)

2 cups water
$1/2$ cup dried apricots

1 cup nonfat yogurt
$1/4$ cup egg substitute

¹/₂ teaspoon
  vanilla extract

2 bananas, sliced
2 egg whites

In a 1-quart saucepan, combine the water and apricots. Bring to a boil, then reduce the heat and simmer for 10 minutes, or until the apricots are tender. Let cool.

In a blender, combine the bananas, yogurt, egg substitute, egg whites, and vanilla. Process until smooth. Add the apricots and process on medium speed until smooth.

Pour into four goblets. Chill or serve immediately.

Serves 4

FRUIT AND BANANA SPLITS

Healing Foods

Bananas
Blueberries
Cottage cheese (low-fat)
Strawberries
Wheat germ

2 cups low-fat
  cottage cheese
3 tablespoons all-
  fruit apricot
  preserves

4 bananas
1 cup sliced
  strawberries
1 cup blueberries
¹/₄ cup toasted
  wheat germ

Puree the cottage cheese in a food processor

until completely smooth (periodically stop to scrape down the sides of the container). Add the preserves and combine well. Transfer to a bowl and chill.

Peel the bananas and split each lengthwise. Set each pair on a plate. Top with apricot mixture, strawberries, and blueberries. Sprinkle with the wheat germ.

Serves 4

FRESH-FRUIT FREEZES

It's easy to make your own sorbets, ice milks, and frozen yogurt from summer-fresh fruit. Start with ripe, naturally sweet produce and add a few complementary flavorings. Then freeze the mixture in a standard ice-cream maker, following the manufacturer's directions.

If you don't have an ice-cream maker, freeze the mixture in a shallow bowl. For the first 2 hours, stir or beat the mixture every 15 to 20 minutes to break up ice crystals and to prevent it from freezing solid too fast. Then allow the mixture to set to the desired texture.

Here's a cornucopia of healthy frozen desserts, all naturally low in fat and calories.

Nectarine Sorbet

4 cups chopped nectarines

2 cups apple juice concentrate

Puree the nectarines in a blender or food processor. Transfer to a large nonmetallic bowl. Stir in the apple juice concentrate.

Freeze as directed above.

Serves 4

Healing Food

• Nectarines

Frozen Pineapple Yogurt

1 1/2 cups chopped pineapple	2 cups nonfat yogurt
1 banana, sliced	2 tablespoons maple syrup

In a food processor, puree the pineapple and bananas. Transfer to a large bowl. Stir in the yogurt and maple syrup.

Freeze as directed above.

Serves 4 to 6

Healing Foods

• Bananas   • Pineapple   • Yogurt (low-fat)

Banana Ice Milk

1 banana, sliced	1/8 teaspoon ground cinnamon
1 1/2 cups skim milk	1 teaspoon vanilla extract
2 tablespoons honey	

In a blender, puree the bananas with 1/2 cup of the milk, the honey, vanilla, and cinnamon. With the motor running, slowly add the remaining milk.

Freeze as directed on page 636.

Serves 4

Healing Foods

- Bananas   • Milk (low-fat)

Strawberry Sherbet

2 cups sliced
  strawberries
1 cup orange juice
3 tablespoons honey

1 tablespoon
  lemon juice
2 cups honeydew
  balls

In a food processor or blender, process the strawberries, orange juice, honey, and lemon juice until smooth.
Freeze as directed on page 636.
Serve over the honeydew.

Serves 4

Healing Foods

- Melons   • Strawberries

Passion-Fruit Freeze

7 ripe passion fruit
2 tablespoons orange
  juice concentrate

1 tablespoon lime
  juice
1 cup nonfat yogurt

Use a sharp paring knife to slice the tops off the passion fruit. Spoon the flesh into the bowl of a food processor.
Add the orange juice concentrate and lime juice. Process until smooth. Fold in the yogurt.

Freeze as directed on page 636.

Serves 4

Healing Foods

- Tropical Fruit   • Yogurt (low-fat)

Tropical Freezes

Even easier are the creamy "ices" you can make from tropical fruit. Simply peel, slice, and freeze your selection. When you're ready for something special, let the fruit soften for a few minutes at room temperature. Process in a food processor or blender until smooth and creamy.

Use your imagination for fruit combinations or try these tasty suggestions.

- *Kiwifruit.* Two kiwis, peeled and sliced, yield about $1/2$ cup of tropical freeze. For a super dessert, fold in $1/2$ cup of nonfat vanilla yogurt.
- *Mango.* One large mango, peeled and sliced, yields about $1^1/3$ cups tropical freeze. When processing, pour in 2 tablespoons of white grape juice. Great as a filling for oatmeal cookies or graham crackers.
- *Pineapple.* Half a small pineapple, about $1^2/3$ cups chopped, makes about 1 cup of tropical freeze. The texture is naturally fluffy, as though eggs had been whipped in. A drop or two of mint extract added during processing is especially refreshing.

PART THREE

PART TWELVE

CHAPTER FIFTEEN

Meals That Heal

What's your individual health goal? Lessening your chance of getting certain types of cancer? Lowering your risk of heart attack or stroke? Easing the discomfort of rheumatoid arthritis? Avoiding osteoporosis? All of the above?

To help you to reach your goals using the healing power of food, we've drawn up meal plans for diseases that often respond well to diet or that may be prevented with the help of certain nutrients. The menus that follow highlight both the 100 healthy foods from chapter 2 and recipes from the succeeding chapters.

We realize that at first glance these menus may seem ambitious. Indeed, few people will actually have the time or inclination to prepare all the dishes listed in each two-week plan. We advise instead that you consider these menus as meal suggestions.

Pick and choose the meals that both tempt you and fit into your schedule. Supplement them with easy-to-prepare variations of other suggested foods. If you're following an osteoporosis (high-calcium) diet and don't have time to make Broccoli and Cheese Pasta, for example, quickly steam some broccoli and serve it sprinkled with grated low-fat cheese. And make it a point to

643

include a wide variety of other high-calcium foods in your diet. Use the menu plans as a starting point to spark your imagination when you find yourself in a culinary rut.

If you have diabetes, high blood pressure, or any other serious problem, remember that its always wise to discuss diet changes with your physician. And use common sense when following any diet plans. If you know that cucumbers give you indigestion or that even an occasional serving of asparagus leads to a flare-up of your gout, by all means steer clear of those items.

Although all the recipes in this book are designed to go light on fat, sodium, and calories, only you know what your personal dietary requirements and limitations are. Reduce portion sizes if you feel a tempting recipe exceeds your allotment of any specific food component.

The menu plans on the following pages were developed by Rodale Food Center nutritionist Anita Hirsch, M.S., R.D. Here is a brief outline of the main dietary principles behind each two-week plan.

Anemia. These meals feature iron-rich foods such as meat, fish, and poultry, plus beans, dried fruits, seeds, and greens to help prevent iron-deficiency anemia. They're also high in vitamin C, which helps the body absorb iron. To get extra iron in your diet, substitute blackstrap molasses for other sweeteners when making baked goods and use iron cookware.

Cancer prevention. Recipes in this section focus on foods that show the most promise in helping to prevent certain types of cancer. They include cruciferous vegetables—such as broccoli and cabbage—as well as foods high in beta-carotene, pectin, calcium, and vitamin C.

Colds. To help prevent or fight colds, these meal plans feature foods high in vitamins A and C, such as citrus fruits and other fresh produce. Some of the recipes also have a nice amount of spicy ingredients to help relieve nasal and sinus congestion.

Diabetes. Although diabetes can't be cured, it can be controlled, often with a diet low in fat and high in complex carbohydrates, similar to the one presented. And because maintaining an ideal weight can help stabilize blood-sugar levels, be sure to tailor portion sizes to your individual calorie allowance.

Digestive Problems. If you're plagued with digestive problems, including *constipation, diverticular disease* and *hemorrhoids,* menus such as the ones given can help you find relief. They're high in insoluble fiber from whole grains, legumes, fruits, and vegetables. For best results, drink lots of liquids on a fiber-rich diet.

Fatigue. To fight chronic fatigue, try to eat meals high in potassium, magnesium, B vitamins, vitamin C, and iron. For extra measure, avoid eating heavy meals late at night. Opt instead for hearty breakfasts to get your day off to the right start.

Gout. Gout sufferers should avoid foods high

in purines, such as sardines, mussels, and herring. And they should limit intake of many other moderate-purine foods, such as dried beans, shellfish, spinach, yeast, meat, fish, and poultry, to one serving a day. These menus give you an idea of what a gout-controlling diet would look like.

Heart disease and stroke. To help lessen the risk of heart disease and stroke, eat foods that are low in fat, cholesterol, and sodium but high in fiber, pectin, potassium, and omega-3 fatty acids. These menus feature such foods, among them fish, lean meats, and poultry, plus fresh produce.

Hiatal hernia. One of the best ways to deal with hiatal hernia is to eat small meals throughout the day and to avoid foods that are fatty, spicy, or acidic. Those same foods can also trigger chronic indigestion. If these problems plague you, the menus given may spell relief.

High blood pressure. These menus are low in sodium but rich in potassium, calcium, and fish oils to help control high blood pressure. They're also light on meat because vegetarians tend to have less trouble with elevated blood pressure.

Immunity building. Meals designed to fight infection include lots of yellow, orange, and dark green fruits and vegetables for their vitamin A content. Equally important are the B vitamins, vitamin C, vitamin E, zinc, and iron—found alone or in combination in foods such as grains, lean meats and poultry, wheat germ, and oysters.

Lactose intolerance. These menus contain almost no dairy products, with the exception of yogurt, which may actually help cure lactose intolerance. They do feature soy foods, broccoli, and dark leafy greens to help supply the calcium that dairy items generally provide. Keep in mind that you can often substitute yogurt with active cultures for other dairy products in many soups, casseroles, and baked goods.

Osteoporosis. These high-calcium meals feature low-fat dairy products, deep green vegetables, soy foods, and fish. To get at least 1,000 milligrams of calcium a day, which some doctors recommend to help prevent osteoporosis, accompany your meals with skim milk rather than empty-nutrient beverages like coffee or soda.

Overweight. These meals are designed to be low in calories but high in hunger-satisying fiber. Fresh fruits and fruity desserts help appease a sweet tooth without tipping the scales the wrong way. And low-fat entrees also keep calories under control. But remember that portion sizes do count, so practice restraint before reaching for seconds.

Rheumatoid arthritis. These meals, especially the dinners, contain a lot of seafood because the omega-3 fatty acids found in fish may help reduce the symptoms of rheumatoid arthritis for some sufferers. These meals are also high in vitamin C—from citrus and other pro-

647

duce—because arthritis sufferers tend to use a lot of aspirin, which can deplete the vitamin.

Wound healing. Diets designed to promote wound healing should include lots of vitamins A and C, plus zinc. The meal plans given incorporate those nutrients by featuring recipes with dark green and yellow fruits and vegetables, such as broccoli, citrus fruits, brussels sprouts, and salad greens. In addition, zinc-rich foods such as oysters and wheat germ are included.

Anemia

Week One

DAY 1

BREAKFAST
Orange juice
Apricot-Quinoa Cereal (p. 334)

LUNCH
Fragrant Borscht (p. 183)
Tuna Tart w/ Basil (p. 145)
Spinach salad topped w/ wheat
   germ and low-fat dressing
Fresh fruit

DINNER
Orange Beef w/ Rice (p. 537)
Brussels Sprouts w/ Mushroom Glaze (p. 594)
Tossed salad w/ low-fat dressing
Marinated Figs and Apricots (p. 608)

DAY 2

BREAKFAST
Prune juice
Frittata w/ apple filling
Cinnamon Buns (p. 294)

LUNCH
Caribbean Bean Casserole (p. 372)
Julienned raw vegetables

Whole wheat bread
Strawberry Sherbet (p. 638)

DINNER
Flounder w/ Pepper Puree (p. 467)
Broccoli w/ Parsley Sauce (p. 562)
Baked Potato
Whole wheat bread
Winter-Jubilee Fruit (p. 623)

DAY 3

BREAKFAST
Blueberries and nonfat yogurt
Prune Muffins (p. 291)

LUNCH
South American Squash Soup (p.174)
Mackerel Salad (p. 442)
Carrot Muffins (p. 292)

DINNER
Moroccan Chicken w/ Chick-Peas (p. 359)
Indian-Style Wilted Greens (p. 568)
Apricot Mousse (p. 634)

DAY 4

BREAKFAST
Grapefruit
Sweet Potato Scones (p. 259)
Orange-Almond Cheese (p. 148)

LUNCH
Irish Vichyssoise (p. 193)
Antipasto w/ Baked Oysters (p. 153)
Sesame-seed crackers
Sliced cantaloupe

DINNER
Black-Eyed Peas w/ Spinach (p. 377)
Orchard Meat Loaf (p. 526)
Mashed potatoes
Strawberries w/ Two Melons (p. 603)

DAY 5

BREAKFAST
Orange Muffins (p. 267)
Nonfat yogurt w/ sunflower seeds and
   dried fruit

LUNCH
Great Northern Soup (p. 357)
Whole-Grain and Seed Bread (p. 273)
Tuna salad w/ light mayonnaise
Cut fresh fruit

DINNER
Mexican Picadillo (p. 549)
Savory Rice Pilaf (p. 329)
Escarole and roasted pepper salad

DAY 6

BREAKFAST
Sliced oranges and bananas
Oatmeal w/ raisins and skim milk

LUNCH
Navy-Bean Soup (p. 378)
Tossed salad w/ low-fat dressing
Potato-Cheese Bread (p. 287)

DINNER
Chicken Canapés w/ Broccoli Stuffing (p. 150)
Pear and Pork Stir-Fry (p. 551)
Steamed rice
Nectarines w/ Sauce Cardinale (p. 616)

DAY 7

BREAKFAST
Orange juice
Fruit and Nut Bread (p. 265)
Millet-Stuffed Apples (p. 327)

LUNCH
Lentil Tacos (p. 383)
Tossed salad w/ low-fat dressing
Melon slices

DINNER
Garlic and Potato Soup (p. 178)
Good-Luck Peas (p. 365)
Smoked Turkey and Grapes (p. 216)
Cran-Apple Sauce (p. 605)

DAY 1

BREAKFAST
Orange juice
Assorted dried fruits and seeds
Nonfat yogurt
Rice-Bran Scones (p. 274)

LUNCH
Black Beans and Rice (p. 348)
Tossed salad w/ low-fat dressing
Fresh fruit

DINNER
Dilled Cabbage Soup (p. 162)
Cod w/ Herbed Potatoes (p. 470)
Steamed broccoli
Spinach w/ citrus slices and
   vinaigrette dressing
Whole wheat bread
Classic Carrot Cake (p. 630)

DAY 2

BREAKFAST
Prune juice
Pineapple Focaccia (p. 255)
Hot cereal w/ raisins and skim milk

LUNCH
Creamy Broccoli Soup (p. 187)
Hummus w/ Pumpkin and
  Pomegranate (p. 373)
Toasted pita triangles
Fresh fruit

DINNER
Vegetables w/ Creamy Garlic Sauce (p. 139)
Grilled Tilefish w/ Bean Salsa (p. 385)
Savoy Puree in Potato Shells (p. 573)
Fruit w/ nonfat yogurt

DAY 3

BREAKFAST
Orange juice
Potato Waffles w/ Peach Sauce (p. 279)
Nonfat yogurt

LUNCH
Korean Hot Beef Soup (p. 185)
Nachos (p. 364)
Apple

DINNER
Spicy Beef w/ Orange Vinaigrette (p. 535)
Peach Chutney (p. 534)
Garden-Puff Potatoes (p. 556)
Baked Prune Compote (p. 609)

DAY 4

BREAKFAST
Stewed dried fruit
Cooked rice-bran cereal
Nonfat yogurt

LUNCH
Tomato-vegetable juice
Whole Wheat Crêpes (p. 270)
Cooked fish filling and sautéed
   mushroom topping
Tropical Compote (p. 612)

DINNER
Diamond Head Turkey w/ Pineapple (p. 489)
Christmas Cabbage (p. 577)
Spinach Risotto (p. 323)
Whole wheat rolls
Fresh fruit cup w/ nuts and seeds

DAY 5

BREAKFAST
Grapefruit
Raisin-Oat Bread (p. 289)
Prune Butter (p. 252)
Cold cereal w/ skim milk

LUNCH
Chick-Pea Chili (p. 356)
Greens and Tangerines (p. 239)
Bran-Flake Muffins (p. 249)
Sliced bananas

DINNER
London Broil w/ Garlic Marinade (p. 524)
Brussels Sprouts w/ Three-Root
    Sauce (p. 566)
Oranges w/ Radishes and Dates (p. 209)
Rice pudding w/ raisins

DAY 6

BREAKFAST
Grapefruit juice
Scrambled egg substitute
One-Hour Oat Bread (p. 261)
Skim milk

LUNCH
Iced Cantaloupe Soup (p. 171)
Poultry Pâté (p. 492)
Sesame-seed crackers
Spicy Shrimp Salad w/ Cool Mango
    Dressing (p. 215)

DINNER
Fragrant Chicken in Bok Choy Leaves (p. 140)
Couscous and Chick-Pea Stew (p. 375)
Assorted greens salad w/ low-fat dressing

DAY 7

BREAKFAST
Baked Prune Compote (p. 609)
Raisin bran cereal w/ skim milk

LUNCH
Main-Dish Antipasto (p. 369)
Sesame-seed bread sticks
Nonfat yogurt and fresh fruit

DINNER
Lean Beef w/ Greens and Feta (p. 208)
Red Beans in Edible Cups (p. 386)
Winter Greens w/ Roasted Garlic (p. 563)
Berry Custard (p. 621)

Cancer Prevention

Week One

DAY 1

BREAKFAST
Orange slices
Hot oatmeal
Apple Breakfast Bread (p. 258)

LUNCH
Escarole Soup (p. 164)
Whole wheat toast
Red-Pepper Bean Spread (p. 381)
Fresh garden salad w/ low-fat dressing

DINNER
Broccoli and Cheese Pasta (p. 301)
Green Beans w/ Walnuts (p. 596)
Lemon Pumpkin Pie (p. 601)

DAY 2

BREAKFAST
Grapefruit
Broccoli omelet

LUNCH
Cajun Soup (p. 176)
Carrot Muffins (p. 292)
Wild-Rice Salad (p. 228)
Fresh fruit

DINNER
Flounder w/ Pepper Puree (p. 467)
Garden-Puff Potatoes (p. 556)
Oriental Gingered Vegetables (p. 571)
Berry Custard (p. 621)

DAY 3

BREAKFAST
Fresh strawberries
Oat-Bran Muesli (p. 294)

LUNCH
Corn Enchiladas (p. 425)
Tossed salad
Green-Herb Dressing (p. 232)
Marinated Figs and Apricots (p. 608)

DINNER
Pumpkin soup (p. 163)
Cabbage-Stuffed Shells (p. 314)
Black-Eyed Peas w/ Spinach (p. 377)
Nectarine Sorbet (p. 636)

DAY 4

BREAKFAST
Fresh fruit cup
Onion frittata
Corn-Bran Bread (p. 248)

LUNCH
Pheasant and Mushroom Soup (p. 168)
Whole Wheat French Bread (p. 283)
Apricot Mousse (p. 634)

DINNER
Monkfish w/ Citrus and Ginger (p. 433)
Acorn Squash Stuffed w/ Cornbread (p. 395)
Chinese Beans w/ Seasame Seeds (p. 581)
Passion-Fruit Freeze (p. 638)

DAY 5

BREAKFAST
Apricot nectar
Wheat-bran cereal w/ blueberries
Orange Muffins (p. 267)

LUNCH
Creamy Corn Chowder (p. 194)
Whole-Grain and Seed Bread (p. 273)
Carrot Spread (p. 251)
Melon balls

DINNER
Braised Leeks w/ Mustard Sauce (p. 136)
Tarragon Chicken w/ Linguine (p. 335)
Tossed salad
Green-Herb Dressing (p. 232)
Stuffed Peaches (p. 631)

DAY 6

BREAKFAST
Fruit and Banana Splits (p. 635)
Pecan-Oat Muffins (p. 275)

LUNCH
Cabbage and Kasha (p. 297)
Citrus-Marinated Carrots (p. 154)
Tropical Compote (p. 612)

DINNER
Watercress Canapés (p. 152)
Turkey Medallions w/ Peaches (p. 518)
Spicy Beet Salad (p. 229)
Creamed Turnips (p. 567)
Classic Carrot Cake (p. 630)

DAY 7

BREAKFAST
Orange juice
Apricot-Quinoa Cereal (p. 334)

LUNCH
Cold Zucchini Soup (p. 179)
Fragrant Chicken in Bok Choy Leaves (p. 140)
Onion Toast (p. 149)
Cran-Apple Sauce (p. 605)

DINNER
Dilled Vegetables (p. 144)
Spaghetti w/ Spinach Chiffonade (p. 307)
Whole Wheat French Bread (p. 283)
Sweet Plums and Oranges (p. 614)

Week Two

DAY 1

BREAKFAST
Sweet Potato Scones (p. 259)
Tropical fruit plate

LUNCH
Broccoli-Buttermilk Soup (p. 188)
Cabbage Noodles (p. 298)
Greens and Tangerines (p. 239)
Peach-Blackberry Pie (p. 610)

DINNER
Jasmine Chicken w/ Strawberry
  Coulis (p. 481)
Bulgur and Sweet-Pepper Salad (p. 207)
Broccoli w/ Parsley Sauce (p. 562)
Cranberry Pears (p. 633)

DAY 2

BREAKFAST
Cranberry juice
Buckwheat Crêpes (p. 270)
Sliced fruit and nonfat yogurt

LUNCH
Summer Chicken Salad Sandwiches (p. 513)
Curried Yogurt and Broccoli (p. 157)
Nectarines w/ Sauce Cardinale (p. 616)

662

DINNER
Seafood Gazpacho (p. 167)
Spicy Stuffed Peppers (p. 413)
Grilled Onion Brochettes (p. 128)
Dilled Carrot Bread (p. 282)
Pineapple Fruit Cocktail (p. 632)

DAY 3

BREAKFAST
Stuffed Peaches (p. 631)
Cold cereal w/ skim milk

LUNCH
Sprouts and Cheese (p. 214)
Fruit and Nut Bread (p. 265)
Strawberry Sherbert (p. 638)

DINNER
Butternut Bisque (p. 166)
Fettuccine w/ Grapes (p. 306)
Carrot Salad (p. 213)
Apple Squares (p. 250)

DAY 4

BREAKFAST
Grapefruit juice
Breakfast Scramble w/ Oven Fries (p. 392)
Orange Muffins (p. 267)

LUNCH
Onion and Pesto Pie (p. 390)
Raw broccoli

Horseradish Dip (p. 145)
Strawberries w/ Two Melons (p. 603)
Popcorn

DINNER
Cool Peach Soup (p. 177)
Snapper w/ Red-Pepper Salsa (p. 461)
Marinated Cauliflower (p. 599)
Italian-Style Fried Rice (p. 412)
Black-Raspberry Pie (p. 606)

DAY 5

BREAKFAST
Citrus sections
Pecan Waffles w/ Strawberry Sauce (p. 288)

LUNCH
Potato Bake w/ Mushroom Stroganoff (p. 414)
Tossed salad w/ broccoli and cauliflower
Cherry-Maple Crunch (p. 634)

DINNER
Carrot Sticks w/ Dill Pesto (p. 125)
Chicken w/ Tropical Fruit (p. 511)
Couscous w/ Sweet Corn (p. 332)
Berries and Greens (p. 230)
Peach Soufflé (p. 607)

DAY 6

BREAKFAST
Winter-Jubilee Fruit (p. 623)
Apple Breakfast Bread (p. 258)

LUNCH
Enchiladas w/ Cheese and Kale (p. 423)
Equinox Salad (p. 235)
Chilled grapes

DINNER
Tuna w/ Orange and Ginger Sauce (p. 452)
Favas w/ Tiny Pasta (p. 363)
Moroccan Carrot Salad (p. 580)
Fresh-Fruit Tart (p. 613)

DAY 7

BREAKFAST
Grapefruit
French Toast w/ Tomato Salsa (p. 254)

LUNCH
South American Squash Soup (p. 174)
Whole Wheat French Bread (p. 283)
Crudités (p. 157)
Pesto Cheese (p. 149)
Blueberry-Apple Crisp (p. 622)

DINNER

Chicken Breasts w/ Harvest
  Vegetables (p. 503)
Winter Greens w/ Roasted
  Garlic (p. 563)
Maple Sweet Potatoes (p. 596)
Watermelon wedges

Colds

Week One

DAY 1

BREAKFAST
Blended banana shake

LUNCH
Pumpkin Soup (p. 163)
Tossed salad
Tomato Vinaigrette (p. 241)
Hot cider

DINNER
Crudités (p. 157)
Horseradish Dip (p. 145)
Skillet Barley and Beef (p. 304)
Cranberry Pears (p. 633)

DAY 2

BREAKFAST
Orange juice
Toasted bagel
Peach Chutney (p. 534)

LUNCH
Apple-Barley Soup (p. 175)
Whole-Grain and Seed Bread (p. 273)
Carrot Spread (p. 251)
Squash Salad w/ Buttermilk
  Dressing (p. 237)
Cut fresh fruit

667

DINNER
Chicken noodle soup
Caribbean Bean Casserole (p. 372)
Winter Greens w/ Roasted Garlic (p. 563)
Melon wedges

DAY 3

BREAKFAST
Cranberry juice
French Toast w/ Tomato Salsa (p. 254)

LUNCH
Fragrant Borscht (p. 183)
One-Hour Oat Bread (p. 261)
Salad greens and julienned vegetables
Lemon Vinaigrette (p. 241)
Strawberries

DINNER
Tarragon Chicken w/ Linguine (p. 335)
Steamed broccoli and carrots with
    Mexican spices

DAY 4

BREAKFAST
Carrot Muffins (p. 292)
Hot cider

LUNCH
Creamy Broccoli Soup (p. 187)
Dilled Carrot Bread (p. 282)

Greens and Tangerines (p. 239)
Banana

DINNER
Chunky Tomato Soup (p. 169)
Spaghetti w/ Spinach Chiffonade (p. 307)
Chinese Beans w/ Sesame Seeds (p. 581)
Sweet Plums and Oranges (p. 614)

DAY 5

BREAKFAST
Grapefruit juice
Hot rice cereal w/ skim milk and berries

LUNCH
Garlic and Potato Soup (p. 178)
Sweet and Spicy Curry Dip (p. 147)
Pita triangles
Oranges w/ Radishes and Dates (p. 209)

DINNER
Escarole Soup (p. 164)
Chili Con Kasha (p. 336)
Rosemary Roasted Peppers (p. 590)
Spiced Apples (p. 618)

DAY 6

BREAKFAST
Peach nectar
Apricot-Quinoa Cereal (p. 334)

LUNCH
Dilled Cabbage soup (p. 162)
Raisin-Oat Bread (p. 289)
Fresh green salad
Hot 'n' Spicy Vinaigrette (p. 242)
Sweet cherries

DINNER
Sweetheart Soup (p. 182)
Broccoli and Cheese Pasta (p. 301)
Far Eastern Rutabagas (p. 557)
Peach Soufflé (p. 607)

DAY 7

BREAKFAST
Grapefruit
Potato Waffles w/ Peach Sauce (p. 279)

LUNCH
Cream of Carrot Soup (p. 172)
Wheat toast
Bulgur and Sweet-Pepper Salad (p. 207)
Kiwifruit slices

DINNER
Eggplant Soup w/ Tiny Pasta (p. 160)
Indonesian Stir-Fry (p. 402)
Indian-Style Wilted Greens (p. 568)
Marinated Figs and Apricots (p. 608)

Week Two

DAY 1

BREAKFAST
Grapefruit juice
Hot cereal w/ skim milk
Sweet Potato Scones (p. 259)

LUNCH
Fresh Pineapple Chutney (p. 533)
New Orleans Red Beans (p. 352)
Blueberries

DINNER
Korean Hot Beef Soup (p. 185)
Steamed Wontons (p. 490)
Oriental Gingered Vegetables (p. 571)
Nectarines w/ Sauce Cardinale (p. 616)

DAY 2

BREAKFAST
Orange juice
Nonfat yogurt
Sliced peaches

LUNCH
Broccoli Buttermilk Soup (p. 188)
Cranberry Bread (p. 293)
Equinox Salad (p. 235)
Banana

DINNER
Creamy Corn Chowder (p. 194)
Pasta w/ Salmon and Sun-Dried
    Tomatoes (p. 303)
Dandelion Greens w/ Beans (p. 225)
Pineapple Fruit Cocktail (p. 632)

DAY 3

BREAKFAST
Hot cereal w/ skim milk
Orange slices

LUNCH
Eight-Vegetable Millet Soup (p. 190)
Orange Muffins (p. 267)
Pear and Hazelnut Salad (p. 201)

DINNER
Clam and Lobster Chowder (p. 191)
Japanese Noodles w/ Spinach
    Ribbons (p. 299)
Strawberries w/ Two Melons (p. 603)

DAY 4

BREAKFAST
Tomato juice
Cinnamon-Scented French Toast (p. 268)

LUNCH
Cream of Mushroom Soup (p. 192)
Cranberry Muffins (p. 263)
Mexican Chicken Salad (p. 198)
Orange sections

DINNER
Chicken and rice soup
Fusilli w/ Fresh Tomato Sauce (p. 324)
Steamed carrots and parsnips
Stuffed Peaches (p. 631)

DAY 5

BREAKFAST
Apple juice
Oat-Bran Muesli (p. 316)

LUNCH
Succotash Chowder (p. 186)
Bran-Flake Muffins (p. 249)
Sprouts and Cheese (p. 214)
Melon wedges

DINNER
Tomato Bisque (p. 172)
Cabbage-Stuffed Shells (p. 314)
French-Style Chard (p. 577)
Cran-Apple Sauce (p. 605)

DAY 6

BREAKFAST
Cranberry juice
Pecan Waffles w/ Strawberry Sauce (p. 288)

LUNCH
Egg-drop soup
Roasted-Garlic Dip (p. 148)
Bread sticks

Corn Salad w/ Lemon-Dill Dressing (p. 212)
Fresh pears

DINNER
Summer-Vegetable soup (p. 184)
Buckwheat Noodles w/ Grilled Tuna (p. 312)
Apricot Mousse (p. 634)

DAY 7

BREAKFAST
Orange sections
Golden French Toast (p. 262)

LUNCH
Cajun Soup (p. 176)
Carrot Muffins (p. 292)
Berries and Greens (p. 230)
Kiwifruit slices

DINNER
Striper Chowder (p. 161)
Linguine w/ Sweet Peppers (p. 302)
Spinach w/ Pistachios (p. 591)
Tropical Compote (p. 612)

Diabetes

Week One

DAY 1

BREAKFAST
Nonfat yogurt
Blueberries
Bran-Flake Muffins (p. 249)

LUNCH
Apple-Barley Soup (p. 175)
Pita crisps
Beans Florentine (p. 381)
Tossed salad
Shallot Vinaigrette (p. 241)
Fresh fruit slices

DINNER
Grilled Tilefish w/ Bean Salsa (p. 385)
Brown rice
Mixed greens
Parsley Vinaigrette (p. 241)
Skim milk
Pineapple Fruit Cocktail (p. 632)

DAY 2

BREAKFAST
Banana Pancakes (p. 285)

LUNCH
Nachos (p. 364)
Greek Spinach and Rice (p. 391)
Orange sections

DINNER
South American Squash Soup (p. 174)
Grilled Chicken and Artichokes w/
  Mixed Greens (p. 505)
Grapes

DAY 3

BREAKFAST
Potato Waffles w/ Peach Sauce (p. 279)

LUNCH
Roast pork tenderloin
Rosemary Roasted Peppers (p. 590)
Brussels sprouts w/ Mushroom Glaze (p. 594)
Zucchini w/ Caraway (p. 561)
Banana slices

DINNER
Snapper w/ Red-Pepper Salsa (p. 461)
Black-Eyed Peas w/ Spinach (p. 377)
Romaine salad
Lemon Vinaigrette (p. 241)
Blueberries

DAY 4

BREAKFAST
Omelet w/ vegetable filling

LUNCH
Russian Vegetable Pie (p. 420)
Greens
Three-Mustard Vinaigrette (p. 241)
Berries and nonfat yogurt

DINNER
White-Bean Gumbo (p. 345)
Sole and Salmon Roulades (p. 138)
Melon balls

DAY 5

BREAKFAST
Winter-Jubilee Fruit (p. 623)
Oatmeal w/ skim milk

LUNCH
Indonesian Stir-Fry (p. 402)
Salad greens
Tomato Vinaigrette (p. 241)
Apple slices

DINNER
Vegetable-beef soup
Sweet Potato Scones (p. 259)
Green salad w/ low-fat cheese and
   low-fat dressing
Grapefruit and orange sections

DAY 6

BREAKFAST
Low-fat cottage cheese
Sliced fruit
Whole-Grain and Seed Bread (p. 273)

LUNCH
Chunky Tomato Soup (p. 169)
Garlic toast
Tossed salad w/ sardines
Tangy Horseradish Dressing (p. 233)
Nectarine slices

DINNER
Spicy Vegetables w/ Tofu (p. 410)
Nonfat yogurt and strawberries

DAY 7

BREAKFAST
Apples and Oat Cereal (p. 329)
Scrambled egg substitute
Whole wheat toast

LUNCH
Navy-Bean Soup (p. 378)
Whole wheat bread
Roasted-Garlic Dip (p. 148)
Tossed salad and low-fat cottage cheese
Parsley Vinaigrette (p. 241)
Cherries

DINNER
Perch w/ Mustard and Thyme (p. 445)
Componata w/ Rigatoni (p. 326)
Kiwifruit slices

Week Two

DAY 1

BREAKFAST
Pineapple sections
Orange Muffins (p. 267)
Orange-Almond Cheese (p. 148)

LUNCH
Salmon Bisque (p. 188)
Bulgur and Sweet-Pepper Salad (p. 207)
Whole wheat bread
Assorted berries

DINNER
Moroccan Chicken w/ Chick-Peas (p. 359)
Crudités (p. 157)
Apple slices

DAY 2

BREAKFAST
Millet-Stuffed Apples (p. 327)

LUNCH
Eight-Vegetable Millet Soup (p. 190)
Hummus Bi Tahini (p. 382)
Pita wedges

Tossed salad
Cider Vinaigrette (p. 241)
Plums

DINNER
Monkfish in Ginger Sauce (p. 459)
Spinach Risotto (p. 323)
Equinox Salad (p. 235)
Strawberries w/ Two Melons (p. 603)

DAY 3

BREAKFAST
Buckwheat Blini (p. 247)

LUNCH
Creamy Broccoli soup (p. 187)
Sliced lean beef
Whole wheat bread
Tossed salad
Hot 'n' Spicy Vinaigrette (p. 242)
Raspberries and nonfat yogurt

DINNER
Baked chicken breasts
Wild-Rice Stuffing (p. 310)
Steamed snow peas
Tossed salad
Garlic Vinaigrette (p. 241)
Skim milk
Papaya and mango cubes

DAY 4

BREAKFAST
Oat-Bran Muesli (p. 316)

LUNCH
Cuban Bean Stew (p. 384)
Warm Salmon Salad (p. 242)
Pear slices

DINNER
Artichoke Quiche (p. 124)
Spinach and mushroom salad w/
   low-fat dressing
Peach slices

DAY 5

BREAKFAST
Orange sections
Caraway Pancakes (p. 278)

LUNCH
Korean Hot Beef Soup (p. 185)
Pecan-Oat Muffins (p. 275)
Tossed salad
Green-Herb Dressing (p. 232)
Banana slices and strawberries

DINNER
Swordfish and Pineapple Brochettes (p. 456)
Chinese Vegetable Pasta (p. 313)
Tropical Compote (p. 612)

DAY 6

BREAKFAST
Scrambled egg substitute
One-Hour Oat Bread (p. 261)

LUNCH
Clam and Lobster Chowder (p. 191)
Tossed salad
Calico Vinaigrette (p. 242)
Spiced Apples (p. 618)

DINNER
Fruited Lamb Curry (p. 552)
Cucumbers w/ Cumin and Coriander (p. 564)
Indian-Style Wilted Greens (p. 568)
Fresh apricots

DAY 7

BREAKFAST
Stuffed Peaches (p. 631)
Raisin bran w/ skim milk

LUNCH
Escarole Soup (p. 164)
Bran-Flake Muffins (p. 249)
Orange-Almond Cheese (p. 148)
Passion-Fruit Freeze (p. 638)

DINNER
Mandarin Chicken w/ Bean Sprouts (p. 516)
Orange sections

Digestive Problems

Week One

DAY 1

BREAKFAST
Orange juice
Millet-Stuffed Apples (p. 327)
Rice-Bran Scones (p. 274)

LUNCH
Cajun Soup (p. 176)
Stuffed Baked Potatoes (p. 527)
Tossed salad
Green-Herb Dressing (p. 232)
Tropical Compote (p. 612)

DINNER
Seafood-Broccoli Terrine (p. 472)
Wild-Rice Pilaf (p. 317)
Berries and Greens (p. 230)
Almond-Topped Baked Plums (p. 623))

DAY 2

BREAKFAST
Prune juice
Pineapple Focaccia (p. 255)
Hot cereal w/ raisins and skim milk

LUNCH
Avocado and Shrimp Salad (p. 220)
Pecan-Oat Muffins (p. 275)

Carrot Spread (p. 251)
Emerald Isle Rice Pudding (p. 605)

DINNER
Polenta (p. 417)
Mediterranean Topping (p. 418)
Greens and Tangerines (p. 239)
Black-Raspberry Pie (p. 606)

DAY 3

BREAKFAST
Grapefruit
Potato Waffles w/ Peach Sauce (p. 279)
Nonfat yogurt

LUNCH
Zucchini-Ricotta Puffs (p. 400)
Spicy Beet Salad (p. 229)
Orange Muffins (p. 267)
Melon wedges

DINNER
Spicy Pork and Chicken w/ Pineapple (p. 541)
Bulgur and Sweet-Pepper Salad (p. 207)
Green Beans w/ Walnuts (p. 596)
Blueberry-Apple Crisp (p. 622)

DAY 4

BREAKFAST
Stewed dried fruit
Cooked rice-bran cereal w/ skim milk

LUNCH
Summer-Vegetable Soup (p. 184)
Carrot Fritters (p. 575)
Oranges w/ Radishes and Dates (p. 209)
Fragrant Pear Charlotte (p. 628)

DINNER
Poached Chicken w/ Pear and
  Kiwifruit (p. 507)
Parsnip-Corn Cakes (p. 589)
Savoy Puree in Potato Shells (p. 573)
Classic Carrot Cake (p. 630)

DAY 5

BREAKFAST
Grapefruit juice
Omelet w/ julienned vegetables
One-Hour Oat Bread (p. 261)

LUNCH
Eight-Vegetable Millet Soup (p. 190)
Lentil and Leek Burritos (p. 428)
Melon sections and berries

DINNER
Crudités (p. 157)
Smoky Cucumber Dip (p. 127)
Herb-Steamed Mussels w/ Rice Pilaf (p. 460)
Dilled Carrot Bread (p. 282)
Pineapple Fruit Cocktail (p. 632)

DAY 6

BREAKFAST
Cranberry juice
Oat-Bran Muesli (p. 316)

LUNCH
Iced Cantaloupe Soup (p. 171)
Asparagus and Shellfish Salad (p. 238)
Cranberry Bread (p. 293)

DINNER
Fruited Lamb Curry (p. 552)
Couscous w/ Sweet Corn (p. 332)
Broccoli w/ Parsley Sauce (p. 562)
Whole wheat pitas
Sweet Plums and Oranges (p. 614)

DAY 7

BREAKFAST
Orange sections
Apples and Oat Cereal (p. 329)
Bran-Flake Muffins (p. 249)

LUNCH
Escarole Soup (p. 164)
Poached Turkey Paprika (p. 480)
Pear and Potato Salad (p. 219)
Carrot Muffins (p. 292)
Grapes

DINNER
Chicken w/ Thai Flavors (p. 494)
Confetti Spaghetti Squash (p. 393)
Dandelion Greens w/ Beans (p. 225)
Cole slaw
Nectarines w/ Sauce Cardinale (p. 616)

Week Two

DAY 1

BREAKFAST
Orange sections
High-fiber bran cereal w/ peaches
   and skim milk
Raisin bread
Prune Butter (p. 252)

LUNCH
Tomato Bisque (p. 172)
Sliced turkey and lettuce sandwich
   on whole wheat bread
Steamed broccoli

DINNER
Mexican Chicken Salad (p. 198)
Steamed sweet potatoes, pears, and raisins
Cranberry muffins (p. 263)
Frozen Pineapple Yogurt (p. 637)
Strawberries and raspberries

DAY 2

BREAKFAST
Prune juice
Frittata w/ sautéed apple filling
Cinnamon Buns (p. 294)

LUNCH
Scallop Salad w/ Pineapple Relish (p. 221)
Whole-Grain and Seed Bread (p. 273)
Blueberry Pudding (p. 624)

DINNER
Mexican Bean Pie (p. 347)
Corn Salad w/ Lemon-Dill Dressing (p. 212)
French-Style Chard (p. 577)
Apricot Mousse (p. 634)

DAY 3

BREAKFAST
Nonfat yogurt w/ blueberries,
   nuts, and seeds
Prune Muffins (p. 291)

LUNCH
Pumpkin Soup (p. 163)
Bread Stuffed w/ Lentils (p. 351)
Tossed salad
Watercress Dressing (p. 231)
Melon wedges

DINNER
Spinach-Stuffed Mushrooms (p. 134)
Barbecued Beef Satay (p. 538)
Herbed Bean Salad (p. 346)
Winter-Jubilee Fruit (p. 623)

DAY 4

BREAKFAST
Grapefruit
Sweet Potato Scones (p. 259)
Orange-Almond Cheese (p. 148)
High-fiber cereal w/ skim milk

LUNCH
Clam and Lobster Chowder (p. 191)
Corn-Bran Bread (p. 248)
Pear and Hazelnut Salad (p. 201)
Sweet cherries

DINNER
Spinach and Feta Pie (p. 389)
Whole wheat pita
Curried Pea Spread (p. 381)
Beets w/ Pecans and Dill (p. 583)
Tossed salad
Garlic Vinaigrette (p. 241)
Black-Raspberry Pie (p. 606)

DAY 5

BREAKFAST
Orange Muffins (p. 267)
Nonfat yogurt w/ sunflower seeds
  and dried fruit

LUNCH
Cabbage and Kasha (p. 297)
Sweet-Corn Fritters (p. 565)
Tossed salad
Tomato Vinaigrette (p. 241)
Strawberries

DINNER
Mandarin Chicken w/ Bean Sprouts (p. 516)
Brown rice
Tossed salad
Hot 'n' Spicy Vinaigrette (p. 242)
Cranberry Pears (p. 633)

DAY 6

BREAKFAST
Sliced oranges and bananas
Oatmeal w/ raisins and skim milk

LUNCH
Garlic and Potato Soup (p. 178)
Spicy Shrimp Salad w/
   Cool Mango Dressing (p. 215)
Whole Wheat French Bread (p. 283)
Apple Tart (p. 616)

DINNER
Vegetarian Sausage Links (p. 406)
Brown rice
Brussels Sprouts w/ Mushroom Glaze (p. 594)
Tossed salad
Low-fat dressing
Fresh fruit plate

DAY 7

BREAKFAST
Baked Prune Compote (p. 609)
Fruit and Nut Bread (p. 265)
Savory Pear Spread (p. 253)

LUNCH
Pinto-Bean Stew (p. 368)
Sprouts and Cheese (p. 214)
Sesame bread sticks

DINNER
Scallops of Veal with Fennel
  and Grapes (p. 544)
Spinach Risotto (p. 323)
Potato and Raspberry Salad (p. 200)
Marinated Figs and Apricots (p. 608)

Fatigue

Week One

DAY 1

BREAKFAST
Baked Prune Compote (p. 609)
Apricot-Quinoa Cereal (p. 334)
Rice-Bran Scones (p. 274)

LUNCH
Summer-Vegetable Soup (p. 184)
Stuffed Baked Potatoes (p. 527)
Pear and Hazelnut Salad (p. 201)
Blueberries and nonfat yogurt

DINNER
Watercress Canapés (p. 152)
Moroccan Turkey (p. 500)
Favas w/ Tiny Pasta (p. 363)
Salad
Honey-Lime Dressing (p. 233)
Peach Soufflé (p. 607)

DAY 2

BREAKFAST
Fruit and Banana Splits (p. 635)
Prune Muffins (p. 291)

692

LUNCH
Summer Chicken-Salad Sandwiches (p. 513)
Herbed Bean Salad (p. 346)
Berry Custard (p. 621)

DINNER
Mexican Bean Pie (p. 347)
Green salad
Hot 'n' Spicy Vinaigrette (p. 242)
Papaya slices

DAY 3

BREAKFAST
Winter-Jubilee Fruit (p. 623)
Oatmeal w/ raisins and skim milk

LUNCH
Fish and Chips (p. 437)
Black-Eyed Peas w/ Spinach (p. 377)
Orange slices

DINNER
Compote of Raspberries and
  Roasted Red Peppers (p. 141)
Turkey Cutlets w/ Pear-Pecan Stuffing (p. 482)
Spinach w/ Pistachios (p. 591)
Citrus-Marinated Carrots (p. 154)
Cherry-Maple Crunch (p. 634)

DAY 4

BREAKFAST
Prune juice
Broccoli omelet
Cinnamon Buns (p. 294)

LUNCH
Salmon Bisque (p. 188)
Pita chips
Creole Bean Dip (p. 380)

DINNER
Spicy Beef w/ Orange Vinaigrette (p. 535)
Brussels Sprouts w/
   Three-Root Sauce (p. 566)
Curried Potato Salad (p. 217)
Cranberry Pears (p. 633)

DAY 5

BREAKFAST
Sweet Plums and Oranges (p. 614)
Nonfat yogurt
Fruit and Nut Bread (p. 265)

LUNCH
Korean Hot Beef Soup (p. 185)
Vegetable Egg Roll-Ups (p. 593)
Lemon Pumpkin Pie (p. 601)

DINNER
Turkey Cacciatore (p. 521)
Green Beans w/ Walnuts (p. 596)
Whole wheat pasta
Pineapple Fruit Cocktail (p. 632)

DAY 6

BREAKFAST
Grapefruit
Sweet Potato Scones (p. 259)
Orange-Almond Cheese (p. 148)

LUNCH
Chicken w/ Kashmiri Rice (p. 478)
Equinox Salad (p. 235)
Carrot Muffins (p. 292)
Almond-Topped Baked Plums (p. 623)

DINNER
Veal Loin w/ Mango Sauce (p. 553)
Red Beans in Edible Cups (p. 386)
Wild-Rice Pilaf (p. 317)
Assorted berries and nonfat yogurt

DAY 7

BREAKFAST
Marinated Figs and Apricots (p. 608)
Orange Muffins (p. 267)
Nonfat yogurt w/ sunflower seeds
  and dried fruit

LUNCH
Dilled Salmon Tart (p. 453)
Tossed salad
Creamy Raspberry Dressing (p. 232)
Fresh-fruit ice

DINNER
Roast Duck w/ Fresh Rosemary (p. 502)
Stuffed Red Beets (p. 574)
Rice Timbales (p. 127)
Apple and Persimmon Cobbler (p. 611)

Week Two

DAY 1

BREAKFAST
Orange juice
Millet-Stuffed Apples (p. 327)
Cranberry Muffins (p. 263)

LUNCH
Orchard Meat Loaf (p. 537)
Whole-Grain and Seed Bread (p. 273)
Berries and Greens (p. 230)
Citrus sections

DINNER
Mushrooms Stuffed w/
  Cheese Soufflé (p. 126)
Sautéed Turkey w/
  Strawberry Puree (p. 514)
Lentil Loaf (p. 349)
Passion-Fruit Freeze (p. 638)

DAY 2

BREAKFAST
Prune juice
Pineapple Focaccia (p. 255)
Hot cereal w/ raisins and skim milk

LUNCH
Roast Chicken w/ Fennel
  and Mustard (p. 479)
Whole wheat bread
Rotini w/ Rosemary Vinaigrette (p. 205)
Nectarines w/ Sauce Cardinale (p. 616)

DINNER
Spicy Vegetables w/ Tofu (p. 410)
Sweet-Corn Fritters (p. 565)
Salad
Three-Mustard Vinaigrette (p. 241)
Emerald Isle Rice Pudding (p. 605)

DAY 3

BREAKFAST

Tropical Compote (p. 612)
Cooked rice-bran cereal w/ skim milk
Nonfat yogurt

LUNCH
Sardines
Mixed green salad and
  raw vegetables and tofu
Balsamic Vinaigrette (p. 241)

Garlic bread
Cran-Apple Sauce (p. 605)

DINNER
Sizzling Fajitas (p. 530)
Broccoli w/ Parsley Sauce (p. 562)
Tomato and Zucchini Gratin (p. 572)
Peach-Blackberry Pie (p. 610)

DAY 4

BREAKFAST
Grapefruit juice
Potato Waffles w/ Peach Sauce (p. 279)

LUNCH
Seafood Gazpacho (p. 167)
Corn chips
Fiesta Bean Dip (p. 382)
Honeydew balls and strawberries

DINNER
Turkey and Shrimp Kabobs
  with Tomatoes (p. 493)
Brussels Sprouts w/ Mushroom Glaze (p. 594)
Tossed salad
Garlic Vinaigrette (p. 241)
Fresh-Fruit Tart (p. 613)

DAY 5

BREAKFAST
Pineapple Fruit Cocktail (p. 632)
Raisin-Oat Bread (p. 289)
Prune Butter (p. 252)
Cold cereal w/ nonfat milk

LUNCH
Honey-Basil Turkey (p. 512)
Savory Lima Beans (p. 362)
Garden-Puff Potatoes (p. 556)
Pecan-Oat Muffins (p. 275)
Strawberries w/ Two Melons (p. 603)

DINNER
Chicken Canapés w/ Broccoli Stuffing (p. 150)
Pear and Pork Stir-Fry (p. 551)
Marinated Cauliflower (p. 599)
Cheesecake Tart (p. 602)

DAY 6

BREAKFAST
Grapefruit
Scrambled egg substitute
One-Hour Oat Bread (p. 261)

LUNCH
Caspian Split Peas (p. 367)
Falafel Pockets (p. 353)
Melon wedges

DINNER
Vegetables w/ Creamy Garlic Sauce (p. 139)
Pan-Fried Noodles w/
   Beans and Beef (p. 543)
Stir-Fry w/ Snow Peas, Celery,
   and Pistachios (p. 582)
Apricot Mousse (p. 634)

DAY 7

BREAKFAST
Stuffed Peaches (p. 631)
Raisin bran w/ skim milk

LUNCH
Butternut Bisque (p. 166)
Salmon Salad w/ Almonds
   and Bok Choy (p. 202)
Blueberry-Apple Crisp (p. 622)

DINNER
Antipasto w/ Baked Oysters (p. 153)
Orange-Scented Roast Goose (p. 485)
Oriental Gingered Vegetables (p. 571)
Fresh fruit plate

Gout
Week One

DAY 1

BREAKFAST
Orange juice
Cooked rice cereal w/ skim milk
Raisins

LUNCH
Pasta w/ marinara sauce
Romaine, carrot, and red onion salad
Green-Herb Dressing (p. 232)
Nectarines with Sauce Cardinale (p. 616)

DINNER
Greek Spinach and Rice (p. 391)
Tossed salad w/ feta cheese
Lemon Vinaigrette (p. 241)
Sweet Plums and Oranges (p. 614)

DAY 2

BREAKFAST
Grapefruit
Cornbread
Baked Prune Compote (p. 609)

LUNCH
Chinese Vegetable Pasta (p. 313)
Mixed-green salad
Tangy Horseradish Dressing (p. 233)
Fresh peach slices

DINNER
Corn Crêpes w/ Bean Filling (p. 397)
Savory Stuffed Snow Peas (p. 143)
Tossed salad w/ low-fat dressing
Strawberries w/ Two Melons (p. 603)

DAY 3

BREAKFAST
Cold rice-flakes cereal w/ skim milk
Winter-Jubilee Fruit (p. 623)

LUNCH
Sablefish w/ Basil Aioli (p. 470)
Date and nut bread
Potato and Raspberry Salad (p. 200)
Tropical Compote (p. 612)

DINNER
Dilled Cabbage Soup (p. 162)
Spaghetti Squash w/ Tomato Sauce (p. 422)
Fresh raw vegetable salad
Shallot Vinaigrette (p. 241)
Apricot Mousse (p. 634)

DAY 4

BREAKFAST
Pancakes and syrup

LUNCH
Noodles w/ nut sauce
Tossed salad
Honey-Lime Dressing (p. 233)
Blueberries

DINNER
Corn-Pone Pie (p. 405)
Crudités (p. 157)
Three-Mustard Vinaigrette (p. 241)
Cranberry Pears (p. 633)

DAY 5

BREAKFAST
Buckwheat Blini (p. 247)
Cottage cheese, peaches, and grapes

LUNCH
Eggs w/ Chili Sauce (p. 404)
Cornbread
Lettuce
Calico Vinaigrette (p. 242)
Kiwifruit slices

DINNER
Apple-Barley Soup (p. 175)
Grilled Chicken w/ Artichokes
  and Mixed Greens (p. 505)
Cabbage Noodles (p. 298)
Low-fat cheesecake w/ strawberries

DAY 6

BREAKFAST
Orange juice
Potato frittata

LUNCH
Cabbage-Stuffed Shells (p. 314)
Biscuits
Prune Butter (p. 252)
Mixed greens
Low-fat dressing
Cran-Apple Sauce (p. 605)

DINNER
Broccoli-Buttermilk Soup (p. 188)
Sizzled Salmon w/ Mint (p. 449)
Spaghetti w/ Guacamole (p. 342)
Peach-Blackberry Pie (p. 610)

DAY 7

BREAKFAST
Corn sticks
Savory Pear Spread (p. 253)
Nonfat yogurt w/ fresh fruit

LUNCH
Scrambled egg substitute
Oven-fried potatoes
Blueberry muffins
Cool Peach Soup (p. 177)

DINNER
Corn Enchiladas (p. 425)
Broccoli w/ Parsley Sauce (p. 562)
Tossed salad
Creamy Vinaigrette (p. 242)
Pineapple Fruit Cocktail (p. 632)

Week Two

DAY 1

BREAKFAST
Sliced oranges and grapefruit
Carrot Muffins (p. 292)

LUNCH
Fettuccine w/ Grapes (p. 306)
Mixed greens
Garlic Vinaigrette (p. 241)
Plums

DINNER
Cream of Carrot Soup (p. 172)
Honey-Basil Turkey (p. 512)
Savory Rice Pilaf (p. 329)
Stuffed Peaches (p. 631)

DAY 2

BREAKFAST
Cranberry juice
Hot rice cereal w/ skim milk
Marinated Figs and Apricots (p. 608)

LUNCH
Broccoli Quesadilla (p. 409)
Spicy Beet Salad (p. 229)
Banana slices

DINNER
Butternut Bisque (p. 166)
Couscous w/ Chicken and Vegetables (p. 320)
Spiced Apples (p. 618)

DAY 3

BREAKFAST
Prune juice
Millet-Stuffed Apples (p. 327)

LUNCH
Iced Cantaloupe Soup (p. 171)
Dilled Shrimp and Rice Salad (p. 469)
Greens and Tangerines (p. 239)
Carrot Cake

DINNER
Mexican Corn Casserole (p. 415)
Stuffed Red Beets (p. 574)
Dill-Zucchini Spears (p. 155)
Berry Custard (p. 621)

DAY 4

BREAKFAST
Orange juice
Apricot-Quinoa Cereal (p. 334)

LUNCH
Lean hamburger
Peas and Pasta (p. 304)
Green salad
Garlic Vinaigrette (p. 241)
Sweet cherries

DINNER
Vegetable Paella (p. 424)
Chinese Beans w/ Sesame Seeds (p. 581)
Oranges w/ Radishes and Dates (p. 209)
Peach Soufflé (p. 607)

DAY 5

BREAKFAST
Tomato juice
Barley Pilaf w/ Grilled Apples (p. 333)

LUNCH
Polenta (p. 417)
Primavera Sauce (p. 419)
Berries and Greens (p. 230)
Lemon Pumpkin Pie (p. 601)

DINNER
Chilled Blueberry Soup (p. 181)
Potato Curry (p. 398)
Corn Pasta w/ Avocado Sauce (p. 322)

DAY 6

BREAKFAST
Grapefruit juice
Apple frittata

LUNCH
Cold Zucchini Soup (p. 179)
Low-fat cheese quiche in
   Potato Pie Shell (p. 401)
Tossed salad

Tomato Vinaigrette (p. 241)
Nectarine Sorbet (p. 636)

DINNER
Greek Garden Kabobs (p. 403)
Fusilli w/ Fresh Tomato Sauce (p. 324)
Blueberry Pudding (p. 624)

DAY 7

BREAKFAST
Peach nectar
Cooked rice-bran cereal w/ skim milk

LUNCH
Monkfish Salad w/ Tomato Chutney (p. 226)
Rice cakes
Carrot Spread (p. 251)
Black and red raspberries

DINNER
Irish Vichyssoise (p. 193)
Onion and Pesto Pie (p. 390)
Carrot Salad (p. 213)
Apple Tart (p. 616)

Heart Disease and Stroke

Week One

DAY 1

BREAKFAST
Orange juice
Barley Pilaf w/ Grilled Apples (p. 333)

LUNCH
Chilled Blueberry Soup (p. 181)
Poached Chicken w/
   Chinese Vinaigrette (p. 486)
Sweet Potato Scones (p. 259)

DINNER
Broiled Salmon w/ Cucumbers (p. 450)
Favas w/ Tiny Pasta (p. 363)
Grilled Onion Brochettes (p. 128)
Peach-Blackberry Pie (p. 610)

DAY 2

BREAKFAST
Fruit and Banana Splits (p. 635)
Orange Muffins (p. 267)

LUNCH
Apple-Barley Soup (p. 175)
Hummus w/ Pumpkin
   and Pomegranate (p. 373)
Orange sections

DINNER
Crudités (p. 157)
Chili Bean Dip (p. 380)
Buckwheat Noodles w/ Grilled Tuna (p. 312)
Winter Greens w/ Roasted Garlic (p. 563)
Cranberry Pears (p. 633)

DAY 3

BREAKFAST
Apple juice
Banana pancakes (p. 285)

LUNCH
Lentil and Leek Burritos (p. 428)
Tossed salad
Green-Herb Dressing (p. 232)
Strawberries w/ Two Melons (p. 603)

DINNER
Garlic-Roasted Turkey Breast (p. 496)
Squash Salad w/
    Buttermilk Dressing (p. 237)
Cucumbers w/ Cumin and Coriander (p. 564)
Apple Tart (p. 616)

DAY 4

BREAKFAST
Sliced bananas in orange juice
Apple Squares (p. 250)

LUNCH
Broccoli Quesadilla (p. 409)
Tossed salad w/ anchovies
Creamy Raspberry Dressing (p. 232)
Cran-Apple Sauce (p. 605)

DINNER
Thyme-Flavored Tuna Steaks (p. 434)
Wild Rice and Raspberries (p. 317)
Apples and Celeriac w/
    Honey-Mustard Dressing (p. 204)
Apricot Mousse (p. 634)

DAY 5

BREAKFAST
Grapefruit
Whole Wheat Crêpes (p. 270)
Applesauce, nonfat yogurt,
    and chopped fruit

LUNCH
Cream of Carrot Soup (p. 172)
Lentil Loaf (p. 349)
Whole wheat bread
Banana slices

DINNER
Rabbit Sauté w/ Mushrooms (p. 506)
East Indian Rice Salad (p. 197)
Broccoli w/ Parsley Sauce (p. 562)
Fragrant Pear Charlotte (p. 628)

DAY 6

BREAKFAST
Orange juice
Apples and Oat Cereal (p. 329)

LUNCH
Polenta (p. 417)
Mediterranean Topping (p. 418)
Tangy Horseradish Dressing (p. 233)
Mango slices and blueberries

DINNER
Spanish Halibut (p. 444)
Corn Salad w/ Lemon-Dill
   Dressing (p. 212)
Asparagus and Bulgur (p. 342)
Tropical Compote (p. 612)

DAY 7

BREAKFAST
Orange juice
Apple frittata

LUNCH
Garlic and Potato Soup (p. 178)
Red Beans in Edible Cups (p. 386)
Whole-Grain and Seed Bread (p. 273)
Mixed fruit cup

DINNER
Veal in Apple-Lemon Sauce (p. 545)
Spaghetti w/ Guacamole (p. 342)

Green Salad
Watercress Dressing (p. 231)
Blueberry Pudding (p. 624)

Week Two

DAY 1

BREAKFAST
Grapefruit
Oat-Bran Muesli (p. 316)
Skim milk

LUNCH
Mushroom and Lentil Soup (p. 358)
Lean Beef w/ Greens and Feta (p. 208)
Whole Wheat French Bread (p. 283)
Grapes

DINNER
Pasta w/ Salmon and
  Sun-Dried Tomatoes (p. 303)
Equinox Salad (p. 235)
Apple and Persimmon Cobbler (p. 611)

DAY 2

BREAKFAST
Spiced Apples (p. 618)
Nonfat yogurt
Oat-bran cereal w/ skim milk

LUNCH
Mackerel Salad (p. 442)

One-Hour Oat Bread (p. 261)
Peach Crisp

DINNER
Venison Brochettes (p. 499)
Black Beans and Rice (p. 348)
Greens and Tangerines (p. 239)
Berry Custard (p. 621)

DAY 3

BREAKFAST
Orange juice
Apple Breakfast Bread (p. 258)

LUNCH
Vegetable Chili (p. 366)
Rice-Bran Scones (p. 274)
Frozen Pineapple Yogurt (p. 637)

DINNER
Chinese Braised Mackerel (p. 435)
Hunan Eggplant (p. 585)
Chinese Vegetable Pasta (p. 313)
Fresh-Fruit Tart (p. 613)

DAY 4

BREAKFAST
Grapefruit juice
Cold cereal w/ apples and skim milk

LUNCH
Antipasto w/ Baked Oysters (p. 153)

Toasted pita chips
Apple slices

DINNER
Stuffed Tofu Triangles (p. 132)
Skillet Barley and Beef (p. 304)
Sesame Snow Peas (p. 593)
Black-Raspberry Pie (p. 606)

DAY 5

BREAKFAST
Cold oat-bran cereal w/ skim milk
Banana slices
Raisin-Oat Bread (p. 289)
Savory Pear Spread (p. 253)

LUNCH
Sardines
Rotini w/ Rosemary Vinaigrette
   (p. 205)
Pecan-Oat Muffins (p. 275)
Marinated Figs and Apricots (p. 608)

DINNER
Tuna and Pepper Bake (p. 468)
Herbed Bean Salad (p. 346)
Cidered Parsnips (p. 597)
Blueberry-Apple Crisp (p. 622)

DAY 6

BREAKFAST

Orange juice
Banana Pancakes (p. 285)

LUNCH
Striper Chowder (p. 161)
Corn-Bran Bread (p. 248)
Tossed salad
Green-Herb Dressing (p. 232)
Nectarines w/ Sauce Cardinale (p. 616)

DINNER
Braised Leeks w/ Mustard Sauce (p. 136)
Corn Pasta with Avocado Sauce (p. 322)
Savory Lima Beans (p. 362)

DAY 7

BREAKFAST
Apple juice
Cinnamon-Scented French Toast (p. 268)

LUNCH
Whole wheat pasta w/ tomato sauce
Berries and Greens (p. 230)
Banana Ice Milk (p. 637)

DINNER
Escarole Soup (p. 164)
Salmon w/ Scallions (p. 449)
Linguine w/ Sweet Peppers (p. 302)
Baked Prune Compote (p. 609)

Hiatal Hernia

Week One

DAY 1

BREAKFAST
Hot oat-bran cereal w/ sweet acidophilus milk
Sliced apples
• *Snack:* Prune Muffins (p. 291)
  Sweet acidophilus milk

LUNCH
Broccoli-Buttermilk Soup (p. 188)
Whole Wheat French Bread (p. 283)
Carrot Spread (p. 251)
Pear and pecan salad
• *Snack:* Popcorn

DINNER
Chinese Braised Mackerel (p. 435)
Cooked barley
Steamed asparagus
Crudités (p. 157)
• *Snack:* Berry Custard (p. 621)

DAY 2

BREAKFAST
Pecan-Oat Muffins (p. 275)
Scrambled egg substitute
• *Snack:* Banana slices
  Sweet acidophilus milk

LUNCH
Chicken and vegetable soup
Steamed Wontons (p. 490)
Hummus w/ Pumpkin
    and Pomegranate (p. 373)
• *Snack:* Fresh peach slices
    Nonfat yogurt

DINNER
Poached Chicken w/
    Chinese Vinaigrette (p. 486)
Baked potato
Broccoli w/ Parsley Sauce (p. 562)
• *Snack:* Sliced pears and kiwifruit

DAY 3

BREAKFAST
Golden French Toast (p. 262)
Nonfat yogurt w/ dried apricots and seeds
• *Snack:* Pear slices
    Sweet acidophilus milk

LUNCH
Chicken noodle soup
Cranberry Muffins (p. 263)
Low-fat cottage cheese
Apple butter
• *Snack:* Plums

DINNER
Julienned pork and vegetables
Angel-hair pasta
Salad w/ low-fat dressing
• *Snack:* Black-Raspberry Pie (p. 606)

DAY 4

BREAKFAST
Fruit and Banana Splits (p. 635)
• *Snack:* Classic Carrot Cake (p. 630)
  Sweet acidophilus milk

LUNCH
Garlic and Potato Soup (p. 178)
Corn-Bran Bread (p. 248)
Sardines
Salad w/ low-fat dressing
• *Snack:* Applesauce
  Pretzels

DINNER
Jasmine Chicken w/ Strawberry Coulis (p. 481)
Steamed potatoes
Green Beans w/ Walnuts (p. 596)
• *Snack:* Apricot Mousse (p. 634)

DAY 5

BREAKFAST
Apple juice
Broccoli omelet
• *Snack:* Whole wheat toast
  Fruit spread
  Sweet acidophilus milk

LUNCH
Eggplant Soup w/ Tiny Pasta (p. 160)
One-Hour Oat Bread (p. 261)
Vegetable Egg Roll-Ups (p. 593)
• *Snack:* Cherry-Maple Crunch (p. 634)

DINNER
Sautéed flounder
Brussels Sprouts w/ Three-Root Sauce (p. 566)
Spinach pasta
- *Snack:* Nonfat yogurt
  Assorted fresh berries

DAY 6

BREAKFAST
Pancakes w/ sliced bananas and maple syrup
- *Snack:* Nonfat yogurt
  Nut and seed mix

LUNCH
Korean Hot Beef Soup (p. 185)
Summer Chicken Salad Sandwiches (p. 513)
- *Snack:* Passion-Fruit Freeze (p. 638)

DINNER
Veal scallops sautéed in apple juice
Mashed potatoes
French-Style Chard (p. 577)
Crudités (p. 157)
Nonfat yogurt dip
- *Snack:* Fruit plate

DAY 7

BREAKFAST
Pecan Waffles w/ Strawberry Sauce (p. 288)
- Snack: Oat-bran muffins
  Sweet acidophilus milk

LUNCH
Sautéed Turkey w/ Strawberry Puree (p. 514)
Cornmeal-Cheese Muffins (p. 260)
Cabbage slaw with apples and pears
• *Snack:* Pita toasts

DINNER
Bluefish in a Sea of Green (p. 451)
Bulgur
Oriental Gingered Vegetables (p. 571)
Salad w/ low-fat dressing
• *Snack:* Banana slices

Week Two

DAY 1

BREAKFAST
Oat-bran cereal w/ sweet acidophilus milk
Banana slices
• *Snack:* Apple squares (p. 250)
    Sweet acidophilus milk

LUNCH
Stuffed Tofu Triangles (p. 132)
Angel-hair pasta
Mushroom-Cheese sauce (p. 339)
• *Snack:* Hummus Bi Tahini (p. 382)
    Pita wedges

DINNER
Apricot-Stuffed Hens (p. 476)
Steamed asparagus
Roasted new potatoes

Whole Wheat French Bread (p. 283)
• *Snack:* Banana Ice Milk (p. 637)
  Graham crackers

DAY 2

BREAKFAST
Prune juice
Oatmeal w/ sliced apples and raisins
• *Snack:* Rice-Bran Scones (p. 274)
  Sweet acidophilus milk

LUNCH
Beef noodle soup
Salmon Salad w/ Almonds
  and Bok Choy (p. 202)
• *Snack:* Prune Muffins (p. 291)

DINNER
Crudités (p. 157)
Shrimp and Roasted Peppers (p. 466)
Chinese Vegetable Pasta (p. 313)
• *Snack:* Blueberry muffins
  Nonfat yogurt w/ sliced pears, almonds
  and yogurt

DAY 3

BREAKFAST
Apple juice
Buckwheat Blini (p. 247)
• *Snack:* Nonfat yogurt
  Granola

LUNCH
Pheasant and Mushroom Soup (p. 168)
Salad
Basic Vinaigrette (p. 241)
Whole-grain bread
• *Snack:* Grapes and sliced mangoes

DINNER
Fragrant Chicken in Bok Choy Leaves (p. 140)
Compote of Raspberries and
   Roasted Red Peppers (p. 141)
Rice
• *Snack:* Apple slices

DAY 4

BREAKFAST
Banana slices
Nonfat yogurt w/ pumpkin seeds
• *Snack:* Raisin-Oat Bread (p. 289)
   Orange-Almond Cheese (p. 148)

LUNCH
Rice Timbales (p. 127)
Tossed salad w/ salmon and vegetables
Cider Vinaigrette (p. 241)
• *Snack:* Popcorn
   Grapes

DINNER
Diamond Head Turkey w/ Pineapple (p. 489)
Wild rice
Green beans w/ julienned peppers
• *Snack:* Crudités (p. 157)
   Nonfat yogurt dip

DAY 5

BREAKFAST
Cooked prunes and apricots
Pineapple Focaccia (p. 255)
• *Snack:* Wheat toast
  Fruit spread
  Sweet acidophilus milk

LUNCH
Vegetables w/ Creamy Garlic Sauce (p. 139)
Greens w/ feta cheese
Raisin-Oat Bread (p. 289)
• *Snack:* Pita crisps
  Red-Pepper Bean spread (p. 381)

DINNER
Baked chicken cutlets w/ oat-bran coating
Carrots and Parsnips (p. 576)
Dandelion Greens w/ Beans (p. 225)
• *Snack:* Fruit compote

DAY 6

BREAKFAST
Rice-Waffle Stack (p. 245)
• *Snack:* Apple wedges
  Low-fat cheese

LUNCH
Bagels
Minced smokey turkey and yogurt cheese
Carrot Salad (p. 213)
• *Snack:* Fruit plate

DINNER
Pan-Fried Noodles w/
  Beans and Beef (p. 543)
Cidered Parsnips (p. 597)
• *Snack:* Frozen Pineapple Yogurt (p. 637)

DAY 7

BREAKFAST
Apricot nectar
Baked apples w/ maple syrup and raisins
• *Snack:* Cranberry Muffins (p. 263)
  Sweet acidophilus milk

LUNCH
Chicken barley soup
Asparagus and Shellfish Salad (p. 238)
Oat-bran bread
• *Snack:* Tropical Compote (p. 612)

DINNER
Broiled Salmon w/ Cucumbers (p. 450)
Steamed cauliflower
Stir-fried peas
• *Snack:* Nectarines w/ Sauce Cardinale (p. 616)

High Blood Pressure

Week One

DAY 1

BREAKFAST
Orange juice
Caraway Pancakes (p. 278)
Skim milk

LUNCH
Minestrone soup
Sliced turkey and tomato
One-Hour Oat Bread (p. 261)
Tossed salad
Green-Herb Dressing (p. 232)
Watermelon wedges
Skim milk

DINNER
Shark and Stars (p. 443)
Spinach Risotto (p. 323)
Equinox Salad (p. 235)
Stuffed Peaches (p. 631)

DAY 2

BREAKFAST
Nonfat yogurt and raspberries
Breakfast Scramble w/ Oven Fries (p. 392)
Whole-Grain and Seed Bread (p. 273)
Skim milk

LUNCH
Mackerel Salad (p. 442)
Pecan-Oat Muffins (p. 275)
Pineapple Fruit Cocktail (p. 632)

DINNER
Butternut Bisque (p. 166)
Polenta (p. 417)
Mediterranean Topping (p. 418)
Tossed salad w/ chick-peas and avocado
Balsamic Vinaigrette (p. 241)
Nectarine Sorbet (p. 636)

DAY 3

BREAKFAST
Cranberry juice
High-fiber cereal w/ banana slices
　and skim milk
Raisin-Oat Bread (p. 289)

LUNCH
Potato Bake w/ Mushroom
　Stroganoff (p. 414)
Berries and Greens (p. 230)
Apricots

DINNER
Grilled Tilefish w/ Bean Salsa (p. 385)
Onions and Apples in a Pumpkin (p. 598)
Tossed salad
Whole Wheat Crêpes (p. 270)
Dried fruit and nonfat yogurt

DAY 4

BREAKFAST
Prune Muffins (p. 291)

LUNCH
Lentil and Leek Burritos (p. 428)
Tossed salad
Hot 'n' Spicy Vinaigrette (p. 242)
Melon balls
Skim milk

DINNER
Bouillabaisse (p. 448)
Brown rice
Salad greens and broccoli
Garlic Vinaigrette (p. 241)
Orange and banana slices

DAY 5

BREAKFAST
Golden French Toast (p. 262)
Skim milk

LUNCH
Bread Stuffed w/ Lentils (p. 351)
Greens and Tangerines (p. 239)
Blueberries and nonfat yogurt

DINNER
Potato Curry (p. 398)
Favas w/ Tiny Pasta (p. 363)
Stuffed Acorn Squash (p. 562)

Green salad
Parsley Vinaigrette (p. 241)
Watermelon wedges

DAY 6

BREAKFAST
Grapefruit juice
Oatmeal w/ raisins and skim milk

LUNCH
Antipasto w/ Baked Oysters (p. 153)
Rice-Bran Scones (p. 274)
Strawberries w/ Two Melons (p. 603)

DINNER
Crudités (p. 157)
Horseradish Dip (p. 145)
Pinto-Bean Stew (p. 368)
Spicy Roasted Potatoes (p. 595)
Winter Greens w/ Roasted Garlic (p. 563)
Apricot Mousse (p. 634)

DAY 7

BREAKFAST
Banana blender drink
Cinnamon Buns (p. 294)

LUNCH
Chicken and vegetables
  in a Potato Pie Shell (p. 401)
Tossed salad w/ low-fat dressing
Sweet Plums and Oranges (p. 614)

DINNER
White-Bean Gumbo (p. 345)
Pita Crisps
Spinach-Stuffed Mushrooms (p. 134)
Parsnip-Corn Cakes (p. 589)
Fresh fruit

Week Two

DAY 1

BREAKFAST
Grapefruit juice
Omelet w/ potatoes and basil

LUNCH
Garlic and Potato Soup (p. 178)
Hummus w/ Pumpkin
  and Pomegranate (p. 373)
Pita wedges
Tossed salad
Marinated Figs and Apricots (p. 608)

DINNER
Vegetarian Sausage Links (p. 406)
Italian-Style Fried Rice (p. 412)
Romaine lettuce and tomato slices
Nectarines w/ Sauce Cardinale (p. 616)

DAY 2

BREAKFAST
Orange juice
Oat-Bran Muesli (p. 316)
Skim milk

LUNCH
Vegetables w/ Creamy Garlic Sauce (p. 139)
Bran-Flake Muffins (p. 249)
Beans Florentine (p. 381)
Fresh-Fruit Tart (p. 613)

DINNER
Savory Stuffed Snow Peas (p. 143)
Chinese Braised Mackerel (p. 435)
Chinese Vegetable Pasta (p. 313)
Banana Ice Milk (p. 637)

DAY 3

BREAKFAST
Sliced peaches
Raisin-bran cereal w/ skim milk

LUNCH
Corn Crêpes w/ Bean Fillings (p. 397)
Tossed salad
Tomato Vinaigrette (p. 241)
Berry Custard (p. 621)

DINNER
Indonesian Stir-Fry (p. 402)
Brown rice
Spinach w/ Pistachios (p. 591)
Cranberry Pears (p. 633)

DAY 4

BREAKFAST
Grapefruit
Oat-bran cereal w/ skim milk
Apple Squares (p. 250)

LUNCH
Mushroom and Lentil Soup (p. 358)
Canned salmon on mixed greens
Honey-Lime Dressing (p. 233)
Dilled Carrot Bread (p. 282)
Tropical Compote (p. 612)

DINNER
Falafel Pockets (p. 353)
Steamed broccoli
Moroccan Carrot Salad (p. 580)
Mango slices

DAY 5

BREAKFAST
Pecan Waffles w/ Strawberry Sauce (p. 288)
Skim milk

LUNCH
Whole Wheat Pizza (p. 408)
Tossed salad
Garlic Vinaigrette (p. 241)
Melon balls

DINNER
Mandarin Chicken w/ Bean Sprouts (p. 516)
Brown rice
Vegetable Egg Roll-Ups (p. 593)
Orange sections

DAY 6

BREAKFAST
Orange juice
Buckwheat Crêpes (p. 270)
Fresh fruit and nonfat vanilla yogurt

LUNCH
Chunky Tomato Soup (p. 169)
Lentil Tacos (p. 383)
Mixed greens
Creamy Vinaigrette (p. 242)
Cantaloupe slices

DINNER
Grilled Florida Snapper (p. 439)
Potatoes w/ Creamy
  Mustard Topping (p. 590)
Rosemary Asparagus (p. 582)
Cherry-Maple Crunch (p. 634)

DAY 7

BREAKFAST
Apricot-Quinoa Cereal (p. 334)
Skim milk

LUNCH
Avocado and Shrimp Salad (p. 220)
Corn-Bran Bread (p. 248)

DINNER
Curried Yogurt and Broccoli (p. 157)
Couscous and Chick-Pea Stew (p. 375)
Spiced Apples (p. 618)

Immunity Building

Week One

DAY 1

BREAKFAST
Pineapple juice
Breakfast Scramble w/ Oven Fries (p. 392)

LUNCH
Mushroom and Lentil Soup (p. 358)
Mackerel Salad (p. 442)
Potato-Cheese Bread (p. 287)
Pineapple Fruit Cocktail (p. 632)

DINNER
Carrot Sticks w/ Dill Pesto (p. 125)
Turkey Medallions w/ Peaches (p. 518)
Savory Rice Pilaf (p. 329)
Chinese Beans w/ Sesame Seeds (p. 581)
Lemon Pumpkin Pie (p. 601)

DAY 2

BREAKFAST
Cranberry juice
Buckwheat Blini (p. 247)

LUNCH
Lentil and Leek Burritos (p. 428)
Green salad
Tomato Vinaigrette (p. 241)
Strawberries w/ Two Melons (p. 603)

DINNER
Orange Beef w/ Rice (p. 537)
Pear and Potato Salad (p. 219)
Banana Ice Milk (p. 637)

DAY 3

BREAKFAST
Orange juice
Apple Squares (p. 250)

LUNCH
Creamy Corn Chowder (p. 194)
Nachos (p. 364)
Greens and Tangerines (p. 239)
Banana slices

DINNER
Curried Chicken Breasts (p. 488)
Brown rice
Winter Greens w/ Roasted Garlic (p. 563)
Fresh Pineapple Chutney (p. 533)
Nectarine Sorbet (p. 636)

DAY 4

BREAKFAST
Grapefruit
Banana Pancakes (p. 285)

LUNCH
Falafel Pockets (p. 353)
Spicy Beet Salad (p. 229)
Frozen Pineapple Yogurt (p. 637)

DINNER
Eight-Vegetable Millet Soup (p. 190)
Oyster Fritters w/
  Tarragon-Mustard Sauce (p. 465)
Tossed salad
Calico Vinaigrette (p. 242)
Winter-Jubilee Fruit (p. 623)

DAY 5

BREAKFAST
Orange sections
Raisin-bran cereal w/ skim milk
Cinnamon Buns (p. 294)

LUNCH
Broccoli-Buttermilk Soup (p. 188)
Stuffed Baked Potatoes (p. 527)
Carrot Salad (p. 213)
Kiwifruit slices

DINNER
Flounder w/ Pepper Puree (p. 467)
Oranges w/ Radishes and Dates (p. 209)
Asparagus and Bulgur (p. 342)
Classic Carrot Cake (p. 630)

DAY 6

BREAKFAST
Grapefruit juice
Potato Waffles w/ Peach Sauce (p. 279)

LUNCH
Vegetable Chili (p. 366)
Apples and Celeriac w/
  Honey-Mustard Dressing (p. 204)
Whole-Grain and Seed Bread (p. 273)
Peach slices

DINNER
Chicken w/ Thai Flavors (p. 494)
Curried Potato Salad (p. 217)
Wild-Rice Pilaf (p. 317)
Tropical Compote (p. 612)
Nonfat yogurt

DAY 7

BREAKFAST
Tomato juice
Caraway Pancakes (p. 278)

LUNCH
Cream of Carrot Soup (p. 172)
Main-Dish Antipasto (p. 369)
Rice-Bran Scones (p. 274)
Apricot Mousse (p. 634)

DINNER
Tomatoes Stuffed w/ Lamb Hash (p. 528)
Steamed green beans
Pasta
Herbed Pepper Sauce (p. 340)
Fresh fruit plate

Week Two

DAY 1

BREAKFAST
Orange juice
Spinach omelet

LUNCH
Oyster Stew (p. 473)
Berries and Greens (p. 230)
Onion Toast (p. 149)
Cantaloupe wedges

DINNER
Spicy Beef w/ Orange Vinaigrette (p. 535)
Emerald Isle Rice Pudding (p. 605)

DAY 2

BREAKFAST
Blended banana drink
Cranberry Bread (p. 293)
Savory Pear Spread (p. 253)

LUNCH
Cajun Soup (p. 176)
Corn Enchiladas (p. 425)
Tossed salad
Hot 'n' Spicy Vinaigrette (p. 242)
Bananas and orange slices

DINNER
Savory Stuffed Snow Peas (p. 143)
Jamaican Chicken (p. 509)
Couscous
Spinach w/ Pistachios (p. 591)
Spiced Apples (p. 618)

DAY 3

BREAKFAST
Orange sections
Apple Breakfast Bread (p. 258)
Oat-Bran Muesli (p. 316)
Skim milk

LUNCH
Navy-Bean Soup (p. 378)
Pita crisps
Artichoke Quiche (p. 124)
Watermelon wedges

DINNER
Fruited Lamb Curry (p. 552)
Brown rice
Indian-Style Wilted Greens (p. 568)
Almond-Topped Baked Plums (p. 623)

DAY 4

BREAKFAST
Grapefruit juice
Oatmeal w/ raisins and skim milk
Carrot Muffins (p. 292)

LUNCH
Creamy Broccoli Soup (p. 187)
Fish and Chips (p. 437)
Tossed salad
Green-Herb Dressing (p. 232)
Cran-Apple Sauce (p. 605)

DINNER
Sausage-Stuffed Zucchini Wheels (p. 142)
Monkfish w/ Citrus and Ginger (p. 433)
Corn Salad w/ Lemon-Dill Dressing (p. 212)
Black-Raspberry Pie (p. 606)

DAY 5

BREAKFAST
Marinated Figs and Apricots (p. 608)
Fruit and Nut Bread (p. 265)
Nonfat yogurt

LUNCH
Sizzling Fajitas (p. 530)
Cranberry Pears (p. 633)

DINNER
Curried Yogurt and Broccoli (p. 157)
Polenta (p. 417)
Asparagus Topping (p. 420)
Herbed Bean Salad (p. 346)
Fruit and Banana Splits (p. 635)

DAY 6

BREAKFAST
Prune juice
Cinnamon-Scented French Toast (p. 268)

LUNCH
Escarole Soup (p. 164)
Sprouts and Cheese (p. 214)
Bran-Flake Muffins (p. 249)

DINNER
Crudités (p. 157)
Sweet and Spicy Curry Dip (p. 147
Swordfish and Pineapple Brochettes (p. 456)
Japanese Noodles w/
  Spinach Ribbons (p. 299)
Peach slices

DAY 7

BREAKFAST
Citrus cup
Pecan Waffles w/ Strawberry Sauce (p. 288)

LUNCH
Seafood Gazpacho (p. 167)
Tossed salad
Garlic Vinaigrette (p. 241)
Orange Muffins (p. 267)
Banana slices

DINNER

Chinese-Style Rabbit (p. 501)
Sweet Potato Scones (p. 259)
Rosemary Asparagus (p. 582)
Stuffed Peaches (p. 631)

Lactose Intolerance

Week One

DAY 1

BREAKFAST
Tomato juice
Scrambled egg substitute
Soy milk

LUNCH
Iced Leek and Orange Soup (p. 173)
Lentil Tacos (p. 383)
Almond-Topped Baked Plums (p. 623)

DINNER
Crudités (p. 157)
Fragrant Chicken in Bok Choy Leaves (p. 140)
Rice
Chinese Beans w/ Sesame Seeds (p. 581)
Banana slices

DAY 2

BREAKFAST
Orange juice
Oatmeal w/ raisins and soy milk

LUNCH
Chunky Tomato Soup (p. 169)
Stuffed Baked Potatoes (p. 527)
Tossed salad
Basic Vinaigrette (p. 241)
Melon balls

DINNER
Lobster w/ Mint Vinaigrette (p. 440)
Steamed greens
Spicy Roasted Potatoes (p. 595)
Cherry-Maple Crunch (p. 634)

DAY 3

BREAKFAST
Grapefruit
Raisin-Oat Bread (p. 289)
Prune Butter (p. 252)
Soy milk

LUNCH
Cold Zucchini Soup (p. 179)
Indonesian Stir-Fry (p. 402)
Blueberries

DINNER
Roast port tenderloin
Vegetables w/ a honey glaze
Couscous
Apple and Persimmon Cobbler (p. 611)

DAY 4

BREAKFAST
Cranberry juice
French Toast w/ Tomato Salsa (p. 254)

LUNCH
South American Squash Soup (p. 174)
Buffalo Chili (p. 515)

Salad greens
Hot 'n' Spicy Vinaigrette (p. 242)
Strawberries

DINNER
Shrimp and Roasted Peppers (p. 466)
Chinese Vegetable Pasta (p. 313)
Nectarine Sorbet (p. 636)

DAY 5

BREAKFAST
Blueberries and nonfat yogurt
Orange Muffins (p. 267)
Savory Pear Spread (p. 253)

LUNCH
Crudités (p. 157)
Orchard Meat Loaf (p. 526)
Lettuce and tomato slices
Whole-Grain and Seed Bread (p. 273)

DINNER
Korean Hot Beef Soup (p. 185)
Chicken Breasts w/
   Harvest Vegetables (p. 503)
Zucchini w/ Caraway (p. 561)
Kale risotto
Spiced Apples (p. 618)

DAY 6

BREAKFAST
Pecan Waffles w/ Strawberry Sauce (p. 288)
Lactose-treated milk

LUNCH
Escarole Soup (p. 164)
Sardines
Tossed salad
Parsley Vinaigrette (p. 241)
Tropical Compote (p. 612)

DINNER
Scallops of Veal w/ Fennel and Grapes (p. 544)
Pasta w/ tomato sauce
Strawberry Sherbet (p. 638)

DAY 7

BREAKFAST
Orange sections
Apple Squares (p. 250)
Cold cereal w/ soy milk

LUNCH
Summer-Vegetable Soup (p. 184)
Salmon Salad w/ Almonds
  and Bok Choy (p. 202)
Cranberry Pears (p. 633)

DINNER
Chicken w/ Kashmiri Rice (p. 478)
Herbed Bean Salad (p. 346)
Savoy Puree in Potato Shells (p. 573)
Black-Raspberry Pie (p. 606)

Week Two

DAY 1

BREAKFAST

Orange sections
Cold cereal w/ apples and lactose-
  treated milk

LUNCH
Navy-Bean Soup (p. 378)
Salmon salad w/ broccoli
Three-Mustard Vinaigrette (p. 241)
Apple slices

DINNER
Roasted Eggplant Hors d'Oeuvres (p. 156)
Orange Beef w/ Rice (p. 537)
Rosemary Asparagus (p. 582)
Peach-Blackberry Pie (p. 610)

DAY 2

BREAKFAST
Grapefruit juice
Pineapple Focaccia (p. 255)

LUNCH
Creamy Broccoli Soup (p. 187)
Lentil Loaf (p. 349)
Whole Wheat French Bread (p. 283)
Watermelon wedges

DINNER
Grilled Tilefish w/ Bean Salsa (p. 385)
Barley Pilaf w/ Grilled Apples (p. 333)
Green Beans w/ Walnuts (p. 596)
Nectarines w/ Sauce Cardinale (p. 616)

DAY 3

BREAKFAST
Prune juice
Breakfast Scramble w/ Oven Fries (p. 392)

LUNCH
Dilled Cabbage Soup (p. 162)
Oyster Fritters w/ Tarragon-Mustard
  Sauce (p. 465)
Tossed salad
Tomato Vinaigrette (p. 241)
Pear slices

DINNER
Stuffed Tofu Triangles (p. 132)
Bouillabaisse (p. 448)
Whole-Grain and Seed Bread (p. 273)
Baked Prune Compote (p. 609)

DAY 4

BREAKFAST
Pineapple Fruit Cocktail (p. 632)
Hot cereal w/ soy milk

LUNCH
Tomato Bisque (p. 172)
Spicy Shrimp Salad w/ Cool Mango
   Dressing (p. 215)
Berries and Greens (p. 230)
Sweet Plums and Oranges (p. 614)

DINNER
Dilled Vegetables (p. 144)
Spicy Pork and Chicken
   w/ Pineapple (p. 541)
Steamed broccoli
Linguine
Fruit plate

DAY 5

BREAKFAST
Orange juice
Apple omelet
Soy milk

LUNCH
Sizzling Fajitas (p. 530)
Corn tortillas
Equinox Salad (p. 235)
Pineapple sections

DINNER
Soft-Shell Sauté (p. 441)
Good-Luck Peas (p. 365)
Savory Rice Pilaf (p. 329)
Blueberry-Apple Crisp (p. 622)

DAY 6

BREAKFAST
Grapefruit
Orange Muffins (p. 267)
All-fruit spread

LUNCH
Cajun Soup (p. 176)
Tropical Chicken Salad (p. 234)
English muffin
Grapes

DINNER
Sole and Salmon Roulades (p. 138)
Black-eyed peas w/ kale
Oranges with Radishes and Dates (p. 209)
Rice pudding made w/ lactose-treated milk

DAY 7

BREAKFAST
High-fiber cereal w/ soy milk

LUNCH
Striper Chowder (p. 161)
Spicy Vegetables w/ Tofu (p. 410)
Cran-Apple Sauce (p. 605)

DINNER
Veal Loin w/ Mango Sauce (p. 553)
Garlic and Eggplant Salad (p. 206)
Mustard greens
Peach Soufflé (p. 607)

Osteoporosis
Week One

DAY 1

BREAKFAST
Orange juice
Breakfast Scramble w/ Oven Fries (p. 392)
Rice-Bran Scones (p. 274)
Skim milk

LUNCH
Salmon Bisque (p. 188)
Corn Crêpes w/ Bean Filling (p. 397)
Nonfat yogurt and blueberries

DINNER
Vegetables w/ Creamy Garlic Sauce (p. 139)
Peaches and Pork (p. 531)
Broccoli and Cheese Pasta (p. 301)
Banana Ice Milk (p. 637)

DAY 2

BREAKFAST
Grapefruit juice
Golden French Toast (p. 262)
Skim milk

LUNCH
Fragrant Borscht (p. 183)
Smoky Cucumber Dip (p. 127)
Raw broccoli florets
Garlic toast
Cheesecake Tart (p. 602)

DINNER
Monkfish in Ginger Sauce (p. 459)
Greens and Tangerines (p. 239)
Cornmeal-Cheese Muffins (p. 260)
Fruit cup
Nonfat yogurt

DAY 3

BREAKFAST
Millet-Stuffed Apples (p. 327)
Prune Muffins (p. 291)
Skim milk

LUNCH
Iced Cantaloupe Soup (p. 171)
Slice turkey
Whole Wheat French Bread (p. 283)
Curried Yogurt and Broccoli (p. 157)
Banana slices

DINNER
Spinach-Stuffed Mushrooms (p. 134)
Oyster Fritters w/ Tarragon-Mustard
   Sauce (p. 465)
Tossed salad w/ yogurt dressing
Cabbage-Stuffed Shells (p. 314)
Melon wedges

DAY 4

BREAKFAST
Cranberry juice
Oat-Bran Muesli (p. 316)
Skim milk

LUNCH
Cream of Carrot Soup (p. 172)
Mexican Chicken Salad (p. 198)
Tossed salad
Green-Herb Dressing (p. 232)
One-Hour Oat Bread (p. 261)
Fresh fruit

DINNER
Seafood-Broccoli Terrine (p. 472)
Peas and Pasta (p. 304)
Tossed salad
Tangy Horseradish Dressing (p. 233)
Ice milk

DAY 5

BREAKFAST
Fruit shake
Orange-Almond Cheese (p. 148)
Whole wheat English muffin
Skim milk

LUNCH
Clam and Lobster Chowder (p. 191)
Zucchini-Ricotta Puffs (p. 400)
Tossed salad
Creamy Raspberry Dressing (p. 232)
Spiced Apples (p. 618)

DINNER
Onion and Pesto Pie (p. 390)
Good-Luck Peas (p. 365)
Passion-Fruit Freeze (p. 638)

DAY 6

BREAKFAST
Apple juice
Broccoli omelet
Bran-Flake Muffins (p. 249)
Skim milk

LUNCH
Enchiladas w/ Cheese and Kale (p. 423)
Berries and Greens (p. 230)
Winter-Jubilee Fruit (p. 623)

DINNER
Savory Stuffed Snow Peas (p. 143)
Stir-fried chicken w/ bok choy, tofu,
    and sesame seeds
Broccoli w/ Parsley Sauce (p. 562)
Berries and nonfat vanilla yogurt

DAY 7

BREAKFAST
Orange juice
Rice-Waffle Stack (p. 245)
Skim milk

LUNCH
New England clam chowder
Roasted-Garlic Dip (p. 148)
Pita wedges
Tossed salad w/ broccoli and chick-peas
Fresh fruit w/ sunflower seeds and raisins

DINNER
Mexican Corn Casserole (p. 415)
Indian-Style Wilted Greens (p. 568)
Strawberries w/ Two Melons (p. 603)

Week Two

DAY 1

BREAKFAST
Orange sections
Whole-grain cereal w/
  almonds and skim milk

LUNCH
Creamy Broccoli Soup (p. 187)
Cheese pizza
Emerald Isle Rice Pudding (p. 605)

DINNER
Vegetarian Sausage Links (p. 406)
Cabbage Noodles (p. 298)
Whole-wheat and molasses muffins
Buttermilk

DAY 2

BREAKFAST
Grapefruit
Cinnamon-Scented French Toast (p. 268)
Skim milk

LUNCH
Antipasto w/ Baked Oysters (p. 153)
Potato-Cheese Bread (p. 287)
Berry Custard (p. 621)

DINNER
Garlic and Potato Soup (p. 178)
Lamb Meatballs w/
    Pear-Turnip Puree (p. 525)
Dilled Split Peas (p. 371)
Brown rice
Apple Tart (p. 616)
Skim milk

DAY 3

BREAKFAST
Apricot-Quinoa Cereal (p. 334)
Skim milk

LUNCH
Chilled Blueberry Soup (p. 181)
Artichoke Quiche (p. 124)
Salad greens
Tangy Horseradish Dressing (p. 233)
Pineapple sections

DINNER
Rice Timbales (p. 127)
Chicken Canapés w/
    Broccoli Stuffing (p. 150)
Potato and Raspberry Salad (p. 200)
Pear-Cheese Pie (p. 625)

DAY 4

BREAKFAST
Potato Waffles w/ Peach Sauce (p. 279)
Skim milk

LUNCH
Watercress Canapés (p. 152)
Oyster Stew (p. 473)
Mackerel Salad (p. 442)
Fruit and Banana Splits (p. 635)

DINNER
Creamy Corn Chowder (p. 194)
Shrimp and Roasted Peppers (p. 466)
Pasta
Mushroom-Cheese Sauce (p. 339)
Frozen Pineapple Yogurt (p. 637)

DAY 5

BREAKFAST
Orange juice
Apples and Oat Cereal (p. 329)
Skim milk

LUNCH
Broccoli-Buttermilk Soup (p. 188)
Warm Salmon Salad (p. 242)
Dilled Carrot Bread (p. 282)
Nonfat yogurt and strawberries

DINNER
Crudités (p. 157)
Sweet and Spicy Curry Dip (p. 147)
Pesto Turkey (p. 497)
Chinese Vegetable Pasta (p. 313)
Skim milk
Marinated Figs and Apricots (p. 608)

DAY 6

BREAKFAST
Apricot nectar
Apple Breakfast Bread (p. 258)
Skim milk

LUNCH
Irish Vichyssoise (p. 193)
Broccoli Quesadilla (p. 409)
Fragrant Pear Charlotte (p. 628)

DINNER
Stuffed Tofu Triangles (p. 132)
Pasta
Spicy Aurora Sauce (p. 339)
Steamed kale w/ lemon rind
Pineapple Fruit Cocktail (p. 632)
Nonfat yogurt

DAY 7

BREAKFAST
Grapefruit juice
Buckwheat Blini (p. 247)
Low-fat cottage cheese and fresh fruit

LUNCH
Potato Bake with Mushroom
  Stroganoff (p. 414)
Corn-Bran Bread (p. 248)
Sardine and lentil salad
Basic Vinaigrette (p. 241)
Lemon Pumpkin Pie (p. 601)
Skim milk

DINNER
Seafood Gazpacho (p. 167)
Whole Wheat French Bread (p. 283)
Horseradish Dip (p. 145)
Pollo Sevilla (p. 491)
Dandelion Greens w/ Beans (p. 225)
Kiwifruit

Overweight

Week One

DAY 1

BREAKFAST
Fruit and Banana Splits (p. 635)
English muffin

LUNCH
Cold Zucchini Soup (p. 179)
Mackerel Salad (p. 442)
Pita triangles
Pineapple chunks

DINNER
Poached Turkey Paprika (p. 480)
Wild Rice and Raspberries (p. 317)
Green salad w/ low-fat dressing
Melon wedges

DAY 2

BREAKFAST
Grapefruit
Scrambled egg substitute
Whole-Grain and Seed Bread (p. 273)
Skim milk

LUNCH
Bulgur-Stuffed Yellow Peppers (p. 315)
Tossed salad w/ low-calorie dressing
Tropical Compote (p. 612)

DINNER
Flounder w/ Pepper Puree (p. 467)
Confetti Spaghetti Squash (p. 393)
Greens and Tangerines (p. 239)
Rice-Bran Scones (p. 274)

DAY 3

BREAKFAST
Golden French Toast (p. 262)

LUNCH
Pheasant and Mushroom Soup (p. 168)
Tossed salad
Lean Vinaigrette (p. 242)
Apple slices

DINNER
Skillet Barley and Beef (p. 304)
Squash Salad w/
   Buttermilk Dressing (p. 237)
Nectarine Sorbet (p. 636)

DAY 4

BREAKFAST
Hot cereal w/ skim milk

LUNCH
Eggs w/ Chili Sauce (p. 404)
Berries and Greens (p. 230)
Cantaloupe balls

DINNER
Diamond Head Turkey w/ Pineapple (p. 489)
Asparagus and Bulgur (p. 342)
Greek Garden Kabobs (p. 403)
Passion-Fruit Freeze (p. 638)

DAY 5

BREAKFAST
Oat-Bran Muesli (p. 316)
Skim milk

LUNCH
Enchiladas w/ Cheese and Kale (p. 423)
Equinox Salad (p. 235)
Nonfat vanilla yogurt w/ raspberries

DINNER
Poached Chicken with
   Chinese Vinaigrette (p. 486)
Chinese Vegetable Pasta (p. 313)
Turnip and carrot sticks
Fresh-Fruit Tart (p. 613)

DAY 6

BREAKFAST
Sweet Plums and Oranges (p. 614)
Shredded wheat w/ skim milk

LUNCH
Millet-Stuffed Apples (p. 327)
Corn Salad w/ Lemon-Dill Dressing (p. 212)
Strawberries

DINNER
Greek Spinach and Rice (p. 391)
Shredded carrot salad
Lean Vinaigrette (p. 242)
Nectarines w/ Sauce Cardinale (p. 616)

DAY 7

BREAKFAST
Buckwheat Crêpes (p. 270)
Low-fat cottage cheese
Fresh fruit

LUNCH
Spicy Stuffed Peppers (p. 413)
Tossed salad w/ low-calorie dressing
Winter-Jubilee Fruit (p. 623)

DINNER
Crudités (p. 157)
Monkfish in Ginger Sauce (p. 459)
Spaghetti w/ Spinach Chiffonade (p. 307)
Spiced Apples (p. 618)

Week Two

DAY 1

BREAKFAST
Orange juice
Raisin bran w/ skim milk and banana slices

LUNCH
Chunky Tomato Soup (p. 169)
Lentil and Leek Burritos (p. 428)
Pear slices

DINNER
Itialian-Style Fried Rice (p. 412)
Three-bean salad
Cheesecake Tart (p. 602)

DAY 2

BREAKFAST
Apples and Oat Cereal (p. 329)

LUNCH
Zucchini-Ricotta Puffs (p. 400)
Herbed Bean Salad (p. 346)
Blueberry Pudding (p. 624)

DINNER
Broccoli-Buttermilk Soup (p. 188)
Chili con Kasha (p. 336)
Kiwifruit slices and strawberries

DAY 3

BREAKFAST
Marinated Figs and Apricots (p. 608)
Hot cereal w/ skim milk

LUNCH
Creamy Broccoli Soup (p. 187)
Spicy Shrimp Salad w/
   Cool Mango Dressing (p. 215)
Whole Wheat French Bread (p. 283)
Strawberry Sherbet (p. 638)

DINNER
Roast Chicken w/ Fennel
  and Mustard (p. 479)
Spaghetti Squash w/ Tomato Sauce (p. 422)
Marinated broccoli and cauliflower florets
Cran-Apple Sauce (p. 605)

DAY 4

BREAKFAST
Grapefruit
Apple Breakfast Bread (p. 258)

LUNCH
Turkey and Shrimp Kabobs
  w/ Tomatoes (p. 493)
Green salad
Lean Vinaigrette (p. 242)
Orange slices

DINNER
Salmon Bisque (p. 188)
Fusilli w/ Fresh Tomato Sauce (p. 324)
Pineapple Fruit Cocktail (p. 632)

DAY 5

BREAKFAST
Stuffed Peaches (p. 631)
Bran-Flake Muffins (p. 249)

LUNCH
Breakfast Scramble w/ Oven Fries (p. 392)
Cornmeal-Cheese Muffins (p. 260)
Nonfat yogurt w/ pineapple chunks

DINNER
Spanish Halibut (p. 444)
Spinach Risotto (p. 323)
Tossed salad
Hot 'n' Spicy Vinaigrette (p. 242)
Apple and pear slices

DAY 6

BREAKFAST
Strawberries w/ Two Melons (p. 603)
Banana Pancakes (p. 285)

LUNCH
Potato Bake with Mushroom
    Stroganoff (p. 414)
Green salad w/ low-calorie dressing
Cranberry Pears (p. 633)
Nonfat yogurt

DINNER
Dilled vegetables (p. 144)
Polenta (p. 417)
Mediterranean Topping (p. 418)
Frozen Pineapple Yogurt (p. 637)

DAY 7

BREAKFAST
Baked Prune Compote (p. 609)
Apricot-Quinoa Cereal (p. 334)

LUNCH
Corn Enchiladas (p. 425)
Indian-Style Wilted Greens (p. 568)
Apricot Mousse (p. 634)

DINNER
Garlic-Roasted Turkey Breast (p. 496)
Pineapple-Rice Stuffing (p. 311)
Rosemary Asparagus (p. 582)
Papaya slices

Rheumatoid Arthritis

Week One

DAY 1

BREAKFAST
Orange juice
Granola w/ nonfat yogurt and fruit

LUNCH
Bulgur-Stuffed Yellow Peppers (p. 315)
Tossed green salad w/ low-fat dressing

DINNER
Iced Leek and Orange Soup (p. 173)
Bluefish in a Sea of Green (p. 451)
Potato and Raspberry Salad (p. 200)
Corn

DAY 2

BREAKFAST
Apple juice
Pecan Waffles w/ Strawberry Sauce (p. 288)

LUNCH
Chilled Blueberry Soup (p. 181)
Tropical Chicken Salad (p. 234)
Bread sticks

DINNER
Tuna and Pepper Bake (p. 468)
Oranges w/ Radishes and Dates (p. 209)
Wild Rice and Raspberries (p. 317)

DAY 3

BREAKFAST
Grapefruit
Hot oatmeal w/ raisins and skim milk

LUNCH
Seafood Gazpacho (p. 167)
Tossed green salad
Parsley Vinaigrette (p. 241)
Banana Ice Milk (p. 637)

DINNER
Dilled Shrimp and Rice Salad (p. 469)
Broccoli w/ Parsley Sauce (p. 562)
Black-Raspberry Pie (p. 606)

DAY 4

BREAKFAST
Melon slices
Banana Pancakes (p. 285)

LUNCH
Corn Enchiladas (p. 425)
Spinach salad
Tomato Vinaigrette (p. 241)
Fresh blueberries and mango slices

DINNER
Compote of Raspberries and
  Roasted Red Peppers (p. 141)
Whole Wheat French Bread (p. 283)
Warm Salmon Salad (p. 242)
Sautéed French chard
Sweet Plums and Oranges (p. 614)

DAY 5

BREAKFAST
Grapefruit juice
Oat-Bran Muesli (p. 316)

LUNCH
Tuna Tart w/ Basil (p. 145)
Curried Yogurt and Broccoli (p. 157)
Fresh fruit

DINNER
Shrimp and Roasted Peppers (p. 466)
Spicy Beet Salad (p. 229)
Fusilli w/ Fresh Tomato Sauce (p. 324)
Strawberry Sherbet (p. 638)

DAY 6

BREAKFAST
Cooked rice-bran cereal w/ skim milk

LUNCH
Striper Chowder (p. 161)
Cranberry Muffins (p. 263)
Garden salad w/ low-fat dressing
Kiwifruit slices

DINNER
Mexican Chicken Salad (p. 198)
Corn Pasta w/ Avocado Sauce (p. 322)
Berry Custard (p. 621)

DAY 7

BREAKFAST
Fresh orange
French Toast w/ Tomato Salsa (p. 254)

LUNCH
Chili con Kasha (p. 336)
Greens and Tangerines (p. 239)
Blueberry Pudding (p. 624)

DINNER
Chinese Braised Mackerel (p. 435)
Tossed salad
Lemon Vinaigrette (p. 241)
Chinese Vegetable Pasta (p. 313)
Kumquats

Week Two

DAY 1

BREAKFAST
Tropical Compote (p. 612)
Cooked wheat cereal w/ skim milk

LUNCH
Salmon Bisque (p. 188)
Red Pepper Canapés (p. 135)
Frozen Pineapple Yogurt (p. 637)

DINNER
Turkey and Shrimp Kabobs
   w/ Tomatoes (p. 493)
Squash Salad with Buttermilk
   Dressing (p. 237)
Sourdough rolls
Fresh-Fruit Tart (p. 613)

DAY 2

BREAKFAST
Orange juice
Toasted English muffin w/ melted low-fat
   cheese and tomato slices

LUNCH
Salmon Salad w/ Almonds
   and Bok Choy (p. 202)
Bread sticks
Peach-Blackberry Pie (p. 610)

DINNER
Sweetheart Soup (p. 182)
Tomatoes Stuffed w/ Lamb Hash (p. 528)
Cabbage Noodles (p. 298)
Cranberry Pears (p. 633)

DAY 3

BREAKFAST
Orange sections
Golden French Toast (p. 262)

LUNCH
Chunky Tomato Soup (p. 169)
Grilled Chicken and Artichokes
   w/ Mixed Greens (p. 505)
Strawberries w/ Two Melons (p. 603)

DINNER
Carrot Sticks w/ Dill Pesto (p. 125)
Spanish Halibut (p. 444)
Berries and Greens (p. 230)
Couscous w/ Sweet Corn (p. 332)
Passion-Fruit Freeze (p. 638)

DAY 4

BREAKFAST
Tomato juice
Cinnamon-Scented French Toast (p. 268)

LUNCH
Eggplant Soup w/ Tiny Pasta (p. 160)
Tossed salad
Watercress Dressing (p. 231)
Fruit and Nut Bread (p. 265)
Pear and low-fat cheese slices

DINNER
Tuna w/ Orange and Ginger Sauce (p. 452)
Pear and Potato Salad (p. 219)
Brussels Sprouts w/
   Mushroom Glaze (p. 594)
Blueberry-Apple Crisp (p. 622)

DAY 5

BREAKFAST
Orange-papaya juice
Apples and Oat Cereal (p. 329)

LUNCH
Dilled Cabbage Soup (p. 162)
Potato-Cheese Bread (p. 287)
Frozen Pineapple Yogurt (p. 637)

DINNER
Madrid Trout (p. 446)
Corn Salad w/ Lemon-Dill Dressing (p. 212)
Steamed fresh vegetables
Sliced peaches
Creamy Raspberry Dressing (p. 232)

DAY 6

BREAKFAST
Grapefruit
Rice-Waffle Stack (p. 245)

LUNCH
Sprouts and Cheese (p. 214)
Cranberry Bread (p. 293)
Frozen nonfat yogurt

DINNER
Clam and Lobster Chowder (p. 191)
Sizzled Salmon w/ Mint (p. 449)
Bulgur and Sweet-Pepper Salad (p. 207)
Nectarines w/ Sauce Cardinale (p. 616)

DAY 7

BREAKFAST
Cold cereal w/ skim milk
Sliced strawberries

LUNCH
Tomato Bisque (p. 172)
Mixed green salad
Honey-Lime Dressing (p. 233)
Whole Wheat French Bread (p. 283)

DINNER
Haddock Black Raven (p. 447)
Cabbage and Kasha (p. 297)
Whole Wheat Crêpes (p. 270)
Chopped fresh fruit and nonfat yogurt

Wound Healing

Week One

DAY 1

BREAKFAST
Orange juice
Fruit and Nut Bread (p. 265)
Cold cereal w/ strawberries and skim milk

LUNCH
Great Northern Soup (p. 357)
Mexican Picadillo (p. 549)
Tortilla crisps
Greens and Tangerines (p. 239)
Peach halves

DINNER
Chicken w/ Tropical Fruit (p. 511)
Cooked carrots and parsnips
Salad greens
Cider Vinaigrette (p. 241)
Apple and Persimmon Cobbler (p. 611)

DAY 2

BREAKFAST
Grapefruit
Breakfast Scramble w/ Oven Fries (p. 392)
Cranberry Muffins (p. 263)
Orange-Almond Cheese (p. 148)

LUNCH
Broccoli, chicken, and cashew stir-fry
Brown rice
Passion-Fruit Freeze (p. 638)

DINNER
Oyster Fritters w/ Tarragon-Mustard
    Sauce (p. 465)
Garden-Puff Potatoes (p. 556)
Rosemary Roasted Peppers (p. 590)
Green salad
Nectarines w/ Sauce Cardinale (p. 616)

DAY 3

BREAKFAST
Orange sections
Oatmeal w/ sunflower seeds, dried
    fruit, and nuts
Nonfat yogurt

LUNCH
Enchiladas w/ Cheese and Kale (p. 423)
Tossed salad
Hot 'n' Spicy Vinaigrette (p. 242)
Marinated Figs and Apricots (p. 608)

DINNER
London Broil w/ Garlic Marinade (p. 524)
Brussels Sprouts w/
    Mushroom Glaze (p. 594)
Pear and Potato Salad (p. 219)
Black-Raspberry Pie (p. 606)

DAY 4

BREAKFAST
Grapefruit juice
Carrot Muffins (p. 292)
Peanut butter
Nonfat yogurt w/ banana slices

LUNCH
Stir-fry of red peppers, mushrooms
  and snow peas
Baked potatoes w/ nonfat yogurt topping
Herbed Bean Salad (p. 346)
Orange slices

DINNER
Chicken Breasts w/
  Harvest Vegetables (p. 503)
Brussels Sprouts w/
  Three-Root Sauce (p. 566)
Brown rice
Equinox Salad (p. 235)
Strawberries

DAY 5

BREAKFAST
Cranberry juice
Golden French Toast (p. 262)
Skim milk

LUNCH
Butternut Bisque (p. 166)
Sweet Potato Scones (p. 259)
Sprouts and Cheese (p. 214)
Cranberry Pears (p. 633)

DINNER
Crown roast of lamb
Sesame Snow Peas (p. 593)
Berries and Greens (p. 230)
Emerald Isle Rice Pudding (p. 605)

DAY 6

BREAKFAST
Sweet Plums and Oranges (p. 614)
Bran-Flake Muffins (p. 249)
Yogurt cheese

LUNCH
Orchard Meat Loaf (p. 526)
Whole-Grain and Seed Bread (p. 273)
French-Style Chard (p. 577)
Moroccan Carrot Salad (p. 580)
Watermelon wedges

DINNER
Monkfish w/ Citrus and Ginger (p. 433)
Onions and Apples in a Pumpkin (p. 595)
Cabbage and Kasha (p. 297)
Peach crisp

DAY 7

BREAKFAST
Orange sections
Buckwheat Blini (p. 247)

LUNCH
Korean Hot Beef Soup (p. 185)
Winter Greens w/ Roasted Garlic (p. 563)
Dilled Carrot Bread (p. 282)

DINNER
Pollo Sevilla (p. 491)
Dandelion Greens w/ Beans (p. 225)
Carrots and Parsnips (p. 576)
Passion-Fruit Freeze (p. 638)

Week Two

DAY 1

BREAKFAST
Orange juice
Pecan Waffles w/ Strawberry Sauce (p. 288)

LUNCH
Mushroom and Lentil Soup (p. 358)
Spicy Beef w/ Orange Vinaigrette (p. 535)
Pita triangles

DINNER
Corn and Onion Pudding (p. 574)
Green Beans w/ Walnuts (p. 596)
Spinach Risotto (p. 323)
Peach Soufflé (p. 607)

DAY 2

BREAKFAST
Oat-Bran Muesli (p. 316)

LUNCH
Broccoli and Cheese Pasta (p. 301)
Cranberry Bread (p. 293)
Tossed salad
Parsley Vinaigrette (p. 241)
Mango slices

DINNER
Swordfish and Pineapple Brochettes (p. 456)
Maple Sweet Potatoes (p. 596)
Brussels sprouts
Bulgur and Sweet-Pepper Salad (p. 207)
Sliced kiwifruit and starfruit

DAY 3

BREAKFAST
Grapefruit
Cinnamon-Scented French Toast (p. 268)

LUNCH
Mackerel Salad (p. 442)
One-Hour Oat Bread (p. 261)
Carrot Spread (p. 251)
Blueberries and nonfat yogurt

DINNER
Stuffed Acorn Squash (p. 562)
Wild Rice and Raspberries (p. 317)
Indian-Style Wilted Greens (p. 568)
Cheesecake Tart (p. 602)

DAY 4

BREAKFAST
Apricot-Quinoa Cereal (p. 334)

LUNCH
Broccoli Quesadilla (p. 409)
Green salad
Honey-Lime Dressing (p. 233)
Berry Custard (p. 621)

DINNER
Pan-Fried Noodles w/
  Beans and Beef (p. 543)
Oranges w/ Radishes and Dates (p. 209)
Strawberry Sherbet (p. 638)

DAY 5

BREAKFAST

Grapefruit juice
Rice-Waffle Stack (p. 245)

LUNCH
Tomato Bisque (p. 172)
Lentil Tacos (p. 383)
Marinated Cauliflower (p. 599)
Apple slices and sunflower seeds

DINNER
Fruited Lamb Curry (p. 552)
Carrot Fritters (p. 575)
Broccoli w/ Parsley Sauce (p. 562)
Tossed salad
Creamy Raspberry Dressing (p. 232)
Melon wedges

DAY 6

BREAKFAST
Fruit and Banana Splits (p. 635)
Oatmeal with skim milk

LUNCH
Oyster Stew (p. 473)
Chinese Vegetable Pasta (p. 313)
Fresh greens
Green-Herb Dressing (p. 232)

DINNER
Curried Yogurt and Broccoli (p. 157)
Apricot-Stuffed Hens (p. 476)
Christmas Cabbage (p. 577)
Chinese Beans w/ Sesame Seeds (p. 581)
Pineapple chunks

DAY 7

BREAKFAST
Citrus medley
Scrambled egg substitute
Pecan-Oat Muffins (p. 275)

LUNCH
Iced Cantaloupe Soup (p. 171)
Savoy Puree in Potato Shells (p. 573)
Classic Carrot Cake (p. 630)

DINNER
Couscous w/ Chicken
   and Vegetables (p. 320)
Apricot Mousse (p. 634)

Index

Page references in **boldface** indicate tables.

A
Acorn squash. *See* Squash (winter)
Alcohol,   24, 31, 50
Allergies,   21–22
Almonds. *See also* Nuts
    Almond-Topped Baked Plums,   623–24
    Cornish Hens Stuffed with
        Apples, Almonds, and Raisins,   520–21
    Orange-Almond Cheese,   148
    Salmon Salad with Almonds and
        Bok Choy,   202
Anemia,   5–6
menu plan for,   644, 649–57
Anise seeds,   318
Antipasto
    Antipasto with Baked Oysters,   153–54
    Main-Dish Antipasto,   369–71
Appetizers. *See also* Dips; Spreads
    Antipasto with Baked Oysters,   153–54
    Artichoke Quiche,   124–25
    Braised Leeks with Mustard Sauce, 136–37
    Carrot Sticks with Dill Pesto,   125
    Chicken Canapés with Broccoli
        Stuffing,   150–51
    Citrus-Marinated Carrots,   154–55
    Compote of Raspberries and
        Roasted Red Peppers,   141
    Crudités   157–58

Appetizers (cont'd)
    Curried Yogurt and Broccoli,   157
    Dilled Vegetables,   144
    Dill-Zucchini Spears,   155
    Fragrant Chicken in Bok Choy Leaves, 140–41
    Grilled Onion Brochettes,   128–29
    Horseradish Dip,   145
    Mushrooms Stuffed with Cheese
        Soufflé   126
    Nachos,   364
    Onion Toast,   149–50
    Orange-Almond Cheese,   148
    Pesto Cheese,   149
    Popcorn,   129–32
    Red Pepper Canapés,   135–36
    Rice Timbales,   127–28
    Roasted Eggplant Hors d'Oeuvres,   156
    Roasted Garlic Dip,   148
    Sausage-Stuffed Zucchini Wheels,   142–43
    Savory Stuffed Snow Peas,   143
    Smoky Cucumber Dip,   127
    Sole and Salmon Roulades,   138–39
    Spinach-Stuffed Mushrooms,   134–35
    Stuffed Tofu Triangles,   132–34
    Sweet and Spicy Curry Dip,   147
    Tuna Tart with Basil,   145–46
    Vegetables with Creamy Garlic Sauce, 139–40
    Watercress Canapés,   152
    Yogurt cheese on canapés,   147–49
Apples,   55
    Apple-Barley Soup,   175–76
    Apple Breakfast Bread,   258–59
    Apples and Celeriac with
        Honey-Mustard Dressing,   204

Apples (cont'd)
 Apples and Oat Cereal,   329
 Apple and Persimmon Cobbler,   611–12
 Apple Squares,   250–51
 Apple Tart,   616–18
 Apple-Tomato Chutney,   534–35
 Barley Pilaf with Grilled Apples, 333–34
 Blueberry-Apple Crisp,   622
 Cornish Hens Stuffed with Apples,
  Almonds, and Raisins,   520–21
 Cran-Apple Sauce,   605
 Millet-Stuffed Apples,   327–28
 Onions and Apples in a Pumpkin, 598
 Spiced Apples,   618
 Veal in Apple-Lemon Sauce,   545–46
Apricots,   55–56, **626**
 Apricot Mousse,   634–35
 Apricot-Quinoa Cereal,   334
 Apricot-Stuffed Hens,   476–77
 Marinated Figs and Apricots,   608–9
Arthritis. *See also* Gout; Rheumatoid arthritis
Artichokes,   56
 Artichoke Quiche,   124–25
 Grilled Chicken and Artichokes
  with Mixed Greens,   505
 Italian-Style Fried Rice,   412
Arugula. *See* Salad greens
Asparagus,   56–57
 Asparagus and Bulgur,   342–43
 Asparagus and Shellfish Salad, 238–39
 Asparagus Topping for polenta,   420
 Rosemary Asparagus,   582–83
Avocados,   57
 Avocado and Shrimp Salad,   220–21

Avocados (cont'd)
  Corn Pasta with Avocado Sauce,   322–23
  Spaghetti with Guacamole,   342

B
Baked Prune Compote,   609
Bananas,   57–58
  Apricot Mousse,   634–35
  Banana Ice Milk,   637–38
  Banana Pancakes,   285–86
  Fruit and Banana Splits,   635
Barbecued Beef Satay,   538–39
Barley, 58 *See also* Grains
  Apple-Barley Soup,   175–76
  Banana Pancakes,   285–86
  Barley Pilaf with Grilled Apples,   333–34
  Skillet Barley and Beef,   304–5
Basic Vinaigrette,   241
Batter-Dipped Fish,   458
Beans (dried), 58–59
    See also Lentils; Split Peas
  Beans Florentine,   381
  Black Beans and Rice,   348–49
  Black-Eyed Peas with Spinach,   377
  Cajun Soup,   176–77
  Caribbean Bean Casserole,   372–73
  Chick-Pea Chili,   356–57
  Chili Beans Ranchero,   374–75
  Corn Crêpes with Bean Filling,   397–98
  Couscous and Chick-Pea Stew,   375–76
  Cuban Bean Stew,   384–85
  Dandelion Greens with Beans,   225
  Dips and spreads,   379–82
  Falafel Pockets,   353–55

Beans (dried) (cont'd)
Fava, 361–62
Favas with Tiny Pasta, 363
flavorings for, 355–56
Good-Luck Peas, 365
Great Northern Soup, 357–58
Hummus Bi Tahini, 382
Hummus with Pumpkin and
Pomegranate, 373–74
Mexican Bean Pie, 347–48
microwave preparation of, 350
Moroccan Chicken with Chick Peas, 359–60
Nachos, 364
Navy Bean Soup, 378
New Orleans Red Beans, 352–53
Vegetarian Sausage Links, 406–7
White-Bean Gumbo, 345–46
Beans (snap), 59–60, **560**
Chinese Beans with Sesame Seeds, 581
Dandelion Greens with Beans, 225
Green Beans and Peppers, 558–59
Green Beans with Walnuts, 596–97
Herbed Bean Salad, 346–47
Pan-Fried Noodles with Beans
and Beef, 543–44
Savory Lima Beans, 362
Succotash Chowder, 186–87
Beef (lean), 60–61
Barbecued Beef Satay, 538–39
Chili con Kasha, 336
Korean Hot Beef Soup, 185–86
Lean Beef with Greens and Feta, 208–9
London Broil with Garlic Marinade, 524
Mexican Picadillo, 549–50

Beef (lean) (cont'd)
    Orange Beef with Rice, 537–38
    Orchard Meat Loaf, 526
    Pan-Fried Noodles with Beans
      and Beef, 543–44
    Sizzling Fajitas, 530–31
    Skillet Barley and Beef, 304–5
    South American Squash Soup, 174–75
    Spicy Beef with Orange Vinaigrette, 535–36
    Stuffed Baked Potatoes, 527
Beets, 61
    Beets with Pecans and Dill, 583–84
    Fragrant Borscht, 183–84
    Spicy Beet Salad, 229
    Stuffed Red Beets, 574
Berries. *See also specific berries*
    Berries and Greens, 230
    Berry Custard, 621–22
    vinegar, 212
Black Beans and Rice, 348–49
Blackberries, 61–62, **627** *See also* Berries
    Peach-Blackberry Pie, 610
Black-Eyed Peas. *See also* Beans (dried)
    Black-Eyed Peas with Spinach, 377
    Good-Luck Peas, 365
Black-Raspberry Pie, 606–7
Blini, Buckwheat, 247–48
Blood pressure, 32–35
    menu plan for, 646, 726–34
Blueberries, 62, **627** *See also* Berries
    Blueberry-Apple Crisp, 622
    Blueberry Pudding, 624–25
    Chilled Blueberry Soup, 181–82

Bluefish. *See also* Fish
    Bluefish in a Sea of Green,   451–52
Bok choy. *See also* Cabbage
    Fragrant Chicken in Bok Choy
      Leaves,   140–41
    Salmon Salad with Almonds and
      Bok Choy,   202
Borscht, Fragrant,   183–84
Bouillabaisse,   448
Braised Leeks with Mustard Sauce,   136–37
Bran,   62–63
    Apples and Oat Cereal,   329
    Bran-Flake Muffins,   249–250
    Corn-Bran Bread,   248–49
    Oat-Bran Muesli,   316
    Prune Muffins,   291
Breads
    Apple Breakfast Bread,   258–59
    Apple Squares,   250–51
    Bread Stuffed with Lentils,   351–52
    Corn-Bran Bread,   248–49
    Cranberry Bread,   293–94
    Dilled Carrot Bread,   282–83
    Fruit and Nut Bread,   265–66
    One-Hour Oat Bread,   261–62
    Potato-Cheese Bread,   287–88
    problems with,   256–58
    Raisin-Oat Bread,   289–90
    seeds in,   319
    Whole-Grain and Seed Bread,   273–74
    Whole Wheat French Bread,   283–85
    yeast for,   276–77
    yeast breads,   281–82

Breakfasts
  Apple Breakfast Bread, 258–59
  Apples and Oat Cereal, 329
  Apricot-Quinoa Cereal, 334
  Banana Pancakes, 285–86
  Breakfast Scramble with Oven Fries, 392–93
  Buckwheat Blini, 247–48
  Caraway Pancakes, 278–79
  Cinnamon Buns, 294–95
  Cinnamon-Scented French Toast, 268
  Crêpes, 269–71
  French Toast with Tomato Salsa, 254
  Oat-Bran Muesli, 316
  Pecan Waffles with Strawberry Sauce, 288–89
  Pineapple Focaccia, 255–56
  Potato Waffles with Peach Sauce, 279–80
  Rice-Waffle Stack, 245–46
Broad beans. *See* Fava beans
Broccoli, 63–64, **559**. *See also* Cruciferous
  vegetables
  Broccoli-Buttermilk Soup, 188
  Broccoli and Cheese Pasta, 301
  Broccoli with Parsley Sauce, 562
  Broccoli Quesadilla, 409–10
  Chicken Canapés with Broccoli
    Stuffing, 150–51
  Creamy Broccoli Soup, 187
  Curried Yogurt and Broccoli, 157
  Irish Vichyssoise, 193
  Seafood-Broccoli Terrine, 472–73
Broiled Salmon with Cucumbers, 450–51
Brussels sprouts, 64. *See also* Cruciferous
  vegetables

Brussels Sprouts (cont'd)
  Brussels Sprouts with
    Mushroom Glaze,   594–95
  Brussels Sprouts with
    Three-Root Sauce,   566–67
Buckwheat, 64–65. *See also* Kasha
  Buckwheat Blini,   247–48
  Buckwheat Crêpes,   270–71
  Buckwheat Noodles with
    Grilled Tuna,   312–13
Buffalo Chili,   515
Bulgur, 65. *See also* Grains
  Asparagus and Bulgur,   342–43
  Bulgur-Stuffed Yellow Peppers,   315–16
  Bulgur and Sweet-Pepper Salad,   207–8
  Cornish Hens Stuffed with Apples,
    Almonds, and Raisins,   520–21
Buns, Cinnamon,   294–95
Burritos, Lentil and Leek,   428–29
Buttermilk Dressing, Squash Salad with,   237–38
Butternut Bisque,   166–67

C

Cabbage, 66. *See also* Bok Choy; Chinese
  cabbage; Cruciferous vegetables
  Cabbage and Kasha,   297–98
  Cabbage Noodles,   298–99
  Cabbage-Stuffed Shells,   314
  Christmas Cabbage,   577
  Dilled Cabbage Soup   162–63
  Fragrant Borscht,   183–84
  Savoy Puree in Potato Shells,   573
Cajun Soup,   176–77
Cake, Classic Carrot,   630–31

Calico Vinaigrette, 242
Canapés
  Chicken Canapés with
    Broccoli Stuffing, 150–51
  Watercress Canapés, 152
  yogurt cheese on, 146–49
Cancer, 6–9
  menu plan for, 658–66
Cantaloupe, *See also* Melons
  Iced Cantaloupe Soup, 171
Caraway
  Caraway Pancakes, 278–79
  seeds, 318
Caribbean Bean Casserole, 372–73
Carrots, 66
  Carrot Fritters, 575–76
  Carrot Muffins, 292
  Carrot Salad, 213
  Moroccan Carrot Salad, 580
  Carrots and Parsnips, 576
  Carrot Spread, 251–52
  Carrot Sticks with Dill Pesto, 125
  Citrus-Marinated Carrots, 154–55
  Classic Carrot Cake, 630–31
  Cream of Carrot Soup, 172
  Dilled Carrot Bread, 282–83
Caspian Split Peas, 367
Cauliflower, 67. *See also* Cruciferous vegetables
  Marinated Cauliflower, 599
Celeriac, Apples and, with Honey-
  Mustard Dressing, 204
Celery, 67–68
  Stir-Fry with Snow Peas, Celery,
    and Pistachios, 582

Celiac disease,   9–10
Cereal
    Apples and Oat Cereal,   329
    Apricot-Quinoa Cereal,   334
    Oat-Bran Muesli Cereal,   316
Charlotte, Fragrant Pear,   628–29
Cheese (low-fat), 68–70, 69–70. *See also*
    Cottage cheese
    Broccoli and Cheese Pasta,   301
    Cornmeal-Cheese Muffins,   260–61
    Enchiladas with Cheese and Kale,   423
    Mushroom-Cheese Sauce,   339
    Mushrooms Stuffed with Cheese
        Soufflé,   126
    Pear-Cheese Pie,   625–26
    Potato-Cheese Bread,   287–88
    Sprouts and Cheese,   214
    Whole Wheat Pizza,   408–9
Cheesecake Tart,   602–3
Cherries,   70–71
    Cherry-Maple Crunch,   634
Chestnuts,   71
    Chestnut Stuffing,   309–10
Chicken, 72–74. *See also* Poultry
    Apricot-Stuffed Hens,   476–77
    breast of
        boneless,   475
        Chicken Breasts with Harvest
            Vegetables,   503–4
        Curried Chicken Breasts,   488–89
        Orange-Scented Chicken Breasts,   517–18
    Chicken Canapés with Broccoli
        Stuffing,   150–51
    Chicken with Kashmiri Rice,   478–79

Chicken (cont'd)

Chicken with Thai flavors,	494–95
Chicken with Tropical Fruit,	511–12
Cornish Hens Stuffed with Apples, Almonds, and Raisins,	520–21
Couscous with Chicken and Vegetables,	320–22
Fragrant Chicken in Bok Choy Leaves,	140–41
Grilled Chicken and Artichokes with Mixed Greens,	505
Jamaican Chicken,	509–10
Jasmine Chicken with Strawberry Coulis,	481–82
Mandarin Chicken with Bean Sprouts,	516–17
Mexican Chicken Salad,	198–99
Moroccan Chicken with Chick-Peas,	359–60
Poached Chicken	
Poached Chicken with Chinese Vinaigrette,	486
Poached Chicken with Pear and Kiwifruit,	507–8
Pollo Sevilla,	491–92
Poultry Pâté,	492–93
Roast Chicken with Fennel and Mustard,	479–80
seeds with,	319
Spicy Pork and Chicken with Pineapple,	541–42
Steamed Wontons,	490–91
Tarragon Chicken with Linguine,	335
Tropical Chicken Salad,	234–35

Chick-Peas. *See also* Beans (dried)
    Chick-pea Chili, 356–57
    Couscous and Chick-Pea Stew, 375–76
    Moroccan Chicken with Chick-Peas, 359–60
Chicory. *See* Salad greens
Chili
    Buffalo Chili, 515
    Chick-Pea Chili, 356–57
    Chili Bean Dip, 380
    Chili Beans Ranchero, 374–75
    Chili con Kasha, 336
    Chili Popcorn, 132
    Eggs with Chili Sauce, 404
    Vegetable Chili, 366
Chilled Blueberry Soup, 181–82
Chinese Beans with Sesame Seeds, 581
Chinese Braised Mackerel, 435
Chinese cabbage. *See also* Cabbage; Cruciferous
    vegetables
    Korean Hot Beef Soup, 185–86
Chinese-Style Rabbit, 501
Chinese Vegetable Pasta, 313
Chives, 588
Chowders. *See also* Soups
    Creamy Corn Chowder, 194
    Striper Chowder, 161–62
    Succotash Chowder, 186–87
Christmas Cabbage, 577
Chunky Tomato Soup, 169–70
Chutneys, 533–35
Cidered Parsnips, 597
Cider Vinaigrette, 241

Cinnamon
    Cinnamon Buns, 294–95
    Cinnamon-Scented French Toast, 268
Citrus fruit. *See specific fruit*
Citrus-Marinated Carrots, 154–55
Clams. *See also* Mollusks
    Asparagus and Shellfish Salad, 238–39
    Clam and Lobster Chowder 191–92
Clarifying soup stock, 194–95
Classic Carrot Cake, 630–31
Cobbler, Apple and Persimmon, 611–12
Cod with Herbed Potatoes, 470–71
Colds, 10–12
    menu plan for, 645, 667–74
Cold Zucchini Soup 179–80
Collard greens. *See* Salad greens
Componata with Rigatoni, 326–27
Compote
    Baked Prune Compote, 609
    Compote of Raspberries and
        Roasted Red Peppers, 141
    Tropical Compote, 612
Confetti Spaghetti Squash, 393–94
Constipation, 12–13
    menu plan for, 645, 683–91
Cool Peach Soup, 177–78
Coriander
    Coriander-Bean Dip, 380
    seeds, 318
Corn, 74, **560**
    Acorn Squash Stuffed with
        Cornbread, 395–96
    Cajun Soup, 176–77
    Corn-Bran Bread, 248–49

Corn (cont'd)
Corn Crêpes with Bean Filling,   397–98
Corn Enchiladas,   425–26
Cornmeal-Cheese Muffins,   260–61
Corn and Onion Pudding,   574–75
Corn Pasta with Avocado Sauce,   322–23
Corn-Pone Pie,   405–6
Corn Salad with Lemon-Dill
    Dressing,   212–13
Couscous with Sweet Corn,   332
Creamy Corn Chowder,   194
Mexican Corn Casserole,   415–16
Parsnip-Corn Cakes,   589
Polenta,   416–20
Succotash Chowder,   186–87
Sweet Corn Fritters,   565–66
Cornbread, Acorn Squash Stuffed with   395–96
Cornish Hens. *See also* Chicken; Poultry
Apricot-Stuffed Hens,   476–77
Cornish Hens Stuffed with Apples,
    Almonds, and Raisins,   520–21
Cornmeal-Cheese Muffins,   260–61
Cottage cheese (low-fat)   74–75, **76**
Buckwheat Blini,   247–48
Cheesecake Tart,   602–3
Fettuccine with Grapes,   306
Greek Spinach and Rice,   391–92
Green-Herb Dressing,   232–33
Millet-Stuffed Apples,   327–28
Mushrooms Stuffed with
    Cheese Soufflé,   126
Onion and Pesto Pie,   390–91
Pasta with Salmon and Sun-Dried
    Tomatoes,   303

Cottage cheese (cont'd)
Pear-Cheese Pie, 625–26
Potatoes with Creamy Mustard Topping, 590
Rice-Waffle Stack, 245–46
Russian Vegetable Pie, 420–21
Spaghetti with Spinach Chiffonade, 307
Spicy Aurora Sauce, 339–40
Spinach-Stuffed Mushrooms, 134–35
Tangy Horseradish Dressing, 233
Zucchini-Ricotta Puffs, 400
Couscous
Couscous with Chicken and
Vegetables, 320–22
Couscous and Chick-Pea Stew, 375–76
Couscous with Sweet Corn, 332
Crab. *See also* Crustaceans
Soft-Shell Sauté, 441–42
Cranberries, 75
Cran-Apple Sauce, 605
Cranberry Bread, 293–94
Cranberry Muffins, 263–64
Cranberry Pears, 633
Crayfish. *See* Crustaceans
Cream of Carrot Soup, 172
Creamed Turnips, 567–68
Cream of Mushroom Soup 192–93
Creamy Broccoli Soup, 187
Creamy Corn Chowder, 194
Creamy Garlic Sauce, Vegetables with, 139–40
Creamy Raspberry Dressing, 232
Creamy Vinaigrette, 242
Creole Bean dip, 380
Crêpes, 269–71
Corn Crêpes with Bean Filling, 397

Crisp. *See also* Crunch
    Blueberry-Apple Crisp,   622
Cruciferous vegetables, 7–8. *See* Broccoli;
    Brussels sprouts; Cabbage; Cauliflower;
    Rutabagas; Turnips
Crudités,   157–58
Crunch. *See also* Crisp
    Cherry-Maple Crunch,   634
Crustaceans, 76–77. *See also* Crab; Lobster;
    Shrimp
Cucumbers,   77–78
    Broiled Salmon with Cucumbers,   450–51
    Cucumbers with Cumin
       and Coriander,   564–65
    Smoky Cucumber Dip,   127
Curly endive. *See* Salad greens
Currants (fresh),   **627**
Curry(ied)
    Curried Chicken Breasts,   488–89
    Curried Pea Spread,   381
    Curried Potato Salad,   217
    Curried Yogurt and Broccoli,   157
    Curry Popcorn,   130
    Fruited Lamb Curry,   552–53
    Sea Kabob Salad with Curry
       Vinaigrette,   236–37
    Sweet and Spicy Curry Dip,   147
Custard, Berry,   621–22
Cystitis. *See* Urinary tract infections

D

Dairy products. *See specific dairy products*
Dandelion Greens with Beans,   225

Dates. *See also* Tropical fruit
  Oranges with Radishes and Dates,   209–10
Dental problems,   13–14
Desserts
  Almond-Topped Baked Plums,   623–24
  Apple and Persimmon Cobbler,   611–12
  Apple Tart,   616–18
  Apricot Mousse,   634–35
  Baked Prune Compote,   609
  Banana Ice Milk,   637–38
  Berry Custard,   621–22
  Black-Raspberry Pie,   606–7
  Blueberry-Apple Crisp,   622
  Blueberry Pudding,   624–25
  Cheesecake Tart,   602–3
  Cherry-Maple Crunch,   634
  Classic Carrot Cake,   630–31
  Cran-Apple Sauce,   605
  Cranberry Pears,   633
  Emerald Isle Rice Pudding,   605–6
  Fragrant Pear Charlotte,   628–29
  Fresh Fruit Freezes,   636–39
  Fresh-Fruit Tart,   613
  Frozen Pineapple Yogurt,   637
  Fruit and Banana Splits,   635
  Lemon Pumpkin Pie,   601–2
  Marinated Figs and Apricots,   608–9
  Nectarine Sorbet,   636–37
  Nectarines with Sauce Cardinale,   616
  Peach-Blackberry Pie,   610
  Peach Soufflé,   607–8
  Pear-Cheese Pie,   625–26
  Pineapple Fruit Cocktail,   632–33
  pizza,   409

Desserts (cont'd)
    seeds in, 320
    Spiced Apples, 618
    Strawberries with Two Melons, 603–4
    Strawberry Sherbet, 638
    Stuffed Peaches, 631–32
    Sweet Plums and Oranges, 614
    Tropical Compote, 612
    Winter-Jubilee Fruit, 623
Diabetes, 14–16
    menu plan for, 645, 675–82
Diamond Head Turkey with Pineapple, 489–90
Diarrhea, bananas and, 58
Digestive problems. *See* Constipation;
    Diarrhea; Diverticular disease; Hemorrhoids
    menu plan for, 645, 683–91
Dill
    Beets with Pecans and Dill, 583–84
    Carrot Sticks with Dill Pesto, 125
    Dilled Cabbage Soup, 162–63
    Dilled Carrot Bread, 282–83
    Dilled Salmon Tart, 453–54
    Dilled Shrimp and Rice Salad, 469
    Dilled Split Peas, 371–72
    Dill-Zucchini Spears, 155
Dips
    bean, 379–82
    Horseradish Dip, 145
    Roasted Garlic Dip, 148
    Smoky Cucumber Dip, 127
    Sweet and Spicy Curry Dip, 147
Dishware, safety in microwave, 137–38
Diverticular disease, 16–17
    menu plan for, 645, 683–91

Dressings for salads, 230–34, 240–42.
  See also specific salads
Duck. *See also* Waterfowl
  Roast Duck with Fresh Rosemary,   502–3

E

East Indian Rice Salad,   197–98
Eggplant,   78
  Componata with Rigatoni,   326–27
  Eggplant Soup with Tiny Pasta,   160–61
  Garlic and Eggplant Salad,   206–7
  Hunan Eggplant,   585
  Roasted Eggplant Hors d'Oeuvres,   156
Eggs,   429–30
  Eggs with Chili Sauce,   404
  Egg substitute,   429–31
Eight-Vegetable Millet Soup,   190–91
Emerald Isle Rice Pudding,   605–6
Enchiladas
  Corn Enchiladas,   425–26
  Enchiladas with Cheese and Kale,   423
Endive. *See* Salad greens
Equinox Salad,   235–36
Escarole. *See also* Salad greens
  Escarole Soup,   164

F

Falafel Pockets,   353–55
Far Eastern Rutabagas,   557–58
Fatigue,   17–19
  menu plan for,   645, 692–700
Fava beans. *See also* Beans (dried)

Fennel
  Scallops of Veal with Fennel and
    Grapes,   544–45
  seeds,   318
Feta
  Lean Beef with Greens and Feta,   208–9
  Spinach and Feta Pie,   389–90
Fettuccine with Grapes,   306
Fibrocystic breast disease,   19–20
Fiesta Bean Dip,   382
Figs,   78–79
  Marinated Figs and Apricots,   608–9
Fish, 79–81, **80**. *See also specific fish*
  baked,   455–56
  Batter-Dipped Fish,   458
  Bouillabaisse,   448
  buying and preparation tips,   454–56
  Fish and Chips,   437–39
  Fish in Foil,   437
  grilled,   436–37
  microwave preparation of,   462–64
  oil, healing qualities   45–47
  Sea Kabob Salad with Curry
    Vinaigrette,   236–37
  seeds with,   319
  steamed,   454–55
Flatulence, fiber and,   20–21
Flavoring for beans,   355–56
Flounder. *See also* Fish
  Fish and Chips,   437–39
  Flounder with Pepper Puree,   467–68
Focaccia, Pineapple,   255–56
Food allergies,   21–22
Fragrant Borscht,   183–84

Fragrant Chicken in Bok Choy Leaves, 140–41
Fragrant Pear Charlotte, 628–29
Freezing fruit, 614–15
French Bread, Whole Wheat, 283–85
French-Style Chard, 577–78
French Toast
    Cinnamon-Scented French Toast, 268
    French Toast with Tomato Salsa, 254
    Golden French Toast, 262–63
Fresh Pineapple Chutney, 533
Fritters
    Carrot Fritters, 575–76
    Sweet Corn Fritters, 565–66
Frozen Pineapple Yogurt, 637
Fruits, **626–28**. *See also specific fruit*
    Chicken with Tropical Fruit, 511–12
    enhancing flavor in microwave, 604
    freezing, 614–15
    Fresh Fruit Tart, 613
    Fruit and Banana Splits, 635
    Fruited Lamb Curry, 552–53
    Fruit Freezes, 636–39
    Fruit and Nut Bread, 265–66
    Oat-Bran Muesli, 316
    pesticides and, 578–79
    pies prepared in microwave, 619–20
    Pineapple Fruit Cocktail, 632–33
    Winter-Jubilee Fruit, 623
Fusilli with Fresh Tomato Sauce, 324

G
Gallbladder problems, 22–23
Game, 81–82
    Buffalo Chili, 515

Game (cont'd)
Chinese-Style Rabbit,   501
Pheasant and Mushroom Soup,   168–69
Rabbit Sauté with Mushrooms,   506
Venison Brochettes,   499–500
Garden-Puff Potatoes,   556–57
Garlic,   82, 587
Garlic and Eggplant Salad,   206–7
Garlic and Potato Soup,   178–79
Garlic-Roasted Turkey Breast,   496
Garlic Vinaigrette,   241
London Broil with Garlic Marinade,   524
Roasted Garlic Dip,   148
Vegetables with Creamy Garlic Sauce,   139–40
vinegar,   211
Gazpacho, Seafood,   167–78
Ginger Sauce, Monkfish in,   459–60
Ginger Turkey with Spicy Tomato Sauce,   508–9
Gluten-free foods,   10
Golden French Toast,   262–63
Good-Luck Peas,   365
Goose. *See also* Waterfowl
Orange-Scented Roast Goose,   485
Gout,   23–25
menu plan for,   645–46, 701–8
Grains, 296. *See also specific grains*
as healing food,   17
Grapes,   83
Fettuccine with Grapes,   306
Scallops of Veal with Fennel
and Grapes,   544–45
Smoked Turkey and Grapes,   216
Summer Chicken Salad Sandwiches,   513
Tropical Compote,   612

Grapefruit, *See also* Citrus fruit 82–83
Great Northern Soup, 357–58
Greek Garden Kabobs, 403
Greek Spinach and Rice, 391–92
Green Beans. *See also* Beans (snap)
   Green Beans and Peppers, 558–59
   Green Beans with Walnuts, 596–97
Green-Herb Dressing, 232–33
Green-Pepper Pesto, 341
Greens. *See* Salad greens
Grilled Chicken and Artichokes with
   Mixed Greens, 505
Grilled Florida Snapper, 439–40
Grilled Onion Brochettes, 128–29
Guacamole, Spaghetti with, 342
Guavas, 115. *See also* Tropical fruit
Gumbo, White-Bean, 345–46
Gum disease, *See* Dental Problems

H
Haddock. *See also* Fish
   Haddock Black Raven, 447
Halibut. *See also* Fish
   Spanish Halibut, 444–45
Hawaiian pizza, 408
Hazelnut Salad, Pear and, 201
Headaches, 25–26
Hearing problems, 26–27
Heart disease, 27–30
   menu plan for, 646, 709–16
Hemorrhoids, 30–31
   menu plan for, 645, 683–91
Herbed Bean Salad, 346–47
Herbed Pepper Sauce, 340–41

Herbs, 83–84. *See also* Spices; Seeds
    Herb-Steamed Mussels with
        Rice Pilaf,   460–61
    herb vinegar,   211
Hiatal hernia,   31–32
    menu plan for,   **646,** 717–25
High blood pressure. *See* Blood pressure
Honey
    Apples and Celeriac with
        Honey-Mustard Dressing,   204
    Honey-Lime Dressing,   233–34
Honeydew. *See also* Melons
    Strawberries with Two Melons, 603–4
    Strawberry Sherbet,   638
Horseradish
    Horseradish Dip,   145–46
    Tangy Horseradish Dressing,   233
Hummus
    Hummus Bi Tahini,   382
    Hummus with Pumpkin and
        Pomegranate,   373–74
Hunan Eggplant,   585

I

Iced Cantaloupe Soup,   171
Iced Leek and Orange Soup,   173–74
Ice Milk, Banana,   637–38
Immune system. *See* Impaired immunity
Impaired immunity,   35–36
    menu plan for,   646–47, 735–43
Indian-Style Wilted Greens,   568–69
Indonesian Stir-Fry,   402–3
Insomnia, cheese and,   70
Irish Vichyssoise,   193

Iron-deficiency anemia. *See* Anemia
Irritable bowel syndrome,   36–37
Italian beans. *See* Beans (snap)
Italian-Style Fried Rice,   412

J
Jamaican Chicken,   509–10
Japanese Noodles with
    Spinach Ribbons,   299–300
Jasmine Chicken with
    Strawberry Coulis,   481–82

K
Kabobs, Greek Garden,   403
Kale,   84–85
    Enchiladas with Cheese and Kale,   423
Kasha
    Cabbage and Kasha,   297–98
    Chili con Kasha,   336
Kidney stones,   38–39
Kiwifruit,   85
    Kiwifruit Freeze,   639
    Poached Chicken with Pear
        and Kiwifruit,   507–8
Korean Hot Beef Soup,   185–86

L
Lactose intolerance,   39–40
    menu plan for,   647, 744–51
Lamb (lean),   85–86
    Fruited Lamb Curry,   552–53
    Lamb Meatballs with
        Pear-Turnip Puree,   525–26
    Tomatoes Stuffed with Lamb Hash,   528

Lean Beef with Greens and Feta, 208–9
Lean Vinaigrette, 242
Leeks, 588
  Braised Leeks with Mustard Sauce, 136–37
  Iced Leek and Orange Soup, 173–74
  Lentil and Leek Burritos, 428–29
Legumes, *See* Beans (dried); Lentils; Peas; Split peas
Lemons, 86. *See also* citrus fruit
  Corn-Salad with Lemon-Dill Dressing, 212–13
  Lemon Pumpkin Pie, 601–2
  Lemon Vinaigrette, 241–42
  Veal in Apple-Lemon Sauce, 545–46
Lentils, *See also* Beans (dried)
  Bread Stuffed with Lentils, 351–52
  Lentil and Leek Burritos, 428–29
  Lentil Loaf, 349–50
  Mushroom and Lentil Soup, 358–59
Lettuce. *See* Salad greens
Lima Beans, **560**
  Savory Lima Beans, 362
Limes, 86. *See also* Citrus fruit
  Honey-Lime Dressing, 233–34
Linguine. *See also* Pasta
  Linguine with Sweet Peppers, 302
  Tarragon Chicken with Linguine, 335
Liver, 5
Loaf
  Lentil Loaf, 349–50
  Orchard Meat Loaf, 526
Lobster. *See also* Crustaceans
  Clam and Lobster Chowder, 191–92
  Lobster with Mint Vinaigrette, 440

London Broil with Garlic Marinade, 524
Low-fat meat. *See* Meat

M

Mackerel. *See also* Fish
  Chinese Braised Mackerel, 435
  Mackerel Salad, 442–43
Macular degeneration, spinach and, 110
Madrid Trout, 446–47
Main-Dish Antipasto, 369–71
Mandarin Chicken with Bean Sprouts, 516–17
Mangoes, 86–77. *See also* Tropical fruit
  Mango Freeze, 639
  Spicy Shrimp Salad with Cool
    Mango Dressing, 215
  Veal Loin with Mango Sauce, 553–54
Maple Sweet Potatoes, 596
Marinades, 487, 529–30
Marinated Cauliflower, 599
Marinated Figs and Apricots, 608–9
Meat (lean), 623–54. *See also specific meats*
  marinades for, 529–30
  moist, preparing in microwave, 539–41
  Orchard Meat Loaf, 526
  in stir-fries, 546–49
Meatballs, Lamb, with Pear-Turnip
  Puree, 525–26
Mediterranean Topping for polenta, 418
Melons, 87, 627. *See also* Cantaloupe; Honeydew
  Strawberries with Two Melons,
Menu plans, 643–784
Mexican Bean Pie, 347–48
Mexican Chicken Salad, 198–99
Mexican Corn Casserole, 415–16

Mexican Picadillo,   549–50
Microwave
  beans (dried) and,   350
  for enhancing flavor of fruit,   604
  fish and,   462–64
  fruit pies and,   619–20
  marinated salads and,   202–3
  moist meat and,   539–41
  muffins and,   264–65
  pasta and,   325–26
  poultry and,   483–84
  safety of dishware in,   137–38
  soups and,   164–66
  spaghetti squash and,   394–95
  vegetables and,   569–70
  yeast breads and,   281–82
Milk (low-fat),   87–88, 89–90
Millet, 88–89. *See also* Grains
  Apricot-Quinoa Cereal,   334
  Eight-Vegetable Millet Soup,   190–91
  Millet-Stuffed Apples,   327–28
Mint Vinaigrette, Lobster with,   440
Mollusks, 90–91. *See also* Clams; Mussels;
  Oysters; Scallops
Monkfish. *See also* Fish
  Monkfish with Citrus and Ginger,   433–34
  Monkfish in Ginger Sauce,   459–60
  Monkfish Salad with
  Tomato Chutney,   226–27
Monounsaturated fat,   94–96, **95**
Moroccan Carrot Salad,   580
Moroccan Chicken with Chick-Peas,   359–60
Moroccan Turkey,   500–1
Mousse, Apricot,   634–35

Muesli, Oat-Bran, 316
Muffins
    Bran-Flake Muffins, 249–50
    Carrot Muffins, 292
    Cornmeal-Cheese Muffins, 260–61
    Cranberry Muffins, 263–64
    microwave preparation of, 264–65
    Orange Muffins, 267
    Pecan-Oat Muffins, 275–76
    Prune Muffins, 291
Mushrooms, 91
    Brussels Sprouts with
      Mushroom Glaze, 594–95
    Cream of Mushroom Soup, 192–93
    Mushroom-Cheese Sauce, 339
    Mushroom and Lentil Soup, 358–59
    Mushrooms Stuffed with Cheese
      Soufflé, 126
    Pheasant and Mushroom Soup, 168–69
    Potato Bake with Mushroom
      Stroganoff, 414
    Rabbit Sauté with Mushrooms, 506
    Spinach-Stuffed Mushrooms, 134–35
Mussels. *See also* Mollusks
    Asparagus and Shellfish Salad, 238–39
    Herb-Steamed Mussels with
      Rice Pilaf, 460–61
Mustard Greens, Indian-Style Wilted, 568–69
Mustard Sauce, Braised Leeks with, 136–37

N
Nachos, 364
Navy-Bean Soup, 378

Nectarines, 91, **627**
   Nectarine Sorbet, 636–37
   Nectarines with Sauce Cardinale, 616
New Orleans Red Beans, 352–53
Night vision, pumpkin and, 105
Noodles. *See also* Pasta
   Buckwheat Noodles with
      Grilled Tuna, 312–13
   Cabbage Noodles, 298–99
   Japanese Noodles with
      Spinach Ribbons, 299–300
   Noodles with Nut Sauce, 300
   Pan-Fried Noodles with
      Beans and Beef, 543–44
Nuts, 92, **93**. *See also specific nuts*
   Fruit and Nut Bread, 265–66
   Noodles with Nut Sauce, 300

O
Oats, 93–94
   Apples and Oat Cereal, 329
   Cinnamon Buns, 316
   Oat-Bran Muesli, 294–95
   One-Hour Oat Bread, 261–62
   Pecan-Oat Muffins, 275
   Raisin-Oat Bread, 289–90
Oil, 94–96, **95**
   monounsaturated, **95**
   olive, 217–19
Olive oil, 217–19
Omega-3 fatty acids, 79–81, **80**, 90, 432–33
One-Hour Oat Bread, 261–62
Onions, 96–97, 586
   Corn and Onion Pudding, 574–75

Onions (cont'd)
    Grilled Onion Brochettes,   128–29
    Onion and Pesto Pie,   390–91
    Onions and Apples in a Pumpkin,   598
    Onion Toast,   149–50
Oranges, 97. *See also* Citrus fruit
    Iced Leek and Orange Soup,   173–74
    Orange-Almond Cheese,   148
    Orange Beef with Rice,   537–38
    Orange Muffins,   267
    Orange-Scented Chicken Breasts,   517–18
    Orange-Scented Roast Goose,   485
    Oranges with Radishes and Dates,   209–10
    Pollo Sevilla,   491–92
    Sizzled Salmon with Mint,   449
    Spicy Beef with Orange Vinaigrette, 535–36
    Sweet Plums and Oranges,   614
    Tuna with Orange and Ginger Sauce, 452–53
Orchard Meat Loaf,   526
Oriental Gingered Vegetables,   571
Osteoporosis,   40–42
    menu plan for,   647, 752–60
Overweight,   43–45
    menu plan for,   647, 761–68
Oysters. *See also* Mollusks
    Antipasto with Baked Oysters,   153–54
    Oyster Fritters with Tarragon-
        Mustard Sauce,   465–66
    Oyster Stew,   473–74

P
Pancakes
    Banana Pancakes,   285–86
    Caraway Pancakes,   278–79

Pan-Fried Noodles with
    Beans and Beef,   543–44
Papayas, 97–98. *See also* Tropical fruit
    Winter-Jubilee Fruit,   623
Parsley,   98
    Broccoli with Parsley Sauce,   562
    Parsley Vinaigrette,   241
Parsnips,   98
    Brussels Sprouts with
        Three Root Sauce,   566–67
    Carrots and Parsnips,   576
    Cidered Parsnips,   597
    Parsnip-Corn Cakes,   589
Passion fruit. *See also* Tropical fruit
    Passion-Fruit Freeze,   638–39
Pasta, 98–99. *See also* Couscous; Noodles
    Broccoli and Cheese Pasta,   301
    Cabbage-Stuffed Shells,   314
    Chinese Vegetable Pasta,   313
    Componata with Rigatoni,   326–27
    Corn Pasta with Avocado Sauce,   322–23
    Eggplant Soup with Tiny Pasta,   160–61
    Favas with Tiny Pasta,   363
    Fettuccine with Grapes,   306
    Fusilli with Fresh Tomato Sauce,   324
    Linguine with Sweet Peppers,   302
    microwave preparation of,   325–26
    Pan-Fried Noodles with
        Beans and Beef,   543–44
    Pasta with Salmon and Sun-Dried
        Tomatoes,   303
    Peas and Pasta,   304
    Rabbit Sauté with Mushrooms,   506
    Rotini with Rosemary Vinaigrette,   205

Pasta (cont'd)
  sauces for, 330–31, 337–41
  Spaghetti with Guacamole, 342
  Spaghetti with Spinach Chiffonade, 307
  Tarragon Chicken with Linguine, 335
Peaches, 99, **628**
  Buckwheat Blini, 247–48
  Cinnamon-Scented French Toast, 268
  Cool Peach Soup, 177–78
  Peach-Blackberry Pie, 610
  Peach Chutney, 534
  Peaches and Pork, 531–32
  Peach Soufflé, 607–8
  Potato Waffles with Peach Sauce, 279–80
  Stuffed Peaches, 631
  Turkey Medallions with Peaches, 518–19
Peanuts.
  Peanut Popcorn, 131
Pears, 100
  Cranberry Pears, 633
  Fragrant Pear Charlotte, 628–29
  Lamb Meatballs with
    Pear-Turnip Puree, 525–26
  Pear-Cheese Pie, 625–26
  Pear and Hazelnut Salad, 201
  Pear and Pork Stir-Fry, 551–52
  Pear and Potato Salad, 219–20
  Poached Chicken with
    Pear and Kiwifruit, 507–8
  Savory Pear Spread, 253
  Turkey Cutlets with
    Pear-Pecan Stuffing, 482–83
Peas, 100. *See also* Legumes; Snow peas
  Bluefish in a Sea of Green, 451–52

Peas (cont'd)
  Curried Pea Spread,   381
  Peas and Pasta,   304
  Potato Curry,   398–99
Pecans. *See also* Nuts
  Beets with Pecans and Dill,   583–84
  Pecan-Oat Muffins,   275
  Pecan Waffles with Strawberry Sauce, 288–89
  Turkey Cutlets with
    Pear-Pecan Stuffing,   482–83
Pectin, weight control and,   43–44
Peppers (chili),   100–1, 426–28
Peppers (sweet), 101. *See also* Red Peppers
  Bulgur-Stuffed Yellow Peppers,   315–16
  Flounder with Pepper Puree,   467–68
  Green Beans and Peppers,   558–59
  Green-Pepper Pesto,   341
  Herbed Pepper Sauce,   340–41
  Linguine with Sweet Peppers,   302
  Rosemary Roasted Peppers,   590–91
  Shrimp and Roasted Peppers,   466–67
  Snapper with Red-Pepper Salsa,   461–62
  Spicy Stuffed Peppers,   413
  Tuna and Pepper Bake,   468
Perch. *See also* Fish
  Perch with Mustard and Thyme,   445–46
Periodontitis. *See* Dental Problems
Persimmons,   101–102
  Apple and Persimmon Cobbler,   611–12
Pesticides, fruits and vegetables and,   578–79
Pesto
  Carrot Sticks with Dill Pesto,   125
  Green-Pepper Pesto,   341
  Onion and Pesto Pie,   390–91

Pesto (cont'd)
Pesto Cheese, 149
Pesto Popcorn, 130
Pesto Turkey, 497
Pheasant and Mushroom Soup, 168–69
Pie. *See also* Tart
Black-Raspberry Pie, 606–7
Corn-Pone Pie, 405–6
fruit, microwave preparation of, 619–20
Lemon Pumpkin Pie, 601–2
Mexican Bean Pie, 347–48
Onion and Pesto Pie, 390–91
Peach-Blackberry Pie, 610
Pear-Cheese Pie, 625–26
Russian Vegetable Pie, 420–21
Spinach and Feta Pie, 389–90
Piecrust
Potato Pie shell, 401
microwave preparation of, 620–21
Rice Crust, 308
Whole Wheat Pie Shell, 272–73
Pilaf
Barley Pilaf with Grilled Apples, 333–34
Savory Rice Pilaf, 329–30
Wild Rice Pilaf, 317
Pineapples, 102
Diamond Head Turkey with Pineapple, 489–90
Fresh Pineapple Chutney, 533
Frozen Pineapple Yogurt, 637
Pineapple Focaccia, 255–56
Pineapple Freeze, 639
Pineapple Fruit Cocktail, 632–33
Pineapple-Rice Stuffing, 311

Pineapples (cont'd)
Scallop Salad with
Pineapple Relish,   221–22
Spicy Pork and Chicken
with Pineapple,   541–42
Swordfish and Pineapple Brochettes, 456–57
Pinto-Bean Stew, 368. *See also* Beans (dried)
Pistachios. *See also* Nuts
Spinach with Pistachios,   591–92
Stir-Fry with Snow Peas, Celery,
and Pistachios,   582
Pizza, Whole Wheat,   408–9
Plums,   102
Almond-Topped Baked Plums,   623–24
Sweet Plums and Oranges,   614
Poached Chicken with Chinese
Vinaigrette,   486
Poached Chicken with Pear
and Kiwifruit,   507–8
Poached fish,   455
Poached Turkey Paprika,   480–81
Polenta,   417–20
Pollo Sevilla,   491–92
Pomegranates,   103
Hummus with Pumpkin
and Pomegranate,   373–74
Popcorn,   103, 129–32
Pork (lean),   104
Peaches and Pork,   531–32
Pear and Pork Stir-Fry,   551–52
Spicy Pork and Chicken
with Pineapple,   541–42
Potatoes,   104–5
Breakfast Scramble with Oven Fries, 392–93

Potatoes (cont'd)
    Brussels Sprouts with Three-
        Root Sauce,   566–67
    Cod with Herbed Potatoes,   470–71
    Curried Potato Salad,   217
    Fish and Chips,   437–39
    Garden-Puff Potatoes,   556–57
    Garlic and Potato Soup,   178–79
    Green Beans and Peppers,   558–59
    Irish Vichyssoise,   193
    Pear and Potato Salad,   219–20
    Potato Bake with Mushroom
        Stroganoff,   414
    Potato-Cheese Bread,   287–88
    Potato Curry,   398–99
    Potatoes with Creamy
        Mustard Topping,   590
    Potato Pie Shell,   401
    Potato and Raspberry Salad,   200
    Potato Waffles with Peach Sauce, 279–80
    Savoy Puree in Potato Shells,   573
    Spicy Roasted Potatoes,   595–96
    Stuffed Baked Potatoes,   527
    Tomatoes Stuffed with Lamb Hash, 528
    whipped, hot topping for,   592–93
Pot cheese. *See* Cheese (low-fat)
Poultry, **72–73**, 475–522. *See also specific types*
    marinades for,   487
    microwave preparation of,   483–84
    Poultry Pâté,   492–93
    preparation tips for,   498–99, 519
Primavera Sauce for polenta,   419
Prunes,   105
    Baked Prune Compote,   609

Prunes (cont'd)
    Prune Butter,   252
    Prune Muffins,   291
Psoriasis. *See* Skin problems
Pudding
    Blueberry Pudding,   624–25
    Corn and Onion Pudding,   574–75
Pumpkin,   105–6
    Hummus with Pumpkin and
        Pomegranate,   373–74
    Lemon Pumpkin Pie,   601–2
    Onions and Apples in a Pumpkin,   598
    Pinto-Bean Stew,   368
    Pumpkin Soup,   163
    seeds,   319

Q
Quesadilla, Broccoli,   409–10
Quiche, Artichoke,   124–25
Quinoa, 106. *See also* Grains
    Apricot-Quinoa Cereal,   334

R
Rabbit
    Chinese-Style Rabbit,   501
    Rabbit Sauté with Mushrooms,   506
Radishes,
    Oranges with Radishes and Dates, 209–10
Raisins,   106–7
    Cornish Hens Stuffed with Apples,
        Almonds, and Raisins,   520–21
    Raisin-Oat Bread,   289–90
Raspberries, 107, **628**. *See also* Berries
    Berry Custard   621–22

Raspberries (cont'd)
  Black-Raspberry Pie   606–7
  Cinnamon-Scented French Toast,   268
  Compote of Raspberries and
      Roasted Red Peppers,   141
  Cool Peach Soup,   177–78
  Creamy Raspberry Dressing,   232
  Golden French Toast,   262–63
  Nectarines with Sauce Cardinale,   616
  Potato and Raspberry Salad,   200
  Wild Rice and Raspberries,   317–18
Red chard. *See* Swiss chard
Red Peppers. *See also* Peppers (sweet)
  Red-Pepper Bean Spread,   381
  Red Pepper Canapés, roasted,   135–36
      Compote of Raspberries and
          Roasted Red Peppers,   141
  Snapper with Red-Pepper Salsa,   461–62
Retinopathy. *See* Diabetes
Rheumatoid arthritis,   45–46
  menu plan for,   647–48, 769–76
Rhubarb,   628
Rice,   107–108
  Black Beans and Rice,   348–49
  brown
      Chicken with Kashmiri Rice,   478–79
      Emerald Isle Rice Pudding,   605–6
      Madrid Trout,   446–47
      Orange Beef with Rice,   537–38
      Rice-Waffle Stack,   245–46
  Caribbean Bean Casserole,   372–73
  Dilled Shrimp and Rice Salad,   469
  East Indian Rice Salad,   197–98
  Greek Spinach and Rice,   391–92

Rice (cont'd)
  Herb-Steamed Mussels with
    Rice Pilaf,   460–61
  Italian-Style Fried Rice,   412
  New Orleans Red Beans,   352–53
  Pineapple-Rice Stuffing,   311
  Pollo Sevilla,   491–92
  Rice-Bran scones,   274–75
  Rice Crust,   308
  Savory Rice Pilaf,   329–30
  Spinach Risotto,   323–24
  Vegetable Paella,   424
  wild
    Apricot-Stuffed Hens,   476–77
    Rice Timbales,   127–28
    Wild-Rice Pilaf,   317
    Wild Rice and Raspberries, 317–18
    Wild-Rice Salad,   228–29
    Wild-Rice Stuffing,   310–11
Ricotta cheese,   **76**
  Zucchini-Ricotta Puffs,   400
Rigatoni. *See also* Pasta
  Componata with Rigatoni,   326–27
Risotto, Spinach,   323–24
Roast Chicken with Fennel
  and Mustard,   479–80
Roast Duck with Fresh Rosemary, 502–3
Roasted Eggplant Hors d'Oeuvres, 156
Roasted Garlic Dip,   148
Roasted Peppers
  Rosemary Roasted Peppers, 590–91
  Shrimp and Roasted Peppers, 466–67
Roast Goose, Orange-Scented,   485

Rosemary
    Rosemary Asparagus, 582–83
    Rosemary Roasted Peppers, 590–91
    Rotini with Rosemary Vinaigrette, 205
Rotini. *See also* Pasta
    Rotini with Rosemary Vinaigrette, 205
Russian Vegetable Pie, 420–21
Rutabagas, 108
    Far Eastern Rutabagas, 557–58

S

Sablefish. *See also* Fish
    Sablefish with Basil Aioli, 470
Salads
    Apples and Celeriac with Honey-
        Mustard Dressing, 204
    Asparagus and Shellfish Salad, 238–39
    Avocado and Shrimp Salad, 220–21
    Bay Scallops with Saffron, 441
    Berries and Greens, 230
    Black-Eyed Peas with Spinach, 377
    Bulgur and Sweet-Pepper Salad, 207–8
    Carrot Salad, 213
    Corn Salad with Lemon-
        Dill Dressing, 212–13
    Curried Potato Salad, 217
    Dandelion Greens with Beans, 225
    Dilled Shrimp and Rice Salad, 469
    dressings, 230–34, 240–42
    East Indian Rice Salad, 197–98
    Equinox Salad, 235–36
    Garlic and Eggplant Salad, 206–7
    Greens and Tangerines, 239–40

Salads (cont'd)
Grilled Chicken and Artichokes,
    with Mixed Greens, 505
Herbed Bean Salad, 346–47
Lean Beef with Greens and Feta, 208–9
Lobster with Mint Vinaigrette, 440
Mackerel Salad, 442–43
Mexican Chicken Salad, 198–99
Monkfish Salad with
    Tomato Chutney, 226–27
Moroccan Carrot Salad, 580
Oranges with Radishes and Dates, 209–10
Pear and Hazelnut Salad, 201
Pear and Potato Salad, 219–20
Potato and Raspberry Salad, 200
Rotini with Rosemary Vinaigrette, 205
Salmon Salad with Almonds and
    Bok Choy, 202
Scallop Salad with Pineapple Relish, 221–22
Sea Kabob Salad with
    Curry Vinaigrette, 236–37
Shrimp and Roasted Peppers, 466–67
Smoked Turkey and Grapes, 216
Spicy Beef with Orange Vinaigrette, 535–36
Spicy Beet Salad, 229
Spicy Shrimp Salad with Cool
    Mango Dressing, 215
Sprouts and Cheese, 214
Squash Salad with
    Buttermilk Dressing, 237–38
Summer Chicken Salad Sandwiches, 513
Tropical Chicken Salad, 234–35
Warm Salmon Salad, 242–43
Wild-Rice Salad, 228–29

Salad greens, 108–109. *See also* Salads

Berries and Greens,	230
Dandelion Greens with Beans,	225
Garlic and Eggplant Salad,	206–7
Greens and Tangerines,	239–40
Grilled Chicken and Artichokes with Mixed Greens,	505
Indian-Style Wilted Greens,	568–69
Lean Beef with Greens and Feta,	208–9
Mexican Chicken Salad,	198–99
Orange Beef with Rice,	537–38
Pear and Hazelnut Salad,	201
Poached Chicken with Chinese Vinaigrette,	486
Smoked Turkey and Grapes,	216
Vegetable Egg Roll Ups,	593–94

Salmon. *See also* Fish

Antipasto with Baked Oysters,	153–54
Broiled Salmon with Cucumbers,	450–51
Dilled Salmon Tart,	453–54
Pasta with Salmon and Sun-Dried Tomatoes,	303
Salmon Bisque,	188–89
Salmon Salad with Almonds and Bok Choy,	202
Salmon with Scallions,	449–50
Sizzled Salmon with Mint,	449
Sole and Salmon Roulades,	138–39
Warm Salmon Salad,	242–43

Sandwiches

Falafel Pockets,	353–55
Summer Chicken Salad Sandwiches,	513

Sapsago cheese. *See* Cheese (low-fat)

Satay, Beef, Barbecued,	538–39

Sauces
    Braised Leeks with Mustard Sauce, 136–37
    Cran-Apple Sauce, 605
    Green-Pepper Pesto, 341
    Herbed Pepper Sauce, 340–41
    Mushroom-Cheese Sauce, 339
    Nectarines with Sauce Cardinale, 616
    for pasta, 330–31, 337–41
    Spicy Aurora Sauce, 339–40
    Vegetables with Creamy Garlic Sauce, 139–40
Sausage
    Sausage-Stuffed Zucchini Wheels, 142–43
    Vegetarian Sausage Links, 406–7
Sautéed Turkey with Strawberry Puree, 514
Savory Lima Beans, 362
Savory Pear Spread, 253
Savory Potato Crust (pie shell), 401
Savory Rice Pilaf, 329–30
Savory Stuffed Snow Peas, 143
Scallops. *See also* Mollusks
    Bay Scallops with Saffron, 441
    Bouillabaisse, 448
    Scallop Salad with Pineapple
      Relish, 221–22
    Seafood-Broccoli Terrine, 472–73
    Seafood Gazpacho, 167–68
    Sea Kabob Salad with
      Curry Vinaigrette, 236–37
Scallops of Veal with Fennel
  and Grapes, 544–45
Scones
    Rice-Bran Scones, 274–75
    Sweet Potato Scones, 259–60

Seafood. *See also* Crustaceans; Fish; Mollusks
    Seafood-Broccoli Terrine, 472–73
    Seafood Gazpacho, 167–68
Sea Kabob Salad with
    Curry Vinaigrette, 236–37
Seeds, 109–110, 318–20. *See also specific seeds*
    Whole-Grain and Seed Bread, 273–74
Sesame seeds, 318–19
    Chinese Beans with Sesame Seeds, 581
Sesame Snow Peas, 593
Shallots, 587–88
    Shallot Vinaigrette, 241
Shark. *See also* Fish
Sea Kabob Salad with
    Curry Vinaigrette, 236–37
    Shark and Stars, 443–44
Shellfish. *See also* Crustaceans: Mollusks
    Asparagus and Shellfish Salad, 238–39
Sherbet, Strawberry, 638
Shrimp, *See also* Crustaceans
    Avocado and Shrimp Salad, 220–21
    Bouillabaisse, 448
    Dilled Shrimp and Rice Salad, 469
Sea Kabob Salad with
    Curry Vinaigrette, 236–37
    Shrimp and Roasted Peppers, 466–67
Spicy Shrimp Salad with Cool
    Mango Dressing, 215
    Stuffed Tofu Triangles, 132–34
Turkey and Shrimp Kabobs
    with Tomatoes, 493–94
Side dishes, 555–99
    Beets with Pecans and Dill, 583–84
    Broccoli with Parsley Sauce, 562

Side dishes (cont'd)

Brussels Sprouts with Mushroom
  Glaze,   594–95
Brussels Sprouts with Three-
  Root Sauce,   566–67
Carrot Fritters,   575–76
Carrots and Parsnips,   576
Chinese Beans with Sesame Seeds,   581
Christmas Cabbage,   577
Cidered Parsnips,   597
Corn and Onion Pudding,   574–75
Creamed Turnips,   567–68
Cucumbers with Cumin and
  Coriander,   564–65
Far Eastern Rutabagas,   557–58
Favas with Tiny Pasta,   363
French-Style Chard,   577–78
Garden-Puff Potatoes,   556–57
Green Beans and Peppers,   558–58
Green Beans with Walnuts,   596–97
Hunan Eggplant,   585
Indian-Style Wilted Greens,   568–69
Maple Sweet Potatoes,   596
Marinated Cauliflower,   599
Moroccan Carrot Salad,   580
Onions and Apples in a Pumpkin,   598
Oriental Gingered Vegetables,   571
Parsnip-Corn Cakes,   589
Potatoes with Creamy
  Mustard Topping,   590
Rosemary Asparagus,   582–83
Rosemary Roasted Peppers,   590–91
Savory Lima Beans,   362
Savoy Puree in Potato Shells,   573

Side dishes (cont'd)
    Sesame Snow Peas,   593
    Spicy Roasted Potatoes,   595–96
    Spinach with Pistachios,   591–92
    Stir-Fry with Snow Peas, Celery,
       and Pistachios,   582
    Stuffed Acorn Squash,   562–63
    Stuffed Red Beets,   574
    Sweet Corn Fritters,   565–66
    Tomato and Zucchini Gratin,   572
    Vegetable Egg Roll-Ups,   593–94
    Winter Greens with Roasted Garlic, 563–64
    Zucchini with Caraway,   561
Sizzled Salmon with Mint,   449
Sizzling Fajitas,   530–31
Skillet Barley and Beef,   304–5
Skin problems,   46–48
Smoked Turkey and Grapes,   216
Smoky Cucumber Dip,   127
Snapper. *See also* Fish
    Bouillabaisse,   448
    Grilled Florida snapper,   439–40
    Snapper with Red-Pepper Salsa, 461–62
Snow Peas. *See also* Peas
    Savory Stuffed Snow Peas,   143
    Sesame Snow Peas,   593
    Stir-Fry with Snow Peas, Celery,
       and Pistachios,   582
Soft-Shell Sauté,   441–42
Sole. *See also* Fish
    Sole and Salmon Roulades,   138–39
Sorbet, Nectarine,   636–37

Soufflés
   Mushrooms Stuffed with Cheese
      Soufflé,   126
   Peach Soufflé,   607–8
Soups
   Apple-Barley Soup,   175–76
   Broccoli-Buttermilk Soup,   188
   Butternut Bisque,   166–67
   Cajun Soup,   176–77
   Chilled Blueberry Soup,   181–82
   Chunky Tomato Soup,   169–70
   Clam and Lobster Chowder,   191–92
   Cold Zucchini Soup,   179–80
   Cool Peach Soup,   177–78
   Cream of Carrot Soup,   172
   Creamy Broccoli Soup,   187
   Creamy Corn Chowder,   194
   Dilled Cabbage Soup,   162–63
   Dilled Split Peas,   371–72
   Eggplant Soup with Tiny Pasta, 160–61
   Eight-Vegetable Millet Soup,   190–91
   Escarole Soup,   164
   Fragrant Borscht,   183–84
   Garlic and Potato Soup,   178–79
   Great Northern Soup,   357–58
   Iced Cantaloupe Soup,   171
   Iced Leek and Orange Soup, 173–74
   Irish Vichyssoise,   193
   Korean Hot Beef Soup,   185–86
   microwave preparation of,   164–66
   Mushroom and Lentil Soup,   358–59
   Navy-Bean Soup,   378
   Pheasant and Mushroom Soup, 168–69
   Pumpkin Soup,   163

Soups (cont'd)
 Salmon Bisque,   188–89
 Seafood Gazpacho,   167–68
 South American Squash Soup,   174–75
 stock,   180–81, 189–90, 194–95
 Striper Chowder,   161–62
 Succotash Chowder,   186–87
 Summer-Vegetable Soup,   184–85
 Sweetheart Soup,   182–83
 Tomato Bisque,   172–73
 vegetable purees added for body to,   170
 White-Bean Gumbo,   345–46
South American Squash Soup,   174–75
Soybeans, 110. *See also* Tofu
 Herbed Bean Salad,   346–47
Spaghetti. *See also* Pasta
 Spaghetti with Guacamole,   342
 Spaghetti with Spinach Chiffonade,   307
Spaghetti Squash. *See also* Squash (winter)
 Confetti Spaghetti Squash,   393–94
 microwave preparation of,   394–95
 Spaghetti Squash with Tomato Sauce,   422
Spanish Halibut,   444–45
Spiced Apples,   618
Spices, 83–84. *See also* Herbs
Spicy Aurora Sauce,   339–40
Spicy Beef with Orange Vinaigrette,   535–36
Spicy Beet Salad,   229
Spicy Pork and Chicken
 with Pineapple,   541–42
Spicy Roasted Potatoes,   595–96
Spicy Shrimp Salad with
 Cool Mango Dressing,   215
Spicy Stuffed Peppers,   413

Spicy Vegetables with Tofu,   410–11
Spinach,   110–11
    Apples and Celeriac with
        Honey-Mustard Dressing,   204
    Black-Eyed Peas with Spinach,   377
    Equinox Salad,   235–36
    Greek Spinach and Rice,   391–92
    Italian-Style Fried Rice,   412
    Japanese Noodles with
        Spinach Ribbons,   299–300
    Rotini with Rosemary Vinaigrette,   205
    Spaghetti with Spinach Chiffonade,   307
    Spinach and Feta Pie,   389–90
    Spinach with Pistachios,   591–92
    Spinach Risotto,   323–24
    Spinach-Stuffed Mushrooms,   134–35
Split Peas. *See also* Legumes
    Caspian Split Peas,   367
    Dilled Split Peas,   371–72
Spreads
    bean,   379–82
    for breads and muffins,   251–53
    Carrot Spread,   251–52
    Hummus Bi Tahini,   382
    Prune Butter,   252
    Savory Pear Spread,   253
Sprouts,   111
    Mandarin Chicken with
        Bean Sprouts,   516–17
    Sprouts and Cheese,   214
Squash seeds,   319
Squash (summer), 111–12. *See also* Zucchini
    Squash Salad with Buttermilk
        Dressing,   237–38

Squash (winter),   112
  Acorn Squash Stuffed
    with Cornbread,   395–96
  Butternut Bisque,   166–67
  Confetti Spaghetti Squash,   393–94
  South American Squash Soup,   174–75
  Spaghetti Squash with Tomato
    Sauce,   422
  Stuffed Acorn Squash,   562–63
Starfruit
  Chicken with Tropical Fruit,   511–12
  Shark and Stars,   443
Steamed fish,   454–55
Steamed Wontons,   490–91
Stew
  Couscous and Chick-Pea Stew,   375–76
  Cuban Bean Stew,   384–85
  Pinto-Bean Stew,   368
Stir-Fry,   546–49
  Pear and Pork Stir-Fry,   551–52
  Stir-Fry with Snow Peas, Celery,
    and Pistachios,   582
Stock,   180–81, 189–90, 194–95
Strawberries, 112–13. *See also* Berries
  Berries and Greens,   230
  Berry Custard,   621–22
  Jasmine Chicken with
    Strawberry Coulis,   481–82
  Pecan Waffles with Strawberry Sauce,   288–89
  Sautéed Turkey with
    Strawberry Puree,   514
  Strawberries with Two Melons,   603–4
  Strawberry Sherbet,   638

Striper. *See also* Fish
    Striper Chowder, 161–62
Stroke Prevention, 48–50
    menu plan for, 646, 709–16
Stuffed Acorn Squash, 562–63
Stuffed Baked Potatoes, 527
Stuffed Peaches, 631
Stuffed Peppers, Spicy, 413
Stuffed Red Beets, 574
Stuffed Shells, Cabbage, 314
Stuffed Snow Peas, Savory, 143
Stuffed Tofu Triangles, 132–34
Stuffings, 309–11
    Chestnut Stuffing, 309–10
    Pineapple-Rice Stuffing, 311
Succotash Chowder, 186–87
Summer Chicken Salad Sandwiches, 513
Summer-Vegetable Soup, 184–85
Sweet Corn Fritters, 565–66
Sweetheart Soup, 182–83
Sweet potatoes, 113
    Maple Sweet Potatoes, 596
    Sweet Potato Scones, 259–60
Sweet and Spicy Curry Dip, 147
Swiss Chard, 113–14
    East Indian Rice Salad, 197–98
    French-style Chard, 577–78
    Indian-Style Wilted Greens, 568–69
    Tropical Chicken Salad, 234–35
Swordfish. *See also* Fish
    Swordfish and Pineapple Brochettes, 456–57

T

Tangerines, 114
  Cheesecake Tart, 602–3
  Greens and Tangerines, 239–40
Tarragon
  Oyster Fritters with Tarragon-
    Mustard Sauce, 465–66
  Tarragon Chicken with Linguine, 335
Tarts
  Apple Tart, 616–18
  Cheesecake Tart, 602–3
  Fresh-Fruit Tart, 613
  Tuna Tart with Basil, 145–46
Three-Mustard Vinaigrette, 241
Thyme-Flavored Tuna Steaks, 434–35
Timbales, Rice, 127–28
Tofu, 114
  Spicy Vegetables with Tofu, 410–11
  Stuffed Tofu Triangles, 132–34
Tomatoes, 114–15
  Bouillabaisse, 448
  Chick-Pea Chili, 356–57
  Chili con Kasha, 336
  Chunky Tomato Soup, 169–70
  Chutney
    Apple-Tomato Chutney, 534–35
    Monkfish Salad with Tomato
      Chutney, 226–27
  Cold Zucchini Soup, 179–80
  Corn-Pone Pie, 405–6
  French Toast with Tomato Salsa, 254
  Greek Garden Kabobs, 403
  Pasta with Salmon and Sun-
    Dried Tomatoes, 303

Tomatoes (cont'd)
  Sauce
    Fusilli with Fresh Tomato Sauce,   324
    Ginger Turkey with spicy Tomato
      Sauce,   508–9
    Spaghetti Squash with Tomato
      Sauce,   422
    Spicy Aurora Sauce,   339–40
  Seafood Gazpacho,   167–68
  Tomato Bisque,   172–73
  Tomatoes Stuffed with Lamb Hash,   528
  Tomato Vinaigrette,   241
  Tomato and Zucchini Gratin,   572
  Turkey Cacciatore,   521–22
  Turkey and Shrimp Kabobs
    with Tomatoes,   493–94
  Vegetable Chili,   366
Toppings
  for polenta,   418–20
  for whipped potatoes,   592–93
Tropical Chicken Salad,   234–35
Tropical Compote,   612
Tropical fruit, 115–16. *See also specific fruit*
  Chicken with Tropical Fruit,   234–35
  freezes made with,   639
  Passion-Fruit Freeze,   638–39
  Tropical Compote,   612
Trout. *See also* Fish
  Madrid Trout,   446–47
Tuna, *See also* Fish
  Buckwheat Noodles with
    Grilled Tuna,   312–13
  Main-Dish Antipasto,   369–71
  Thyme-Flavored Tuna Steaks,   434–35

Tuna (cont'd)
  Tuna with Orange and
    Ginger Sauce,   452–53
  Tuna and Pepper Bake,   468
  Tuna Tart with Basil,   145–46
Turkey, 116. *See also* Poultry
  Diamond Head Turkey
    with Pineapple,   489–90
  Garlic-Roasted Turkey Breast,   496
  Ginger Turkey with Spicy
    Tomato Sauce,   508–9
  Moroccan Turkey,   500–1
  Pesto Turkey,   497
  Poached Turkey Paprika,   480–81
  Poultry Pâté,   492–93
  Sausage-Stuffed Zucchini Wheels,   142–43
  Sautéed Turkey with
    Strawberry Puree,   514
  Smoked Turkey and Grapes,   216
  Smoky Cucumber Dip,   127
  Turkey Cacciatore,   521–22
  Turkey Cutlets with Pear-Pecan
    Stuffing,   482–83
  Turkey Medallions with Peaches,   518–19
  Turkey and Shrimp Kabobs
    with Tomatoes,   493–94
Turnips,   116
  Creamed Turnips,   567–68
  Lamb Meatballs with Pear-
    Turnip Puree,   525–26
20-Minute Pizza (Whole-Wheat),   407–9

U
Urinary tract infections,   50–51

V

Veal (lean),   116–17
   Scallops of Veal with Fennel
      and Grapes,   544–45
   Veal in Apple-Lemon Sauce,   545–46
   Veal Loin with Mango Sauce,   553–54
Vegetables, **559–61**. *See also specific*
vegetables; Side dishes;
Vegetarian main meals
   Chicken Breasts with Harvest
      Vegetables,   503–4
   Chinese Vegetable Pasta,   313
   Couscous with Chicken and
      Vegetables,   320–22
   Crudités,   157–58
   Dilled Vegetables,   144
   Eight-Vegetable Millet Soup,   190–91
   Mediterranean Topping for polenta,   418
   microwave preparation of,   569–70
   Oriental Gingered Vegetables,   571
   and pesticides,   578–79
   Primavera Sauce for polenta,   419
   purees added to soups for body,   170
   Russian Vegetable Pie,   420–21
   seeds with,   319–20
   Spicy Vegetables with Tofu,   410–11
   Summer Vegetable Soup,   184–85
   Vegetable Chili,   366
   Vegetable Egg Roll-Ups,   593–94
   Vegetable Paella,   424
   Vegetables with Creamy Garlic Sauce,   139–40
Vegetarian main meals,   388–431
   Acorn Squash Stuffed with
      Cornbread,   395–96

Vegetarian main meals,
Black Beans and Rice,	348–49
Breakfast Scramble with Oven Fries,	392–93
Broccoli Quesadilla,	409–10
Caribbean Bean Casserole,	372–73
Caspian Split Peas,	367
Chick-Pea Chili,	356–57
Chili Beans Ranchero,	374–75
Confetti Spaghetti Squash,	393–94
Corn Crêpes with Bean Filling,	397–98
Corn Enchiladas,	425–26
Corn-Pone Pie,	405–6
Couscous and Chick-Pea Stew,	375–76
Eggs with Chili Sauce,	404
Enchiladas with Cheese and Kale,	423
Falafel Pockets,	353–55
Good-Luck Peas,	365
Greek Garden Kabobs,	403
Greek Spinach and Rice,	391–92
Hummus with Pumpkin and Pomegranate,	373–74
Indonesian Stir-Fry,	402–3
Italian-Style Fried Rice,	412
Lentil and Leek Burritos,	428–29
Lentil Loaf,	349–50
Mexican Bean Pie,	347–48
Mexican Corn Casserole,	415–16
New Orleans Red Beans,	352–53
Onion and Pesto Pie,	390–91
Pinto-Bean Stew,	368
Polenta,	416–20
Potato Bake with Mushroom Stroganoff,	414
Potato Curry,	398–99
Russian Vegetable Pie,	420–21

Vegetarian main meals (cont'd)
    Spaghetti Squash with Tomato Sauce,   422
    Spicy Stuffed Peppers,   413
    Spicy Vegetables with Tofu,   410–11
    Spinach and Feta Pie,   389–90
    Vegetable Chili,   366
    Vegetable Paella,   424
    Vegetarian Sausage Links,   406–7
    Whole Wheat Pizza,   408–9
    Zucchini-Ricotta Puffs,   400
Vegetarian Sausage Links,   406–7
Venison Brochettes,   499–500
Vichyssoise, Irish,   193
Vinaigrette dressings,   240–42
Vinegar,   210–12

W
Waffles
    Pecan Waffles with Strawberry Sauce,   288–89
    Potato Waffles with Peach Sauce,   279–80
    Rice-Waffle Stack,   245–46
Walnuts. *See also* Nuts
    Green Beans with Walnuts,   596–97
Warm Salmon Salad,   242–43
Watercress, 117. *See also* Salad greens
    Watercress Canapés,   152
    Watercress Dressing,   231
Waterfowl, 117. *See also* Duck; Goose
Wax beans. *See* Beans (snap)
Weight control. *See* Overweight
Wheat. *See also* Couscous; Whole wheat
    Bran (*see* Bran)
    germ,   118

Whole-grain. *See also specific grains*
　Whole-Grain and Seed Bread,　　273–74
Whole wheat
　flour,　　118–19
　Whole Wheat French Bread,　　283–85
　Whole Wheat Pie Shell,　　272–73
　Whole Wheat Pizza,　　408–9
Wild Rice. *See* Rice, wild
Wilted Greens, Indian-Style,　　568–69
Winter-Jubilee Fruit,　　623
Wontons, Steamed,　　490–91
Wound healing,　　51–52
　menu plan for,　　648, 777–84

Y

Yeast (baker's),　　276–77
Yeast bread. *See* Breads
Yellow Peppers. *See also* Peppers (sweet)
　Bulgur-Stuffed Yellow Peppers,　　315–16
Yogurt (low-fat)　　119
　cheese,　　146–49
　Curried Yogurt and Broccoli,　　157
　Frozen Pineapple Yogurt,　　637

Z

Zucchini. *See also* Squash (summer)
　Cold Zucchini Soup,　　179–80
　Dill-Zucchini Spears,　　155
　Emerald Isle Rice Pudding,　　605–6
　Sausage-Stuffed Zucchini Wheels,　　142–43
　Tomato and Zucchini Gratin,　　572
　Zucchini with Caraway,　　561
　Zucchini-Ricotta Puffs,　　400